Understanding the Political Economics on China's Development

Understanding the Political Economics on China's Development

Hailiang Gu

Tianyi Wang

World Scientific

NEW JERSEY • LONDON • SINGAPORE • BEIJING • SHANGHAI • TAIPEI • CHENNAI

Published by

World Scientific Publishing Co. Pte. Ltd.

5 Toh Tuck Link, Singapore 596224

USA office: 27 Warren Street, Suite 401-402, Hackensack, NJ 07601

UK office: 57 Shelton Street, Covent Garden, London WC2H 9HE

Library of Congress Cataloging-in-Publication Data
Names: Gu, Hailiang, editor | Wang, Tianyi, editor.
Title: Understanding the political economics on China's development / [edited by] Hailiang Gu, Peking University, China, Tianyi Wang, Party School of the CPC Central Committee, China.
Other titles: Du dong zhong guo fa zhan de zheng zhi jing ji xue. English
Description: New Jersey : World Scientific, [2025] | Translation of: Du dong zhong guo fa zhan de zheng zhi jing ji xue, published in 2017 by Zhong guo ren min da xue chu ban she. | Includes bibliographical references and index.
Identifiers: LCCN 2024059688 | ISBN 9789819801404 (hardcover) | ISBN 9789819801411 (ebook) | ISBN 9789819801428 (ebook other)
Subjects: LCSH: Economic development--Political aspects--China. | Communism--China. | Socialism--China.
Classification: LCC HC427 .D8213 2025 | DDC 330.951--dc23/eng/20240225
LC record available at https://lccn.loc.gov/2024059688

British Library Cataloguing-in-Publication Data
A catalogue record for this book is available from the British Library.

读懂中国发展的政治经济学
Originally published in China Renmin University Press

B&R Book Program

For any available supplementary material, please visit
https://www.worldscientific.com/worldscibooks/10.1142/14058#t=suppl

Desk Editors: Soundararajan Raghuraman/Lum Pui Yee

Typeset by Stallion Press
Email: enquiries@stallionpress.com

About the Authors

Gu Hailiang is a Boya Chair Professor and a professor at the School of Marxism at Peking University. He is also the director of the Peking University "Marx Collection" Compilation and Research Center. In addition, he serves as a consultant and chief expert for the Central Project for Research and Construction of Marxist Theory, the director of the Expert Committee on Philosophy and Social Sciences (Marx Project) of the National Textbook Committee, and the vice chairman of the Social Sciences Committee of the Ministry of Education. Since 1984, he has been engaged in teaching and research at the Institute of the Development of Marxism-Leninism at Renmin University of China, and was appointed as a professor in 1994. He successively held the positions of deputy director and director of the institute. From 1996 to 2001, he served as the deputy director of the Office of the Academic Degrees Committee of the State Council and the director of the Department of Social Sciences of the Ministry of Education. From 2001 to 2010, he was the secretary of the Party Committee and president of Wuhan University. From 2010 to 2013, he was a member of the Party Group of the Ministry of Education and the president of the National School of Administration. His research focuses mainly on the history of Marx's economic thought, the history of the development of Marxism, and the political economy of socialism with Chinese characteristics.

Wang Tianyi, a professor and doctoral supervisor at the School of Economics at the Central Party School of China, is also a recipient of the special government allowance from the State Council. He serves as the vice president of the China Research Association of Capital, the vice chairman of the Capital Economists Forum, and a part-time professor at a number of key universities across the country, including Tsinghua University and Peking University. His main research areas are Marxist political economy and the reform and development of the Chinese economy. He has published over 300 articles in newspapers such as the *People's Daily* and academic journals such as *Chinese Social Sciences* and has authored or co-authored more than 20 books and textbooks.

Contents

Chapter 1

The Development of China's Political Economics

The political economics of socialism with Chinese characteristics represents the development of China's political economics. The development of China's political economics takes into account the political and economic factors, institutions, and policies that shape and drive China's growth and progress over time. It is the result of extracting and summarizing the patterns of China's socialist economic relations development in real time and grounded in China's unique national conditions and the practical aspects of its socialist economic construction. This systematic economic theory has been developed based on practical experience, and it helps to promote the new development of Marxist political economics. Since the Communist Party of China's 18th National Congress was held in 2012, the Party Central Committee and its leader, Comrade Xi Jinping, have been committed to persisting on the path of socialism with Chinese characteristics and developing it further through hands-on practice and innovation. This approach has so far encouraged the formation of new concepts, ideas, and strategies for governing the country. These new governance strategies have provided scientific theoretical guidance and action guidelines for furthering economic reform and accelerating socialist modernization under this new social-political context. These new developments in the socialist political economics with Chinese characteristics have brought new advancements to Marxist political economics.

1. Based on the Economic Reality of Chinese Economic Reform and Opening Up

Marxist political economics has consistently maintained the imperative of commencing analysis from the "actual economic situation"[1] of the country, that is, from real and existing economic relationships and facts. The primary stage of socialism is the most important and fundamental economic relationship and reality in contemporary China. The political economics of China's development is based on the exploration of China's economic reality at the primary stage of socialism, with a backdrop that combines Chinese economic realities, history, and theory. The economic relations, policies, and systems associated with the primary stage of socialism are the main subjects of study of Chinese political economics.

Deng Xiaoping astutely grasped this basic characteristic of the political economics of China's development. In 1984, when referring to the *CPC Central Committee's Decision on Economic Restructuring* adopted by the Third Plenary Session of the 12th Central Committee of the Party, he stated, "the socialist economy is a market economy based on central planning and public ownership." His statement was a new concept that suited the economic reality of China at the time. This new concept marked the beginning of Chinese political economics, which Deng defined as "a political economics that combines the basic principles of Marxism with the practice of China's socialism." Deng further stated, "In the past, we could not have written such a document. Without the experience of previous years, it would have been impossible to write such a document. Even if it was written, it wouldn't have been easy to pass, and it might have been regarded as 'heretical'. We use our own experience to answer new questions that arise in new circumstances."[2] The "first draft of the political economics" of China's development was written during this special time when new concepts were allowed to be explored, and past "heretical" ideas were turning "mainstream."

Based on the practice and facts of economic system reform, the political economics of China's development has formed an innovative theory stating that "the market economic system must be combined with certain basic social economic policies." The initial definition of the socialist market economy given at the 14th National Congress of the Communist Party

[1] *Collected Works of Marx and Engels*, Vol. 1. People's Publishing House, 2009, p. 156.

[2] *Selected Works of Deng Xiaoping*, Vol. 3. People's Publishing House, 1993, p. 83, 91.

of China emphasized that "the socialist market economic system we want to establish should enable the market to play a fundamental role in resource allocation under the macro-control of the socialist country." This definition strongly emphasized that "the socialist market economic system must be combined with the basic socialist policies."[3] The term "combined" here implies that "China is practicing a socialist market economic system, and we still believe in the superiority of our socialist system and the active role of the Party and the government."[4] This statement points out the importance of properly handling the relationship between the market and the government and discussing the issue of whether the market or the government should play a decisive role in resource allocation. Making the market play a decisive role in resource allocation does not exclude the role of the government; it's important to recognize that both are important in the socialist market economy and both have to collaborate and complement each other. As Xi Jinping pointed out, "In understanding the socialist market economy, we should adopt a dialectical and dichotomous approach that leverages both visible and invisible hands.[5] The roles of the government and the market are not antagonistic but complementary. Neither of their roles should be reduced. Ideally, they should combine, collaborate, coordinate, and complement each other."[6] By investigating the truth and studying the issue from a dialectical and dichotomous approach, the way to effective collaboration between the market and government can be found. This way, the socialist market economy can make full use of the advantages of the market and the government, showcasing the features and advantages of the socialist market economic system. "Strive to form a pattern of organic unity between the market and government, mutually complementing, coordinating, and promoting their roles."[7] The refined

[3]Party Literature Research Center of the CPC Central Committee (Ed.) (2008). *Selected Important Documents of Thirty Years of Reform and Opening Up,* Vol. I. Central Party Literature Press, pp. 659–660.

[4]Party Literature Research Center of the CPC Central Committee (Ed.) (2014). *Selected Important Documents since the 18th CPC National Congress,* Vol. I. Central Party Literature Press, p. 500.

[5]Publicity Department of the CPC Central Committee (Ed.). (2016). *General Secretary Xi Jinping Important Speech Series* (2016 Edition). Learning Publishing House and People's Publishing House, p. 62.

[6]*Ibid.*, p. 64.

[7]*Ibid.*, p. 62.

theoretical positioning of the government–market relationship is based on China's economic reality and economic reform practices. It is a rational improvement of this practical experience and an important presentation of the development theme of socialist political economics with Chinese characteristics.

Based on the realities of China's economy, it is essential to adopt a methodology that focuses on "problem awareness." Focusing on "problem awareness" means identifying and addressing the unique challenges in the development of the political economics of socialism with Chinese characteristics. In the commentary on the *Decision of the CCCPC on Some Major Issues Concerning Comprehensively Deepening the Reform*, which was adopted at the Third Plenary Session of the 18th Central Committee of the Communist Party of China, Xi Jinping emphasized, "A strong problem awareness is essential. We must prioritize addressing the most important challenges, concentrate on identifying and studying key problems, and make concerted efforts to resolve the various pressing conflicts and difficulties that China faces in its development."[8] By emphasizing the importance of "problem awareness" and Xi Jinping directly addresses the challenges faced in our economic development. Notable challenges include uneven, uncoordinated, and unsustainable growth; limited capacity for technological innovation; an irrational industrial structure; resource-intensive development methods; and significant disparities in urban and rural regional development, as well as income distribution among residents. In the development of the socialist market economy, strengthening our awareness of these issues involves a clear understanding of the following: "After more than twenty years of practice, China's socialist market economy system has been initially established. However, numerous problems persist, such as unregulated market order with widespread instances of individuals seeking economic benefits through improper means; an underdeveloped market for factors of production, where idle resources coexist with unmet demands; inconsistent market rules, with a high prevalence of sectoral and regional protectionism; and insufficient market competition, hindering the elimination of inferior enterprises and structural adjustments, among others. Without adequately addressing these challenges, it would be difficult to form a well-functioning socialist market economy system."[9]

---

[8]Party Literature Research Center of the CPC Central Committee (2014), *Op. cit.*, p. 497.
[9]*Ibid.*, p. 500.

The foundation of effective problem-solving is being aware of problems and directly addressing them. By adopting a "pressure-induced impetus," we can further increase external pressure and internal motivation for economic reforms, in turn effectively advancing the reform process. Xi Jinping emphasizes, "As Chinese Communists, our work in revolution, nation-building, and reform has always been focused on solving the real and pressing issues of China. It can be said that reforms are driven by problems and are improved through the continuous resolution of these issues."[10] From fostering "problem awareness" to employing a "pressure-induced impetus," both serve as a strategic method for tackling China's economic development challenges and forging the path for China's economic reform while emphasizing the distinctiveness of the political economics of China's development.

Identifying and addressing problems necessitates taking into account both the historical context and relevant theoretical frameworks. The integration of reality, history, and theory constitutes the fundamental method and position of Marxist political economics. Engels asserted, "The conditions under which people produce and exchange differ in every country and even more so among various generations within each country. As a result, political economics cannot be universally applicable to all countries and historical periods."[11] Essentially, political economics is a historical science, and the integration of reality with history and theory is an intrinsic aspect of its methodology.

"History is the best textbook." In his explanation of the "Decision" passed at the Third Plenary Session of the 18th CPC Central Committee, Xi Jinping emphasized: "Considering both historical lessons and current necessities, since the 18th National Congress, the Central Committee has repeatedly stressed that reform and opening up is the key move that determines contemporary China's destiny, and it is also the key move to achieve the 'Two Centennial Goals' and the great rejuvenation of the Chinese nation."[12] "Historical experience" not only reveals the origins of the current economic reality but also forecasts its future trends. It serves as both a mirror of reality and a source of theoretical insight. In his analysis of the development of the socialist market economy, Xi Jinping emphasized: "In 1992, the 14th National Congress of the Party proposed

---

[10] *Ibid.*, p. 497.

[11] *Collected Works of Marx and Engels*, Vol. 9. People's Publishing House, 2009, p. 153.

[12] Party Literature Research Center of the CPC Central Committee (2014), *Op. cit.*, p. 494.

that the goal of China's economic system reform is to establish a socialist market economy and to allow the market to play a fundamental role in resource allocation under the state's macro-control. This major theoretical breakthrough has played an extremely important role in China's reform, opening up, and socioeconomic development."[13] According to Marx, "studying the contributions of economic theories throughout history involves exploring how economic laws were initially revealed and how they evolved over time."[14]

The political economics of China's development is based on China's economic facts and realities, and it takes into account the combination of economic reality with history and theory. It focuses on issues specific to China, addresses the challenges of China's development, and proposes theories and strategies for effectively solving China's problems, managing its affairs, and constructing and developing its economy. As a result, it forms a contemporary Chinese Marxist political economics that is suitable for the country's unique conditions and characteristics during the initial stage of socialism.

2. New Research and Application of the Basic Principles of Marxist Political Economics

As a Sinicized Marxist political economics, the political economics of socialism with Chinese characteristics serves dual purposes. Firstly, it represents the process of adapting Marxist political economics to the Chinese context, applying its fundamental principles to the specific realities of China's reform and opening up, and using it to analyze and solve real-world problems in China's socialist economy. As Mao Zedong said, it aims to "make Marxism relevant in China by adapting the principles of Marxism in a way that is specific and applicable to the unique context and conditions of China."[15] Secondly, it also represents the process of Sinicizing Marxist political economics, transforming the practical understanding gained from the development of China's socialist economy and reform and opening-up practices into new concepts and ideas. This helps achieve the integration of Marxism into political economics and forms a

[13] *Ibid.*, p. 498.

[14] *Collected Works of Marx and Engels*, Vol. 33. People's Publishing House, 2004, p. 417.

[15] *Selected Works of Mao Zedong*, Vol. 2. People's Publishing House, 1991, p. 534.

new meaning, theory, and form of Marxist political economics with Chinese characteristics. This aligns with Mao Zedong's idea of "integrating the important experiences and knowledge gained from the Chinese revolution into a Marxist framework."[16]

Applying the fundamental principles of Marxist political economics in contemporary China entails addressing two key considerations: the need for a scientific approach in its application to the present context and the imperative to advance the development of Marxist political economics within China. When adopting a "scientific approach," we must differentiate between four aspects: (a) determining which fundamental Marxist principles must be upheld in the long term, (b) identifying theoretical judgments that need to be enriched and developed in light of new realities, (c) dismantling dogmatic interpretations of Marxism, and (d) clarifying misconceptions falsely attributed to Marxism. Regarding further developing Marxist political economics in China, it is crucial to have a comprehensive understanding of its core principles. This includes in-depth research on a series of important economic ideas by Marx and Engels that were previously unknown to us. Such research promotes the advancement of political economics of socialism with Chinese characteristics and demonstrates the contemporary relevance of Marxist political economics.

The concept of productive forces is a central aspect of Marxist political economics. In Marxism, science and technology have always been considered part of the productive forces. Over a hundred years ago, Marx emphasized that natural science should be consciously integrated into the development and improvement of machine production. He also asserted that "productive forces encompass science,"[17] as can be seen in his *Economic Manuscripts of 1857–1858*. This long-overlooked theoretical perspective by Marx has gained new significance in the context of China's economic reforms. It has become one of the most important theoretical viewpoints within the political economics of socialism with Chinese characteristics, demonstrating the ongoing relevance of Marxist thought.

Concerning the evolution of social and economic systems, the economic formation of society theory is a fundamental principle of Marxist political economics. Since the implementation of economic reforms and the opening-up policy, Marx's theory of the three forms of human development, as proposed in his manuscript *Grundrisse: Foundations of the*

---

[16] *Ibid.*, 1993, p. 374.

[17] *Selected Works of Deng Xiaoping*, Vol. 2. People's Publishing House, 1994, p. 87.

Critique of Political Economics, has become the focus in the study of Marxist theories on the economic formation of society. During the progression of socio-economic relations, shifts in "social conditions" drive the growth of human productive forces, with the first major form being characterized by "human dependency." At this stage, human productive capacity develops only within limited scopes and isolated locations, as people rely on nature to directly sustain themselves. The formation of human independence, based on material dependency, characterizes the second major form. On one hand, all fixed dependencies among individuals in production have been dissolved; on the other hand, a comprehensive interdependence among unrelated individuals gives rise to social connections among them. The universally developed product exchange relationship serves as the bond that unites these social connections. In this context, human social relations are transformed into tangible, material relations, and human abilities are converted into practical resources contributing to production and societal development. In this widespread material exchange network, people develop a wide range of relationships, diverse needs, and a versatile set of skills and abilities. The third major form is characterized by the development of personal freedom. In this social formation, "personal freedom" has two defining aspects: first, the well-rounded development of each individual, and second, individuals' collective productive abilities contribute to their overall social wealth.[18] The theory of the three major forms of human development laid the theoretical groundwork for the establishment of the socialist market economic system, providing intellectual methods and fundamental ideas for a development concept centered around human development.

In the latest exploration of Marx and Engels' ideas about socialist societies, Marxist political economics reveals the meaning behind Engels' theory. Engels said that a "socialist society" shouldn't be viewed as static but instead as a society that always evolves and improves, just like any other social system.[19] After the early 1870s, Marx and Engels further investigated capitalist economic relations through the lens of global history, considering the broader context and historical patterns. They explored the social development paths of economically underdeveloped countries and raised the issue of "Leaping Over the Caudine Forks of

---

[18] See *The Complete Works of Marx and Engels*, Vol. 30. People's Publishing House, 1995, pp. 107–108.

[19] *Collected Works of Marx and Engels*, Vol. 10. People's Publishing House, 2009, p. 588.

Capitalism." In the early 1880s, Marx raised the question of whether Russia could "leap over the Caudine Forks of capitalism" and apply all the positive outcomes created by the capitalist system to their socialist society. In other words, he asked if Russia could bypass the capitalist stage and still benefit from the positive aspects created by capitalism.[20] Fundamentally, Marx posed the question of whether economically underdeveloped countries, under specific historical conditions, could find a path that avoids the disastrous consequences of capitalist development while still benefiting from all the positive achievements of capitalism. In current China, the question has become more concrete and is asking the specifics of whether the "positive achievements" of the capitalist system, such as the commodity economy, market economy, share capital, and financial capital, can be effectively incorporated and adopted within the socialist economic practices and theories that characterize China's unique approach to socialism. Marx and Engels' theoretical concept of "leaping over the Caudine forks of capitalism" has influenced China's highly successful economic reforms and formed a political economics theory with Chinese characteristics that emphasizes international engagement and cooperation.

The concept of achieving balance and harmony between humans and nature is a crucial component of Marxist political economics. As Engels pointed out, "We should not be too complacent with our victories over nature. For every such victory, nature retaliates against us." He specifically stated, "With every step we take, we must remember: we do not dominate nature in the same way conquerors dominate foreign peoples, nor do we control it as if we were outside of it. Instead, we, along with our flesh, blood, and minds, belong to nature and exist within it. Our entire control over nature lies in our ability to understand and apply its laws more effectively than any other living being."[21] Once we understand this deeply, we can better appreciate the following principle: "We must build an ecological system that respects nature and promotes green development. While humans can use and change nature, we are ultimately part of it, and must protect it without trying to dominate it. We need to tackle the problems brought about by industrial civilization. Our goal should be harmonious existence between humans and nature, which will lead to

[20] See *Ibid.*, Vol. 3, p. 575, 587.

[21] *Ibid.*, Vol. 9, pp. 559–560.

sustainable global development and well-rounded human development."[22] The theories about ecological civilization in the political economics of socialism with Chinese characteristics give new intellectual vitality to Marx and Engels' important concepts and make these concepts more relevant to today's world.

3. The "Terminological Revolution" in the Political Economics of China's Development

Engels, when evaluating the scientific achievements of Marx's *Das Kapital*, once noted: "Every new insight introduced by a science involves a revolution in the terminology of that science."[23] Marx greatly appreciated the scientific value of the "revolution in terminology" found in *Das Kapital*. He believed that the three "novel elements"[24] in the first volume of *Das Kapital* were reflected in the "revolution in terminology" related to surplus value, the dual nature of labor, and the category of wages. Marx made two types of terminological revolutions. The first type involved creating and introducing new terminology, such as the dual nature of labor, surplus value, constant and variable capital, social capital reproduction, and production prices. The second type involved critically redefining existing terminologies, such as wages, exchange value, money, capital, profit, interest, and rent. His ultimate aim was to critically evaluate the popular terminology used in political economics at the time.

Engels highlighted two fundamental features in his description of the "terminological revolution" within Marx's political economics. The first pertains to the methodological dimension of this revolution. Engels provided a critique of the prevailing "conventional political economics" during his time for its failure to recognize the limitations of confining itself to a specific range of ideas represented by certain terms. These terms were never subject to systematic evaluation.[25] Marx's "terminological

[22] Xi Jinping. (2015). Working together to forge a new partnership of win-win cooperation and create a community of shared future for mankind. *People's Daily* (Overseas Edition), September 29, 2015.

[23] *Collected Works of Marx and Engels*, Vol. 5. People's Publishing House, 2009, p. 32.

[24] *Ibid.*, Vol. 10, p. 275.

[25] *Ibid.*, Vol. 5, p. 33.

revolution" in political economics, however, utilized the materialist conception of history to analyze capitalist economic relations comprehensively. Second is the social and historical perspective of the "terminological revolution." Engels believed that the terminology used in political economics, which viewed modern capitalist production as merely a temporary stage in human economic history, was necessarily different from the terminology used by authors who regarded this form of production as eternal and final.[26] The popular economic theories of the time erased the essential differences between various historical periods of economic history. These theories used fishermen, hunters, or Robinson Crusoe stranded on a deserted island as examples or representations of humans in relation to economic activities. However, these examples lack historical and social specificity, turning economic categories into hollow "creeds" that fail to account for the complexities of real-world economic systems. Engels' elaboration on the overall methodology and social-historical significance of the "terminological revolution" in Marx's political economics accurately captured the essence of this "terminological revolution."

In discussing the significance of the "terminological revolution" in the history of scientific development, Thomas Kuhn made a similar argument in *The Structure of Scientific Revolutions*. He believed that "scientific revolutions entail shifts in the interconnected concepts used by scientists to perceive the world," "embracing a new paradigm frequently necessitates redefining the associated science," and "when the criteria for determining valid problems, concepts, and explanations are altered, the entire discipline undergoes a transformation."[27] The evolution of political economics of socialism with Chinese characteristics is primarily characterized by the "terminological revolution" and the establishment of a distinct Chinese discourse framework.

Marx's fundamental principle, present in both historical materialism and political economics, states that "the social relations of production into which men enter when they develop their productive forces materially correspond to a definite stage of development of their material forces of production."[28] During the early stages of the reform and opening-up, Deng Xiaoping suggested that "the main goal of socialism is to grow the

---

[26]*Ibid.*, p. 33.

[27]Thomas Kuhn. (2012). *The Structure of Scientific Revolutions*. Peking University Press, 2012, p. 88, 91.

[28]*Collected Works of Marx and Engels*, Vol. 1. People's Publishing House, 2009, p. 724.

economy and steadily improve people's living standards."[29] Later, he emphasized the importance of thoroughly considering and actively promoting both the liberation and growth of economic productivity.[30] This focus on economic productivity demonstrates a practical understanding and use of a key principle in Marxist political economics, which deals with the balance between the resources used in production and the social structure that governs production. At the 16th National Congress of the Communist Party of China, Jiang Zemin stressed the significance of "prioritizing the liberation and development of productive forces" and positioned it as a crucial responsibility of the Chinese Communist Party in governing and revitalizing the nation. During the 18th National Congress, Hu Jintao identified "unleashing and nurturing social productive forces" as the "fundamental prerequisite" to secure a new triumph for socialism with Chinese characteristics.

Following the 18th National Congress of the Communist Party, Xi Jinping proposed the idea of "liberating and stimulating the immense potential hidden in science and technology."[31] This idea serves as the primary productive force and provides a new perspective on the contemporary significance of turning scientific and technological advancements into practical productive forces. In advancing the construction of an ecological civilization, Xi Jinping introduced the belief that protecting the environment preserves productivity, while improving the environment develops productivity.[32] These concepts, "preserving productivity" and "developing productivity," have become the theoretical foundation and practical direction for planning the development of an ecological civilization. Regarding his view on the new normal of China's economic development, Xi Jinping emphasized the importance of enhancing innovation-driven development capacity, improving industrial competitiveness, and increasing the quality and efficiency of economic growth, which is a new way to understand and plan for the changes in the

[29] *Selected Works of Deng Xiaoping*, Vol. 3. People's Publishing House, 1993, p. 116.

[30] *Ibid.*, p. 370.

[31] *Xi Jinping: The Governance of China*. Foreign Languages Press, 2014, p. 121.

[32] Xi Jinping emphasizes adherence to the basic national policy of resource conservation and environmental protection, striving toward a new era of socialist ecological civilization during the sixth collective study session of the CPC Central Committee's Political Bureau. *People's Daily*, May 25, 2013.

economy.[33] His goal is to achieve a significant leap in China's overall social productivity levels.

The transition from "addressing overall productivity" to "achieving an overall leap in social productivity levels" depicts the fundamental framework of China's economic reform and development. This also represents a "terminological revolution" in the area of productivity. In the explanation of this "terminological revolution" and its Chinese discourse, several aspects have been clarified and expanded:

- The primary challenge facing socialist societies is the need to reconcile the ever-growing material and cultural needs of the populace with the slower pace of growth in social production. A nuanced understanding of this challenge has enhanced our comprehension of the economic characteristics and underlying principles that shape the initial phase of socialism.
- A more profound comprehension of socialism's core has been reached, setting the primary objective and guiding values of socialism as the pursuit of shared wealth and prosperity.
- The theoretical basis for the party's initial phase of socialism, which is centered on economic construction, has been thoroughly examined and clarified. The core objective of the economic development strategy is to achieve socialist modernization. This is accompanied by clear strategic planning and a series of well-defined steps.
- The understanding of the distribution of productive forces and the diverse economic relations in the initial stage of socialism has been clarified. This has formed the theoretical basis for the structure of ownership and distribution systems during this stage.
- By enhancing the understanding of the relationship between economic growth and development, a basic approach for transforming the mode of economic development has been formed. This approach serves as a foundation for improving the economic growth and development of the country.
- The concept of openness to the outside world has been broadened, leading to the development of new viewpoints on international economic relations in the context of globalization.

---

[33] CPC Central Committee Holds Forum with Non-CPC Personages. *People's Daily*, July 30, 2014.

The development of China's political economics has undergone a unique "terminological revolution," which has resulted in the creation of original terms such as the initial stage of socialism, the primary contradiction in socialist society, economic system reform, the essence of socialism, the "Three Favorables," the household responsibility system, the concepts of "getting rich first" and "common prosperity," the socialist market economy, state-owned enterprises, private enterprise, building a moderately prosperous society, development ideology, and opening up to the outside world. These achievements in "terminological revolution" have become prominent markers of contemporary Marxist political economics and academic paradigm in China.

In the development of political economics in China, there has been a "terminological revolution" with a critical and inheritable nature, including terms like resource allocation, macroeconomic analysis, and microeconomic analysis. This raises the question of how to scientifically deal with various foreign economic theories and trends. We need to value the essence of various economic theories, while rejecting and criticizing their undesirable elements. We should not underestimate or blindly follow foreign economic theories, nor should we be arrogant and dismissive of them without studying and learning from them. Contemporary foreign economic theories and trends have shed new light on issues such as the role of markets in resource allocation, market regulation and mechanisms, market failure and macroeconomic instability, government regulation of micro and macroeconomic issues, and policy implementation. They have formed and put forward many new knowledge and academic viewpoints that have practical significance. These are also essential aspects of the development of contemporary socialist political economics with Chinese characteristics. When adopting foreign economic theories, particularly those with a monopolistic capitalist ideology like neoliberalism, caution is required. We should critically analyze and evaluate them, and distinguish between what is beneficial and what is harmful.

4. "The First Draft" of the Development of China's Political Economics

Looking back at history, Mao Zedong's speech "On the Ten Major Relationships" in April 1956 was the origin of China's socialist political economics with Chinese characteristics. The publication of this speech coincided with a crucial historical turning point in China's socialist development. In this speech, Mao Zedong proposed the idea of "adopting a policy of active and rational development"[34] based on the principles of "following the laws of natural and economic development."[35] He also adhered to the method of "viewing from the perspective of development"[36] and provided the initial theoretical interpretation of the basic issues of China's socialist political economics. This had a significant and long-lasting impact on the formation and development of China's socialist political economics with Chinese characteristics.

In a speech commemorating the 120th anniversary of Mao Zedong's birth, Xi Jinping highlighted how Mao used lessons from the Soviet Union to create new theories for China. He emphasized Mao's success in realizing "the second round of efforts" to integrate the basic tenets of Marxism-Leninism with China's realities, and in finding the right path for the country's socialist revolution and development.[37] Xi Jinping commended the contributions of Mao Zedong's "On the Ten Major Relationships" in generating novel theoretical frameworks and literary works through the lens of "the second round of efforts" to integrate Marxism-Leninism with China's unique circumstances. In 2015, Xi Jinping discussed the original ideas Mao and other Chinese communists proposed for China's economic development during a study session on Marxist political economics. These ideas included recognizing the challenges in socialist society, emphasizing overall planning and balanced development, and coordinating agriculture and industry with a focus on agriculture as the foundation and industry as the leading sector. Xi Jinping lauded these ideas as creative developments in Marxist political economics.[38] He praised the theoretical essence of socialist political economics found in "On the Ten Major Relationships" and its innovative development. Xi Jinping's evaluations show that "On the Ten Major Relationships" is a ground-breaking work of socialist political economics

---

[34] *Ibid.*, p. 540.

[35] Central Compilation and Translation Bureau of the Communist Party of China (Ed.) (2013). *Chronology of Mao Zedong (1949–1976)*, Vol. 2. Central Literature Publishing House, 2013, p. 535.

[36] *Selected Works of Mao Zedong*, Vol. 7. People's Publishing House, 1999, p. 44.

[37] Party Literature Research Center of the CPC Central Committee (2014), *Op. cit.*, p. 691.

[38] Based on China's realities and development practices, advance Marxist political economics in contemporary China. *People's Daily*, November 25, 2015.

with Chinese characteristics, providing valuable guidance for the continued development of socialism in China.

The development of socialist political economics with Chinese characteristics emerged and grew during the period of economic reform and opening up. Before the 18th National Congress of the Communist Party of China, an initial draft of this political economics had taken shape. It was based on the study of the economic system during the early stages of socialism, focused on the establishment and improvement of the socialist market economy system, and covered key topics such as the nature of the economic system, economic system reform, economic development, and opening up to the outside world.

The first aspect of China's socialist political economics is the theory of the basic economic system of the primary stage of socialism. Deng Xiaoping addressed the question of "what is socialism and how to build socialism" by stating: "A dominant public ownership and the common prosperity are the fundamental principles of socialism that we must uphold. We are determined to implement and achieve these socialist principles."[39] These two fundamental principles represent the essence of the economic system in the initial phase of socialism.

During the initial phase of socialism in China, the basic economic system consisted of diverse forms of ownership side-by-side with a dominant public ownership. The public ownership of the means of production is the foundation of the socialist economic system. Public ownership plays a pivotal role in society, as evidenced by the prevalence of public assets among the total assets. The state-owned economy controls the country's economic lifelines and leads the way in driving economic development. The implementation methods and approaches of public ownership can and should be diversified. Accelerating the reform and development of modern enterprise systems for state-owned enterprises is crucial, and the shareholding system is one of the primary forms of public ownership that should be further developed. The two essential principles for maintaining and improving the socialist economic systems are consolidating and developing the public ownership economy, while simultaneously encouraging, supporting, and guiding the development of the non-public ownership economy. These principles ensure the balanced and sustainable development of the economy, promoting both efficiency and equity. They are critical to achieving the long-term goal of common prosperity for all.

[39] *Selected Works of Deng Xiaoping*, Vol. 3. People's Publishing House, 1993, p. 111.

The innovation in the distribution theory of socialist political economics with Chinese characteristics can be attributed to its adherence to a distribution system that mainly focuses on distribution according to work. At the same time, it allows for the utilization of various distribution methods. This approach provides flexibility and efficiency in the distribution process, leading to the achievement of socialist goals while promoting social equity. The distribution theory of socialist political economics with Chinese characteristics innovatively combines distribution based on labor with distribution according to production factors. This system improves the way different factors such as labor, capital, technology, and management are involved in distribution, based on their respective inputs. By encouraging some individuals to become wealthy first, this system lays the foundation for achieving the ultimate goal of common prosperity for the entire society. To uphold and improve the distribution system during the early stages of socialism, it is essential to strike a balance between efficiency and fairness. This applies to both primary distribution and redistribution. In redistribution, greater emphasis should be placed on fairness. Gradually increasing the proportion of residents' income in national income distribution and the share of labor remuneration in primary distribution helps to reverse the trend of widening income disparities.

The second aspect of China's socialist political economics is the theory of the socialist market economy system. The theory of socialist market economy is the core of economic system reform and it is guided by the reform theory. Reform is not about minor adjustments to the existing economic system; instead, it represents a complete transformation of the economic system. The nature of reform, like past revolutions, aims to eliminate obstacles to the development of productive forces and help China overcome poverty and underdevelopment. From this perspective, reform can also be described as a revolutionary, radical transformation. Fundamentally, reform involves adjusting socialist economic relations. Innovation is essential to the improvement and development of the socialist economic system.[40]

The theory of the socialist market economy system reform must be thoroughly examined and taken into account in the process of selecting the target model for China's economic system reform. Prior to the 14th National Congress of the Communist Party of China, there were

---

[40] *Ibid.*, p. 135.

various economic systems being explored, such as a planned economy with market regulation as a supplement, a planned socialist commodity economy, and an approach that combines both planned and market economy. After the 14th National Congress, the target model for the socialist market economy system was established, which provided initial guidance on the definition and construction of a socialist market economy system. The *Decision on Several Issues Concerning the Establishment of a Socialist Market Economy System* passed at the Third Plenary Session of the 14th CPC Central Committee outlined the basic framework for the socialist market economy system. It provided specific regulations for reforms, including the establishment of modern enterprise systems, fostering a market system, transforming government functions, creating a macroeconomic regulation system, and setting up a social security system.

The 15th National Congress of the Communist Party of China emphasized the importance of adhering to the reform direction of the socialist market economy. It also emphasized the need to integrate the development of a market economy and the process of economic marketization with the initial phase of socialism. Its goal is to promote innovation in the socialist market economy system reform to achieve significant breakthroughs in major system reforms that impact overall economic and social development. At the 17th National Congress, the proposal to deepen the understanding of the laws governing the socialist market economy was put forward, with the aim of better leveraging the market's fundamental role in resource allocation through institutional arrangements. Additionally, the Congress emphasized the need for the establishment of a macroeconomic regulation system that promotes scientific development. The Congress also called for accelerating the formation of a unified, open, competitive, and orderly modern market system; developing various production factor markets; and establishing a modern financial system featuring diverse ownership and business forms, a reasonable structure, comprehensive functions, and high efficiency and security.

The third aspect of China's socialist political economics is the theory of socialist economic development. Deng Xiaoping said that "development is the absolute principle" and "China's main goal is development." Later, during the Third Generation of the CPC Central Leadership under Jiang Zemin, it was emphasized that "development must be the top priority for the Party's governance and national rejuvenation." This reflects the profound insights of the Communist Party of China on the issue of development. Since the 16th National Congress was held in 2002, with

Hu Jintao as the General Secretary of the CPC Central Committee, the Party has focused on major issues such as "what kind of development to achieve and how to develop." It has proposed the major strategic concept of scientific development, emphasizing that development is still the top priority. The main principle is to prioritize the needs of the people, while the basic requirement is to achieve comprehensive, coordinated, and sustainable development. The fundamental approach is to take all factors into consideration and strive for balance.

To advance socialist modernization, it is important to scientifically formulate and refine the "three-step" development strategy in accordance with the national conditions of the initial phase of socialism. To build a moderately prosperous society in all respects, it is necessary to accelerate the transformation of the economic development model. To speed up the transformation of economic development model, it's necessary to focus on the strategic adjustments of the economic structure. Technological progress and innovation provide crucial support for the transformation process, while ensuring and improving people's livelihoods is the cornerstone and ultimate goal of this transformation. Building a resource-saving and environmentally friendly society is its key focus, and reform and opening up is its powerful driving force.

The fourth aspect of China's socialist political economics is the strategy of integration with the global economy. Engaging with the global economy is a fundamental approach to China's socialist modernization and an essential component of socialism with Chinese characteristics in the field of political economics. Since the reform and opening up, the Communist Party of China has adopted a basic approach of opening up and formed a strategy of integration with the global economy that aligns with its socialist policies. This strategy covers various aspects and sectors and is not limited to just one area. To achieve mutual benefits in the global economy, China must continue to improve its level of openness and speed up the implementation of the "going global" strategy. It's essential to actively participate in global economic governance and regional cooperation while creating new advantages for international economic cooperation and competition. While maintaining an open economy, China should focus on promoting independent innovation and achieving self-reliance, leveraging its own strengths. Additionally, China needs to protect its own economic interests and ensure economic stability by guarding against risks posed by globalization and other external factors.

5. Theoretical Advancement Toward the Decisive Victory of Building a Moderately Prosperous Society in All Respects

Since the 18th National Congress of the Communist Party of China held in 2012, under the leadership of Xi Jinping, the Party Central Committee has set achieving a moderately prosperous society in all respects as its strategic goal. The Party has analyzed and evaluated the trends and specific characteristics of China's contemporary economic relations within the framework of new governance concepts, ideas, and strategies. In addition, the Party has fully understood and grasped the changing features and basic tendencies of contemporary international economic relations. Amid the changing economic landscape, China has sustained steady and continuous economic growth by adapting to the evolving conditions. As a result, it has further advanced its socialist political economics with Chinese characteristics and opened a new chapter in the country's economic development.

The fundamental belief of contemporary Chinese Marxist political economics is to adopt a problem-oriented approach, focusing on resolving main problems and addressing weaknesses, while also listening to and responding to the needs of the people to ensure that they benefit from the outcomes. As summarized by Xi Jinping: "We must stick to the people-oriented development ideology which is the fundamental stance of Marxist political economics. The goal of economic development should be to improve the well-being and promote the comprehensive development of people, and to steadily move toward common prosperity for all. This should be the primary concern and the foundation of all economic development efforts. The deployment of economic work, the formulation of economic policies, and the advancement of economic development must be firmly guided by this fundamental stance."[41]

Since the founding of the People's Republic of China, and especially since the reform and opening up, China's political economics has been characterized by a set of new development concepts: innovation, coordination, environmental sustainability, openness, and sharing. These concepts summarize the theoretical framework that guides China's economic and social development. These concepts offer a fresh approach to the crucial strategic question of "what type of development and how to

---

[41] People's Daily (2015), *Op. cit.*

achieve it" and are an integral part of China's new concepts and strategies for governance and administration.

Innovation is the primary driving force for development. To promote innovation, we need to establish a supportive system and prioritize leading-edge development driven by innovation, which can take advantage of the first-mover benefit. In order to achieve sustainable and healthy development, coordination is essential across various aspects, such as economic, social, and environmental, to ensure balanced and harmonious development. To create a more harmonious and sustainable society, we need to pursue regional collaboration, urban–rural integration, and balanced social and economic development, while also integrating economic and national defense construction. By coordinating these efforts, we can expand our development opportunities and address areas of weakness. Environmental sustainability is a crucial element of long-term development and an essential aspect of people's pursuit of a better life. To achieve this, we must prioritize environmentally friendly approaches and ensure that they contribute to the economic prosperity of the country and the well-being of the people. We should also strive to provide more high-quality, eco-friendly products and promote sustainable living patterns. By working together, we can help achieve a prosperous, powerful, and beautiful China. Openness is an essential path to achieving national prosperity and development. We must expand the scope of openness by increasing our level of engagement with the outside world and working together to promote strategic trust, economic and trade cooperation, and cultural exchanges. By embracing new opportunities and fostering deep, mutually beneficial relationships, we can create a more integrated and cooperative global community that benefits all parties involved. Sharing is an essential requirement of socialism with Chinese characteristics. We need to prioritize attaining social fairness and justice, so that everyone can benefit from the fruits of reform and development. This is crucial as it demonstrates the superiority of the socialist system.

The political economics of socialism with Chinese characteristics has adhered to its fundamental position and development concepts while making various expansions in constructing and developing a "systematic economic theory." This theory aims to provide a comprehensive understanding of the economy. It incorporates ideas from Marxism and Chinese traditions and practices. The theory is constantly evolving to adapt to new challenges and circumstances.

First and foremost, it is essential to prioritize the adherence to and improvement of the basic economic system. This requires a steadfast commitment to consolidating and developing the public ownership economy, as well as providing unwavering encouragement, support, and guidance for the growth of non-public ownership economies. This approach aims to promote mutual development and the sharing of strengths and weaknesses among different forms of ownership. China is a socialist country led by the Chinese Communist Party, and it has developed its public ownership economy over the long-term national development process. This system has made significant contributions to national construction, defense security, and the improvement of people's livelihoods. The public ownership economy, as a collective resource, is seen as a valuable asset that benefits everyone in the country. The dominant position of public ownership and the leading role of the state-owned economy must not be undermined, as these are institutional guarantees for ensuring that people of all ethnic groups in China share the fruits of development. The role of the state-owned economy is also crucial in consolidating the Party's ruling position and maintaining China's socialist system. Xi Jinping emphasizes that maintaining public ownership as the dominant form is a major policy established by the Chinese Communist Party. However, this policy also allows for the co-development of diverse ownership economies. The public ownership system is an essential component of socialism with Chinese characteristics and a necessary requirement for improving the socialist market economy.[42] It is essential for the public ownership economy to improve and continue playing a role in reform, opening up, and modernization.

Over an extended period, the non-public ownership economy in China has experienced rapid growth, assuming a significant role in promoting innovation, stabilizing economic growth, generating employment opportunities, and enhancing people's livelihoods. The non-public ownership economy is an essential foundation for economic stability, a primary area for expanding employment, a vital source of national tax revenue, an essential body for technological innovation, an important support for financial development, and a crucial force for steady and healthy economic development. Focusing on strengthening and expanding the public

---

[42]Xi Jinping. (2016). Unwavering adherence to China's basic economic system to promote healthy development of enterprises under diverse forms of ownership. *People's Daily*, March 9, 2016.

ownership economy while simultaneously encouraging, supporting, and guiding the growth of the non-public ownership economy represents an organic unity, rather than a contradiction. Public and non-public ownership economies should complement and benefit each other, not exclude or offset each other. Xi Jinping stated, "Both public and non-public ownership economies experience some contradictions and problems during their development, and they face various difficulties and challenges that require our joint efforts to solve. However, we must not focus on a single issue and lose sight of the overall situation. Any viewpoint aiming to negate either the public ownership economy or the non-public ownership economy does not align with the fundamental interests of the majority of people, nor does it meet the demands of our country's reform and development, and therefore, it is incorrect."[43]

Secondly, we must commit to and refine the socialist basic distribution system. We have to align residents' income growth with economic growth and synchronize the rise in labor compensation with improved labor productivity. We need to consistently enhance systems and policies, adjust the national income distribution patterns, steadily increase the income of urban and rural residents, and gradually reduce income gaps. It's crucial to make sure that development benefits are distributed more equitably among everyone, moving our society steadily toward common prosperity.

Thirdly, we must focus on developing a socialist market economy, enabling the market to have a decisive influence on resource allocation while improving the government's role. Balancing the relationship between the government and the market is central to economic reform. Highlighting the market's decisive function in resource allocation is a new breakthrough in understanding the principles of building socialism with Chinese characteristics. This perspective helps establish a proper understanding of the government–market relationship, transition to new economic development models, transform government functions, and curb negative corruption. It's crucial to maintain the direction of socialist market economy reforms and continue integrating the basic socialist system with the market economy. We must make effective use of both the "invisible hand" and the "visible hand" to maximize the benefits of both aspects.

Fourthly, China's economy is moving toward a new stage of development, which is recognized as the new normal for economic development.

---

[43] Xi Jinping (2016), *Op. cit.*

The strategic assessment of this new normal is based on the changes in the country's overall social productivity and the fundamental principles of promoting the liberation and development of productive forces. Achieving a significant increase in China's overall social productivity level is both the beginning and the end goal for this new normal of economic development. Understanding, adapting to, and leading the new normal are vital to China's current and future economic development. Entering this new normal doesn't change the fact that China's development still has significant strategic opportunities for progress; however, it does alter the nature and conditions of these opportunities. It doesn't change the overall positive trajectory of China's economic development but instead changes its mode and structure. It doesn't change the fundamental task and principle of liberating and developing productive forces, but it does change the methods and approaches for developing social productivity. Marx believed that social reproduction occurs "continuously and concurrently." Examining the time continuity and spatial coexistence of economic processes is an important aspect of Marxist political economics. A comprehensive understanding of the temporal and spatial dimensions of social productivity patterns is essential for this new normal of economic development. In other words, Marx's theory of social reproduction refers to the process by which a society reproduces itself both materially and socially, including the reproduction of its social classes, relationships, and ideologies. According to Marx, this process is continuous and occurs concurrently, meaning that it happens repeatedly and simultaneously.[44] The examination of the temporal continuity and spatial coexistence of economic processes is an important aspect of Marxist political economics because it allows us to understand how the economic system works over time and space (different historical times and geographical locations/countries), and how it reproduces itself through these processes. A comprehensive understanding of the temporal and spatial dimensions of social productivity patterns is also essential for this new normal of economic development. This means that we need to have a clear understanding of how the economy is evolving over time and space in order to effectively promote economic growth and development in the current phase. This new normal creates fresh strategic opportunities and offers new resources, conditions, methods, and environments for progress. To achieve the desired outcomes, it is necessary to actively drive the reforms forward

[44] *Collected Works of Marx and Engels*, Vol. 6. People's Publishing House, 2009, p. 117.

across various fields. Additionally, it is important to effectively complete the tasks of transforming and adjusting the economic development model to meet current needs. Finally, it's very crucial to achieve steady, high-speed economic growth while enhancing the quality and efficiency of production, improving technology and innovation, and moving toward more advanced and sophisticated industries.

The new normal of economic development is a constantly evolving process with a defined goal. Xi Jinping has stated that during the "13th Five-Year Plan" period, the notable characteristic of China's economic development was its entry into a period of new normal. This phase is a necessary stage in the evolution of China's economy toward more advanced stages of development, more efficient allocation of labor resources, and a more balanced economic structure. This significant transformation presents a new and immense challenge that must be addressed by adapting to, coming to grips with, and leading this new phase throughout the entire development process. China's economic development has always undergone a continuous emergence of new states, patterns, and stages throughout its long history. China's transition to the new normal phase aligns with the natural law of ascending spiral progression and development of objects. Therefore, achieving steady, high-speed economic growth while improving the quality and efficiency of production, enhancing technology and innovation, and upgrading industries to more advanced and sophisticated levels is critical to meet the challenges and demands of the new normal.[45]

To lead the new normal of economic development, the new approach to supply-side structural reform is the fundamental measure for promoting the overall improvement of China's social productivity level. While moderately expanding total demand, the focus should be on strengthening the supply-side structural reform, improving the quality and efficiency of the supply system, and enhancing the steady growth momentum of the economy. It is necessary to make an effort to promote structural reform of the economy and make the supply system more adaptable to changes in demand. Supply-side structural reform is a fundamental measure for promoting the overall improvement of China's social productivity level, which involves expanding effective supply, satisfying effective demand,

[45] Focus on implementing the spirit of the fifth plenary session to ensure the timely and comprehensive completion of building a moderately prosperous society. *People's Daily*, January 19, 2016.

and accelerating the reform of the economic system, mechanisms, and development modes. This reform is closely linked to the economy's current phase of development and emphasizes both structural reform on the supply side and changes in demand structure. It highlights the decisive role of the market in resource allocation while also emphasizing the government's role, as well as the importance of developing social productivity and improving social production relations. Ultimately, the aim is to adhere to the principle of liberating and developing social productivity, and to make timely and progressive new interpretations of the new normal of economic development.

Fifth, we must adhere to the path of new "four modernizations" with Chinese characteristics, which is a theory about promoting the coordinated development of new industrialization, informatization, urbanization, and agricultural modernization. This path emphasizes the deep integration of informatization and industrialization. It also focuses on the positive interaction between industrialization and urbanization, and the coordination between urbanization and agricultural modernization. The integration of urban and rural development is an inevitable requirement for the development of industrialization, urbanization, and agricultural modernization at a certain point in their progress, and it is an important symbol of national modernization. To build a moderately prosperous society in all respects, we need to accomplish these things: make China's industries fully developed, greatly improve the use of information technology, significantly enhance the quality of urban life, make agriculture more modernized, and build better rural communities under socialist principles.

Sixth, we must adhere to the basic national policy of opening up to the outside world and maintain a skillful balance between domestic economic development and engagement in the global economy. We should make good use of both the domestic and international markets and resources, implement a more proactive opening-up strategy. We should aim to achieve a high level of economic development and adopt a high degree of openness to international trade and investment. The strategy of opening up to the outside world will enable China to optimize its economic and social development potential through the maximal exploitation of the advantages granted by engaging with the global economy. We must build a more dynamic open economic system and participate actively in global economic governance. At the same time, we need to protect our country's development interests, guard against risks, and enhance our ability to withstand international economic risks to ensure national economic security.

Xi Jinping believes that Marxist political economics is an important component of Marxism and China must adhere to it and further develop it.[46] The process of achieving a moderately prosperous society in all respects offers a rare historical opportunity for the innovative development of socialist political economics with Chinese characteristics. We must develop new characteristics while implementing new practices. We should develop new ideas and explore new frontiers of Marxist economics in modern China. By doing so, we can contribute "Chinese wisdom" to the innovation and development of Marxist political economics.

[46]People's Daily (2015), *Op. cit.*

Chapter 2

Major Principles of Political Economics of Socialism with Chinese Characteristics

Political economics of socialism with Chinese characteristics contains a series of important theoretical achievements, such as the theory on the essence of socialism, the theory on the basic economic system in the primary stage of socialism, the theory on innovation, coordination, green, openness, and sharing of new development philosophy, the theory on developing socialist market economy, making the market play a decisive role in resource allocation and giving better play to the role of the government, the theory that China's economic development has entered a new normal, the theory on promoting the coordination of new industrialization, informatization, urbanization, and agricultural modernization, the theory on making good use of international and domestic markets and resources, and the theory on promoting social fairness and justice and gradually realizing the common prosperity of all people. The major principles of political economics of socialism with Chinese characteristics run through the formation and development of the series of theories, embody the inherent characteristics and fundamental spirit of this theoretical system, and profoundly explain the theoretical logic of economic reform and development of socialism with Chinese characteristics.

1. People-Centered Principle

Placing the people at the center is the theoretical principle that dominates the development process of socialist economy with Chinese characteristics and reflects the development trend of socialist economy with Chinese characteristics. It is an abstract criterion summarized from the theory, which gathers the fundamental value of the theory, reflects the research stance of political economics of socialism with Chinese characteristics, and is the "soul" of socialist political economics theory with Chinese characteristics. As pointed out by Xi Jinping, "We must adhere to the people-centered philosophy of development. This is the fundamental stance of Marxist political economics."[1]

The "fundamental stance" of research determines the purpose, method, and value orientation of research. In China's academic circles, some scholars put forward the problem of "depoliticization" in the study of contemporary economics, emphasizing that the study should stay at the level of resource allocation, without considering institutional changes and social and economic relations. In the final analysis, this is the research stance, that is, the research is "for whom," "for whom to speak," and "for whom to advocate." If the study of economics only pursues theoretical and logical satisfaction, then this kind of study will be far away from reality and lose its due significance and value. The superstructure of any social concept is a reflection of a certain social and economic form and the political system determined by it. "The ruling ideas of each age have ever been the ideas of its ruling class."[2] It is impossible for the study of Marxist political economics to "depoliticize." The study of political economics of socialism with Chinese characteristics, as a component of Marxist political economics, not only reflects the interests of the social ruling class but also reflects the interests of the wide mass of the people as social subjects consistent with the interests of the ruling class. Therefore, to study the political economics of socialism with Chinese characteristics, we must stand and adhere to the people-centered fundamental stance. "We must persist in improving people's well-being, promoting people's all-round development, and steadily advancing towards common prosperity as the starting point and objective of economic development. We must firmly adhere to this fundamental stance in deploying economic work, formulating economic policies, and promoting economic development."[3] To dismiss the significance of social and economic relations of Marxist political economics and solely conduct "pure research" is to contradict both history and reality.

---

[1] Based on China's realities and development practices, advance Marxist political economics in contemporary China. *People's Daily*, November 25, 2015.
[2] *Collected Works of Marx and Engels*, Vol. 2. People's Publishing House, 2009, p. 51.
[3] *People's Daily* (2015), *Op. cit.*

The people-centered principle should run through the study of political economics of socialism with Chinese characteristics from beginning to end, highlighting its inherent characteristics and fundamental spirit and reflecting its development direction. When understanding and grasping this principle, we must make clear the understanding of "people" in the development of socialism with Chinese characteristics. Mao Zedong made a profound interpretation of "people" in *On Correctly Processing Contradictions among the People*. He pointed out: "The concept of people has different contents in different countries and different historical periods of each country. Take China's situation as an example. During the War of Resistance against Japan, all anti-Japanese classes, hierarchies and social groups belonged to the people, and Japanese imperialism, traitors and Japanophile were enemies of the people. During the War of Liberation, American imperialism and its bureaucratic bourgeoisie, landlord class and Kuomintang reactionaries representing these classes, were enemies of the people. All classes, hierarchies and social groups that opposed these enemies belong to the people. During the period of building socialism, all classes, hierarchies and social groups that support, uphold and participate in the cause of socialist construction belong to the scope of the people."[4] Mao Zedong's exposition is significant in guiding us to understand the people-centered principle. The concept of people in the context of China's development of socialism with Chinese characteristics refers to the basic members of society, with the working masses as the main body. This term encompasses all individuals who support, uphold, and participate in socialist construction. Placing the people at the center entails placing all the working masses who support, uphold, and participate in socialist construction at the center, and placing the fundamental interests of these working masses who support, uphold, and participate in socialist construction at the center.

Placing the people at the center reflects the direction and focus of the study of political economics of socialism with Chinese characteristics, which is reflected in the basic theory, structural system, and practical problems. Rather than being abstract theoretical regulations, what is presented to the people are the tangible outcomes of socialist economic development with Chinese characteristics. These outcomes are recognized by the people due to their prioritization of addressing the vital interests of

[4] *Collected Works of Mao Zedong*, Vol. 7. People's Publishing House, 1999, p. 205.

the populace and their resilience under the scrutiny of economic practice activities involving the wide mass of people. Placing the people at the center emphasizes that the Communist Party of China should realize, safeguard, and develop the fundamental interests of the overwhelming majority of the people, and insist that development is for the people, development depends on the people, and development achievements are shared by the people, so that all the people have more sense of gain in co-construction and sharing of development. Studying the political economics of socialism with Chinese characteristics with people as the center combines the principles of Marxist economics with the concrete practice of contemporary China through understanding the process of economic movement, grasping the law of social and economic development, and knowing the process of scientifically answering major theoretical and practical problems in China's economic development. It is also a process based on China's national situation and development practice, upgrading the people's practical experience into a systematic economic theory, revealing the new characteristics and laws of China's economic development, and refining and summarizing the regular achievements of China's economic development practice. It can be seen that placing people at the center as a major principle of political economics of socialism with Chinese characteristics is scientific, which lies in that it concretizes the political or ideological nature of contemporary Chinese Marxist political economics into the theory and practice of realizing, maintaining, and developing the fundamental interests of the overwhelming majority of people.

Placing the people at the center is the essential provision of political economics of socialism with Chinese characteristics. Political economics of socialism with Chinese characteristics has no significance and value without the people. In 2014, when talking about the "people's principal position" of socialist literature and art in his speech at the Symposium on Literature and Art Work, Xi Jinping pointed out: "The people are the source of literary and artistic creation. If literature and art detach themselves from the people, they will become rootless duckweed, disease-free moan and soulless body."[5] This exposition on the essence of socialist literature and art is also applicable to the study of political economics of

[5]Party Literature Research Center of the CPC Central Committee (Ed.) (2016). *Selected Important Documents since the 18th CPC National Congress,* Vol. II. Central Party Literature Press, p. 128.

socialism with Chinese characteristics. In essence, political economics of socialism with Chinese characteristics is the political economics of the Chinese people, which needs to solve the problems of "for whom, who to rely on and who I am."[6] To begin with, it is imperative to put people in the first place. In the process of China's revolution and construction, Mao Zedong reminded the whole party many times that the line of the Communist Party is the line of mobilizing the masses and strengthening the people's strength. At the closing ceremony of the 7th CPC National Congress, he also emphasized that "the whole Chinese people" are the "God" of the Communist Party of China.[7] Only by relying on the people can we accomplish the great historical tasks of the new democratic revolution, socialist revolution, and construction. The people are the creators of history and also the main body of socialist economic practice. In fact, political economics of socialism with Chinese characteristics is to reflect the practical experience with the people as the main body and upgrade it to a systematic economic theory. Secondly, we should seek benefits for the people. The focus of people's principal position is people's interests.[8] Political economics of socialism with Chinese characteristics embodies people's principal position, which is based on the people, for the people, toward the people, responsible for the people and beneficial to the people. On the one hand, we should take the stance and attitude of the overwhelming majority of the people as the starting point and objective, pay attention to the voices, needs and expectations of the people, study major theoretical and practical issues involving reform and development, and incorporate people's thoughts and feelings, world outlook, and people's spirit into the research. On the other hand, we should aim at realizing the interests of the overwhelming majority of people, adhere to the development concept that the development fruits are shared by the people, and earnestly protect the interests of the people. Finally, people's satisfaction should be the only criterion. The people are the main force of socialist economic construction and also the main objects for which socialist economic construction seeks benefits. Therefore, it is inevitable to regard the people as the ultimate judges of the effectiveness of socialist economic development with Chinese characteristics. In the historical process of the development

[6] *Ibid.*, p. 131.

[7] See *Selected Works of Mao Zedong*, Vol. 3. People's Publishing House, 1991, p. 1102.

[8] See Mind the overall situation, grasp the general trend, focus on major events, and strive to do a better job in propaganda and ideological work. *People's Daily*, August 21, 2013.

of the socialist market economy, we must take "whether the people uphold or not," "whether the people approve or not," "whether the people are happy or not," and "whether the people allow or not" as the starting point and destination for formulating various principles and policies, and take whether the people are satisfied or not as the fundamental yardstick for measuring the effectiveness of development. The measurement standard of people's primacy, benefit for the people, and people's satisfaction has become the concrete manifestation of the people-centered principle of political economics of socialism with Chinese characteristics.

2. Principle of Liberating and Developing Productive Forces

Liberating and developing productive forces is the essential requirement of socialism, the fundamental task of the primary stage of socialism, and the major principle of political economics of socialism with Chinese characteristics. This principle is a regular achievement refined and summarized from China's fundamental realities and economic development practice of reform and opening-up. Besides, it is an important leap in theoretical understanding of the CPC's exploration of the development practice of socialism with Chinese characteristics that meets the requirements of the development and progress of China and the evolving times.

Productive forces are the decisive factor of social development and the driving force of human social development. When discussing the development of productive forces, we must also talk about liberating productive forces. Both aspects should be considered. In the decisive stage of building a moderately prosperous society in all respects, liberating and developing productive forces is closely related to correctly handling the relationship between fairness and efficiency. Liberating and developing productive forces first shows that socialist development must stress efficiency, that is, "to stress socialism, we must first develop productive forces, which is the main thing,"[9] "to adhere to the socialist system, the most fundamental thing is to develop social productive forces," and "the superiority of socialism should ultimately be reflected in the better development of productive forces."[10] However, in the process of socialist reform and opening-up, liberating and developing productive forces also

[9]*Selected Works of Deng Xiaoping*, Vol. 2. People's Publishing House, 1994, p. 314.
[10]*Ibid.*, Vol. 3, 1993, p. 149.

implies that the development of socialism must pay attention to fairness. Fairness is the conceptual expression of existing economic relations, which develops and changes with the development and change of social and economic relations. As far as China's realistic economic relations are concerned, the fairness that meets the requirements of the development of socialist market economy must be the fairness that is consistent with efficiency. Liberating and developing productive forces shows that we should pay attention to fairness in the pursuit of efficiency, that is, we must reform the relations of production that constrain the development of productive forces and the superstructure that does not adapt to the economic base in the development of productive forces. The unity of liberating and developing productive forces embodies the unity of efficiency and fairness, which indicates that only by liberating and developing productive forces can we truly embody the essential requirements of socialism. In addition, the unity also emphasizes that the primary stage of socialism must attach importance to both the development of productive forces and the liberation of productive forces, so as to be more conducive to people's construction and development of socialism.

Liberating and developing productive forces reflects the unity of resource allocation and resource development and utilization in socialist economic construction. In terms of resource allocation, efficiency depends not only on the activity ability and tools of the subject, but also directly on the activity mode, and more on the enthusiasm, initiative, and creativity of people's activities. The dynamic factors, namely the enthusiasm, initiative, and creativity of people's activities that determine efficiency are usually determined by fairness. The more reasonable a society's fairness is, the more consistent the contribution of the society member will be with his income, and the higher his labor enthusiasm, initiative, and creativity will be; otherwise, the lower it will be. To a certain extent, fairness improves "efficiency" by arousing people's enthusiasm, initiative, and creativity, and fairness has become the fundamental guarantee of efficiency. As far as the development and utilization of resources are concerned, efficiency must also be unified with fairness. Modern society is facing more and more pressure from population, resources, and environment, so we can't just pursue efficiency without paying attention to fairness. There is no doubt that the relationship between humans and nature is profoundly manifested in productive forces. If we only pursue efficiency but overlook environmental protection and development and utilization of resources in the development of productive forces, there will be a large number of unfair phenomena, such as generational unfairness and intergenerational unfairness, which will bring profound disasters to people and far-reaching turbulence and destruction to society. If the development and utilization of natural resources in the development of productive forces in China only pursues efficiency but does not pay attention to fairness, it will inevitably be punished by disasters such as drought, water shortage, water and soil loss, and sandstorm, which will damage the interests of more people. Therefore, liberating and developing productive forces is to pursue efficiency and pay attention to fairness. The law of human social development determines that liberating and developing productive forces always run through the development of human society and socialism. If the study of political economics of socialism with Chinese characteristics does not take liberating and developing productive forces as a major principle, it will lose its guiding significance to the real economic construction.

Liberating and developing productive forces, as an important principle, is determined by the study object of political economics of socialism with Chinese characteristics. Political economics of socialism with Chinese characteristics takes the economic relations in the primary stage of socialism in China as the study object. It is necessary to study the economic relations system in the primary stage of socialism, including the essential relationship and concrete realization form, as well as the economic operation and development in the primary stage of socialism. Economic relations and productive forces are inseparable. The purpose of studying economic relations is to liberate and develop productive forces, promote the deepening of China's reform, and opening-up and the development of socialist economic construction practice. The study of economic operation and economic development in the primary stage of socialism aims to advance the study of economic relations, which is to promote the development and perfection of economic relations by liberating and developing productive forces.

Starting from the most important and basic "economic facts" in contemporary China, namely, the national conditions in the primary stage of socialism, political economics of socialism with Chinese characteristics focuses on the economic relations in the primary stage of socialism and strives to explore and reveal the laws of socialist economic system and economic operation with Chinese characteristics. For the socialist system established on the basis of backward economy and culture, and for a socialist country that has gone through detours in socialist economic construction, the main contradiction in the primary stage of socialism is the contradiction between the people's increasing material and cultural needs and backward social production. This is not only a problem of developing productive forces but also of liberating them. "After the establishment of the basic socialist system, it is necessary to fundamentally change the economic system that constrains the development of productive forces, establish a socialist economic system full of vigor and vitality, and promote the development of productive forces."[11] Regarding the liberation of productive forces, we are referring to reform and the adjustment of productive relations at this stage. Revolution is to liberate productive forces, just as reform aims to do. Xi Jinping emphasized that "to promote the modernization of the national governance system and governance capacity, it is necessary to adapt to the changing times. We should not only reform the institutional mechanisms, laws and regulations that do not meet the requirements of practical development, but also constantly build new institutional mechanisms, laws and regulations to make all aspects of the system more scientific and perfect."[12] That is to say, liberating productive forces means solving the problem of coordination between productive forces and productive relations in the reform, and handling the problem of overall connection between productive forces and economic and social relations. Developing productive forces is about economic development. Although the reform has liberated the bound productive forces and promoted their significant advancement, it is not the development of productive forces itself which has its own laws. Therefore, when studying the economic relations in the primary stage of socialism, political economics of socialism with Chinese characteristics should not only study the economic relations themselves, but also the productive forces, as well as development of productive forces and liberation of productive forces. As Deng Xiaoping clearly pointed out at the beginning of China's reform and opening-up: "In the past, it was incomplete to talk only about developing productive forces under socialist conditions, but not about liberating productive forces through reform. We should consider both liberating productive forces and developing productive forces."[13] Only by liberating

---

[11] *Ibid.*, p. 370.

[12] Party Literature Research Center of the CPC Central Committee (Ed.) (2014). *Selected Important Documents since the 18th CPC National Congress*, Vol. I. Central Party Literature Press, p. 549.

[13] *Selected Works of Deng Xiaoping*, Vol. 3. People's Publishing House, 1993, p. 370.

and developing productive forces can we truly embody the essence of socialism.

Liberating and developing productive forces is the inherent requirement of political economics of socialism with Chinese characteristics, which is embodied in all theories. Without the implementation of the major principle of liberating and developing productive forces, it is impossible to form a new summary of the essence of socialism, reveal the main contradictions in socialist society, and establish a new strategy for socialist economic development and understand the new normal of economic development. Then, in the practice of socialist economic development with Chinese characteristics, it would merely be empty rhetoric to adhere to the economic construction as the center, take the five development concepts of innovation, coordination, green, openness, and sharing as the theme, comprehensively promote the construction of "the five-sphere integrated plan" and realize the comprehensive, coordinated, and sustainable development centered on the people. Liberating and developing productive forces is the main thread running through political economics of socialism with Chinese characteristics. It is in this sense that political economics of socialism with Chinese characteristics is manifested as a "systematic economic theory" of liberating and developing productive forces.

Liberating and developing productive forces is the fundamental task of socialist economic development with Chinese characteristics in the primary stage of socialism, which constitutes a continuous thread throughout this stage. Xi Jinping pointed out: "To build a moderately prosperous society in all respects, realize socialist modernization and bring about the great rejuvenation of the Chinese nation, the most fundamental and urgent task is to further liberate and develop social productive forces."[14] Over the course of more than 60 years of socialist construction in New China, the historical landscape of an economically and culturally underdeveloped China has been completely transformed. Especially since the 3rd Plenary Session of the 11th CPC Central Committee, through reform and opening-up, China's productive forces have greatly developed, people's living standards have been greatly improved, comprehensive national strength has been significantly enhanced, and China's international status and influence have been significantly improved. China's economic aggregate ranks second in the world, while the output of industrial and agricultural

[14]Party Literature Research Center of the CPC Central Committee (2014), *Op. cit.*, p. 549.

products takes the top position globally. The production of steel has risen from 26th in the early days of liberation to 1st place, crude oil output has jumped from 27th to 5th, power generation has leaped from 25th to 2nd, and the trade volume of goods has surged from 6th to 1st. In 2015, China's total grain output reached 621 million tons, which was 5.5 times higher than the output in the early days of liberation. Qualitative changes took place in the living standards of urban and rural residents. The per capita disposable income of rural residents in China increased from RMB 44 in the early days of liberation to RMB 11,422 in 2015, an increase of nearly 260 times. In 2015, the total retail sales of consumer goods in China exceeded RMB 30 trillion, and the contribution rate of consumption to national economic growth reached 66.4%.[15] The development achievements of socialist construction in the past 60 years in New China, especially the performance made in the past 30 years of reform and opening-up, show that liberating and developing productive forces is the foundation for the survival and development of socialism, and is the thinking logic and historical logic of the theory and practice of political economics of socialism with Chinese characteristics.

3. Principle of Public Ownership as the Main Form and Common Prosperity

In the historical process of reform and opening-up, Deng Xiaoping emphasized many times that "a dominant public ownership and the common prosperity are the fundamental principles of socialism that we must uphold."[16] Public ownership as the main form embodies the socialist nature of China and also reflects the actual requirements of economic reform, that is, the immaturity of socialism in the primary stage inevitably requires the development of non-public sectors of the economy while developing public sector of the economy. Common prosperity is the fundamental feature that distinguishes the socialist system from other social systems, and it is the criterion for the success or failure of China's reform and opening-up. When presiding over the 28th collective learning of the Political Bureau of the Central Committee on the basic principles and methodology of Marxist political economics, Xi Jinping emphasized:

---

[15] Compiled from the data published by the National Bureau of Statistics.

[16] *Selected Works of Deng Xiaoping*, Vol. 3. People's Publishing House, 1993, p. 111.

"We must uphold and improve the basic socialist economic system, unswervingly consolidate and develop the public sector of the economy, unswervingly encourage, support and guide the development of the non-public sector of the economy, and drive various forms of ownership to learn from each other's strengths, promote each other and develop together. At the same time, the dominant position of public ownership and the leading role of state-owned economy cannot be shaken, which is an institutional guarantee to ensure that people of all ethnic groups in China share the fruits of development, and also an important guarantee to consolidate the reigning position of the Party and adhere to China's socialist system. It is necessary to adhere to and improve the socialist basic distribution system, strive to promote the synchronization of residents' income growth and economic growth, labor remuneration improvement and labor productivity improvement, constantly improve institutional mechanisms and specific policies, adjust the national income distribution pattern, continuously increase the income of urban and rural residents, and continuously narrow the income gap."[17] A dominant public ownership and the common prosperity are the fundamental principles of Marxist political economics and also the major principles that political economics of socialism with Chinese characteristics must adhere to.

Public ownership as the main form is the essential requirement of China's socialist basic economic system, which is based on China's concrete reality. After the Third Plenary Session of the 11th CPC Central Committee, based on the reality of the primary stage of socialism in China, the Communist Party of China made an ideological breakthrough in understanding the planned economic system and single public ownership, and formed a socialist basic economic system in which diverse forms of ownership develop side-by-side with the dominant public ownership. Public ownership as the main form first explains the main nature of the position of public ownership in this ownership structure. It is conducive to amplifying the function of state-owned capital, maintaining and increasing its value and improving its competitiveness to actively explore the effective realization form of public ownership as the main form and develop the mixed ownership economy. Public ownership as the main form also shows that public sector of the economy exists in the ownership structure that develops together with non-public sectors of the economy. As public ownership remains the primary form, the vigorous development

[17] *People's Daily* (2015), *Op. cit.*

of non-public sectors of the economy constitutes a significant aspect of the basic socialist economic system. China's non-public sectors of the economy, based on the socialist system, are guided and restricted by public sector of the economy. Therefore, the 18th CPC National Congress clearly pointed out: "We must unswervingly consolidate and develop public sector of the economy, promote various forms of public ownership, deepen the state-owned enterprise reform, improve various state-owned asset management systems, promote more state-owned capital to invest in important industries and key areas related to national security and the lifelines of the national economy, and continuously enhance the vitality, control and influence of the state-owned economy. We should unswervingly encourage, support and guide the development of non-public sectors of the economy, and ensure that all kinds of ownership economies use production factors equally according to law, participate in market competition fairly, and are equally protected by law."[18] "Two Unwavering" clearly states the importance of the principle of public ownership as the main form in the development of socialist economic theory and practice with Chinese characteristics.

Common prosperity stands as both the essential requirement and goal of socialism, serving as the key criterion to assess the success or failure of socialist construction. At the beginning of reform and opening-up, Deng Xiaoping emphasized that "the purpose of socialism is to make the people of the whole country prosperous together rather than promoting polarization," and that "certain regions and individuals can get prosperous first, and then drive and help other regions and other people to gradually achieve common prosperity."[19] Common prosperity is neither average prosperity nor synchronous prosperity but refers to the universal prosperity of all people on the basis of eliminating polarization and poverty. The essential significance of common prosperity lies in that it not only emphasizes comprehensive prosperity including material life and spiritual life but also emphasizes "common," that is, all people finally achieve the universality of prosperity through hard work and mutual help. If there is no "commonness" of prosperity, it is a poor society. If there is no "common" prosperity, it is an unfair society. Neither a poor society nor an unfair society is a socialist society. Only common prosperity is the crucial distinction between socialism and capitalism and can ultimately enable

[18] Party Literature Research Center of the CPC Central Committee (2014), *Op. cit.*, p. 16.

[19] *Selected Works of Deng Xiaoping*, Vol. 3. People's Publishing House, 1994, pp. 110–111, 149.

socialism to triumph over capitalism. Therefore, Xi Jinping clearly proposed: "Common prosperity is the fundamental principle of socialism with Chinese characteristics, so it is necessary to make development results fairer and benefit all the people to make steady progress towards common prosperity."[20] As the essential requirement of socialism, common prosperity is the consistent fundamental value orientation of the Communist Party of China.

Public ownership as the main form is the economic basis for realizing common prosperity. If we talk about common prosperity without this economic basis, we cannot correctly understand the scientific significance of common prosperity, nor can truly realize common prosperity. In the primary stage of socialism in China, adhering to public ownership as the main form is the fundamental guarantee for realizing common prosperity, because only by adhering to public ownership as the main form can we promote the rapid development of social productive forces, safeguard the common and long-term interests of the people, and realize the desire for common prosperity of the whole society as soon as possible. Political economics of socialism with Chinese characteristics is a political economics ideology that seeks development and benefits for the people. To study political economics of socialism with Chinese characteristics well, we must apply the major principle of public ownership as the main form and common prosperity to all aspects of socialist economic development with Chinese characteristics.

First of all, the important principle of public ownership as the main form and common prosperity must run through the study of the basic socialist economic system theory and socialist distribution system theory. These two theories formed in the economic development practice of China's reform and opening-up promote the development of the public sector of the economy by developing non-public sectors of the economy, increase the vitality of economic and social development, and enhance the vitality, control, and influence of state-owned economy. By focusing on addressing income inequality and preventing polarization, the development achievements can be shared fairly and benefit all individuals so as to overcome the "middle-income trap" by stabilizing growth, adjusting structure, benefiting people's livelihood, and promoting reform in the process of building a moderately prosperous society in all respects. Public ownership as the main form and common prosperity ensures the equitable

---

[20] *Xi Jinping: The Governance of China*. Foreign Languages Press, 2014, p. 13.

sharing of development outcomes among all individuals through the system and upholds the socialist system and the socialist path of China's economic development.

Second, the important principle of public ownership as the main form and common prosperity must run through the study of the new development philosophy of socialism. Only by emphasizing the goal of taking public ownership as the main form and common prosperity to promote the practice of economic development can we adhere to innovative, coordinated, green, open, and shared development concepts, address the persistent challenges of imbalanced, uncoordinated, and unsustainable development, eradicate issues such as weak innovation capacity in the development model, excessive overcapacity in some industries, and declining enterprise efficiency, solve the economic development problems such as the development gap between urban and rural areas, tight resource constraints and deteriorating ecological environment, and continuously foster a new phase of economic development.

Third, the important principle of public ownership as the main form and common prosperity must run through the study of the new normal theory of economic development. The new normal of economic development implies that China's economic growth should not solely focus on the growth rate and must persist in prioritizing the enhancement of economic development's quality and efficiency, diligently fulfill the historical mission of transforming the development mode and adjusting the economic structure, achieve medium- and high-speed economic growth, move toward the middle and high-end industries, effectively safeguard fairness and justice, effectively guarantee and improve people's livelihood, and promote stable and healthy economic and social development. If we do not adhere to the principle of public ownership as the main form and common prosperity, we cannot understand, adapt to, and lead the new normal.

Fourth, the important principle of public ownership as the main form and common prosperity must run through the study of the theory of promoting the coordinated development of new industrialization, informatization, urbanization, and agricultural modernization. The development of these four core areas is a complex systematic project requiring deep integration and interaction between them. They are not developed in isolation but in an interrelationship, and their functions are not played alone but realized through integration, interaction, and coordination. To adhere to the new road of these four core areas with Chinese characteristics and the direction of their synchronous development, we must handle the relationship between them and playing the decisive role of the market, the relationship between the four core areas and government governance, and the relationship between the core areas and people sharing development achievements. To grasp and study the theory of these four core areas, it is crucial to maintain a steadfast commitment to public ownership as the main form and the pursuit of common prosperity.

Fifth, the important principle of public ownership as the main form and common prosperity must run through the study of supply-side structural reform theory. At present, China's economy is experiencing a slowdown, which may appear as insufficient effective demand but is, in fact, a result of insufficient effective supply. "Supply side + structural + reform" means to implement structural optimization from the perspective of supply while moderately expanding total demand, correct the mismatch of supply and demand structure and distortion of factor allocation, reduce ineffective and low-end supply, expand effective and high-end supply, promote factor flow and optimal allocation, and attain a higher level of balance between supply and demand. The purpose of implementing supply-side structural reform is to improve the quality and efficiency of the supply system, boost the driving force for sustainable economic growth, and propel a comprehensive advancement of China's social level of productive forces. To conduct an in-depth study of the supply-side structural reform theory, it is necessary to adhere to the important principle of taking public ownership as the main form and common prosperity.

To put it in a nutshell, the important principle of public ownership as the main form and common prosperity reflects the nature, starting point, process, and foothold of socialist economic development with Chinese characteristics. It is not a matter of choice but rather holds indispensable guiding and regulatory functions for the development of socialist economic theory and practice with Chinese characteristics. Without this important principle, the development of socialist economy with Chinese characteristics will lose its way. In the theory and practice of the development of socialism with Chinese characteristics, we must unswervingly adhere to the important principle of public ownership as the main form and common prosperity, which is an inevitable requirement of China's socialist economic development and a fundamental lesson derived from the CPC's experience in reform and opening-up. It is bound to become the theoretical logical force and ideological innovation power in building a moderately prosperous society in all respects and develop a prosperous, strong, democratic, civilized, and harmonious socialist modern power and promote China's social development and progress of the times.

4. Principle of Socialist Market Economy Reform

Socialist market economy is an unprecedented system, and it is an unprecedented great revolution to establish, develop, and perfect the socialist market economy system. Since the 14th CPC National Congress in 1992 formally established that "the goal of China's economic system reform is to establish a socialist market economic system," China has successfully realized the transformation from a highly centralized planned economic system to a vibrant socialist market economic system, a turning point from closed and semi-closed to all-round opening-up, a historic leap in people's life from adequate food and clothing to a well-off life, and a historic leap in the economic aggregate ranking second in the world. Adhering to the socialist market economy reform in the exploration of socialism with Chinese characteristics is a great pioneering work in the practice of reform and opening-up led by the Communist Party of China, which embodies the dialectical unity of theoretical logic of Marxist political economics and historical logic of contemporary Chinese social development. As the "soul" of the theory of political economics of socialism with Chinese characteristics, it has opened up a new realm of theoretical development and made important innovations to Marxist political economics.

Political economics of socialism with Chinese characteristics must adhere to the major principle of socialist market economy reform. The key lies in achieving a harmonious combination of the basic socialist system and the market economy system, allowing the seeds of the market economy to be sown in socialist soil, to take root, and to flourish. The socialist market economy reform has ignited tremendous enthusiasm and creativity among the people, greatly promoted the development of social productive forces, and significantly enhanced the vitality of the national economy. It has enabled the Chinese people to steadily march on the journey of building a moderately prosperous society in all respects, basically achieving modernization, and realizing the Chinese dream of the great rejuvenation of the Chinese nation under the leadership of the Communist Party of China.

Socialist market economy is the combination of the socialist basic system and the market economic system. In the early stage of China's economic system reform, Deng Xiaoping once discussed the problem that "socialism can also engage in market economy." He pointed out: "It is definitely incorrect to say that market economy only exists in capitalist society and only capitalist market economy exists. Why should socialism be precluded from participating in a market economy? Such engagement cannot be deemed synonymous with capitalism."[21] Deng Xiaoping's exposition reveals the institutional provisions of market economy as the "method" of economic operation. In the early 1990s, Deng Xiaoping expounded on the relationship between market economy and basic social system more clearly and concisely. He pointed out: "The distinction between capitalism and socialism does not lie in the juxtaposition of a market economy versus a planned economy. A planned economy does not exclusively signify socialism, as capitalism also incorporates planning mechanisms. Likewise, a market economy does not solely represent capitalism, as socialism can also encompass market dynamics. Planning and market mechanisms are economic tools used by both systems."[22] This exposition, which later became a famous saying and has been repeatedly cited by people, makes a clearer explanation of the institutional provisions of the market economy. Deng Xiaoping's exposition on the socialist market economy separates the market economy from the capitalist system to form an abstract market economy category while emphasizing that the market economy system must be combined with certain social basic economic system and puts forward a new concept of socialist market economy system. As Xi Jinping pointed out, "This major theoretical breakthrough has played an extremely important role in China's reform, opening-up and economic and social development."[23] The combination of the socialist basic system and the market economic system emphasizes that the socialist market economy is combined with the socialist basic system, and it is an economy in which the market plays a decisive role in resource allocation under the macro-control of the state. Obviously, the market economy reform combined with the basic socialist system, which plays a decisive role in resource allocation under the state macro-control, is the basic requirement for China's economic development. It runs through the theory and practice of socialist economic development with

[21] *Selected Works of Deng Xiaoping*, Vol. 2. People's Publishing House, 1994, p. 236.
[22] *Ibid.*, Vol. 3, 1993, p. 373.
[23] Party Literature Research Center of the CPC Central Committee (2014), *Op. cit.*, p. 498.

Chinese characteristics from beginning to end, revealing the essence of socialism and the path of socialist economic development.

To persist in socialist market economy reform, the core issue is to handle the relationship between the government and the market. Over the past two decades of developing the socialist market economy, the Communist Party of China has made scientific positioning on the relationship between the government and the market based on practice expansion and deep understanding. This point is fully illustrated in the 15th CPC National Congress, as it pronounced "making the market play a fundamental role in resource allocation under the state macro-control," to the 16th CPC National Congress, which stressed on "giving full play to the basic role of the market in resource allocation," to the 17th CPC National Congress, which focused on "giving full play to the basic role of the market in resource allocation from the system," to the 18th CPC National Congress, which expanded to "giving full play to the basic role of the market in resource allocation to a greater extent and in a wider scope," and then to the Third Plenary Session of the 18th CPC Central Committee, which laid emphasis on "making the market play a decisive role in resource allocation and give better play to the role of the government." From the "basic role" to the "decisive role" of the market and "giving full play to the role of the government," it embodies the general law that the market determines resource allocation, which will definitely play an extremely important role in China's reform, opening-up, and economic and social development. At the same time, it is important to note that the "decisive role" does not imply an "all-encompassing role," but rather underscores the necessary commitment to maintaining the direction of reform towards a socialist market economy. Only by fully embodying the superiority of the socialist system and giving full play to the positive role of the Party and the government can we ensure the correct direction of China's reform and opening-up and economic and social development. From the "basic role" to the "decisive role" of the market and "giving better play to the role of the government," it fully shows that the CPC has not only further clarified the basic idea for deepening economic system reform but also further put forward the practical path of perfecting and promoting the development of the socialist market economy. Therefore, political economics of socialism with Chinese characteristics can clearly create the theory and practice of economic development by combining the socialist basic system and the market economic system and promote

China's socialist economic development by grasping the advantages of the government and market.

Since the 18th CPC National Congress in 2012, Xi Jinping has repeatedly stressed the socialist market economy reform multiple times. He emphasized that it is necessary to make the market play a decisive role in resource allocation and give better play to the role of the government. Both are organically unified, not mutually exclusive, and cannot be separated and opposed. To deal with the relationship between the government and the market, "in fact, it is necessary to deal with the problem whether the market plays a decisive role or the government plays a decisive role in resource allocation. The objective of economic development is to enhance the allocation efficiency of resources, particularly scarce resources, to produce a maximum amount of goods and services while utilizing minimal resources and generating the most benefits possible."[24] In the final analysis, the relationship between the government and the market is about how to accurately position the government and the market. As far as the market is concerned, it is about how to position its function in improving economic efficiency, realize the effective resource allocation by price determination mechanism, and improve the enthusiasm and economic efficiency of micro-subjects. As for the government, it is about how to position its function in macroeconomic guidance, grasp the development direction of market economy from the top-level design, and guide the sound development of the market economy from the perspective of macro-control. The government needs to find a delicate balance, ensuring it doesn't become absent, misaligned, or overly intrusive in its approach. For China's economic system reform to progress effectively, it is crucial to strike the right balance between the government and the market. This entails allowing the market to fulfill its role in resource allocation while enabling the government to effectively carry out macro-control and supervision. By achieving this equilibrium, the in-depth development of the economic system reform, a healthy socialist market economy, and a continuously advancing socialist economy with Chinese characteristics can be ensured on the correct path.

"We must adhere to the direction of socialist market economy reform," the reaffirmation of the goal of socialist market economy system reform by the Third Plenary Session of the 18th CPC Central Committee

[24] *Ibid.*, p. 499.

is another major theoretical breakthrough and practical promotion of the CPC in the socialist economic construction with Chinese characteristics, and it is also the basic compliance for comprehensively deepening the reform. While studying and solving the problems existing in the development of a socialist market economy, such as the absence of a standardized market order, lagging development of production factor market, inconsistent market rules, and insufficient market competition, political economics of socialism with Chinese characteristics must adhere to the direction of socialist market economy reform. Moreover, the political economics of socialism with Chinese characteristics must persist in the direction of socialist market economy reform in the research of new development philosophy, reform and development of state-owned enterprises, innovation-driven development strategy, the "Belt and Road" development strategy, and supply-side structural reform. Adhering to the socialist market economy reform ensures the socialist reform direction of China's market economy leads to the success or failure of China's socialist economic development and determines the scientific and accurate formation of the theoretical achievements of political economics of socialism with Chinese characteristics. Looking ahead to the development of theory and practice, the principle of socialist market economy reform is not only the compass to promote the development of the socialist economy with Chinese characteristics but also the beacon for the study of political economics of socialism with Chinese characteristics.

5. Principle of Opening to the Outside World

Persisting in opening to the outside world is an important decision for China to build a great modern socialist country, and it is also a long-term basic state policy of China. Since the initiation of reform and opening-up, China has witnessed significant achievements in its comprehensive and profound economic system reform, which has extended from rural areas to urban centers and expanded from scattered initiatives to nationwide implementation. Notably, remarkable progress has been made in opening up to the global arena, leading to a transformative shift from a closed or semi-closed economy to all-round openness. This has resulted in a cascading pattern of opening, extending from coastal regions to riversides and borders, and from the east to the central and western regions. Furthermore, China has achieved a continuous expansion in its opening strategy, progressing from trade-oriented policies to encompass investment, and from the exchange of goods to the facilitation of service trade. These developments reflect a new trend of opening, transitioning from a small-scale and low-quality approach to a larger-scale and higher-quality one. According to incomplete statistics, by the end of 2015, China had established 219 state-level economic and technological development zones, 149 state-level high-tech industrial development zones, 63 state-level export processing zones, 45 state-level comprehensive bonded zones, and 17 state-level border economic cooperation zones. These economic and technological development zones have become new growth points of economic development in their regions, which have effectively promoted the development of China's economy, society, and opening to the outside world. In 2015, China achieved a total import–export volume of services of USD 713 billion, an increase of 14.6% over the previous year. Among them, exports were USD 288.19 billion, an increase of 9.2%; imports reached USD 424.81 billion, an increase of 18.6%.[25] These economic achievements fully prove that opening to the outside world is the road to a country's prosperity. Its meaning has gone far beyond "being able to possess all its positive achievements without experiencing the terrible twists and turns of capitalist production."[26] It has expanded into a long-term basic state policy and a "strategic issue"[27] and has become "a key measure to determine the destiny of contemporary China" and "a key measure to realize the 'two centenary goals' and realize the great rejuvenation of the Chinese nation."[28]

The principle of opening to the outside world in political economics of socialism with Chinese characteristics is rooted in facts and development process and is a systematic achievement refined and summarized from China's basic national conditions and economic development practice. At present, China's foreign economic situation has undergone major changes. Some domestic industries have overcapacity and the dependence on foreign resources and energy continues to rise. The processing trade mode of "three-plus-one," which relies on preferential treatment and

---

[25] Compiled from the data published by the National Bureau of Statistics.

[26] *Collected Works of Marx and Engels*, Vol. 3. People's Publishing House, 2009, p. 51.

[27] *Selected Works of Deng Xiaoping*, Vol. 3. People's Publishing House, 1993, p. 32.

[28] Publicity Department of the CPC Central Committee (Ed.) (2016). *General Secretary Xi Jinping Important Speech Series* (2016 Edition). Learning Publishing House and People's Publishing House, pp. 67–68.

resources, can no longer adapt to China's social and economic development. China has now stood at a new starting point of implementing a new round of high-level opening-up. This new starting point includes: comprehensively promoting two-way opening-up, promoting orderly flow of domestic and international factors, efficient allocation of resources, and deep integration of markets; accelerating the cultivation of new advantages in international competition and improving the strategic layout of opening up to the outside world; improving the business environment of rule of law, internationalization, and convenience, perfecting the system and mechanism conducive to win–win cooperation and adaptation to international investment and trade rules, and improving the new system of opening up to the outside world; emphasizing sincerity and goodwill, persisting in the principle of joint construction and sharing, carrying out pragmatic cooperation with relevant countries and regions in various fields for mutual benefit and win–win, creating a new pattern of comprehensive opening-up with linkage between land and sea and two-way opening between east and west, and promoting the construction of the "Belt and Road"; promoting the reform and improvement of the international economic governance system, actively guiding the global economic agenda, safeguarding, and strengthening the multilateral trading system, promoting the development of the international economic order in the direction of equality, justice, and win–win cooperation, jointly meeting global challenges and actively participating in global economic governance. The goal of China's opening to the outside world lies in enriching the connotation of opening to the outside world, improving the level of opening to the outside world, promoting strategic mutual trust, investment, economic and trade cooperation, and people-to-people exchanges, striving to form a deeply integrated and mutually beneficial cooperation pattern, creating a new situation of opening to the outside world and building a new pattern of all-round opening through the construction of the "Belt and Road."

The decision-making framework for opening to the outside world is deeply integrated into the socialist economic development with Chinese characteristics led by the CPC. During the early stages of China's reform and opening-up, Deng Xiaoping emphasized on numerous occasions that both China's own experiences and the experiences of other nations had demonstrated the impossibility of achieving success by isolating oneself from the world. Nowadays, with the accelerated development of economic globalization and the great changes in the world's political and economic structure, the CPC should unswervingly persist in opening to the outside world and align with the changing times to expand opening to the outside world.[29] Today, with great achievements in opening to the outside world, Xi Jinping further pointed out: "Today's world is a world of change, a world where new opportunities and challenges emerge one after another, a world in which the international system and international order are deeply adjusted, and a world in which the international power has undergone profound changes and is conducive to peace and development." Under such a world environment, China "will continue to deepen reform in various fields, adhere to the basic state policy of opening to the outside world, unswervingly pursue the mutually beneficial and win–win opening strategy, continue to draw development momentum from the world, and make China's development better benefit the world," and "China will improve the level of open economy in a wider scope, in a wider field and at a deeper level."[30] "Community with a shared future for mankind,"[31] the "Belt and Road," and "free trade area strategy" have become major strategic ideas for China to implement a new round of high-level opening-up. China needs the world and opening to the outside world is a secret of China's economic take-off and an inevitable choice to realize the Chinese dream of the great rejuvenation of the Chinese nation. The world also needs China and persists in opening to the outside world. The world can also get the goods and services it needs from China, providing a broader stage for the development of all countries. The greater development space of China's economy and the world economy will surely be expanded in opening up to the outside world.

Since the reform and opening-up, China's achievements in opening to the outside world and the decision-making arrangement of the CPC in opening to the outside world have profoundly demonstrated that opening to the outside world has penetrated into the practice of socialist economic development with Chinese characteristics, and China's economic development, social progress, and China's contributions to the world are inseparable from opening to the outside world. Only by persisting in opening to the outside world can the socialist economy with Chinese characteristics really develop and can make it possible to coordinate the two

---

[29]Central foreign affairs working conference held in Beijing. *People's Daily*, November 30, 2014.

[30]Xi Jinping meets foreign representatives of the international conference on understanding China. *People's Daily*, November 4, 2015.

[31]*Xi Jinping: The Governance of China*. Foreign Languages Press, 2014, p. 114.

major domestic and international situations, make use of international and domestic markets and resources, develop a higher-level open economy, actively participate in global economic governance, safeguard China's development interests, actively prevent various risks, and ensure national economic security. As pointed out in the *CPC Central Committee's Recommendations for the 13th Five-Year Plan for Economic and Social Development* (hereinafter referred to as the "Recommendations"): "Opening-up is the only way for the country to prosper and develop."[32]

Opening to the outside world runs through the theory of political economics of socialism with Chinese characteristics like a red line and promotes the theoretical research and practical guidance of political economics of socialism with Chinese characteristics. China's opening to the outside world is not merely an end in itself but a means to an end. In the process of construction, it is to make China open the doors, better learn to make full use of external conditions for construction, make full use of international and domestic markets and resources, constantly enrich the forms and contents of opening to the outside world, continuously expand the breadth and depth of opening to the outside world, continuously improve the quality and level of opening to the outside world, and continuously enhance China's economic structure and core competitiveness while taking a domestic foothold and expanding the domestic demand as the long-term strategy of economic development, thus continuously providing a powerful driving force for building a moderately prosperous society in all respects and realizing the great rejuvenation of the Chinese nation. In the course of developing the socialist economy with Chinese characteristics, steadfastly embracing openness to the outside world allows China to extend its reach globally and soar toward broader horizons. We should firmly grasp the major principles of opening to the outside world to study the theory of political economics of socialism with Chinese characteristics. Only in this way can we make the theory of socialist essence, the theory of basic economic system in the primary stage of socialism, the new development philosophy, the theory of socialist market economy, the theory of economic development entering a new normal, and the theory of coordination of the four core areas, as well as the theory of international and domestic markets and resources and the theory of common prosperity really perfected based on the development of practice, and make practice develop under the guidance of theoretical innovation.

---

[32]Party Literature Research Center of the CPC Central Committee (2016), *Op. cit.*, p. 792.

Chapter 3

Commitment to the New Development Philosophy of Innovative, Coordinated, Green, Open, and Shared Development

The Fifth Plenary Session of the 18th CPC Central Committee underscored the need to steadfastly adhere to and effectively implement the new development philosophy of innovative, coordinated, green, open, and shared development to achieve the objectives set forth in the 13th Five-Year Plan (2016–2020). This approach seeks to overcome development obstacles while consolidating the nation's development strengths. In this context, Xi noted, during the 28th collective study of the Political Bureau of the CPC Central Committee, that the five development concepts are an essential outcome of the study of political economics. "These concepts embody a political economics that is responsive to contemporary Chinese realities and bears the imprint of the times. Not only do they provide robust guidance for the economic development practices of China but also open up new vistas in Marxist political economics."[1] In *CCCPC's Explanations for the 13th Five-Year Plan for Economic and Social Development*, Xi affirmed that "the five development concepts constitute a concentrated reflection of China's development perspectives, priorities, and directions for the 13th Five-Year Plan and beyond, represent a summation of China's development experience during the past three decades of Reform and Opening-up, and reflect the Party's innovative understanding of China's development laws."[2]

[1] Based on China's realities and development practices, advance Marxist political economics in contemporary China. *People's Daily*, November 25, 2015.

[2] Party Literature Research Center of the CPC Central Committee (Ed.) (2016). *Selected Important Documents since the 18th CPC National Congress*, Vol. II. Central Party Literature Press, pp. 774–775.

1. Understanding the Significant Implications of the New Development Philosophy

The development philosophy plays a pivotal role in governing the overall situation, fundamental principles, directional focus, and long-term strategy of development. It is a strategic, programmatic, and visionary framework that holds immense significance in determining the effectiveness and success of developmental outcomes. The concepts of innovative, coordinated, green, open, and shared development serve as a concentrated embodiment of the strategies, directions, and key priorities of China's development for the forthcoming five years and beyond, providing profound insight into the imperative course for attaining higher quality, greater efficiency, increased equity, and sustainable development.

An in-depth understanding of the five development concepts holds significant theoretical and practical implications. First and foremost, these concepts represent a strategic choice that conforms to the trend of the times, seizes development opportunities, and consolidates development advantages. Despite the unchanged theme of peace and development in the world, global trends, such as economic globalization, cultural diversity, and social informatization, are undergoing profound changes. Although the number of unstable, uncertain, and uncoordinated factors has increased, the pursuit of faster domestic development and stronger international competitiveness remains the common goal of all nations. Particularly with respect to mitigating the profound impact of the international financial crisis and enhancing development quality and efficiency, many countries are actively innovating development concepts and perfecting development strategies, striving to win the future of development with new ideas and strategies. Therefore, economic and social development issues are primarily conceptual problems and development strategy competition is, in essence, a competition of development concepts. The five development concepts proposed at the Fifth Plenary Session of the 18th CPC Central Committee are in line with the requirements of the times, draw lessons from the experiences and lessons of other countries, and achieve transcendence on the basis of reference while creating their own unique characteristics. By establishing and implementing the five development concepts, China can occupy the commanding heights of the times, maintain and leverage the critical strategic opportunities and win greater development advantages in the increasingly intense international competition.

Second, the five development concepts have creatively answered the significant questions of what kind of development we need to achieve and how to achieve it under new circumstances. Since the 18th National Congress of the Communist Party of China, the Party Central Committee has put forward the "Two Centenary Goals," which are to build a moderately prosperous society in all respects by the centenary of the Communist Party of China in 2020 and to realize the great rejuvenation of the Chinese nation by the centenary of the founding of the People's Republic of China in 2050. We are now in the decisive phase of building a moderately prosperous society in all respects and development has always been the fundamental requirement and top priority. However, the concepts of development should also evolve according to new practices and requirements. Meanwhile, we should also recognize that the development environment in the 13th Five-Year Plan period underwent new changes and adapting to and leading the new normal of economic development is a critical trend to grasp. To achieve new breakthroughs in the new normal, innovative concepts are necessitated. The five development concepts proposed by our Party grasp the new features of changes in development speed, structural optimization, and power conversion, respond to the new requirements of promoting the economy's sustained medium to high-speed growth and upgrading industries to the medium- to high-end level, and reveal new paths to tackle development challenges. By fully enabling the leading role of the five development concepts, we can promote the transformation of development mode and improve development quality and efficiency so as to achieve the goal of building a moderately prosperous society in all respects on schedule.

Third, the five development concepts represent a significant elevation of the theoretical understanding of development within the Communist Party of China. The CPC has always placed great emphasis on theoretical guidance and innovation. Over the past 30 years of Reform and Opening-up, the Party has timely put forward corresponding development concepts and strategies based on the changes in situations and tasks, leading the practices of development. From initially focusing on economic development and placing development in overriding importance, to making development the top priority of the Party's governance of the country, to upholding the scientific outlook on comprehensive, balanced and sustainable development, to insisting on the implementation of the Five-Sphere Integrated Plan, every innovation and improvement in development philosophy has promoted new leaps in achieving growth. It is precisely because of the guidance of correct concepts and continuous updating of the same that our development path has remained steady and far-reaching, becoming ever broader as we proceed. Since the 18th National Congress of the Communist Party of China, the Party under the core leadership of General Secretary Xi Jinping has developed a series of new concepts, new ideas, and new strategies based on new development practices. The five development concepts put forward at the 5th Plenary Session of the 18th Central Committee of the Communist Party of China embody a profound insight into the basic characteristics of the new development stage and reflect a scientific grasp of the socialist essence requirements and development direction. This marks a new height in our Party's understanding of the laws of economic and social development.

In sum, the new development philosophy of innovative, coordinated, green, open, and shared development represents a significant enrichment and progress of our Party's development theories. As an important component of the socialist theoretical system with Chinese characteristics, the philosophy serves as a crucial guideline for China's long-term economic and social development. Therefore, we must have an in-depth understanding of the significant implications of the five development concepts and ensure that they become a true basis for creating development practices and a better future.

2. Scientific Comprehension of the Basic Connotations of the New Development Philosophy

General Secretary Xi Jinping's important speeches and the "Recommendations" have provided profound explanations on the basic connotations and practical requirements of the five development concepts. In summary, it is essential to learn that innovation is the primary driving force for development and must be placed at the core of national development, permeating all aspects of the Party's and the country's work and becoming a prevailing trend throughout society. Coordination is an inherent requirement for sustained and sound development, and it is essential to firmly grasp the overall plan for advancing socialism with Chinese characteristics, correctly handle significant relationships in development, and continuously enhance the overall integrity. The concept of green development represents a prerequisite for sustainable development and an essential expression of the people's pursuit of a better life. We must resolutely follow the path of a civilized development approach that promotes production, prosperity, and ecological harmony, and advance the construction of a beautiful China. Openness is the only path leading to national prosperity and development, and we must adhere to an open strategy that promotes mutual benefits and win–win cooperation, and develop a higher level of open economy. Finally, the concept of sharing is an essential requirement of socialism with Chinese characteristics, where development is for the people, relies on the people, and its outcomes are shared by the people, steadily advancing toward common prosperity.

First, the five development concepts embody the essential requirements of the Party's ideological guiding principles and contain the ideological connotations of emancipating the mind and advancing with the times. Embracing and implementing the five development concepts is a profound transformation that affects the overall development of our country. It signifies a fundamental shift in traditional development ideas and modes and inevitably accompanies the liberation of thought and the updating of concepts. It is essential to view things from the perspective of the Party's ideological guiding principles and focus on problem-solving through ideological methods and ways of thinking. We must bring home to our hearts that development is an ongoing process, and the environment and conditions for development are constantly changing, thus development concepts should naturally evolve as well. In the face of new development practices, what was once effective may not be so now, what was once out of date may now be essential, and what was once insurmountable may now require breakthroughs. Leaders and cadres must regard the emancipation of thought as a general switch, establish a mindset that is adapted to the times and practical development, firmly discard outdated ideas such as the pursuit of GDP at all costs, competing for resources and inputs, emphasizing cities over rural areas, pollution-first approach and efficiency-over-fairness mentality, and instead, embrace new development concepts to guide new development practices. Adopting and implementing the five development concepts cannot be limited to mere rhetoric but should serve as a yardstick for action. We must consciously compare and test our actual work against the concepts, encouraging and supporting the ones that align and rejecting and discarding those that do not. This way, we can keep up with the times by liberating our thoughts and winning new development through transforming our perspectives.

Second, the five development concepts are derived from the profound insights gained from both successful experiences and lessons learned, embodying the practical logic of respecting and following laws and regulations. In terms of development issues, we have both successful experiences and profound lessons to learn from. Our successful experiences mainly stem from adhering to reality and acting according to objective laws and regulations, whereas our lessons are mainly reflected in the deviation from reality. In recent times, some regions have pursued one-sided and distorted development, exploited resources recklessly, ignored the well-being of the people, and neglected the need to share profits with them, resulting in numerous conflicts and problems. Xi emphasized that our development must follow the scientific laws of economic development, the sustainable laws of nature, and the inclusive laws of society. The Fifth Plenary Session of the 18th CPC Central Committee put forward the five development concepts, which fundamentally aim to establish development on the basis of comprehending and abiding by the laws of development, thereby achieving development of higher quality and greater standards. To fully implement the five development concepts, it is essential to enhance our awareness of the laws of development and understand the new connotations and requirements of development in studying and comprehending the laws. Meanwhile, it is necessary to focus on adapting to and leading the new normal of economic development, adhere to the organic unity of development speed, quality, and efficiency, and coordinate efforts to stabilize growth, promote reform, adjust structure, benefit the people, and prevent risks. Furthermore, emphasis should be placed on the green development that benefits both the state and the people's livelihood. By respecting, conforming to, and protecting the ecological environment, the formation of a green development mode and lifestyle can be facilitated. Additionally, we need to strengthen social construction, innovate social governance, and unify the intensity of reform and development speed with social sustainability, to ensure that the fruits of reform and development are more extensive and benefit all people more equitably. In the process of building a moderately prosperous society in all respects, we must always proceed from realities, avoid uniformity and hasty actions, refrain from making local governments take excessive policy steps, and avoid making promises that cannot be fulfilled. Instead, we must take a step-by-step approach and make adjustments according to local conditions and the situation at hand to conduct our work.

Thirdly, the five development concepts are put forward in response to the prominent issues and problems in China's development, showing a distinctive problem-oriented feature. Finding and solving problems in practice is an important way for us to understand and change the world. The five development concepts are problem-oriented and directly point to the prominent issues and problems in China's development. Innovative development focuses on solving the problem of the driving force of development, coordinated development focuses on solving the problem of unbalanced development, green development focuses on solving the problem of harmony between humans and nature, open development focuses on solving the problem of internal and external linkage of development, and shared development focuses on solving the problem of social fairness and justice. It can be seen that the five development concepts not only grasp the crux that restricts development but also provide a good solution to problems. To implement the five development concepts, we should also improve the awareness of the problem, stress the importance of providing problem-oriented solutions, aim at and follow the problems, and achieve new progress in solving development problems. We should also intensify efforts to shore up weak links in order to find the problems and firmly grasp the weak points and do our best to make up for them. Whether it is to formulate specific plans, launch policies and measures, or improve the system and mechanism, efforts should be made to complement weaknesses and solve problems, so as to enhance the synergy and balance of economic and social development in tackling difficulties.

Fourth, the five development concepts adhere to the principle that development is for the people, development depends on the people, and development achievements are shared by the people, highlighting the value orientation of putting people first. The question of whom development serves and benefits is the fundamental issue to be solved in development, and also a litmus test to measure the nature of a political party and a country. As a socialist country under the leadership of the Communist Party, China should, of course, take the realization, maintenance, and development of the fundamental interests of the overwhelming majority of the people as the fundamental starting point and foothold of development. Five development concepts with the distinctive feature of being people-oriented and well-being-oriented reflect the fundamental purpose of remaining loyal to the Party and faithful to the people. We should always adhere to the people's dominant position, adhere to the people-centered development concept, and take the realization of people's happiness as the goal and destination of development. The more we develop to a higher level, the more we must adhere to the principle of ensuring everyone's participation, everyone's efforts and everyone's enjoyment, and the more we must adhere to the common prosperity of all people. We should fully grasp and promote the implementation of policies and measures for shared development. We should do everything we can for the benefit of the people, and resolutely refrain from doing anything that harms the interests of the people, so that the process of building a moderately prosperous society in all respects becomes a process of improving people's well-being and promoting fairness and justice. We should focus on resolutely winning the "13th Five-Year Plan" poverty alleviation battle and make great efforts to solve the outstanding problems such as the large income gap, the insufficient supply of public services, the lagging social security, the uneven education and employment opportunities so as to make development more equitable and inclusive, and let the people have more sense of fulfillment and happiness.

Fifthly, five development concepts are a collection of internal links, reflecting dialectical thinking and scientific methodology of overall consideration. innovative, coordinated, green, open, and shared development concepts are interlinked and mutually promoted, and have profound internal links. These five development concepts, with the same themes and goals, are unified in the "four comprehensives" strategic layout and the Five-Sphere Integrated Plan overall layout, in the practice of adhering to and developing Socialism with Chinese Characteristics, in the historical process of achieving the Two Centenary Goals and realizing the Chinese dream of the great rejuvenation of China. These five development concepts have their own emphasis and support each other. Together, they constitute a top-level design that opens up future development prospects and a systematic logical system. To grasp the Five-Sphere Integrated Plan, we should establish a comprehensive and systematic way of thinking, master the scientific and coordinated working methods, and implement them in a balanced manner. We can neither ignore one thing nor lose another, nor replace each other.

3. Innovation, the First Driving Force for Development

Innovation has always been an important force to promote the development of a country and a nation. Innovation is development and is the future. "Innovation must be placed at the core of the overall development of the country." The Fifth Plenary Session of the 18th Central Committee put forward five development concepts, the first of which is "innovative development." If traditional development just additional, then innovative development provides a multiplier effect. Innovative development helps solve the problem of development impetus.

During "the 12th Five-Year Plan" period, especially since the 18th CPC National Congress, the spirit of reform and innovation permeated all areas of governance. Whether it is economic transformation and upgrading or accelerating the implementation of innovation-driven development strategy, the intensive launch of reform measures in registered residence, justice, education, and other aspects, or the proposal of a series of new concepts, new ideas, and new explorations such as "Internet plus" and "Made in China 2025," all these have constantly opened up new horizons for China's development.

Looking ahead, China's development situation has pushed us to the cusp of innovative development. A new round of scientific and technological revolution and industrial transformation has to follow. Developed countries have promoted a high starting point of "reindustrialization." Our development conditions and comparative advantages have undergone profound changes. We must accelerate the transformation from factor-driven to innovation-driven. At present, China's overall level of scientific and technological development is not high, the supporting capacity of science and technology for economic and social development is insufficient, and the contribution rate of science and technology to economic growth is far lower than that of developed countries, which is the prominent weakness of China's large economy. Without effectively leveraging the path of innovation and development, the driving force of development will fail to undergo the transformation, placing us at a disadvantage in global economic competition. To this end, we must, in accordance with the requirements of the Fifth Plenary Session of the Central Committee, take innovation as the first driving force to lead development and take talents as the first resource to support development and accelerate the formation of an economic system and development model with innovation as the main guide and support.

To adhere to innovative development, we must focus on innovation, form an institutional framework to promote innovation, and shape a leading development that relies more on innovation-driven and gives more play to first-mover advantages. Taking the seven points for innovative development, which are put forward at the Fifth Plenary Session of the Central Committee, as the focus of economic development, including cultivating new impetus for development, expanding new space for development, deepening the implementation of innovation-driven development strategy, vigorously promoting agricultural modernization, building a new industrial system, building a new system for development, and innovating and improving macro-control methods, have given a roadmap for implementing innovative development in the next five years. Guided by the blueprint drawn at the Fifth Plenary Session of the Central Committee, innovation and development can make new breakthroughs and reach a new level.

To promote innovation and development during the "13th Five-Year Plan" period, we should make innovation run through all the work of the Party and the country and form an atmosphere of integrated innovation into common practice in the whole society. The innovative development measures put forward at the Fifth Plenary Session of the Central Committee cover all aspects of economic and social development; it ranges from promoting mass entrepreneurship and innovation to implementing the strategy of strengthening the country through the Internet, from putting forward and organizing international big science plans and big science projects to accelerating the transformation of agricultural development mode, from accelerating the construction of a powerful manufacturing country to deepening the reform of the administrative system and so on. Only by implementing the spirit of the Fifth Plenary Session of the Central Committee can we continue to promote innovation in theory, system, science and technology, culture, and other aspects, so as to improve the quality, efficiency, and structure of development.

Innovation is the soul of a nation's progress, the inexhaustible driving force for the prosperity of a country, and the deepest national endowment of the Chinese nation. With the increasingly fierce international competition and the urgent need to transform China's development momentum, the importance of innovation has become increasingly prominent. In view of the significance of innovative ideas, Xi Jinping pointed out that "to break through bottlenecks and solve deep-seated contradictions and problems in China's economic development, the fundamental way is innovation, and the key is scientific and technological strength."[3] The "Recommendations" further point out that "We must put innovation at the core of the overall development of the country, constantly promote

[3]Innovation drives China's great wheel — The progress of scientific and technological reform and development since the 18th CPC national congress. *Science and Technology Daily*, November 15, 2013.

theoretical innovation, institutional innovation, scientific and technological innovation, cultural innovation and other aspects of innovation, so that innovation runs through all the work of the Party and the country and create an atmosphere of innovation in the whole society."[4]

To achieve innovative development, the Fifth Plenary Session of the 18th Central Committee clearly pointed out that "we must put the development base on innovation, form an institutional framework to promote innovation, and shape a leading development that relies more on innovation and gives more play to the first-mover advantage."[5] We should achieve the innovative development by following seven aspects, including cultivating new impetus for development, expanding new space for development, deepening the implementation of innovation-driven development strategy, vigorously promoting agricultural modernization, building a new industrial system, building a new system for development, and innovating and improving macro-control methods. For example, we should promote mass entrepreneurship and innovation. We should form a vertical and horizontal economic axis belt dominated by the economic belt along the coast and the river and cultivate and expand a number of key economic zones. The strategy of network power and the action plan of "Internet plus" also need to be complemented. We need to accelerate the construction of a manufacturing power and implement the action plan of "Made in China 2025." Xi also put forward clear requirements for promoting innovation-driven development from a practical perspective. It includes effectively managing the relationship between the government and the market, aligning the innovation chain with the industrial chain and the capital chain, eliminating the isolated nature of scientific and technological innovation, enhancing the organizational integration of innovation-driven development, formulating top-level design and implementing related tasks, adopting an "asymmetric strategy" to leverage inherent advantages, and focusing resources and strategic planning on key areas and critical issues.

To give full play to the leading role of scientific and technological innovation, we must deeply implement the innovation-driven development strategy, constantly deepen the reform of the scientific and technological system, stimulate the vitality of innovation subjects, and improve

---

[4]Party Literature Research Center of the CPC Central Committee (2016), *Op. cit.*, p. 792.

[5]The fifth plenary session of the 18th central committee was held in Beijing. *People's Daily*, October 30, 2015.

the efficiency of the use of innovation elements. Under the new economic normal, China should adhere to the multi-dimensional open system led by independent innovation. On the one hand, it is to comprehensively implement the innovation-driven strategy with independent innovation with Chinese characteristics as the core, and on the other hand, it is to promote the all-round opening-up to the external economy. To shift to an innovation-driven development, we need to realize three major changes. The first is to shift from imitation innovation to independent innovation. Second, change from following innovation to leading innovation and enter the same starting line of innovation with developed countries, and control the commanding heights. The third one is to shift from technological innovation to scientific and technological innovation, taking scientific discovery as the source, market as the orientation, and industry–university–research collaborative innovation. To realize innovation and development, we should break down the obstacles of the system and the mechanism and establish an institutional environment conducive to the efficient allocation of innovation resources and the full release of innovation potential. A market environment of fair competition should be created, which needs us to correct the price distortions of production factors and resource-based products and enhance the impetus for enterprise innovation and development. More attention show be paid to intellectual property protection and law enforcement. Innovation and development is a systematic project, which requires overall planning, multiple strategies, and joint efforts.

4. Coordination, the Internal Requirement of Sustainable and Healthy Development

The key to building a moderately prosperous society in all respects is "in all respects." In the "five development concepts" proposed at the Fifth Plenary Session of the 18th Central Committee, "coordinated development" emphasizes the word "in all respects" and focuses on solving the problem of unbalanced development. In order to fully realize the development goals of the 13th Five-Year Plan period, we must firmly grasp the overall layout of the cause of socialism with Chinese characteristics, correctly handle the major relations in development, promote coordinated development, form a balanced structure, and constantly enhance the integrity of development.

Coordination is the internal requirement of sustainable and healthy development. The disharmony of China's development is a long-standing problem, which is highlighted in the relationship between rural development and urban development, material and spiritual civilization, economic construction, and national defense construction. If the main task for a period of time is to run fast when the level of economic development is backward, then after running a certain distance, we should pay attention to adjusting the relationship and the overall efficiency of development; otherwise the "Cannikin law" will become more apparent and a series of social contradictions will continue to deepen. To plan for economic and social development during the "13th Five-Year Plan" period, we must make breakthroughs in optimizing the structure and complementing the weaknesses and strive to improve the coordination and balance of development.

Building a moderately prosperous society in all respects emphasizes not only "moderately prosperous," but also "in all respects." The term "moderately prosperous" refers to the level of development, while the term "in all respects" refers to the balance, coordination, and sustainability of development. If we have completed the task in terms of total volume and speed by 2020, but the problems of unbalanced, uncoordinated, and unsustainable development are more serious, and the shortcomings are more prominent, we can't really achieve the goal. The Party and the state proposed to enhance the coordination of development, focusing on promoting the coordinated development of urban and rural areas, promoting the coordinated development of economic and social, and promoting the synchronous development of new industrialization, informatization, urbanization, and agricultural modernization, while strengthening the national hard power, and paying attention to enhancing the national soft power. In accordance with this spirit, we should further study and focus on key problems, put forward feasible ideas and practical measures, and promote the coordinated development of all links and aspects of modernization.

A moderately prosperous society in all respects is a common moderately prosperous society in urban and rural areas, a moderately prosperous society that benefits all the people, and the progress in all respects of the Five-Sphere Integrated Plan: economic, political, cultural, social, and ecological civilization. Can more than 50 million rural poor people be moderately prosperous at the same time? How can 250 million permanent urban residents equally enjoy public services? How to improve the supply capacity of high-quality ecological products while rapidly expanding the production capacity? The "Recommendations" point out that in view of some obvious shortcomings in China's social development, ecological environment protection, livelihood security, and other aspects at this stage, we must adhere to regional coordination, urban–rural integration, equal emphasis on material civilization and spiritual civilization, and the integration of economic construction and national defense construction to further strengthen the integrity of development. In fact, the shorter the aspect is, the more advantage it has. The more efforts are made on the weak links, and the more efforts are made to solve the obvious problems and weaknesses, the better the "well-leveraged" effect can be achieved so as to solve the development problems, strengthen the development momentum, deeply root in the advantages we owned, and constantly open up new horizons for development.

The Fifth Plenary Session of the 18th CPC Central Committee elaborated on coordinated development from the following four aspects: promoting coordinated regional development, promoting coordinated urban and rural development, promoting coordinated development of material and spiritual civilization, and promoting the integration of economic and national defense construction. In terms of regional coordinated development, on the basis of the implementation of the three strategies of the "Belt and Road," the coordinated development of Beijing, Tianjin, and Hebei, and the Yangtze River Economic Belt, the Central Economic Work Conference injected new meaning into it: "To promote regional development, we should pay more attention to the balance of population, economy, resources, and environment." In terms of coordinated urban and rural development, we should improve the institutional mechanism of urban–rural integrated development, and the long-term mechanism of rural infrastructure investment and we will promote the extension of urban public services to rural areas and improve the level of building a new socialist countryside. In terms of the coordinated development of material civilization and spiritual civilization, we should speed up cultural reform and development, strengthen the construction of socialist spiritual civilization, build a country with socialist culture, strengthen ideological and moral construction and social integrity construction, enhance national awareness, legal awareness, and social responsibility awareness, advocate scientific spirit, and carry forward traditional Chinese virtues. In terms of promoting the integrated development of economy and national defense, we should adhere to the unity of development and security, enrich the country and strengthen the military, implement the military–civilian integration development strategy, and form an in-depth integration development of military and civilian pattern with all elements, multiple fields, and high efficiency.

For the four aspects of coordinated development, it is necessary to deal with ten pairs of relations, namely, the coordination of economic and social development, the coordination of speed and efficiency development, the coordination of regional development, the coordination of urban and rural development, the coordination of human and natural development, the coordination of public and private development, the coordination of the development of the rich and common rich, the coordination of material and spiritual development, the coordination of technological and institutional development, and the coordination of internal and external development. These four aspects of coordinated development form an interconnected and mutually reinforcing organic whole. In practice, we are required to comprehensively grasp and coordinate these aspects without neglecting any of them or treating them as interchangeable substitutes.

In the "13th Five-Year Plan," it is imperative that we approach national development as a strategic chess game, with the coordination of various aspects being the key to achieving victory in the decisive battle. As we stand at a historic moment, akin to a relay race, where the final push is crucial, we will steer development by embracing new development concepts. Furthermore, we will expand the scope of development through coordinated efforts and prioritize strengthening development in weaker areas. By doing so, we are poised to write a more resolute and compelling chapter in the realization of the Chinese Dream and the great rejuvenation of the Chinese nation.

5. Green Concept Is a Necessary Condition for Sustainable Development and an Important Embodiment of People's Pursuit of a Better Life

The ecological environment is the key to the all-round moderately prosperous society. The Fifth Plenary Session of the 18th CPC Central Committee takes "green development" as one of the five development concepts and focuses on balancing the harmony between humans and nature. During the "13th Five-Year Plan" period, we must adhere to the basic national policy of saving resources and protecting the environment, firmly follow the path of civilized development of production development, prosperous life, and good ecology, and work together to promote the prosperity of the people, the power of the country, and the beauty of China, and form a new pattern of people and nature development harmony in modern construction.

A good ecological environment is the most equitable public product and the most inclusive livelihood. At present, resource constraints are tightening, and environmental pollution and ecosystem degradation are becoming increasing serious in China. The people have a strong demand for fresh air, clean water, safe food, and a beautiful environment is increasingly strong. The deterioration of the ecological environment and its impact on people's health is our prominent livelihood issue. Reversing the deterioration of the environment and improving the quality of the environment is an urgent and important work related to an overall well-off society and development.

To adhere to green development, we must adhere to the principle of "enriching the country and benefiting the people," promote the formation of green development and lifestyle, and provide more high-quality ecological products for the people. To promote the harmonious coexistence of human beings and nature, accelerate the construction of main functional areas, promote low-carbon circular development, comprehensively save and efficiently use resources, strengthen environmental governance, and build ecological security barriers, the Fifth Plenary Session of the CPC Central Committee made a series of careful arrangements from these six aspects, which pointed out the direction of efforts for green development. Guided by the blueprint drawn at the Fifth Plenary Session of the CPC Central Committee, we can integrate the concept, principles, and objectives of ecological civilization into all aspects of economic and social development and implement them in all kinds of plans and work at all levels, so that we can write a new chapter of green development.

To advance the cause of green development, we must strive diligently to achieve our objectives. Further improving the weight of importance of green indicators in all indicators of the 13th Five-Year Plan and taking the protection of people's health and improvement of environmental quality as more restrictive hard indicators, which are the policy and institutional guarantees for promoting green development. They encompass the implementation of robust environmental protection systems and water resource management practices, as well as the establishment of vertical management structures for monitoring, supervision, and enforcement at regional levels. Furthermore, we must implement comprehensive action plans to prevent and control air, water, and soil pollution, while also undertaking ecological protection and restoration projects. These efforts are crucial in swiftly halting the deterioration of our ecological environment and establishing a solid foundation for sustainable green development.

With a deep understanding of the principles of development, more and more people realize that lucid waters and lush mountains are invaluable assets, protecting the ecological environment is protecting productivity, and improving the ecological environment is developing productivity. Green, circular, and low-carbon development is the direction of scientific and technological revolution and industrial transformation in the current era and is the most promising development area. China has considerable potential in this area, and many new economic growth points will arise, which can add strong "green power" to economic transformation and upgrading. We can fully achieve a win–win situation of economic development and ecological improvement by seizing the opportunity of green transformation, promoting the energy revolution, accelerating energy technology innovation, promoting the green transformation of traditional manufacturing industries, and constantly improving the green level of China's economic development.

An optimal ecological environment serves as the foundation for the sustainable development of humanity and society. Ecological environmental protection is a cause that yields benefits for both the present and the future. It is imperative to firmly embrace the principles of green development, safeguard the boundaries set by ecological civilization, and expedite the establishment of a society that conserves resources and fosters environmental friendliness. Through these efforts, we will assuredly attain the development objective of "overall enhancement of the quality of the ecological environment," leaving behind a magnificent abode characterized by azure skies, verdant landscapes, and pristine waters for generations to come. This will pave the way for a promising future of sustainable development for the Chinese nation.

Green development is a sustainable development that follows the laws of nature. The construction of ecological civilization is an inevitable requirement for accelerating the transformation of economic development mode and realizing green development. The "Recommendations" state: "The Green concept is a necessary condition for sustainable development and an important manifestation of the people's pursuit of a better life.

We must adhere to the basic national policy of saving resources and protecting the environment, adhere to sustainable development, firmly follow the path of civilized development of production development, prosperous life, and good ecology, accelerate the construction of a resource-saving and environment-friendly society, form a new pattern of modernization construction of harmonious development between humans and nature, promote the construction of a beautiful China, and make new contributions to global ecological security."[6] In the Central Comprehensively Deepening Reforms Commission's 14th meeting, Xi Jinping highlighted, "We must base ourselves on China's basic national conditions and the new characteristics of development, with the goal of building a beautiful China and addressing prominent ecological and environmental issues as our guiding principle. We should clarify the guiding ideology, basic concepts, important principles, and overall objectives that must be adhered to in the reform of the ecological civilization system. We should also propose reform tasks and measures to provide institutional and systemic guarantees for the construction of ecological civilization."[7] The "Recommendations" put forward the proposition to "adhere to green enrichment and green benefits for the people, provide the people with more high-quality ecological products, promote the establishment of a green development and lifestyle, and jointly promote the prosperity of the people, the wealth of the nation, and the beauty of China."[8]

To achieve green development, the Fifth Plenary Session of the 18th CPC Central Committee emphasized the need to establish a scientific and rational urbanization pattern, agricultural development pattern, ecological security pattern, and natural shoreline pattern. It is imperative to promote the establishment of a green, low-carbon, and circular development industrial system, focusing on six key aspects: fostering harmonious coexistence between humans and nature, accelerating the construction of main functional areas, promoting low-carbon circular development, ensuring comprehensive resource conservation and efficient utilization, strengthening environmental governance, and establishing a robust ecological security barrier. During his investigation in Yunnan in January 2015, Xi Jinping

---

[6] Party Literature Research Center of the CPC Central Committee (2016), *Op. cit.*, p. 792.

[7] Put 'Three Stricts and Three Realities' through the whole process of reform and strive to be an active participant in the comprehensive deepening of reform. *People's Daily*, July 2, 2015.

[8] Party Literature Research Center of the CPC Central Committee (2016), *Op. cit.*, p. 804.

underscored the significance of "placing ecological environment protection in a prominent position, likening it to the protection of our own eyes and the preservation of life itself."[9]

The concept of green development is one of the highlights of the five development concepts, with profound meaning and broad connections. In terms of its meaning, the concept of green development includes green economy, green environment, and green political ecology. As far as its connection is concerned, it includes following the path of agricultural modernization with high output efficiency, product safety, resource conservation, and environmental friendliness in innovative development, carrying resources and environment in a coordinated development, actively participating in global climate change negotiations in open development, and actively participating in the 2030 Agenda for Sustainable Development. All of these truly reflect the integration of ecological civilization construction into all aspects, forming the five-sphere integrated plan.[10] In addition, the modernization of ecological governance has opened up a new space for China's economic transformation. The strategic emerging industries supporting the future ecological economy should include: the ecological industries of traditional industries, the new energy industries with internalized costs, the ecological industries that meet green consumption, and the cultural industries with traditional endowment advantages. Green water and green mountains are golden mountains and silver mountains. Once the resources are exhausted and the environment is damaged, it is difficult to repair them. To build a moderately prosperous society in all respects, we must let the people gain a sense of happiness from development and must not sacrifice the environment.

6. Opening-up Is the Only Way to National Prosperity and Development

Opening-up is the only way for the country's prosperity and development, and closing will only stifle its own vitality. It is an inevitable choice for China to take on the world stage by examining the situation from a global

---

[9]Our province strives to be the leader of ecological civilization construction. *Spring City Evening News*, January 29, 2015.

[10]Referring to Implementing the five development concepts and realizing the centennial goals. *People's Daily*, October 30, 2015.

perspective and making plans on a global scale. "We must comply with the trend of China's deep integration into the world economy and pursue an open strategy of mutual benefit and win–win results, develop a higher level of open economy, actively participate in global economic governance and the supply of public goods, improve China's institutional voice in global economic governance, and build a broad community of shared interests."[11] The Fifth Plenary Session of the 18th CPC Central Committee puts forward the concept of "open development" and strives to achieve win–win cooperation. The focus is on solving the problem of internal and external linkage of development, which will enrich the process of opening-up, improve the level of opening-up, inject new impetus, add new vitality, and expand new space for development.

During the initial stages of China's reform and opening-up, Deng Xiaoping cautioned the entire party about the futility of isolating oneself and focusing solely on internal development. The successful experience of China's reform and development lies in promoting progress through opening-up. In the period of the "12th Five-Year Plan," particularly after the 18th National Congress of the Communist Party of China, we have pursued a more proactive opening strategy. This has entailed expediting the establishment of a new open economic system, advancing the construction of the "Belt and Road" initiative, accelerating the implementation of the "going out" strategy, and establishing free trade zones. As a result, the scope and scale of China's opening-up have significantly broadened, paving the way for the emergence of a more advanced and comprehensive pattern of openness.

"Simple action without comprehensive consideration is impractical." The current global economic landscape is undergoing significant transformations, characterized by evolving patterns of international economic cooperation and competition. This dynamic environment necessitates substantial adjustments to the global economic governance system and rules. The scale, scope, and pace of engagement with the international community have reached unprecedented levels. The challenges of managing external economic risks and safeguarding national economic security have also intensified. In response, the Fifth Plenary Session of the CPC Central Committee emphasized the importance of "adhering to a comprehensive approach encompassing both domestic and international considerations." This strategic direction aims to foster development based on

[11] Party Literature Research Center of the CPC Central Committee (2016), *Op. cit.*, p. 792.

global economic interconnectedness, enhance the capacity for global resource allocation, and embrace a broad international perspective.

Embracing a comprehensive perspective and embarking on a new trajectory, China has entered a phase of profound interaction with the global community. As the world's largest exporter and the second largest importer, the world's largest foreign investor and the second largest foreign investor, China's development cannot be separated from the world, and the world's prosperity cannot be separated from China. At present, the level of China's opening-up to the outside world is not high enough, the ability to make good use of both international and domestic markets and resources is not strong enough, the ability to cope with international economic and trade frictions and strive for the right to speak in the international economic forums is relatively weak, and the ability to apply international economic and trade rules is not strong enough. If we want to make the best of our strengths and avoid our weaknesses in the next step of development, we must carefully study how to improve the quality of opening-up and the internal and external linkage of development, and form a mutually beneficial cooperation pattern with deep integration between China and the world, so as to promote the reform and improvement of the global economic governance system, guide the global economic agenda, and take the path of open development.

The door that China opens will never be closed. Adhering to open development means adhering to the basic national policy of opening-up, pursuing the win–win strategy of opening-up, deepening people-to-people and cultural exchanges, improving the regional layout of opening-up, the layout of foreign trade, and the layout of investment, so as to promote innovation, reform, and development by expanding opening-up. The Fifth Plenary Session deployed opening-up and development from six aspects: improving the strategic layout of opening-up, forming a new system of opening-up, promoting the construction of the "Belt and Road," deepening cooperation and development between the mainland and Hong Kong, Macao, the mainland and Taiwan, actively participating in global economic governance, and actively assuming international responsibilities and obligations. Adhering to the long-term struggle according to such a deployment, we can achieve win–win cooperation through open development and inject strong and positive energy into the development of China and the world.

Since the initiation of the reform and opening-up policy, China has embarked on a continuous journey of expanding and deepening its engagement with the global community. Starting with the establishment of special economic zones and progressing through initiatives such as promoting foreign trade, attracting foreign investment, and eventually joining the World Trade Organization (WTO), China's development trajectory has been closely intertwined with its commitment to opening-up. In the present era, upholding the principles of open development and fostering win–win cooperation, we have the confidence to navigate the "China" ship toward broader horizons, securing one triumph after another and achieving even greater victories.

Open development solves the problems of how China's development can connect with the world's development, how to make good use of both international and domestic markets and resources, and how to force domestic reform and development with opening-up. The "Recommendations" adopt a global perspective and propose the concept of open development: "Opening up is the only way for the country's prosperity and development. We must comply with the trend of China's deep integration into the world economy, pursue the win–win strategy of opening-up, adhere to the coordination of internal and external needs, balanced imports and exports, equal emphasis on bringing in and going global, and the introduction of foreign investment, technology, and intelligence. It is essential to develop a higher level of open economy, actively participate in global economic governance and the supply of public goods, improve China's institutional voice in global economic governance, a broader community of shared interests."[12] We need to take a holistic view and macro-control and continue to promote the opening-up to a higher level.

7. Sharing Is the Essential Requirement of Socialism with Chinese Characteristics

Socialism with Chinese characteristics is the cause of hundreds of millions of people. Only by adhering to the principle that development is for the people, development depends on the people, and development achievements are shared by the people can an all-round well-off society truly benefit all the people.

Ensuring that the people can enjoy the benefits of reform and development is an intrinsic demand of socialism, a clear manifestation of the

---

[12]Party Literature Research Center of the CPC Central Committee (2016), *Op. cit.*, p. 792.

advantages of the socialist system, and an unwavering commitment of our Party to wholeheartedly serve the people. The Fifth Plenary Session of the 18th CPC Central Committee put forward the concept of shared development, which focuses on solving the problem of social fairness and justice, and also reveals the fundamental starting point and foothold of contemporary China's development and progress.

The principle of inclusive participation, collective endeavor, and shared benefits guides the journey toward building a moderately prosperous society in all respects. This trajectory also encompasses the pursuit of social equity and justice. On one hand, it is crucial to ensure that every individual has access to development opportunities and can partake in the fruits of progress, thereby fully mobilizing their enthusiasm, initiative, and creativity in promoting development. On the other hand, as China's economic prosperity continues to expand, issues of unequal distribution become more pronounced, with notable income disparities and discrepancies in public service levels between urban and rural areas. Consequently, the current state of shared development faces imperfections in its practical implementation and systemic design. In response, the Fifth Plenary Session of the CPC Central Committee has devised eight plans to enhance the provision of public services, implement poverty alleviation initiatives, improve educational quality, foster employment and entrepreneurship, narrow income gaps, establish a more equitable and sustainable social security system, advance the construction of a healthy China, and promote balanced population development. These plans not only serve as effective institutional arrangements for shared development but also represent pivotal focal points in our efforts to advance the cause of shared development.

To adhere to shared development, we must first highlight the people's dominant position. A moderately prosperous society in all respects is a well-off society that benefits all the people. It is to make all the people move steadily toward common prosperity. There must be no phenomenon that "the rich are burdened with millions, while the poor eat chaff." At present, the poverty alleviation of more than 70 million rural poor people is the most prominent weakness. Therefore, we should take extraordinary measures to implement the poverty alleviation project and take the poverty alleviation of rural poor people as the basic sign of building a moderately prosperous society in all respects. China has a specific population of about 18 million people depending on basic living allowance, more than 130 million people over 65 years old, more than 200 million migrant workers working in cities and towns, tens of millions of college graduates employed in megacities, and more than 9 million unemployed people. We should stick to the bottom line, highlight the key points, improve the system, guide the expectations, pay more attention to the fairness of opportunities, strive to ensure the basic livelihood of the people, and find ways to help them solve practical problems in view of their specific difficulties.

To adhere to shared development, the key is to make more effective institutional arrangements, step up the construction of systems that play a major role in ensuring social fairness and justice, gradually establish a social fairness security system with fair rights, fair opportunities and fair rules as the main content, and strive to create a fair social environment to ensure people's equal participation and equal development rights. To make development achievements highly equitable for the benefit of all people, in the final analysis, we should implement them through the system. With a fair and just system, shared development can have a solid foundation.

Shared development is a development concept highly related to the overall construction of a moderately prosperous society. Whether sharing can be achieved on the basis of prosperity is a question that needs to be highly concerned and addressed during the "13th Five-Year Plan" or an even longer period. The "Recommendation" state, "Sharing is the essential requirement of socialism with Chinese characteristics. We must adhere to the principle that development is for the people, that development depends on the people, and that the fruits of development are shared by the people. We must make more effective institutional arrangements so that all people have a greater sense of gain in jointly building and sharing development, enhance the momentum for development, enhance people's unity, and make steady progress towards common prosperity."[13] At the Central Conference on Ethnic Affairs held in September 2014, Xi emphasized that the fundamental purpose of economic development is to enable the people of all ethnic groups to live a good life.[14]

Only by sharing the development achievements fairly can we achieve a comprehensive well-off society; Only by making the people happy and healthy can China move steadily on the road of modernization. By making

[13] Party Literature Research Center of the CPC Central Committee (2016), *Op. cit.*, p. 793.

[14] The central ethnic work conference and the sixth national conference for the recognition of national unity and progress of the state council were held in Beijing. *People's Daily*, September 30, 2014.

development warmer and happiness more qualitative through shared development, we will be able to continuously enhance the momentum of development, constantly enhance the unity of the people, and make more than 1.3 billion Chinese people steadily advance toward the goal of common prosperity.

The new development philosophy of innovation, coordination, green, openness, and sharing is our Party's profound understanding and theoretical summary of the laws of social and economic development in the new era and is the concentrated embodiment of China's wisdom. "The five development concepts are interconnected and mutually reinforcing, and they are a collection of internal links. They should be implemented in a unified way and cannot be ignored or replaced by each other."[15] The five development concepts have made a comprehensive response to the problems of the purpose, mode, path, focus, measurement, and sharing of development, which can be seen as the further deepening and expansion of the scientific outlook of development, and will be the guiding ideology guiding our development in the next five years or more. At the same time, the proposal of the five development concepts is also an important contribution that China has made to the development of all humankind. The five development concepts, like a slowly rising ideological banner, guide us toward a new era of development.

[15]The decisive guiding principle for building a moderately prosperous society in all respects. *People's Daily*, October 31, 2015.

Chapter 4

Consolidating and Developing the Basic Economic System of the Primary Stage of Socialism

During the "Two Sessions" of 2016, Xi Jinping made an unequivocal statement regarding the basic economic system of China: "The basic economic system whereby public ownership plays a dominant role and economic entities under diverse forms of ownership develop side by side, is a pivotal political guideline established by the Communist Party of China. It is a vital component of the socialism with Chinese characteristics, as well as an indispensable requirement for improving the socialist market economy system."[1] The consolidation and expansion of the system hold significant theoretical and practical implications for advancing the socialist market economy system, fostering sustainable and robust economic and social development, and achieving the goal of building a moderately prosperous society in all respects.

1. Establishment and Continuous Improvement of the Basic Socialist Economic System

Given China's current position in the primary stage of socialism and the objective requirements for the development of a socialist market economy, ongoing adjustments to the ownership structure have been made in the pursuit of the Reform and Opening-up policy. While continuously

[1]Xi Jinping. (2016). Unwavering adherence to china's basic economic system to promote healthy development of enterprises under diverse forms of ownership. *People's Daily*, March 9, 2016.

developing and strengthening the public-owned sector of the economy, we have also actively promoted the non-public sector. The basic economic system, whereby public ownership plays a dominant role and economic entities under diverse forms of ownership develop side by side, represents a significant theoretical achievement of China's Reform and Opening-up. Furthermore, it is a major contribution made by the Communist Party of China to Marxism in the basic economic system of socialism.

1.1. *Evolution of China's ownership structure and the establishment of the basic socialist economic system*

Prior to the founding of the People's Republic of China, the country had a semi-colonial and semi-feudal economy with a variety of economic components, including foreign capital (imperialist economy), feudal economy, capitalist economy (including bureaucratic capitalism and national capitalism), and individual economy of farmers and self-employed craftsmen. The dominant and ruling economic components were the imperialist economy, feudal economy, and bureaucratic capitalist economy.

From the founding of the People's Republic of China in 1949 to the end of 1978 preceding the Reform and Opening-up, China's ownership economy had undergone several major changes. During the early years, the newly established government abolished imperialist privileges in China, eliminated feudal land ownership, and confiscated bureaucratic capital. This led to the development of an economic structure dominated by state-owned enterprises, with self-employed and private businesses as the main components and with the coexistence of multiple economic elements. Based on relevant data, it can be observed that as of the end of 1952, state-owned enterprises accounted for 19.1% of China's economy, with collective enterprises representing 1.5%, joint public–private enterprises accounting for 0.7%, private capitalist enterprises comprising 6.9% and individual enterprises in agriculture and handicrafts amounting to 71.8%. Subsequently, the years from 1953 to 1956 witnessed the socialist transformation of agriculture, handicraft industry, and capitalist industry and commerce, giving rise to fundamental changes of the ownership structure of China's economy, and forming the economic system led by state-owned enterprises, with collective enterprises acting as the mainstay and the coexistence of diverse forms of ownership. As per available data, by the end of 1956, state-owned enterprises accounted for 32.2% of China's economy, with collective enterprises representing 53.4%, joint public–private enterprises accounting for 7.3%, private enterprises comprising 1%, and individual enterprises making up 7.1%. However, during the period from 1957 to 1978, China pursued a policy of rapid economic development, which resulted in a misguided and superficial approach known as the "pauper's transition" (referring to the transition in China's agricultural cooperatives, where the ownership structure in rural areas shifted from small collectives to large ones and from collective ownership to public ownership before the necessary conditions were in place). At the heart of this approach was the mistaken belief that a larger and more pure state-owned economy was a more socialist one. Consequently, our country developed a one-sided economy that focused solely on state ownership, while disregarding and even impeding the growth of other forms of economic ownership. Toward the end of 1978, the state-owned sector constituted 56% of the Chinese economy, with the collective sector accounting for 43% and individual enterprises representing less than 1% of the total. Private enterprise had been entirely eliminated. In addition, the industrial structure in China during this epoch was dominated by state-owned enterprises, which accounted for 77.6%, while collective enterprises represented 22.4%. It has been proven through experience that a single state-owned economic structure that surpasses the due stage of development is not in line with China's existing productivity, nor does it facilitate the growth of social productive forces. As Deng Xiaoping astutely observed, "Between 1958 and 1978, a full two decades, the incomes of peasants and workers experienced little increase, the standard of living remained low, and our productivity barely saw any major progress."[2]

Since initiating the Reform and Opening-up policy, China's basic economic system has been continuously adjusted, along with the liberation of thought and the deepening of reforms. In December 1978, at the closing ceremony of the Central Committee's working conference, Deng Xiaoping stated that, "First, we need to emancipate our minds. Only when our minds are liberated can we correctly use Marxism-Leninism and Mao Zedong Thought as a guide to solve the legacy issues and emerging challenges. We can reform the production relations and the superstructure that are not compatible with the rapid development of productive forces,

[2] *Selected Works of Deng Xiaoping*, Vol. 3. People's Publishing House, 1993, p. 115.

and based on China's actual conditions, we can determine the specific path, principles, methods, and measures to achieve the Four Modernizations" (The Four Modernizations were goals first set forth by Deng Xiaoping to strengthen the fields of agriculture, industry, defense, and science and technology in China).[3] In October 1981, the *Decisions on Expanding Opening-up, Vitalizing the Economy, and Solving Urban Employment Issues* was passed by the Central Committee of the Communist Party of China and the State Council. It was the first time that the policy of "a certain scope of individual economy of laborers is a necessary supplement to the socialist public ownership economy, and it is necessary to implement multiple economic forms and modes of operation on the basis of the fundamental premise that the public ownership economy is dominant for a long time" was proposed. In December 1982, the General Principles of the Constitution of the People's Republic of China were passed, which stipulate that the basis of China's socialist economic system is the public ownership of the means of production, namely, the ownership by the whole people, and the collective ownership by the working masses. Article 7 states that the state-owned economy is the socialist economy of the whole people's ownership, which is the dominant force in the national economy, and the state guarantees the consolidation and development of the state-owned economy. Article 8 sets out that various forms of cooperative economy in industries such as handicrafts, industry, construction, transportation, commerce, and service in urban areas are socialist collective ownership economies of the working masses. Articles 9 and 10 state that urban land belongs to the state. Natural resources such as mineral deposits, water resources, forests, mountains, grasslands, wasteland, and tidal flats are owned by the state, namely, the whole people, except for those belonging to collective ownership as prescribed by law. Article 11 specifies that, within the scope prescribed by law, the individual economy of urban and rural workers is a necessary supplement to the socialist public ownership economy. The state protects the legitimate rights and interests of the individual economy. This was the first time the legal status of the individual economy was established at the level of the fundamental law of the country. In April 1988, the First Amendment to the Constitution of China made supplements to Article 11 and established, for the first time, the role and position of the private sector in the country's

[3] *Ibid.*, Vol. 2, 1994, p. 141.

socialist economy. The amendment stipulates that the state permits the existence and development of the private sector within the limits of the law and that it serves as a supplement to the socialist public ownership economy. Furthermore, the state protects the legitimate rights and interests of the private sector and implements its guidance, supervision, and management. In October 1992, the first formal announcement of China's economic system reform was made at the 14th National Congress of the Communist Party of China. The goal was to establish a socialist market economy system combined with the socialist basic system. The ownership structure is characterized by the predominance of public ownership, complemented by individual, private, and foreign-invested enterprises. These diverse economic elements are encouraged to develop in a coordinated and sustainable manner, with the option to establish voluntary associations among different ownership types.

1.2. *Establishment of the basic economic system of the primary stage of socialism*

On the basis of continuous practice and exploration, the report of the 15th National Congress of the Communist Party of China in September 1997 officially proposed the "basic economic system of the primary stage of socialism whereby public ownership plays a dominant role and economic entities under diverse forms of ownership develop side by side."[4] The report also made clear definitions on the meaning of the public ownership economy and its dominant position, the diversity of forms of public ownership, and the status of the non-public ownership economy. The key points are as follows: The public ownership economy not only encompasses state-owned and collective-owned economies but also contains the state-owned and collective-owned components in the mixed economy. Public ownership as the mainstay means that public assets hold a significant share of the total social assets, and the state-owned sector governs the lifeblood of the national economy, playing a leading role in the economy. This is the case nationwide, although variations may exist across regions or industries. To ensure the dominant role of public assets, it is essential

[4]Party Literature Research Center of the CPC Central Committee (Ed.) (2000). *Selected Important Documents since the 15th CPC National Congress*, Vol. I. People's Publishing House, p. 500.

to not only focus on quantity but also prioritize improving their quality. The primary strength of the state-owned economy lies in its ability to exercise control. By steadfastly upholding public ownership as the mainstay, the state can effectively govern the lifeblood of the national economy, enhancing both control and competitiveness within the state-owned sector. Under this premise, even if the proportion of state-owned economy decreases, it will not affect the nature of China's socialism. The forms of public ownership can and should be diversified, and all management methods and organizational forms that reflect the laws of socialized large-scale production can be boldly utilized. We should strive to find forms of public ownership that can greatly promote the development of productive forces. The joint-stock system is an equity ownership structure commonly found in modern enterprises. It cannot be simply classified as public or private ownership. The crucial aspect lies in identifying the entity or individuals who wield the controlling power over the equity. The joint-stock cooperative system is a new phenomenon in the reform process and should be actively guided and supported. The joint-stock cooperative system, which is based on the labor union and the laborer's capital union, belongs to a new type of collective ownership and should be encouraged and supported. Non-public ownership, such as individual and private enterprises, is an important component of the socialist market economy, which should be encouraged, supported, and guided to promote healthy development.

The establishment of the basic economic system of the primary stage of socialism is mainly based on two key factors. The first basis is the condition of our productive forces. As a general rule governing human society's development, the level of productivity determines the production relations, which in turn must be adapted to the development level of productive forces. This also serves as the fundamental theoretical basis for establishing the basic socialist economic system. China's socialism was not built on a highly developed capitalist economy but rather on the poor foundation of a semi-colonial and semi-feudal society with backward productive forces. The level of productive forces was extremely low and unbalanced, comprising both a socially integrated large-scale production based on advanced technology and a significant number of underdeveloped production forces that were semi-mechanized or even reliant on manual labor. This condition necessitated the implementation of a mixed ownership system with public ownership as the mainstay and the simultaneous development of diverse forms of ownership. Secondly, the requirements of the development of a market economy are also an important factor for establishing the basic economic system of the primary stage of socialism. In this primary stage, only by implementing a market economy could social productivity develop rapidly. The ownership base for the existence and development of a market economy must be the joint development of diverse forms of ownership. Over the past 40 years of Reform and Opening-up in China, we have transformed from a highly centralized planned economic system to a socialist market economy system. This process has also led to the formation and improvement of a basic economic system that is featured by the predominance of public ownership and the simultaneous development of diverse forms of ownership. The development of a market economy requires the establishment of a diversified market subject, which, in turn, necessitates the existence and growth of a diverse ownership economy.

Following the 15th National Congress of the Communist Party of China, which established the basic socialist economic system of the primary stage of socialism, the 16th, 17th, and 18th CPC National Congresses have all emphasized the need to consolidate and develop the basic economic system. The proposal and continuous enrichment of the basic economic system reflect the creative application of Marxist basic theories by the CPC members in the great practice of socialism with Chinese characteristics. It has also developed Marxist political economics, enhanced the confidence in our chosen path, in our guiding theories, in our political system, and in our culture, effectively promoting the development of the public and non-public sectors of China's economy. On the one hand, the state-owned sector of the economy has continuously made great achievements in reform and development, with its scale and strength significantly increasing, and its development vitality constantly growing. Its leading role and international influence continue to expand. In 2014, the total assets of state-owned enterprises (excluding financial ones) nationwide reached 102.1 trillion yuan, with net assets of 35.6 trillion yuan, a total profit of 2.5 trillion yuan, and tax contributions of 3.8 trillion yuan. These figures represent increases of 141 times, 73 times, 38 times, and 65 times, respectively, compared to the beginning of the Reform and Opening-up. Eighty-four out of the 94 Chinese companies listed in the Fortune 500 are state-owned enterprises (excluding Hong Kong, Macao, and Taiwan). On the other hand, the non-public sector has developed expeditiously as well. In 2014, the proportion of the non-public economy to China's GDP exceeded 60%, with its tax revenue exceeding 50%, and its new employment exceeding 90%. It has played an increasingly important role in supporting growth, increasing tax revenue, expanding employment, and promoting innovation. In the great practice of building socialism with Chinese characteristics in economic development, the basic economic system, as a major theoretical and practical innovation, has proved irreplaceable in establishing and improving the socialist market economy system, propelling the rapid growth of China's social productivity and the speedy enhancement of comprehensive national strength.

Upon examining the evolution of China's ownership structure over more than half a century since the founding of the People's Republic of China, we can see a close correlation between the ownership structure and economic development. Empirically, China's comparatively successful economic development during both the "First Five-Year Plan" period and the Reform and Opening-up period was characterized by the adherence to a primary emphasis on public ownership as the mainstay, coupled with the concurrent development of diverse forms of ownership. The difference between these two development periods lies in the driving forces behind them. The former period was propelled by the energy released from the transformation from private ownership to public ownership, while the latter period was driven by the energy released from the transformation from a single form of public ownership to a diverse range of ownership structures. Regardless of how we approach this phenomenon, we can draw a common conclusion: adhering to a primary emphasis on public ownership while developing diverse forms of ownership is the key to mobilizing all aspects of society and achieving rapid economic development. Conversely, any single ownership structure, be it private or public, hinders the mobilization of society's full potential, and thus hinders China's economic growth. Therefore, adhering to public ownership as the mainstay while developing diverse forms of ownership is a necessary adaptation to the law of production relations conforming to the level of production forces, especially at the primary stage of socialism in line with China's national conditions.

The "13th Five-Year Plan" period marks the decisive stage in achieving the goal of building a moderately prosperous society in all respects. It is crucial to fully comprehend the significance of the predominance of public ownership and the concurrent development of diverse forms of ownership. It is essential to comprehensively grasp and earnestly implement the new ideas, new concepts, and new strategies of governance put forward by the Central Committee of the Communist Party of China, with

Comrade Xi Jinping at its core. It is imperative to accurately grasp the profound changes in the connotations of the strategic opportunities for development and truly unify our thoughts and actions around the strategic deployment of building a moderately prosperous society in all respects.

2. Consolidating and Developing the Basic Economic System, Promoting Concurrent Development of the Public and Non-public Sectors

The *Decision of the CCCPC on Some Major Issues Concerning Comprehensively Deepening the Reform* adopted at the Third Plenary Session of the 18th Central Committee of the Communist Party of China pointed out that, "both the public and non-public sectors are key components of the socialist market economy, and are important bases for the economic and social development of China. We must unswervingly consolidate and develop the public economy, persist in the dominant position of public ownership, give full play to the leading role of the state-owned sector, and continuously increase its vitality, controlling force and influence. We must unwaveringly encourage, support and guide the development of the non-public sector, and stimulate its dynamism and creativity."[5]

2.1. *Unwaveringly consolidate and develop the public ownership economy*

Xi Jinping noted that "Our country is a socialist country led by the Communist Party of China. The public ownership economy has been formed over a long period of time in the course of national development, and has made outstanding contributions to such aspects as national construction, national defense and the betterment of people's lives. It is a precious wealth of the entire people, and of course, it must be developed well to continue to contribute to the reform and opening-up, as well as modernization."[6]

---

[5]Party Literature Research Center of the CPC Central Committee (Ed.) (2014). *Selected Important Documents since the 18th CPC National Congress*, Vol. I. Central Party Literature Press, p. 515.

[6]Xi Jinping (2016), *Op. cit.*

The existence and development of the public ownership economy is a fundamental characteristic of the socialist economy. To maintain and develop the basic economic system of socialism in the primary stage, it is crucial to uphold public ownership as the mainstay. The unwavering commitment to consolidating and developing the public ownership economy is determined by the nature of our socialist economy, because it serves as a guarantee for the realization of the essential socialist relationship, which is the elimination of exploitation, the eradication of polarization, and the gradual achievement of common prosperity. It constitutes the backbone of our nation's economic and social development. Only by steadfastly consolidating and developing the public ownership economy, maintaining its dominant position, and fully leveraging the leading role of the state-owned economy, can we safeguard the fundamental interests of the people and promote the consolidation and development of the socialist system. While the relationship among different ownership economies should be based on equal competition in terms of market development and exchange, their positions and roles within the socialist market economy exhibit notable distinctions when viewed through the lens of production relations. The public ownership economy serves as the foundation of the socialist economic system and the driving force for the concurrent development of diverse ownership economy. Thus, the consolidation and development of such an economy play a vital role in achieving the socialist goals of eliminating exploitation, eradicating polarization, and realizing common prosperity. It also promotes the coordination of macro- and micro-economic returns, long-term and short-term interests, and the synergy between basic and high-tech industries, as well as the rapid expansion of key enterprises, thus achieving a leapfrog development driven by informatization and industrialization.

For a big developing socialist country like China, unwaveringly consolidating and developing the public ownership economy is an important condition for achieving stable, sustained, and independent economic and social development. While emphasizing the unwavering consolidation and development of the public ownership economy, we must also develop a modernized understanding of the predominant feature of public ownership.

Firstly, "public ownership as the mainstay" refers to the collective public ownership of diverse forms of the economy as a whole, rather than the traditional understanding of a single form of public ownership. Public ownership points to the ownership form where the means of production are commonly owned by the society (or collective) of all laborers. Since the Reform and Opening-up, China's ownership structure has undergone significant changes, and public ownership has taken on various forms. This includes both state-owned and collective-owned sectors of the economy, as well as state-owned and collective-owned components of mixed economies. Therefore, "public ownership as the mainstay" should not be simply interpreted as state-owned sector being the mainstay, nor should it be understood as a single and pure form of public ownership being the mainstay.

Secondly, it should be noted that the notion of public ownership as the mainstay of the economy refers to the national economy as a whole and not necessarily every sector, region, or enterprise. Given the considerable disparities in the level of productive forces among different sectors, regions, and enterprises in China, it is necessary to allow for varying degrees of ownership in different economic fields, regions, and enterprises for a significant period in the current and future stages of development.

Thirdly, the predominance of public ownership is mainly reflected in the fact that public assets have an advantage over the total social assets. While a certain "quantity" of public assets is required, the emphasis lies in their "quality." Without a certain "quantity," it is difficult to become the mainstay, but if we solely focus on the "quantity," it can easily lead to a misconception that the more significant the proportion of public ownership, the more secure its dominant position is. Once the quantity decreases, there may be concerns about losing its dominant position. While this concern seems reasonable, upon careful analysis, it appears unnecessary. For instance, during the traditional planned economy period, the public ownership economy was not only the mainstay but the entire economy. However, at that time, our country's economic development was not fast, and people's living standards did not improve significantly for a long time. Since the initiative of Reform and Opening-up, with the development of other economic components, the proportion of public ownership in the economy has been decreasing continuously. Nevertheless, social productivity has vigorously developed, and the national economic strength has increased profoundly, with people's living standards improving rapidly.

Fourthly, the predominance of public ownership must be closely linked to the leading role of state-owned sector in the economy. The leading role of the state-owned sector serves as the foundation and guarantee of the dominant position of public ownership economy. Without the leading role, it is difficult to maintain the dominant position. Looking at the current economic situation and development trends in China, how to better exert the leading role of the state-owned sector is an arduous task that we must consistently face and solve.

Fifthly, public ownership as the mainstay of the economy is realized through market competition. A market economy requires fair competition, and neither public nor private enterprises should be granted any privileges. In market competition, public and private enterprises alike face two options: either adapt to market competition and continuously develop and grow through their own advantages, or gradually be eliminated by market competition if they cannot adjust. To maintain its dominant position, public ownership must enhance its vitality through competition and truly assert its dominant status through joint development with other economic components.

2.2. *Unwaveringly encourage, support, and guide the development of the non-public sector of the economy*

Xi Jinping highlighted, "The non-public sector of the Chinese economy has flourished through the CPC's policy guidance since the initiation of Reform and Opening-up. It is a trajectory that has been forged under the Party's leadership."[7] The 15th CPC National Congress made it clear that the non-public sector is an important component of China's socialist market economy. The 16th CPC National Congress called for the resolute consolidation and development of the state-owned sector while encouraging, supporting, and guiding the development of the non-public sector. The 18th CPC National Congress further emphasized the unshakable commitment to encouraging, supporting, and guiding the development of the non-public sector, ensuring that all forms of ownership have equal legal rights, fair market competition, and equal protection under the law. The Third Plenary Session of the 18th CPC Central Committee proposed that both state-owned and non-public sectors of the economy are essential components of China's socialist market economy and are critical foundations for the country's economic and social development. Property rights of both the state-owned and non-public sectors are inviolable, and the state must protect the legitimate rights and interests of all forms of

[7] *Ibid.*

ownership, with equal rights, opportunities, and rules for all. The Fourth Plenary Session called for the establishment of a property protection system centered on the principle of fairness, strengthening the protection of the property rights of all forms of ownership, and the elimination of any laws or regulations that violate fairness. The Fifth Plenary Session of the 18th Central Committee emphasized the need to encourage private enterprises to enter more fields in accordance with the law, introduce non-state capital to participate in state-owned enterprise reforms, and stimulate the vitality and creativity of the non-public sector. Xi emphasized that the non-public sector's position and role in China's economic and social development have not changed, and the CPC's policy directive to encourage, support, and guide the development of the non-public sector remains unwavering. He also underlined that the Party is committed to creating a favorable environment and providing more opportunities for the development of the non-public sector.[8]

Clearly, the accurate treatment and proper development of the non-public sector bear direct significance to the advancement of China's socialist market economy, the adjustment and reform of the public sector economy, and the development and improvement of the socialist economic system. First, the non-public sector has a natural connection with the market economy. Its clearly defined property rights, autonomous decision-making, and flexible operation mechanisms are naturally in line with the requirements of a market economy. Its existence and development are not only conducive to promoting the optimal allocation and utilization of resources but also help to form a market transaction order and a market competition system. Second, "three types of enterprises" (Sino-foreign joint ventures, Sino-foreign cooperative enterprises, and wholly foreign-owned enterprises), which are important components of the non-public sector, play an increasingly important role on the international competitive stage. In the context of economic globalization, the rapid flow of information, capital, and technology worldwide, the integration of capital among countries, and the optimization and sharing of resources on a global scale are unstoppable trends in the development of economies worldwide. The integration of domestic and foreign capital and technology is a necessary condition for China's market economy to integrate into the world's economic big market and achieve accelerated development. Third, in the socialist market economy dominated by the

[8] *Ibid.*

public sector, the non-public sector is attached to the public sector. Although private and foreign economies themselves have capitalist exploitative properties and strong spontaneity and utilitarianism, they need to be guided and managed in their development. However, their existence and development will not only affect the nature of the socialist economy but also be conducive to full market exchange and equal competition, conducive to the incentive mechanism and vitality within the public sector economy, conducive to the enhancement of the overall strength of the national economy, and conducive to the prosperity and development of the socialist market economy. Fourth, the non-public sector provides necessary conditions for the normal operation and development of China's market economy. They adapt to the internal operating mechanisms of the market and provide a reference for the reform of public enterprises. They absorb laid-off workers from state-owned enterprises and a large surplus labor force in society, opening up a broad employment field. They provide financial support and new impetus for the development of the national economy, making outstanding contributions to the development of the national economy. From these aspects, the non-public sector is an indispensable and important component of China's socialist market economy, and it can even be said that without the existence and development of various ownership economies, we would not have the prosperity of our national economy today. Fifth, the non-public sector has long-lasting vitality. First, the non-public sector has strong compatibility with the market economy. It not only grows in the environment of the market economy but also is an important institutional condition for the existence and development of the market economy. In a sense, without public ownership, there would be no socialism, and without non-public ownership, it would be difficult to build a socialist economy with Chinese characteristics. Secondly, the Chinese economy has already integrated into the world economic system. Public and non-public economies not only coexist among enterprises but also merge within enterprises, and this integration is increasingly international in nature. Finally, economic development itself has two parallel and non-contradictory tendencies of centralization and decentralization. On the one hand, as production scales continue to expand, social division of labor also deepens. This not only involves the increasing specialization of tasks between different production departments but also the specialization of various products and even individual stages within the production of a single product. This characteristic of the development of social productive forces has led to the possibility and inevitability of the coexistence of enterprises with different scales and ownership structures. As Xi summarized, "The growth of China's non-public sector economy, from small to large and from weak to strong, has been achieved under the guidance of our Party and state policies. For a long time, the rapid growth of the non-public sector of China's economy has played an indispensable role in stabilizing growth, promoting innovation, increasing employment, and improving people's livelihoods. The non-public sector of the economy is an important foundation for economic stability, a key source of national tax revenue, a major driver of technological innovation, an important support for financial development, and a crucial force for sustainable economic growth."[9]

To further enhance the role of the non-public sector in advancing national economic development, our Party has put forward a series of significant measures to support the healthy development of the non-public sector.

The first major initiative that our Party has put forward to enable the non-public sector to play a greater role in promoting national economic development is the abolition of various unreasonable regulations that had previously hindered the healthy development of non-public enterprises. In the past, there were numerous restrictive conditions targeted at the non-public sector in the establishment and registration of enterprises, such as excessively high registration criteria, excessive pre-approval procedures, and overly strict capital-raising methods. These constraints have limited the development of the non-public sector. Additionally, there were some unreasonable charging standards and items targeted at non-public enterprises in tax collection and management, resulting in a heavier tax burden for these enterprises. "The Decision" adopted at the Third Plenary Session of the 18th CPC Central Committee states that it is necessary to start from the system design, accelerate the modification and improvement of various laws and policies that are unfavorable to the development of the non-public sector, and propose the implementation of unified market access rules. The non-public sector can legally and equally enter areas beyond the negative list of the market, and implement the principle of "non-prohibited entry" and "nulla poena sine lege." These measures will effectively eliminate various institutional barriers that affect the development of the non-public sector and expand its development space.

---

[9] *Ibid.*

The second initiative aims to eliminate various hidden barriers that hinder the healthy development of the non-public sector. For instance, there exist pervasive phenomena such as the "glass door," "spring door," and "revolving door" in the implementation of policies toward the non-public sector. Xi Jinping expressly pointed out, "Some government departments still possess low efficiency in handling affairs for private enterprises, and private enterprises, especially small and medium-sized ones and micro-enterprises, face obstacles such as narrow financing channels, tight capital chains, and so on. Some private entrepreneurs describe the difficulties they encounter as facing the 'Three Mountains': the ice mountain of the market, the high mountain of financing, and the volcanic mountain of transformation. While many of these issues primarily stem from deficiencies in policy implementation, their impact on the efficacy of policies necessitates resolute resolution. Firstly, policies need to be improved to enhance their value and feasibility. For another, policy implementation must be intensified to ensure that policies are fully implemented. Issues such as policy non-implementation, inadequate implementation, or distorted implementation mainly arise from the 'last mile' problem. It is often said that the worth of any plan lies in its implementation. It is imperative for all regions and departments to ground themselves in reality, refine and quantify policy measures, devise relevant supporting measures, facilitate policy implementation and refinement, and ensure that private enterprises genuinely benefit and experience the positive outcomes of these policies."[10]

The third challenge is to overcome a series of hurdles that obstruct the development of the non-public sector. To begin with, we need to tackle the issue of inadequate financing for small and medium-sized enterprises by refining and strengthening the financial system and providing dependable, efficient, and hassle-free financing services. Secondly, we must remove restrictions on market entry, and encourage private investors to participate in all industries and domains that are not explicitly prohibited by laws and regulations. All areas that have been opened or promised to be opened to foreign capital by the Chinese government should be accessible to domestic private capital as well. Thirdly, we need to expedite the construction of public service systems that cater to the private sector's needs. We should promote the development of common technology service platforms that facilitate private enterprises' independent innovation and actively foster

[10] *Ibid.*

technology markets. Technical support and specialized services should be provided to assist private companies in this regard. Fourthly, we should guide private enterprises to leverage the property rights market to bring private capital together and engage in cross-regional and cross-industry mergers and acquisitions. This would facilitate the emergence of a group of large enterprise groups that possess unique characteristics and substantial market competitiveness. Lastly, we must strive to streamline administrative approval processes related to private investment management and reduce enterprise-related fees. To this end, we need to standardize intermediary organizations' behavior in the middle links, which would alleviate the burden and costs borne by private companies.

2.3. *Two "Unwavering Commitments" reunified in the process of socialist modernization*

The practice of China's Reform and Opening-up has fully demonstrated that the public and non-public sectors of the economy are not mutually exclusive or irreconcilable. In the development of a socialist market economy, they can be combined and unified. This combination and unity are manifested at the macro level by the coexistence and mutual development of state-owned, collective, individual, private, and foreign-funded economies under the premise of state-owned sector controlling the lifeblood of the national economy, which represents the diversification of the national economy in the macro sense. At the micro level, it is reflected in the diversification of enterprise investment subjects, namely the diversification of enterprise internal property rights. Based on the mutual inclusion of the diversification of the national economic composition and the diversification of enterprise property rights, the strengths of different ownership economic components can be brought into play, complementing each other's weaknesses.

Since it is required at the macro level that the state-owned sector controls the lifeblood of the national economy, transferring a portion of state-owned equity to the non-public sector while maintaining state-owned capital's controlling stake will not weaken but instead significantly strengthen the state-owned capital's dominant position in these areas. In a market economy, enterprises operate on capital, which can only maintain or increase its value in motion. Therefore, the development of the state-owned economy is dynamic, rather than static. If a state-owned enterprise is in a low-profit condition, abandoning a portion of its equity or even its entire stake, or purchasing a portion of private equity in a high-profit non-public sector, will not weaken but rather invigorate state-owned capital, and enhance its quality and efficiency.

Following an extended period of reform and opening-up, encompassing both practical endeavors and perceptual shifts, notable advancements have been achieved in our comprehension of the dialectical relationship between the public and non-public sectors during the primary stage of socialism. In the socialist market economy, on the one hand, the public and non-public sectors have their respective basis for existence and development and can leverage their respective advantages in various fields. Therefore, they should and can achieve joint development through coexistence in the long run. On the other hand, the integration of the public and non-public sectors within enterprises must be accomplished through specific means, giving rise to mixed-ownership property organizational forms. The essence of the market economy is an open economy, which manifests itself in the coexistence and common development of different economic entities, as well as in the continuous integration and reorganization of property rights among them in mutual openness. This further leads to the modern enterprise system characterized by property rights diversification. However, we must continue to liberate our thinking and deepen our understanding of the dialectical relationship between the two sectors. Only by doing so can we ensure that the public and non-public sectors can continue to develop in a coordinated and complementary manner, and jointly contribute to the prosperity of the socialist market economy.

As our understanding of the non-public sector continues to deepen, and as the Party and government policies to promote its development are implemented, the non-public sector is expected to experience rapid growth over the foreseeable future. While the proportion of the state-owned sector in the national economy may decline as a result of this trend, the absolute size of the state-owned sector will increase significantly as reform deepens, and its overall quality and competitiveness will continue to improve. Over the long term, the state-owned and non-public sectors will form a new situation of mutual integration, mutual promotion, and common development. Of course, both sectors face contradictions, problems, difficulties, and challenges in their development within the context of socialist modernization. However, it is important not to be shortsighted and overlook the broader perspective. Any attempt to negate the state-owned or non-public sectors is contrary to the fundamental interests of the vast majority of the people and runs counter to the requirements of China's reform and development. Therefore, such views are erroneous.

3. Mixed Ownership Economy, an Important Form of Implementing the Basic Economic System

The "Decision" adopted at the Third Plenary Session of the 18th Central Committee of the Communist Party of China pointed out that the mixed-ownership economy is an important form of implementing the basic economic system. The active development of a mixed-ownership economy, characterized by cross-shareholding and mutual integration of state-owned, collective, and non-public capital, holds significant advantages in terms of enhancing the functions, preserving and augmenting the value, and improving the competitiveness of state-owned capital. It also helps various forms of capital to complement each other's strengths and weaknesses, promote each other, and achieve common development.

3.1. *Meaning and significance of the active development of mixed ownership economy*

The mixed ownership economy refers to an economic component formed by the alliance, integration, or mutual participation of capital with different attributes. It emerged in the process of developing a socialist market economy in China and has become a strengthened economic form in the continuous search for the realization of public ownership. Since the initiative of Reform and Opening-up, the Communist Party of China has been exploring effective forms of public ownership and the basic economic system. In 1993, the *Decision of the Central Committee of the Communist Party of China on Some Issues concerning the Improvement of the Socialist Market Economy* pointed out that with the flow and restructuring of property rights, there will be more and more economic entities with mixed property ownership, which will form a new structure of property ownership. The report to the Party's 15th National Congress in 1997 further elaborated on the relationship between public ownership and mixed ownership, stating that the forms of public ownership can and should be diversified, and efforts should be made to find forms of public ownership that can greatly promote the development of productive forces. It also clearly stated that the joint-stock system is a form of capital organization for modern enterprises, which is conducive to the separation of ownership and management rights and can improve the efficiency of enterprise and capital operations. Both capitalism and socialism can use it. The public ownership economy not only includes state-owned and collective sectors but also the state-owned and collective components in the mixed ownership economy. In 1999, the *Decision of the Central Committee of the Communist Party of China on Several Major Issues Concerning the Reform and Development of State-owned Enterprises* proposed that advantage enterprises, especially large and medium-sized state-owned enterprises, should be transformed into joint-stock companies through standardizing listing, domestic and foreign joint ventures, and mutual participation of enterprises to develop the mixed ownership economy. The report to the Party's 16th National Congress in 2002 emphasized that, except for a few enterprises that must be operated solely by the state, all other enterprises should actively promote the joint-stock system and develop the mixed ownership economy. The *Decision of the Central Committee of the Communist Party of China on Several Issues Concerning the Improvement of the Socialist Market Economic System*, passed at the Third Plenary Session of the 16th Central Committee of the Communist Party of China in 2003, proposed that in order to adapt to the trend of continuous development of economic marketization, we should further enhance the vitality of the public ownership economy, vigorously develop the mixed ownership economy with state-owned capital, collective capital, and non-public capital as the participants, realize diversified investment subjects, and make the joint-stock system the main form of public ownership. In 2013, the *Decision of the Central Committee of the Communist Party of China on Some Major Issues Concerning Comprehensively Deepening Reform* proposed to actively develop the mixed ownership economy and for the first time clarified that the mixed ownership economy with cross-holding and integration of state-owned, collective, and non-public capital is the main form of the basic economic system.

We should support and encourage the development of mixed-ownership economy, where state-owned and other forms of ownership can coexist. State-owned capital investment projects should allow non-state-owned capital participation, and mixed-ownership enterprises should be allowed to implement employee stock ownership plans, creating a common interest between capital owners and laborers. Xi Jinping pointed out in his explanation of the "Decision" at the Third Plenary Session of the

18th CPC Central Committee that actively developing mixed-ownership economy is an important way and a necessary choice to uphold the dominant position of public ownership, enhance the vitality, control, and influence of the state-owned economy in new circumstances.

Actively developing a mixed-ownership economy is an inevitable requirement for China's development of a socialist market economy. The partnership and joint-stock companies in Western market economies are generally based on private ownership, with private partnerships and private stockholders. However, China's mixed-ownership economy can be clearly seen from its origins and development process, which mainly stems from the reform of state-owned enterprises, the search for forms and ways of combining public ownership, especially state-owned capital, with a market economy, and the basic economic system of developing multiple ownerships together with public ownership as the mainstay that is adapted to China's national conditions at the present stage. It is recognized that the objective of state-owned enterprise reform is to establish a modern enterprise system, and the typical form of a modern enterprise system is a joint-stock company, which is characterized by diversified ownership. The direction of state-owned enterprise reform is to transform traditional state-owned enterprises into diversified joint-stock companies. This reform process necessitates, in addition to the existing state-owned capital, maximizing the inclusion of non-state-owned capital as strategic investors to the greatest extent possible. Additionally, it seeks to attract as much private and foreign capital as possible for equity participation. The practice of reform has also fully proved that by actively developing a mixed-ownership economy, it is entirely possible to achieve an organic combination of public ownership and a market economy, enabling state-owned enterprises to find a form of implementation that can effectively promote the development of productive forces and meet the requirements of the development of a market economy.

Indeed, this is the case in reality. Since the 1990s, China has implemented policies allowing domestic private capital and foreign investment to participate in the reform, reorganization, and transformation of state-owned enterprises, including the listing of many state-owned enterprises, such as commercial banks. The development of mixed ownership economy has greatly promoted the development of state-owned enterprises. According to data from the China Banking Regulatory Commission, by the end of 2012, private capital accounted for 45% of the total share capital of joint-stock commercial banks, with the proportion of private capital in the total share capital of urban commercial banks exceeding 50%, and the proportion of private capital in the share capital of rural small and medium-sized financial institutions exceeding 90%. In addition, a significant proportion of China's listed companies are controlled or participated in by state-owned capital, and they represent typical mixed ownership economy entities. According to the *China Taxation Yearbook*, the contribution of mixed ownership economy to national tax revenue has been increasing year on year from 1999 to 2011. In 1999, it accounted for 11.68%, in 2005, it raised to 36.57%, and in 2011, it took up 48.52%, which reflects the actual situation of the development of a mixed ownership economy in China. In September 2013, the State Council Executive Meeting proposed to introduce a batch of projects suitable for industrial transformation and upgrading to private capital as soon as possible in the fields of finance, oil, electricity, railways, telecommunications, resource development, and public utilities, with the aim of generating demonstration and driving effects and promoting the development of mixed ownership economy in the process of structural reform.

Developing a mixed-ownership economy is conducive to amplifying the functions of state-owned capital, preserving and increasing its value, and enhancing competitiveness. By vigorously introducing private capital into public construction projects, state-owned capital can be directly enlarged and the diversification of investment entities can improve the corporate governance structure of state-owned enterprises, thereby enhancing their overall efficiency and comprehensive competitiveness. For example, the Beijing Metro Line 4 project was jointly invested and constructed by Beijing Capital Group and Hong Kong MTR Corporation, with a total investment of RMB 15.3 billion, of which the Hong Kong side invested RMB 4.6 billion, and the subway is currently operating smoothly and efficiently. Another example is when the Beijing Municipal Party Committee and Municipal Government proposed in July 2013 to open 126 projects to social capital in six areas, including rail transportation, integrated transportation hubs, urban roads, sewage treatment, solid waste treatment, and city heating network. The total investment was RMB 338 billion, of which more than RMB 130 billion was drawn from social capital. This measure greatly improved the construction speed and quality in the field of municipal infrastructure.

In line with the "Decision" and *Outline of the 13th Five-Year Plan for National Economic and Social Development of the People's Republic of China* adopted at the Third Plenary Session of the 18th CPC

Central Committee, mixed-ownership reform enables the implementation of employee stock ownership plans, creating a community of shared interests between capital owners and laborers. Furthermore, the development of mixed-ownership reform is strongly encouraged, particularly for non-publicly owned capital controlling mixed-ownership enterprises. Additionally, a portion of state-owned capital will be transferred to social security funds to better cope with the possible inadequacies of the pension fund caused by China's aging population trend. The social security fund, as a new subject in state-owned capital, will become an important force in the future development of mixed-ownership reform. It is anticipated that with the progressive implementation of the Party's policies for actively developing mixed-ownership reform, more state-owned and other forms of ownership economies will develop into mixed-ownership economies in the future.

3.2. *Modern property rights system, the foundation for actively developing a mixed ownership economy*

Property rights refer to the right to use, manage, and dispose of property for the purpose of obtaining economic benefits. The legal recognition and protection of property rights reflect economic relationships. Once a person's property ownership relationship is recognized and protected by law, property rights become exclusive, independent, divisible and transferable. The fundamental requirements of a modern property rights system entail unambiguous attribution, clear rights and responsibilities, strict protection, and smooth transfer.

The modern property rights system is the institutional prerequisite for the formation and development of a mixed-ownership economy. For starters, establishing a modern property rights system is an inherent requirement for consolidating and developing the basic economic system. In the historical process of China's reform and opening-up, with the continuous development of the socialist market economy, the types of property have also increased, and the proportion of intangible assets such as knowledge, patents, and trademarks has also expanded. Individual, private, foreign capital, and private property of urban and rural residents have also grown rapidly. China's single public ownership has been replaced by diversified ownership including public ownership, private ownership, and various forms of mixed ownership. In the new situation, further defining various types of property and protecting them according to law has become the foundation for the development of various economic components, especially mixed ownership. Establishing a modern property rights system is conducive to protecting public property rights, consolidating the dominant position of the public ownership economy; it is also conducive to protecting private property rights, promoting the development of the non-public sector of the economy; and it is conducive to the flow and restructuring of various types of property rights, promoting the development of a mixed-ownership economy.

Second, establishing a modern property rights system is conducive to a standardized modern enterprise system. The core and primary feature of a modern enterprise system is clear property rights. Only when property rights are clearly defined can an enterprise truly become a legal person entity with civil rights and responsibilities. This allows the enterprise to use all of its property for autonomous operations and take responsibility for profits and losses in accordance with the law, while also assuming the responsibility to increase the value of its capital for its investors. The smooth flow of property rights is not only beneficial to the enterprise's capital operations and improving economic efficiency but also to the restructuring, mergers, acquisitions, and joint ventures between capital of different forms. This is also conducive to achieving diversified investment and enterprise property rights, and ultimately constructing a standardized corporate governance structure, thereby truly establishing an enterprise management mechanism that meets the requirements of market economic development.

Third, establishing a modern property rights system is beneficial for enhancing the enthusiasm of various enterprises, operators, and laborers in entrepreneurship, innovation, and creative labor, as well as unleashing the full vitality of all production factors such as labor, capital, technology, knowledge, and management. Based on clear property rights, obtaining more income through property rights operation and owning more property rights is the power source for various market entities, including enterprises, operators, and laborers, to creatively carry out production and business activities under market economy conditions. A clear definition of property rights, unambiguous property rights relationships, strict legal protection of property rights, and institutional guarantees for property rights holders to maximize their economic benefits can effectively stimulate the enthusiasm of all sectors of society. This, in turn, can unlock the potential of every production factor and fully utilize all resources for wealth creation. Such an approach can contribute to sustained and healthy economic development as well as comprehensive social progress.

Fourth, establishing a modern property rights system is an essential condition for forming a sound functional system and market order. Property rights are the foundation for the establishment of a credit system, and the essence of market exchange is the exchange of property rights between market players. Only when property rights are clearly defined and effectively protected can a fair and orderly market competition environment and market order be created, providing the premise for the standardized operation of property rights and a solid social foundation for building a good social credit system. Therefore, establishing a modern property rights system provides us with a strategic opportunity to strengthen the construction of the social credit system from the perspective of property rights.

In summary, the establishment of a modern property rights system is conducive to the fluidity and restructuring of various production factors, the interpenetration and complementarity of diverse forms of ownership, and the mobilization of entrepreneurial and innovative initiatives among various types of enterprises, businesspeople, capital owners, and laborers. Hence, it is instrumental in promoting the continuous development and refinement of the mixed-ownership economy.

3.3. *Ensuring legal protection of all types of property rights serves as the institutional guarantee for the healthy development of the mixed ownership economy*

Establishing a comprehensive legal framework for protecting all types of property rights is the institutional guarantee for the normal development of the mixed-ownership economy. The effective protection of property rights in accordance with the law is crucial for safeguarding public ownership, consolidating the dominant position of state-owned sector, protecting private property rights, and safeguarding the legitimate rights and interests of the non-public sector, thereby promoting the healthy development of the non-public sector. It also helps to regulate investment activities, enhance the entrepreneurial initiative of enterprises and various sectors of society, and create a sound social credit system and market order. However, it is worth noting that the effective protection of property rights remains a weak link in our country's current legal framework. In response to this challenge, Xi has repeatedly emphasized "the importance of protecting the property rights of both public and non-public sectors. The state must protect the property rights and legitimate interests of all types of ownership, uphold equality in rights, opportunities, and rules, abolish unreasonable provisions and implicit barriers against the non-public sector, and stimulate the vitality and creativity of the same."[11] At the Fourth Plenary Session of the 18th CPC Central Committee, it was proposed to establish a property rights protection system with fairness as the core principle, strengthen the protection of property rights of various types of ownership organizations and natural persons, and eliminate any provisions in laws and regulations that violate the principles of fairness.

Building a healthy and orderly market for property rights transactions on the basis of protecting property rights, establishing sound property transaction rules and regulatory systems, and maintaining an orderly flow of property rights is a prerequisite for improving the efficiency of production factor allocation and promoting the healthy development of mixed-ownership economy. The free flow of property rights under a sound legal, regulatory, and institutional environment is an important aspect of a modern property rights system. Through various forms of property rights transactions and transfers, such as auctions, acquisitions, mergers, leasing, investment in equity, and debt-to-equity swaps, it is conducive to improving the operational efficiency of capital and enhancing the economic and social benefits of enterprises. Currently and in the future, we must work to remove institutional and policy barriers arising from such factors as ideology, political-business relationships, ownership nature, administrative subordination, and geographic location, in property rights flow, and promote the flow and restructuring of various property rights in a wider field and with higher efficiency. It is necessary to speed up the clearance of trading institutions, regulate trading behaviors, establish and improve a set of legal regulations that involve the entire transaction process, including the confirmation of transaction subject qualifications, the standardization of transaction process operations, and the fairness and reasonableness of transaction results, while strengthening supervision to ensure the fairness and effectiveness of property rights transactions.

Strictly enforcing property rights laws and regulations and holding violators accountable under the law is a fundamental principle that all businesses must adhere to. Regardless of their nature, all enterprises, whether public or private, must prioritize compliance and integrity as the

[11] *Ibid.*

foundation of their operations. They should conduct their business activities, govern their enterprises, and safeguard their rights in accordance with the law. The bottom line of the law cannot be breached, and all businesses must resolutely refrain from illegal activities such as tax evasion, smuggling, counterfeiting, and fraud, as well as unethical practices such as cutting corners, shortchanging customers, and charging high prices for low-quality products. Since the 18th CPC National Congress, our party has increased efforts to crack down on violations of property rights, bringing many illegal and disciplinary activities to justice. Strict enforcement of property rights laws and regulations also helps to purify the economic environment and to bring the market back to its original state by streamlining market order.

Chapter 5

Strengthening the Reformation and Development of the State-Owned Economy

State-owned economic reform advances in tandem with China's opening-up. It is intricately linked to the reform of state-owned enterprises and the transformation of the national economy. Additionally, it interacts with the overall development of the nation's economy.

As an integral component of the state-owned economy, state-owned enterprises serve as the organizational framework for realizing and managing ownership of the means of production. As Xi Jinping pointed out, "State-owned enterprises are an important force in growing the nation's overall strength and defending the interests of the people, and must be justified in being stronger, better, and larger, continually enhancing their vitality, influence, and risk resistance, and achieving value-added preservation of state-owned assets."[1]

1. State-Owned Economy Is the Economic Backbone of Socialism with Chinese Characteristics

The state-owned economy, which falls under the category of ownership of the means of production, is made up of a variety of property rights, management rights, operation rights, and income rights jointly owned by citizens in a society that the state entrusts to the appropriate departments for direct management on behalf of citizens. In an economic society, ownership of the means of production is a form of wealth ownership, that is,

[1] Justify strengthening, improving, and expanding state-owned businesses to produce new outcomes as soon as possible in critical sectors and key links of SOE reform. *People's Daily*, July 5, 2016.

who owns, disposes of, and uses the wealth. In contrast, in a state-owned economy, the resources are jointly owned, used, and disposed of by the members of society, and they are run and managed by the appropriate state agencies on their behalf.

State-owned enterprises embody the material presence of the state-owned economy. The quantity, quality, structure, and vitality of state-owned enterprises are a good representation of the state-owned economy's dimensions. "State-owned enterprises represent a key material and political foundation of socialism with Chinese characteristics, as well as an important pillar and dependable force of our Party in governance and in bringing prosperity to the country,"[2] Xi Jinping noted. The state-owned economy will also be regenerated, enhanced, enlarged, and strengthened if state-owned enterprises are improved and expanded. The reform and growth of state-owned enterprises are necessary for the reform and growth of the state-owned economy, which is itself dependent on the reform and growth of state-owned enterprises. Examining state-owned enterprises entails examining the state-owned economy.

1.1. *The state-owned economy is an important part of the public ownership economy*

The foundation of production relations is determined by the system of ownership of the means of production. Production relations are influenced by the type of ownership and superstructure adapted to it. Accordingly, the superstructure will also determine the production relations.

China has historically been an authoritarian nation with low productivity and a small-scale peasant economy as its primary economic structure for a long time. In modern times, prolonged wars devastated the country, causing significant displacement of people and severe economic destruction. It was the Communist Party of China (CPC) that served as the people's leader throughout their heroic battle. After a prolonged period of arduous armed conflicts and diverse struggles, the Chinese people successfully overcame the oppressive forces of imperialism, feudalism, and bureaucrat-capitalism, known as the "Three Mountains"

---

[2] Staunchly adhere to the party's leadership of state-owned companies to establish a new environment for party construction of state-owned firms. *People's Daily*, October 12, 2016.

under the leadership of the CPC. They achieved a significant triumph in the new democratic revolution and established New China. The Chinese people seized control of the state's authority and rose to power. Under the direction of the Communist Party of China since the founding of the People's Republic of China in 1949, China has steadily built a "people's democratic dictatorship led by the working class and based on the alliance of workers and peasants,"[3] which is, in essence, the dictatorship of the proletariat.

Article 6 of the Constitution stipulates: "The basis of the socialist economic system of the People's Republic of China is socialist public ownership of the means of production, namely, ownership by the whole people and collective ownership by the working people. The system of socialist public ownership supersedes the system of exploitation of man by man; it applies the principle of 'from each according to his ability, to each according to his work.' In the primary stage of socialism, the State upholds the basic economic system in which public ownership is dominant and diverse forms of ownership develop side by side and keeps to the distribution system in which distribution according to work is dominant and diverse modes of distribution coexist."[4]

Early in its history, China accomplished the transition to public ownership of the means of production, abolished the system of man-to-man exploitation, and instituted a socialist economy. Since then, a basis of socialist ownership with Chinese characteristics was established.

---

[3]Article 1 of the Constitution of the People's Republic of China (PRC): "The People's Republic of China is a socialist state under the people's democratic dictatorship led by the working class and based on the alliance of workers and peasants. The socialist system is the basic system of the People's Republic of China. Disruption of the socialist system by any organization or individual is prohibited."

[4]The Constitution of the People's Republic of China was adopted at the fifth session of the Fifth National People's Congress on December 4, 1982, and was promulgated and implemented by the National People's Congress on December 4, 1982. The Constitution was amended in accordance with the Amendment to the Constitution of the People's Republic of China adopted at the first session of the Seventh National People's Congress on April 12, 1988, the Amendment to the Constitution of the People's Republic of China adopted at the first session of the Eighth National People's Congress on March 29, 1993, the Amendment to the Constitution of the People's Republic of China adopted at the second session of the Ninth National People's Congress on March 15, 1999, and the Amendment to the Constitution of the People's Republic of China adopted at the second session of the Tenth National People's Congress on March 14, 2004.

1.2. *The effectiveness of the operation of the state-owned economy determines the efficiency of the public economy*

Economic efficiency is a measure of the quality of economic operation, which refers to the output per unit of time or the output per unit of production factors. Economic efficiency is a relatively comparative indicator. Generally speaking, the more output per unit of time, the higher the efficiency. The more output per unit of input factors, the higher the efficiency.

There is the efficiency principle formula, that is, the input–output relationship as follows:

$$\eta = n/m$$

where η is the efficiency index

n the output

m the input

The input–output efficiency index is key to measuring an economy's efficacy and efficiency. The efficiency of the economic system corresponds with increasing index values. The higher this indicator is, be it measuring an economic organization or an enterprise, the more active the enterprise (or economic organization) is, and the more competitive the market is, which places it in a more favorable position in the industry.

The quantity or quality of outputs or the quantity or quality of inputs can be increased or decreased in order to increase the efficiency of outputs, and both changes can be made under the condition that the quality is maintained.

Article 7 of the Constitution provides that, "The State-owned economy, namely, the socialist economy under ownership by the whole people, is the leading force in the national economy. The State ensures the consolidation and growth of the State-owned economy." The goal of China's public ownership economic system is to use the means of production more effectively, put them to use more effectively, promote social equity more effectively, and allocate resources more effectively in order to mobilize the various economic forces in society, produce and create social wealth as quickly as possible, distribute social wealth as fairly as possible, and provide each member of society with the opportunity to participate fully in society.

Presently, the existing forms of social and economic systems in the world are "public" vs "private," "planned economy" vs "market economy," and "socialism" vs "capitalism." The conventional method used by economic scholars is to monitor the condition of these two types of economic forms using "symmetric analysis" and "comparative analysis," and to separate the advantages and disadvantages by contrasting the traits and operational effectiveness between them. In reality, the state's selection of an economic system is the result of a very intricate historical evolutionary process. The decision-making groups select the economic system best suited for their own development in this process as a result of the convergence of numerous factors and the demands of long-term development. This is by no means a wholly pure economic concept, just as economic phenomena cannot be observed or understood entirely in terms of economics. A wide and broad range of perspectives should be taken into consideration, including areas of geography, politics, economy, society, culture, history, nature, resources, and ethnicities. They must be compared and assessed from a historical viewpoint.

An effective and efficient public economy depends on a number of factors, including whether the state-owned economy is effective and efficient, whether state-owned enterprises are effective and efficient, and whether state-owned enterprises contribute to the social economy in an effective and efficient way.

1.3. *The competitiveness of state-owned enterprises is an indicator of the state-owned economy's competitiveness*

Early on in its development, New China's economy was in dire straits, which made it difficult to feed the population and maintain political stability. It was necessary to feed the nation and stabilize the society on the one hand; however, there was also a need to deal with foreign hostile forces and defend the frontier, so there was tremendous pressure both from within and from the outside. In response to these extraordinary circumstances, the state implemented a planned economic management system and operation mechanism during this time. State-owned enterprises became the main economic force, the state-owned economy became the primary economic sector, and the state-owned economy and the collective economy formed the absolute composition of the social economy. State-owned enterprises and collective economies played a crucial part in the national economy when there were very few resources available. State-owned enterprises in particular were dispersed over all crucial regions and significant industries, acting as the backbone of the nation. The social climate was optimistic during this period, "grasp revolution, promote production, promote work, promote preparation for war" was the slogan at that time. Everyone pooled their efforts together, dedicated themselves to building the newly founded country, and worked toward progression. Policies such as "taking grain as the key link" and "taking steel as the outline" resulted in the gradual resolution of the fundamental problem of feeding the nation and led to the establishment of the basic national industrial system. According to statistics, by 1955, the gross domestic product was RMB 91.16 billion yuan, and the national population reached 614.6 million; by 1960, the gross domestic product was RMB 147.01 billion yuan, the national population reached 662 million, and the grain output reached 143.857 million tons. By 1965, the GDP was 173.40 billion yuan, the population reached 726 million, the grain output reached 194.5250 million tons, the per capita grain intake was 272 kilograms, and the added value of the secondary industry was 60.85 billion yuan. China's economic development achieved notable strides during this time: the 10,000-ton hydraulic press was finished in December 1961, and an atomic bomb successfully detonated on October 16, 1964, along with the active promotion of urban infrastructure construction and the steady increase in grain production. China transitioned from a backward and flawed China to a prosperous new China and started down the socialist path.

State-owned enterprises take the form of factories, with production as their primary function. Their products are distributed by national planning agencies. State-owned enterprises operate with exceptional efficiency, contributing to the overall efficiency of the state-owned economy. State-owned enterprises continued to "grasp the revolution and promote production" even during the 10-year "Cultural Revolution" period in order to supply goods for the nation.

China underwent reform and opening-up following the Third Plenary Session of the Eleventh Central Committee of the Party in December 1978. Enterprises were granted business functions. As the state's system of distributing social goods was gradually abolished, businesses started interacting directly with the market, goods started interacting directly with consumers, production and consumption connected directly, and factories gradually evolved to become corporates. "Supply–Production–Sales" were the three main ties that connected businesses, and "people-finance-goods" were the three domains of management. What is the current state of business operations? How should businesses be run? How should businesses expand and grow? These inquiries pose new challenges.

Due to their "lack of functions and talents," "lack of mechanisms and resources," "lack of ideas and strategies," and other factors, factories were completely unable to adapt to market-oriented operations. As a result, their ability to grow and significantly increase their efficiency was severely constrained. Additionally, the idea of "market competition" had not yet been established, particularly for global enterprises and the global market, which made it improbable to compare the efficiency of state-owned enterprises and global multinational enterprises. In light of this situation, significant adjustments were required.

2. Progressive Reforms to Encourage the Transformation of the State-Owned Economy

Since 1979, China has initiated a momentous endeavor, embarking on the new Long March of reform and opening-up. Reform and opening-up started off with the approach of "allocating farm output quotas to individual households." The grain output increased significantly in just four years, and the agricultural sector advanced quickly. In 1982, grain output reached 3,504,500,000 tons, with a total agricultural output value of 186.530 billion yuan; in 1983, grain output reached 387,275,000 tons, with a total agricultural output value of 207.447 billion yuan; in 1984, grain output reached 407,305,000 tons, with a total agricultural output value of 238.015 billion yuan. The momentum of reform and opening-up proved to be a catalyst for economic growth, resulting in "four consecutive increases" in agricultural production.

Since then, enterprise reform has also slowly begun to take place in cities. Its principal strategy is to bring the fundamental lessons learned during rural reform to urban settings. We shall gradually examine the reform objectives, reform steps, and reform methods and procedures, starting with the contracted operations of enterprises.

2.1. *The objective of state-owned economic reform is to boost productivity and enhance the framework*

How exactly do the reforms of the state economy and state-owned enterprises function? At the time, the situation was not quite clear. Enterprises were only discovered to be insufficiently dynamic and ill-suited to the market economy, particularly the internationalized market economy in contrast to the other enterprises in the market. Businesses also had a tough time adapting to the market, be it through strategic decision-making, project investment, market operation, company model, technical innovation, product production, industry standards, etc. Reforms were therefore meant to address these issues. Their objectives underwent a continuous evolution, transitioning gradually from local to global perspectives, initially starting with simpler tasks before progressing to more complex endeavors.

First, reforms should be focused on reforms of market operations. Opening-up and reform coexist. Reform spurs opening-up, and opening-up fosters reform. Production will immediately be in direct contact with consumption after enterprises enter the market, and enterprises will directly face consumers. The enterprise's production operations currently have to compete with the consumers' consumption activities since the national plan's unified allocation is absent. As a result, the company's original, singular production function is insufficient. Enterprises must improve the functions of operation, investment, technology, and product innovation as well as research and development. Achieving these functions requires a combination of institutional arrangements and effective allocation of personnel and resources. The reform aims to facilitate the integration of these elements into the production process.

Second, reforms should be oriented toward institutional innovation. It is essential to establish a range of institutional arrangements and mechanisms for macro, meso, and micro-management. In order to effectively fulfill their regulatory role, fiscal and monetary policies need to be employed. Shifting from direct regulation to indirect regulation necessitates innovative systems and mechanisms. The central government's management of the national economy and the local government's management of the local economy both require a clear division of labor. Through ongoing exploration, China has come to recognize that the objective of reform is to construct a socialist market economy system.

Third, reforms should be directed to improve efficiency. It is challenging to implement efficiency if an enterprise's market-oriented capability is insufficient and the mechanism is inactive. Therefore, it is essential to reform enterprises' internal operating systems, including market information discovery system, quick response system to market signals, crisis response systems for unforeseen events, investment decision systems, product and technology innovation motivation systems, employee incentive and restraint systems, dynamic salary systems, market-oriented selection and withdrawal mechanisms of employees, professional manager management, capital structure optimization mechanism, etc. The aim of these mechanism reforms is to activate and enhance the various components of production, increasing their functionality and effectiveness.

Fourth, reforms should be focused on structural optimization. It is necessary to distribute the limited state-owned resources in the most necessary fields and links because the state-owned economy does not encompass the entire society. To achieve this, it is imperative to reconfigure the framework, optimize the structure, and fully harness the leverage of the state-owned economy. By strategically "linking various units" and "exerting a multiplier effect," the state-owned economy can effectively assume its leading, demonstrative, and driving roles. In order for other economic components to have the room and opportunity to play their roles and then mobilize various beneficial factors to participate in the social and economic construction, state-owned enterprises should also withdraw from some fields, some industries, and some departments throughout the economy.

The main goal of reforms is to increase the operating effectiveness of state-owned capital and the competitiveness of state-owned businesses. Give full play to the key leadership role of the state-owned capital in the national economy so as to improve the contribution rate of the state-owned economy to the national financial resources.

2.2. *Approach state economic reform by advancing in stages*

The transformation of the state-owned economy and state-owned enterprises in China can be divided into three main phases. These phases, namely "revitalizing state-owned companies," "enhancing state-owned capital," and "strengthening the state-owned economy," represent the key stages of China's state-owned economic reform and development. Throughout these stages, the state-owned economy in China has undergone a progressive transformation.

The initial stage, characterized by the transition from a factory model to a corporate model, primarily focused on revitalizing state-owned enterprises. Following the Third Plenary Session of the 11th CPC Central Committee in 1979, the corporatization and transformation of state-owned enterprises began as part of the state-owned economy's reform. The adoption of contract management of state-owned assets, the conversion of factories into firms, and the autonomy of enterprise management were the primary reform initiatives during this time. Enterprises started to perform multiple types of production instead of just one, and they started to have independent managerial autonomy. Before the reform, businesses only had a production function; the state produced and distributed the goods through a plan, and businesses didn't need to worry about the distribution sector or have a managerial role. In light of the adjustment in the national macroeconomic management system and the gradual elimination of planned economic practices such as centralized distribution and marketing practices, and the introduction of market mechanisms, it became imperative for businesses to directly enter the market and engage in direct interaction with consumers. This shift necessitated a closer connection between production and marketing through market mechanisms in order to facilitate exchange. As a result, businesses were compelled to enhance their operational capacities and actively participate in market competition. Due to market forces and the principle of survival of the fittest, businesses were pushed to change, which started the reform process. Economic authorities began learning from the experience and practice of rural reform, the introduction of contract management, that is, the enterprise entrusted by the business managers to implement contract management, in accordance with the annual predetermined indicators, in order to assess the efficiency and effectiveness of enterprises, change the problem of the absence of the main body of enterprises, and explore ways to improve the operational efficiency of enterprises. Although the primary structure of the business is in place, some short-term tactics may unavoidably surface during the implementation phase in order to meet the annual target. In response to this circumstance, a few improvement techniques to investigate the lengthening of the contract period started to emerge. However, due to a lack of resources, talent, and long-term development plans, the vigor of the businesses to engage in market competition is still insufficient, and the economic benefits are not as satisfactory.

The second stage, encompassing the transition from a corporate model to a listed company model, placed significant emphasis on improving state-owned capital. The reform of the state-owned economy entered the stage of social transformation of state-owned capital and socialization of enterprise equity structure with the introduction of the two major stock markets in 1991. On December 1, 1990, the Shenzhen Stock Exchange was founded, and on July 3, 1991, it was formally inaugurated. On November 26, 1990, the Shanghai Stock Exchange was founded, and on December 19, 1990, it was formally inaugurated. The establishment of China's two main stock exchanges has given businesses the chance to reform the socialization of capital and provided a window and a platform for the socialization of corporate capital. From the level of management to the level of capital structure, the reform of state-owned businesses has started to progress. A number of state-owned businesses have undergone capital structure reform and successfully listed their shares, creating new financing avenues and paving the way for this process. The Shenzhen Stock Exchange, which had 1,063 listed companies, 91.1 million investor securities accounts, a total market value of 7.17 trillion yuan, and cumulative stock financing of 1.03 trillion yuan[5] as of the end of August 2010, had initially established three major systems: a main board, a small and medium-sized enterprise board, and a growth enterprise board. The Shanghai Stock Exchange has 870 listed businesses as of the end of 2009, and the market value of all the equities was RMB 1,846,523 million.[6] The advent of listed state-owned businesses has disrupted the established capital structure of state-owned businesses in the traditional sense, changing the single state-owned capital structure into a multi-capital structure and creating a new environment for state-owned economic reform.

The third and final stage, involving the transition from a listed company to an international business, was aimed at bolstering the state-owned sector of the economy. State-owned businesses started the process of becoming global following the 18th Party Congress in 2013, and the corporate market started to embrace globalization. The availability of general products in perfectly competitive industries has significantly increased, and the number of product categories in complete shortage has started to decrease. With the development of large-scale and batch production in the production field, the problem of insufficient supply has been fundamentally solved, the shortage that afflicted the domestic economy for a long time has ended, and the main aspects of the contradiction between market and supply have been resolved. On the one hand, there is excess supply capacity in some fields, and the main pressure on economic activity comes from the supply side; on the other hand, the non-state economy is growing quickly, and in some fields, the private economy is already in an unquestionably dominant position (such as the catering industry, the garment processing industry, the retail industry, the information terminal

---

[5] Shenzhen Stock Exchange official website, September 30, 2010.

[6] *Ibid.*, August 30, 2010.

industry, the mobile communication industry, etc.). Private enterprises have also made significant strides in other fields (e.g. Huawei, ZTE, Skyworth, etc.). As a result, when the distribution of the state-owned economy changes, the entire national economic structure will likewise shift. The state-owned economy may decline in some regions and make room for other economic sectors, particularly the private economy. The state-owned economy should be developed in some regions while being strengthened in others by focusing on people, financial, and material resources. Additionally, state-owned businesses should broaden their market reach from the domestic to the international level in order to absorb excess capacity. At the same time, they should improve their capacity for innovation, develop new goods and technologies that the market requires in order to meet changing consumer demands, increase the operational effectiveness of state-owned capital, and emphasize the contribution of the state-owned economy to internationalization and innovation.

2.3. *Reform: A perpetual journey of progress*

Change and invariance represent relative states of entities, and there exists a functional relationship among time, state, and disturbance factors. State variables persist as long as time and disturbance variables are present. The state variables undergo alterations corresponding to changes in time and disturbance variables. Change refers to a significant transformation in the state of entities relative to time variables, resulting in a sensitive and intolerable response from the subject, thereby disrupting comfort. Invariance, on the other hand, denotes a minor state alteration in entities relative to time variables, where the overall degree of response from the subject of entities is not sensitive enough to be intolerable, thereby preserving comfort. Entities strive to transition to a new, comfortable state when faced with changes.

The world is characterized by perpetual change, where the concept of constancy is relative and synonymous with change itself. As long as there exists any form of motion, things will inevitably undergo continuous transformations.

State-owned enterprises serve as the material carriers of state-owned capital. These enterprises are required to continually adapt their development trajectory and strategic deployment in order to remain competitive in the market, particularly in the face of competition from large multinational organizations. This process of adaptation is perpetual and ongoing, as long as a market economy exists. The advancement of science and technology will consistently drive the development of more sophisticated technology and equipment. Concurrently, efforts to enhance operational efficiency within businesses and modify productivity and production relationships will persist. Reform, therefore, is an ongoing process characterized by proactive behavior change and adjustment in response to evolving circumstances.

3. Internationalization Gives State-Owned Economic Transformation Additional Impetus

What is the driving force behind the new wave of reforms? What are the objectives and directions of these reforms? Which rules and guidelines are being employed? What methods and measures are being implemented? These concerns are shared across all sectors of society.

Following the 18th National Congress of the Communist Party of China, the Central Committee of the Communist Party of China issued a series of reform documents, which stipulated the direction and objectives of the reform. For example, the *Central Committee of the Communist Party of China's Decision on Comprehensively Deepening Reform* adopted at the Third Plenary Session of the 18th CPC Central Committee, *Decisions of the Central Committee of the Communist Party of China on Major Issues Concerning the Enhancement of All-Round Law-Based Governance* adopted at the Fourth Plenary Session of the 18th CPC Central Committee, the *Central Committee of the Communist Party of China's Recommendations on the 13th Five-Year Plan for Economical and Social Development* adopted at the Fifth Plenary Session of the 18th CPC Central Committee, the *Central Committee of the Communist Party of China and the State Council's Guiding Opinions on Deepening the Reform of State-owned Enterprises* (August 2015), the *Central Committee of the Communist Party of China and the State Council's Opinions on Revitalizing Old Industrial Bases in Northeast China in an All-round Way* (April 2016), *Guiding Opinions of General Office of the State Council on Promoting the Structural Adjustment and Reorganization of Central Enterprises* (July 2016), and so on. These documents outline the necessary steps to further the reform of the state-owned economy and state-owned businesses from many angles and to give fresh development momentum.

According to President Xi Jinping, "We should unwaveringly deepen the reform of state-owned enterprises, focus on innovative institutional mechanisms, accelerate the establishment of a modern enterprise system, display the enthusiasm, initiative, and creativity of all types of talents in state-owned enterprises, and stimulate the vitality of various elements."[7]

The new round of reforms is generally concentrated on the capital and organization of the state-owned economy, but it is more inclined to improve the structure and efficiency through the flow of state-owned capital, to advance through the creation of major development themes, and to seek development through adaptation to internationalization than it is to merely change the organization of state-owned enterprises. With significant changes to state-owned businesses, state-owned capital, and even the state-owned economy, the new round of reforms is innovative, even subversive. "In line with the principles of innovative, coordinated, green, open, and shared development, it is important to promote structural adjustment, foster innovative development, and optimize the overall layout. This approach will empower state-owned enterprises to spearhead the supply-side structural reform."[8] "To make state-owned enterprises the most dependable force for the Party and the State to rely on, an important force in resolutely implementing the Party Central Committee's decisions and plans, an important force in implementing the concept of innovative development and comprehensively deepening reform, an important force in implementing the strategy of going global and building the 'One Belt, One Road' and other major strategies, become a significant force in strengthening overall national power, fostering economic and social progress, securing and enhancing people's means of subsistence, and strengthening our Party's ability to prevail in the great struggle with many new historical characteristics."[9]

---

[7]Justify strengthening, improving, and expanding state-owned businesses to produce new outcomes as soon as possible in critical sectors and key links of SOE reform. *People's Daily*, July 5, 2016.

[8]*Ibid.*

[9]Staunchly adhere to the party's leadership of state-owned companies to establish a new environment for party construction of state-owned firms. *People's Daily*, October 12, 2016.

3.1. *Promote reform through effective management of state-owned capital*

In the Third Plenary Session of the 18th CPC Central Committee, President Xi Jinping outlined the *Decision of the CCCPC on Some Major Issues Concerning Comprehensively Deepening the Reform*. He highlighted that, "The state-owned assets management system will be enhanced, with capital management at the core, to strengthen oversight of state-owned assets. The authorized operation mechanism for state-owned capital will undergo reform. State-owned capital investment operations should align with the strategic goals of the state, prioritizing increased investment in key industries and areas essential to national security and economic vitality. Emphasis will be placed on providing public services, developing important and forward-looking strategic industries, safeguarding the ecological environment, supporting scientific and technological progress, and ensuring national security. A portion of state-owned capital will be transferred to social security funds. Moreover, the proportion of state-owned capital gains turned over to public finance will be increased, with the aim of utilizing these funds to guarantee and enhance people's livelihoods."[10] He also emphasized that, "The policy of promoting deepening reform and enhancing the management of state-owned enterprises must be upheld to preserve and augment the value of state-owned assets, bolster the competitiveness of the state-owned economy and the role of state-owned capital. Additionally, the supervision of state-owned capital should be strengthened. It is crucial to steadfastly enhance the strength, efficiency, and size of state-owned enterprises."[11]

The direction and objectives of the next state-owned economic reform are indicated by President Xi Jinping's statement: focus on the adjustment of the stock of state-owned capital, focusing on increasing the flow of state-owned capital, focusing on maximizing the increment of state-owned capital, and driving the adjustment of the stock by doing so. Reform the state-owned economy by moving from the level of enterprise

---

[10]Party Literature Research Center of the CPC Central Committee (Ed.) (2014). *Selected Important Documents since the 18th CPC National Congress*. Vol. I. Central Party Literature Press, p. 501.

[11]Staunchly adhere to the party's leadership of state-owned companies to establish a new environment for party construction of state-owned firms. *People's Daily*, October 12, 2016.

organization to the level of state-owned capital; utilize the liquidity, changeability, flexibility, and adaptability of capital; and apply capital regulation mechanisms.

The first focus is the adjustments of stocks. The quantity and quality of the current allocation of state-owned capital in the sector must be changed, and state-owned capital must be concentrated and then concentrated again. Under the circumstances of the planned economy, the distribution of state-owned capital was extensive, with state-owned capital in nearly all industries and state-owned enterprises in all fields, both spatially and industrially, all of which were unaccounted for and created a situation that blossomed everywhere. State-owned capital has been reduced and withdrawn from various industries after more than 30 years of reform and opening-up, making room for other economic factors. On the one hand, this action has increased the involvement and vigor of other economic factors, created new elements in the economic structure, engaged different production factors in the economy and society to take part in the nation's construction, improved output capacity, and increased employment opportunities and channels for people to increase their income; on the other hand, the shaky state of the state-owned economy. Nevertheless, some industries continue to operate as de facto monopolies due to areas that are still heavily dominated. For instance, state-owned banks virtually monopolize the banking sector; state-owned oil companies monopolize the oil industry; state-owned telecommunications companies monopolize the telecommunications sector; state-owned power grids monopolize the electric power sector; state-owned enterprises monopolize the military production sector; and there is an absolute monopoly in the tobacco sector. In addition, state-owned businesses also create "quasi-monopolies" in other industries like steel, metallurgy, and non-ferrous metals.

Market competition can be classified as perfect competition, monopolistic competition, oligopoly, and monopoly. When it comes to promoting a business's ability to innovate, only the introduction of a competition mechanism will do. This will also encourage the enterprise to react to market changes and continually improve its operations and management practices in order to increase the quality of its output. Businesses in monopolistic positions in monopolistic markets (or industries) will not stimulate ongoing innovation, which will cause a lag in their innovation actions. As a result, businesses will unavoidably remain dull, and no one will be highly motivated to take the initiative to improve their behavior.

Such businesses have operated in a comparatively stable environment for a considerable amount of time, not having to worry about things like food, drink, income, or money, and leading relatively comfortable lives. As a result, they have developed a set of business management habits and a "seeking stability and fearing chaos" corporate culture. The enterprise's decision-making mechanisms, investment mechanisms, business opportunity capture mechanisms, management mechanisms, product and technology research and development mechanisms, product or service market response mechanisms, etc., are inevitably pushed to their breaking point once such a business venture enters the global market and competes directly with foreign multinational corporations.

As the stock of state-owned capital undergoes adjustments through acquisitions, reorganizations, mergers, withdrawals, and stock listings, the focus of state-owned capital will be redirected toward key areas. These areas encompass national construction, critical sectors, leading industries, foundational sectors, security domains, and public service sectors. This strategic shift aims to promote the operation of a competitive market economy in a wider range of areas and enable enterprises to exercise greater autonomy.

The second is to optimize the increment. By directing the movement and flow of capital, the new state-owned capital investment should play a prominent role in sending out signals to society and making clear what the state supports, encourages, and changes. Instead of being restricted to local competition, state-owned capital investment and operation should support its worldwide strategic goals and involvement in international competition (in fact, industries that form monopolies in the domestic market are largely free of bitter competition). The state's legitimacy serves as the basis for the credibility associated with the state-owned economy and state-owned enterprises. Consumers exhibit confidence in purchasing products from these enterprises due to their commitment to legal compliance, emphasis on credibility, robust management and operational systems, and production of genuine and high-quality goods. These enterprises prioritize safeguarding citizens' and the country's security interests, even if it entails compromising efficiency or effectiveness. Without a doubt, this reliable cash flow contributes significantly to the stability of economic growth.

The national economy's lifeblood and crucial sectors associated with national security should receive more investment from the state-owned sector of the economy. Owing to the opening-up, several sectors of the domestic market now permit foreign money and the private economy to participate, creating variable degrees of indirect competition. In light of this, it is incumbent upon the state-owned economy to shoulder its national responsibility, leverage state-owned capital's advantages of scale and aggregation, and proactively safeguard the domestic market position.

The development of significant, forward-looking strategic industries, the support of advancing science and technology, the preservation of the environment, and the maintenance of national security should all be the main goals of state-owned capital investment. State-owned capital should support the growth of the private economy and provide basic services in the area of social platforms. State-owned capital should also play a part in big national special projects, national heavy weapons, and science and technology initiatives. For instance, in the sectors of nuclear power and nuclear power, spacecraft, airplanes, satellites, high-speed trains, large vessels, aircraft carriers, submarines, aviation engines, space engines, and so on. In general, state-owned money isn't permitted to enter industries that are targeted toward the daily needs of average people.

The third is to improve the flow. As the saying goes, "running water is never stale, and a door hinge never gathers termites." It is imperative to consistently infuse industries with capital to ensure their continuous advancement and increased productivity. The revitalization of state-owned capital and its ability to preserve and appreciate value can only be achieved through a regular and continuous flow of funds.

The three main parameters of capital liquidity are flow volume, flow direction, and flow rate.

Flow volume refers to the number of elements of economic activity measured in terms of the volume of the monetary amount, measured in monetary terms, with the currency unit measured in RMB, or in international statistical currency units (e.g. USD, EUR, etc.), with the basic unit of RMB being Chinese Yuan.

Flow direction refers to the direction in which capital flows in or out. Capital inflows are usually represented as investments and the counted objects as an increase in the quantity of capital. Capital outflows are generally represented as withdrawals and the counted objects as a decrease in the quantity of capital.

The rate of flow is the magnitude of the volume of capital flows (including outflows or inflows) per unit of time.

During the planned economy period, state-owned capital primarily lacked liquidity, and investments and new businesses were strictly regulated by official plans. However, with the onset of reform and opening-up, state-owned capital gradually began to release liquidity. This was characterized by a strategy of "one retreat and one advance, more retreats, and fewer entries." Specifically, state-owned capital withdrew from certain sectors such as small and medium-sized state-owned enterprises and some perfectly competitive industries, while simultaneously entering other crucial investment areas of the state.

State-owned capital functions as a sizable "reservoir," and revitalizing the state-owned economy entails continuously adding fresh water, removing stale water, and maintaining the pool's water level. The improvement of the state-owned asset management system, management of capital as the primary focus, strengthening of state-owned asset supervision, and reform of the approved management of state-owned capital are the areas of reform that will be prioritized in the future years. Policy arrangements and operating arrangements coexist, with new capital being more investment-focused and outgoing capital being more operations-focused. Controlling the flow, flow rate, and speed of the incremental amount of state-owned capital affects the capital quantity, and regulating the operating impact of the stock of state-owned capital directs the incremental amount. The state-owned capital is continually adjusted to become the best assets, the most efficient assets, and the most competitive assets.

3.2. *Promote reform by focusing on key development themes*

Reform is the redistribution of interests and resources, and the promotion of the economy from low-end to high-end operation. Reform is also the revolution that brings about rebirth.

There are two types of reforms: "oppositional reforms" and "congruent reforms." Previous empirical studies have demonstrated that "congruent reforms" hold more positive implications and exhibit a proactive nature. They provide a greater number of alternative approaches, allow for a more flexible timeline, and entail relatively fewer difficulties and costs compared to "oppositional reforms."

In the subsequent era, the reform of the state-owned economy will be supported through the establishment or introduction of significant development themes. This reform will encompass systemic connections rather than being limited to specific areas. The restructuring of state-owned businesses should align with the prevailing trends, enabling them to propagate, drive, leverage, and align with such trends.

Five key development themes have been developed by the nation: the first is the construction of the "free trade zone," the second is "Belt and Road," and the third is "open finance" (internationalization of the RMB). The fourth theme is "building international collaboration platforms," while the fifth theme is "building Chinese multinational enterprises." These five themes represent unquestionably the key opportunities for furthering the reform of the state-owned economy as well as the key topics for the development and reform of state-owned enterprises ("the five-sphere integrated plan," internationalization).[12]

First, we will employ the theme of free trade zone construction to encourage the expansion of the state-owned economy's liquidity. By realizing the "internationalization of the domestic economy" and "internationalization of domestic enterprises," both in the domestic and international markets, this theme will further broaden the scope of opening-up. State-owned enterprises will enjoy protection through preferential policies, and the state-owned economy can invest in any sector in accordance with actual needs. This facilitates the entry and exit of state-owned businesses from the global market as well as the entry and exit of state-owned capital in significant areas, thereby facilitating the flow of state-owned capital, maximizing its efficacy, and effectively advancing the reform of the state-owned economy in the area of capital stock and increment.

The second is to effectively leverage the "Belt and Road" initiatives in order to promote the expansion of the state-owned sector in inland regions. The "Belt and Road" is an abbreviation of the "Silk Road Economic Belt" and the "21st Century Maritime Silk Road," and it refers to the country's strategic deployment in the new era to increase its chances of survival and development, increase its strategic influence, and it serves as a crucial platform for China's full integration into the global community. With such a platform, the state-owned economy and state-owned businesses will flourish, especially in the central and western regions, where they are "looking west" and "moving westward," establishing local economic hubs and acting as polarizing regional hubs that propel the economic growth of the surrounding regions and have an impact on neighboring nations. Playing a prominent role in this process will greatly encourage the state-owned economy to further its transformation in the inland areas.

---

[12] See Zhang Yujie. (2016). *Open Economy*. Xinhua Publishing House, p. 1.

Third, make excellent use of the theme of open finance to highlight the state-owned economy's dominant position in the global economy. The financial industry is the last sector to open, therefore it makes sense. The internationalization of the RMB has caused a financial opening that will fundamentally alter the global economic system. The nerve center of a nation's economic lifeline is its currency. A nation's currency serves as an international medium of exchange, signaling growth in its national economic power and international credit. There are very few non-state-owned banks in China's banking system, which is almost entirely state-owned. Since China's state-owned banks are all business groups with substantial assets and are among the top 500 global corporations, they have the capacity to engage in international capital operations and competition, giving them a wide range of potential applications as an international currency. Hence, there are many sectors where the RMB can be used as a global currency, and doing so will be advantageous. These factors will also greatly support the systematic reform of the state-owned banking sector.

Fourth, promote the deep integration of the state-owned economy into the global economy by making excellent use of the theme of building international cooperation platforms. The two main themes in global socio-economic development are "bilateral cooperation" and "win–win out-comes." China has taken part in the formation of numerous international cooperation organizations, including leading and leading the development of some of these organizations, the formation of "bilateral" and "multilat-eral" cooperation mechanisms, and the creation of a sizable international cooperation platform. For example, the Group of Twenty (G20), Asia-Pacific Economic Cooperation (APEC), the BRICS countries (Brazil, Russia, India, China, South Africa), China and ASEAN ("10+1"), China, Japan, South Korea, and ASEAN ("10+3"), Asian Infrastructure Invest-ment Bank (AIIB) Infrastructure Investment Bank (IIB), Silk Road Fund, etc. By the end of March 2016, China had forged economic cooperation links with 173 nations, including the number of nations with which it has diplomatic ties.[13] The various kinds of economic cooperation with other nations have created a framework for China's economic integration into the global economy and have actively encouraged the deep integration of the state-owned economy into global economic changes.

Fifth, the building of multinational corporations serves as a catalyst for state-owned enterprises to pursue global expansion. The evolving

[13] See Official Website of the Ministry of Foreign Affairs. Retrieved March 15, 2016.

growth and expansion of state-owned capital and enterprises have established favorable conditions for their international presence. State-owned enterprises should possess not only the capability to "step out" and enter global markets but also to "venture into," "carry on" within, and "move up" the international market.

"Stepping out" entails entering the international market, and this encompasses not only products but also technology, business models, brands, standards, and capital.

"Venturing into" refers to gaining acceptance overseas, gaining a foothold, establishing a base, and taking root. Rather than short-term conduct, "carrying on" refers to the capacity to endure and advance overseas over an extended period of time. "Moving up" means moving from low-end to middle- and high-end industries, which are more technological and capital-intensive. The process of "stepping out" entails the internationalization of businesses, the growth of their global markets, and the collaboration of their global production capacities. The largest industrial capacity in the world is held by a collection of Chinese state-owned companies, which also have the potential to export people, capital, and technology. There will undoubtedly be an oversupply if these capabilities are simply used on the domestic market. Stepping out into the international market will not only free up excess capacity but also test the companies' resilience on the global market, improving their own management, their product performance and quality, and their overall level of corporate management. This will in turn strongly support the international transformation and development of state-owned enterprises.

3.3. *Driving reforms via international requirements*

In the past, the impetus for reform was from internal sources. State-owned enterprises had little to no operational autonomy and lacked the necessary corporate functions. The reforms were implemented with the aim of acquiring autonomy. The objectives and mission of reforms are both accomplished once the firms regain their managerial autonomy.

The motivation for reform now and in the future will come more from sources other than state-owned enterprises. One development topic after another keeps appearing as the country's overall tendency toward reform and opening-up continues to grow. The areas of activity for the state-owned economy and state-owned enterprises are more varied. Innovative development and adapting to global development have quite distinct requirements. The strongest among the enterprises will continue to prevail, different economic factors will demonstrate their immense power, and the weakest will be destroyed. The question of how the state-owned economy maintains its place and fulfills its mission can only be addressed during the reform; there is no other way to find out.

President Xi Jinping noted, "State-owned enterprises are an important force in moving national modernization forward and guaranteeing the common interest of the people. Through many years of reform, State-owned enterprises generally have assimilated into the market economy. At the same time, State-owned enterprises have also accumulated a number of problems, some malpractices exist, which require further reform."[14] The state will then push for a number of reforms, such as increasing the investment of state-owned capital in public welfare enterprises; implementing reforms in naturally occurring monopolies in which state-owned capital continues to hold a controlling interest, with the separation of government enterprises, separation of government capital, franchising, and government supervision as the main elements, the implementation of the separation of networks and transportation, and liberalizing competitive businesses according to the characteristics of different industries. The state will also enhance the effectiveness of the checks and balances in the corporate governance framework; create a system of professional managers, and enhance entrepreneurship; a long-term incentive and restraint system should be established, and state-owned businesses' operating and investment accountability should be strengthened; Investigate the promotion of state-owned enterprises' financial budget and other important information disclosure; state-owned enterprises to logically increase the proportion of market-based hiring and selection; logically determine and logically strictly regulate the level of compensation of managers of state-owned enterprises; and logically treat jobs, position-related consumption, and business-related consumption.[15] With the help of these reforms, state-owned enterprises will be encouraged to enhance the contemporary enterprise system, increase operational effectiveness, exercise appropriate social responsibility, and more effectively fulfill their roles as state-owned enterprises and holders of state capital.

---

[14] Party Literature Research Center of the CPC Central Committee (2014), *Op. cit.*, p. 501.
[15] *Ibid.*

The first is to establish a global business. Globalized markets, resources, talents, and capital are the four distinguishing characteristics of international businesses. "Globalized market"[16] denotes that business management is expanding globally and that the goods or services are offered to international consumers.

The term "globalized resources" refers to the fact that the firm uses resources from around the world, not just its own country, for its raw materials, technical equipment, and auxiliary materials. "Global talent" refers to the fact that every employee is from a different country, ethnic group, race, color, and religion, and that they all work together. "Global capital" denotes that the company's operating money is derived from a variety of sources, not just one specific nation, bank, currency, or group. Funds are obtained through financing on the stock market, financing through international credit, etc.

As of the end of August 2016, only a small percentage of domestic Chinese businesses had adopted "globalization," particularly among the group of state-owned enterprises. According to this viewpoint, the state-owned enterprise and economic reforms that have been implemented over the past 40 years have primarily been local reforms, as opposed to changes focused on the global market. The problems left over from the history of state-owned companies in some regions have not yet been fully resolved, and state-owned enterprises are still confined to reforms in some areas. For instance, some businesses in the northeast region struggle with collective management, inadequate retirement plans, historical debts, sizable operating losses, aging business models, a lack of innovation capacity, etc. These businesses still face heavy burdens, and enhancing their competitiveness remains a difficult task.

The new cycle of reform should concentrate on components of the reform that are incompatible with enterprise internationalization, particularly "enterprise reengineering," or the process of re-establishing a state-owned economic management system and a collection of state-owned enterprises. The domestic market-oriented enterprise reform is just the beginning, and the foreign market-oriented enterprise reform is the more advanced stage, of the reform of state-owned businesses. The previous round of reform consisted primarily of ongoing improvement and

[16] See Zhang Yujie (2016), *Op. cit.*, p. 284.

adjustment to the fundamental structure, but the present round of reform aims to build a new system from scratch. The previous period's reform was only to adjust and improve the original foundation, whereas the new round's reform is to recreate a new system; the previous period's reform is to begin in the field of operation and management, primarily at the level of enterprise organization, whereas the new round's reform is to begin in the field of capital operation, primarily at the level of reform of the distribution structure of state-owned capital, project investment, and mergers and the development of new enterprises. Previously, reform efficiency was primarily focused on single state-owned firms, whereas the efficiency of the present cycle of reform is primarily focused on mixed economic components.

The second is to create a mixed-ownership economy. The economic components generated by the combining, integration, or mutual equity involvement of diverse capital are referred to as mixed ownership economies. It is a viable and unavoidable option for enhancing the vitality, control, and impact of the state-owned economy. The establishment of a mixed-ownership economy is an unavoidable prerequisite for the growth of a market economy in Socialism with Chinese characteristics. The Decision at the 18th CPC Central Committee's Third Plenary Session Resolution said that a mixed ownership economy is an important type of fulfillment of China's core economic structure. The active development of a mixed-ownership economy encourages the capital of diverse ownership systems to complement each other's strengths, promote each other, and develop together.

In terms of form, establishing a mixed ownership economy can take four forms: "state–private" "state–foreign," "state–state," and "state–private–foreign."

"State–private" refers to the combination of state-owned and private economies; "state–foreign" refers to the combination of state-owned and foreign-funded economies; and "state–state" refers to the combination of state-owned and state-owned economies, which is cross-industry and cross-regional. Although both are classified as state-owned enterprises, they are managed differently and have different interests. A community of economic components of this type also falls into the category of combination. This understanding, of course, needs to be investigated and tested in practice. A combination of the three kinds is referred to as "state–private–foreign."

The following considerations should be considered while developing a mixed ownership system:

First, the goal of constructing a mixed-ownership economy is to increase the competitiveness of state-owned firms and the state-owned economy, and reforms are meaningless unless they improve the competitiveness of state-owned enterprises.

Second, the development of mixed ownership is the daily management of the enterprise's strategic behavior, not merely understood as a policy action. This is an opportunity for the development of enterprises to operate the behavior, not to engage in campaigns. This is not a "one size fits all," nor should we be "jumping on the bandwagon." Rather, it should be tailored to enterprises and specific cases.

Third, it's crucial to take the initiative to move toward a mixed-ownership structure rather than do it passively. While passive mixing can cause intangible assets to deteriorate or even vanish, proactive actions can keep intangible assets like brands from losing value.

Fourth, combinations should be explored in increments and not by combining stocks. There is no baggage involved with incremental mixes; while stock mixes have a higher historical legacy, making them harder to operate.

Fifth, be selective about development opportunities. It is only necessary to adopt mixed ownership in an enterprise with a major development theme, rather than pulling it out of thin air. New ventures, new project investments, international mergers and acquisitions, and stock market listings are the four main operating scenarios. Follow the trend when there is a chance for business growth; otherwise, it isn't appropriate to move into a mixed-ownership structure.

Sixth, mobilize private consortium power to take part in the mixed ownership system's construction. The ability to participate in the development of mixed ownership of state-owned enterprises is only possible when the development of private capital is sufficiently large. When the volume of private capital is too small, there is no power to do so. Thus, running a mixed ownership system should not be done hastily.

The third aspect involves striving to become a powerful economy.[17] The term "powerful economy" refers to the growth of the factors of production and the resulting increase in the market power of businesses.

---

[17]Zhang Yujie. (2012). *Corporate Strategy Planning and Execution*. Enterprise Management Publishing House, pp. 93–103.

This is a manifestation of the corporate economy phenomena and a key indicator of the efficiency of the factors of production.[18]

Scale economy is a term used to describe the growth in product output and the resultant decrease in cost per unit of product. It is a manifestation of the factory economy and a key indicator of the effectiveness of labor input.

When an enterprise changes from being a factory to being a corporate, its indicators for measuring efficiency will also change. It moves from measuring internal efficiency to measuring external efficiency, from measuring the efficiency of production costs to measuring the efficiency of production factors, from measuring the efficiency of production costs to measuring the efficiency of production factors, from measuring the efficiency of production to measuring the efficiency of operation, from pursuing the advantage of minimizing production costs to pursuing the advantage of maximizing market power, and from pursuing the advantage of owning resources to pursuing the ability to integrate resources.

The transition from a factory-model economy to a corporate-model economy, and then to an international corporate-based economy, is known as the process of enterprise internationalization. Enterprises must adapt to these changes in order to survive and grow in this process because there are significant changes to their legal, policy, cultural, economic, and environmental environments. Enterprises that don't do this will wither and withdraw.

The economy of scale is merely a tool used by multinational corporations to further their pursuit of the economy of power. As the factory follows the company, so does the internal follow the external, as does the product follow the commodity, as does the technology follow the market, does the adequacy of resources follow the integration of resources, and so does the economy of scale follow the economy of power.

Hence, it is very important to understand, respect, and apply the economic law of the "power economy" when deepening reform and development. As a result, this rule will serve as a "guiding beacon" and "motto" for the deepening of reform and development of state-owned enterprises.

---

[18] Zhang Yujie. (2012). Research on potential economy. *China Industrial Economics* (1).

Chapter 6

Persisting and Improving the Socialist Basic Distribution System

The basic economic system in China establishes the dominant role of public ownership, while economic entities under diverse forms of ownership develop side by side. This framework also influences the distribution system, where labor-based distribution holds a dominant position, complemented by various alternative distribution modes. Distributing income based on labor reflects the socialist principle of public ownership. In order to demonstrate the dominant position of public ownership and the socialist nature of China's basic economic system, it is essential to maintain the primary position of distributing income based on labor.

1. The Basic Socialist Economic System Is the Foundation of China's Basic Distribution System

1.1. *The ownership of the means of production forms the basis of the distribution relationship*

The ownership of the means of production is the foundation of the production relationship. In other words, who owns the means of production determines how the work is organized and how the products are distributed. This is a basic principle of Marxism and an objective fact validated by various economic practices throughout human history. The ownership of different means of production determines the position and relationship of the owners of the factors of production in the production process, which in turn determines the distribution methods and relationships between them. "The way that goods and services are distributed is not just based on economic factors, but also on social and political factors that are shaped by the productive conditions and the relationships between the producers. The way resources and income are distributed is not solely determined by current policies or decisions, but is also influenced by the historical and social context in which the economic system operates."[1] "How products are distributed among consumers is a result of how the productive resources are owned and controlled. Furthermore, the way the means of production are distributed reflects the underlying nature and characteristics of the particular economic mode of production. This implies that any changes or adjustments made in the distribution of consumer goods must be based on the ownership and distribution of the means of production in order to effectively address any unfairness or problems in the distribution system."[2] The ownership of the means of production is essential for labor production. It plays a significant role in allowing workers to own the products they produce. "If we assume that production and society are founded solely on the exchange of labor, we are mistaken. The reproduction of the laborer is influenced by the laborer's ownership relationship to the means of production, which is never purely determined by their labor. This is because the laborer's ownership relationship is a prerequisite for their labor, rather than a result of it."[3] In other words, ownership of the means of production is crucial for workers to benefit from their labor. Without ownership or independent access to the necessary materials and resources, workers are unable to produce goods and services on their own terms and may not receive a fair share of the value they create. The principle of "earning what one works for" is not always true because it depends on whether the worker has ownership or access to the materials and resources required for production. In short, owning the means of production is essential for workers to have control over their labor and to benefit from the value they create.

Marx examined how workers cannot own the products they make in situations where they don't control the tools and materials needed for production. He gave examples of slaves and serfs to show that when personal production conditions are controlled by those who own the materials needed for production, workers cannot own the things they produce.

---

[1] *Collected Works of Marx and Engels*, Vol. 7, People's Publishing House, 2009, p. 998.

[2] *Ibid.*, Vol. 3, p. 436.

[3] *Ibid.*, Vol. 30, 1995, p. 511.

In other words, the relationship between workers and the means of production is important for workers to have control over the value they create. Marx compared independent small producers with wage laborers, revealing the key reason why the former can obtain all the products created by their labor while the latter cannot. He pointed out that in the production mode of homesteaders, "the possession of land is a condition for laborers to own their labor products."[4] Independent small producers "are able to own all the products of their labor themselves. The surplus value of their products that exceeds the average price is not owned by a third party, such as a boss. This is not achieved through their labor (in this respect, they are no different from other workers), but only by their ownership of the means of production. Therefore, only because of the ownership of the means of production, can their own surplus labor belong to them."[5]

The principle that ownership determines distribution relations is a common law derived from various different social and economic systems and will not become invalid with changes in social systems. As Marx said: "When a group of people in a society monopolize the means of production, laborers are required to work additional hours beyond what is necessary to sustain themselves. This applies to both free and unfree laborers. The additional work is necessary to produce goods for the owners of the means of production. This has been observed in various societies throughout history, such as Athenian aristocrats, Etruscan religious and political leaders, Roman citizens, Norman barons, American slave owners, landlords of Wallachia, modern landowners, and capitalists."[6] Despite the changes that have occurred in society over thousands of years, from ancient Greek slavery to the modern capitalist system, including changes in technology, productivity, social relations, economic relations, and political relations, one basic law remains unchanged — that distribution relations are determined by ownership. Even today, although the scientific and technological development of modern capitalist society is rapid and its ownership rights system has indeed undergone tremendous changes compared to hundreds of years ago, the basic law of obtaining a portion of benefits through ownership still exists in the distribution relations.

---

[4]*Ibid.*, Vol. 7, p. 911.

[5]*Ibid.*, Vol. 8, p. 415.

[6]*Ibid.*, Vol. 5, p. 272.

1.2. *The socialist market economy should uphold and improve the basic distribution system*

Since the start of the reform and opening-up policy, China has been transitioning from a planned economy to a market economy, and a new ownership structure with public ownership as the mainstay and the co-development of diverse forms of ownership has gradually taken shape. The distribution relations of the entire society have also shifted from a distribution system based on distribution according to work to one where distribution according to work is still the mainstay but coexists with multiple other distribution methods. Different production and labor factors, such as capital, technology, and land, are increasingly participating in the value distribution of the whole society. The participation of various factors of production (such as labor, capital, technology, and natural resources) in the distribution of value has challenged the traditional labor theory of value. As a result, in order to explicate the underlying rationale behind the participation of these diverse factors in the distribution process within a socialist market economy, an increasing number of experts and scholars have proffered the theory of factor distribution. According to both Marxist economics and Western new institutional economics theory, the ownership of factors of production is the primary determinant of their participation in the distribution process. The actual contribution made by each factor only affects the proportion of distribution among the different factors but not the overall distribution itself. In other words, who owns the factors of production decides how the benefits produced by the factors of production are distributed, while the amount of work or contribution made by each factor determines only the share of the value received by that factor.

During the Primary Stage of Socialism, a distribution principle that combines distribution according to work and distribution according to factors is implemented. This distribution principle is chosen because it is suitable for the property rights system during this phase of socialism, as it accommodates diverse forms of ownership and their implementation. In a complete public ownership system, workers cannot gain benefits from the privileges of production materials. Instead, they can only distribute their deserved share from the collectively owned products based on their individual labor input. In private economies, production factors are owned by different entities. Ownership that is legally protected has various exclusive functions. When engaging in production, one must acknowledge the ownership of factors and pay a certain price to obtain the consent of the factor owners to use these factors for production. For example, capitalists must first acquire the services of workers before they can put them to work. In order to obtain the rights of possession and use of factors such as money and land, industrial capitalists must also obtain the consent of these factor owners in advance, sign contracts with them, and transfer a portion of the surplus product to them as a payment. Ownership comes with important functions such as exclusive rights protection, monopoly profits, and transfer sharing, which apply to both human and material factor owners. Therefore, under the condition that production factors belong to different owners, a system of distributing the resulting profits according to ownership rights will naturally emerge.

Under the socialist market economy system, the number of non-public enterprises is increasing. In private-property-based enterprises, people own different and varying amounts of production factors. To protect ownership and safeguard the interests of factor owners and motivate them, it is necessary to distribute according to factors. In mixed ownership enterprises, distribution is combined based on labor and factors according to the different property rights structures. Distributing profits or benefits based on the ownership of production factors (such as land, capital, and labor) safeguards the interests of property rights holders. At the same time, it encourages factor owners to use them in an efficient and effective manner to maximize their own returns. This in turn also prevents their misuse and overuse and promotes the rational allocation of social resources. To ensure the effective use of resources, it's important for users to gain a surplus after the cost of resource usage has been covered. In order to achieve this, users will naturally aim to minimize their use of resources and maximize their efficiency. Marx once pointed out, "Interest is net profit, as Ramsay calls it, which the ownership of capital yields as such, either simply to the lender, who remains outside the reproduction process, or to the owner who employs his capital productively. But in the latter's case, too, capital yields this net profit to him not in his capacity of productive capitalist, but of money-capitalist, of lender of his own capital as interest-bearing capital to himself as to a functioning capitalist."[7]

[7] *Collected Works of Marx and Engels*, Vol. 7. People's Publishing House, 2009, p. 425.

2. The Reform and Improvement Process of China's Socialist Basic Distribution System

2.1. *Exploring the reform of China's basic distribution system during the early stages of reform and opening-up*

In December 1978, the Third Plenary Session of the 11th Central Committee of the Communist Party first proposed the need to overcome egalitarianism. Before the reform and opening-up, due to the long-term influence of the "leftist" ideology, China's income distribution policy was mainly based on a simple distribution according to work under the planned economy system and serious egalitarianism. During this period, the income distribution policy was characterized by the principle of "equal pay for equal work" regardless of the level of effort, performance, or employment status. Notable examples of this policy included the practices of "free-riding" and "big-pot rice" (meaning income is distributed equally among all members of society, regardless of individual productivity or effort). The egalitarian distribution method under the planned economy system severely damaged the enthusiasm and creativity of the majority of workers, gravely undermined productivity, and significantly hindered national economic development. In response to this situation, the Third Plenary Session of the 11th Central Committee of the Communist Party made a proposal, where the focus of the Party's effort should shift from class struggle to economic construction. The Party also put forward the banner of "overcoming egalitarianism." The rural areas were chosen as the starting point, where various economic responsibility systems were experimented with.

As China's economic system reform shifted its focus from rural to urban areas, the central government proposed the establishment of multiple economic responsibility systems and the idea of common prosperity. In October 1987, the 13th National Congress of the Communist Party pointed out that China was in the primary stage of socialism, and the main ownership structure must be public ownership. The statement further clarified that in the primary stage of socialism, there should not be only one type of distribution method. The main distribution method should be "distribution according to work"; however, other distribution methods must coexist with it. This approach introduced new ways of income distribution and moved away from the previous single form of income distribution principles. This change demonstrated a willingness to accept and implement other distribution methods alongside the existing one. The 13th National Congress of the Communist Party's report mentioned that when companies issue bonds to raise funds, they receive interest based on creditors' rights. With the introduction of the equity-based economy, there will be dividend distribution, and income for enterprise operators includes partial risk compensation. Private enterprises that employ a certain number of workers will bring the owner some non-labor income (passive income). The report stated that as long as these incomes are legal, they should be allowed.[8] This was a significant improvement in China's income distribution theory as it further specified various distribution methods.

2.2. *Reform and improvement of China's basic distribution system after the establishment of the socialist market economy system*

In 1992, the 14th National Congress of the Communist Party decided to establish a socialist market economy system as the direction of China's economic system reform. The distribution system was reformed and improved to adapt to this new system, and it mainly went through the following stages:

At the 14th National Congress of the Communist Party in 1992, the party reiterated the principle of "distribution according to work as the mainstay, complemented by other distribution methods." This principle refers to the idea that the majority of income should be distributed based on the amount of labor contributed by each individual, with other distribution methods as complementary means. The Party's emphasis on striking a balance between efficiency and fairness was highlighted for the first time. They acknowledged the need to use a variety of regulatory means, including the market, to encourage progress and promote efficiency. The Party also recognized the importance of reasonably widening the income gaps while preventing polarization and gradually achieving common prosperity. One of the key aspects of the socialist market economy system, as emphasized by the Congress, was the reform and improvement of the distribution system and social security system. This was done to ensure a

[8] Party Literature Research Center of the CPC Central Committee (Ed.) (2008). *Selected Important Documents of Thirty Years of Reform and Opening Up*, Vol. I. Central Party Literature Press, p. 487.

fairer and more effective system. The Congress also emphasized the importance of balancing the interests of the state, collective, and individuals. It stressed the need to clarify the distribution relationship between the state and enterprises, as well as between the central and local governments. To achieve this, the Congress proposed the gradual implementation of the separation of profits and taxes, as well as the adoption of a tax-sharing system. As part of the reform and improvement of the distribution and social security system, the Congress also emphasized the need to accelerate the reform of the wage system. This included gradually establishing wage systems and normal wage growth mechanisms that are more suitable for the unique characteristics of enterprises, institutions, and government agencies. Additionally, the Congress actively advocated for the establishment of social security systems to address unemployment, pensions, medical care, and other areas. Efforts were also made to promote the reform of urban housing systems.[9]

In September 1997, the 15th National Congress of the Communist Party highlighted the importance of both "distribution according to work" and "distribution according to production factors" based on the "mainstay-coexistence" principle proposed at the 14th National Congress. This was a significant step forward since it recognized other distribution methods and allowed for the participation of capital and other production factors belonging to individuals in the distribution of profits.[10]

In November 2002, the 16th National Congress of the Communist Party further elaborated on the distribution principle based on production factors, which was first proposed in the previous congress. The Congress proposed the principle of labor, capital, technology, and management, and other production factors participating in distribution according to their contributions. This improved the distribution system, which was mainly based on labor, and coexisted with various distribution methods. The principle acknowledged the role of labor in wealth creation and recognized the contribution of other essential production factors. It illustrated the integration of the socialist system and market economy in distribution policies, which is an innovation in income distribution theory. It also signifies the maturity of China's income distribution policies, implying that China has made significant progress in its income distribution policies. The 16th Congress report emphasized the principle of prioritizing

---

[9] *Ibid.*, p. 660, 661.

[10] Party Literature Research Center of the CPC Central Committee (2008), *Op. cit.*, p. 902.

efficiency while taking fairness into account. It stated that the primary distribution method should prioritize efficiency and reward individuals who contribute to the economy through honest labor and legal operations, which can lead to higher income and potentially wealth accumulation. The report also proposed that in order to achieve fairness, redistribution should be implemented and the government's regulatory function in income distribution should be strengthened. The focus should be on addressing excessive income gaps, which could help create a more equitable distribution system.[11]

The 17th National Congress of the Communist Party suggested that both primary distribution and redistribution should balance efficiency and fairness. This proposal is different from the 16th Congress, which emphasized efficiency in primary distribution and fairness in redistribution. The 17th Congress believes that both distribution processes should consider fairness and efficiency equally, but with a greater emphasis on fairness in redistribution. Additionally, the 17th Congress proposed the idea of "creating conditions to allow more people to have property income,"[12] which is an innovative development in the distribution system and a significant example of distribution based on production factors.

2.3. *Further advancements in the socialist basic distribution system after the 18th National Congress*

During the Second Plenary Session of the 18th Central Committee, Xi Jinping highlighted the complexity and challenges involved in reforming the income distribution system. He emphasized the importance of all regions and departments recognizing the significance of advancing the reform of the income distribution system. This includes implementing income distribution systems, increasing the income of urban and rural residents, reducing income distribution gaps, and standardizing income distribution order. It is important to focus on resolving the issues that people are concerned about.

Income distribution is an important institutional component of the economic and social systems. It plays a crucial role in meeting the demands of developing a socialist market economy, as it promotes the

---

[11] *Ibid.*, p. 1254.

[12] *Ibid.*, p. 1732.

overall growth of the national economy. Furthermore, income distribution must correspond to the increasing needs of the people and promote the development of a harmonious society. Thus, it is necessary to coordinate the improvement of the socialist basic distribution system with economic development and social construction. Reform must be advanced in a balanced manner to ensure the fair distribution of resources.

In February 2013, the Central Committee of CPC issued *Several Opinions on Advancing the Reform of the Income Distribution System*, which outlined the overall requirements and specific directions for the reform. The objectives of the reform are to adjust the income distribution structure during development and create an open, fair, and just system. The income distribution system will adhere to the labor-based distribution as the mainstay while allowing for various distribution methods to coexist. Additionally, the primary distribution and redistribution are equally important. The primary distribution mechanism will continue to improve, with labor, capital, technology, and management participating in distribution according to their contributions. Efforts will be made to expedite the improvement of the redistribution adjustment mechanism, which primarily relies on taxes, social security, and transfer payments. The main focus of the reform is to increase the income of urban and rural residents, narrow the income distribution gap, and standardize the income distribution order. The effort aims to ensure that the growth of residents' income is in line with economic development, and that labor remuneration grows in parallel with labor productivity improvements. The ultimate goal is to establish a reasonable and orderly income distribution pattern, which promotes sustained and healthy economic development, as well as social harmony and stability.

The income distribution system is of great importance to the public's well-being and is responsible for upholding socialist principles of fairness and justice. Its ultimate goal is to achieve common prosperity for all people. During the Fifth Plenary Session of the 18th Communist Party of China Central Committee, Xi Jinping emphasized the importance of upholding the socialist basic economic and distribution system. He stressed that in order to maintain social fairness and justice, the nation need to adjust the income distribution pattern, as well as improve redistribution adjustment mechanism by using mainly taxes, social security, and transfer payments as the means for distribution. Additionally, he highlighted the need to address the issue of income disparity to make sure that the benefits of development are distributed more fairly to all people.

3. Building a Moderately Prosperous Society in All Respects and Further Improving China's Basic Distribution System

Currently, China is in a crucial phase of building a moderately prosperous society. Regarding income distribution, Xi Jinping proposed that during the "13th Five-Year Plan" period, there are two key areas of focus.[13] The first area of focus is to fully mobilize the enthusiasm, initiative, and creativity of the people, and make concerted efforts to advance the cause of socialism with Chinese characteristics, continually expanding the overall size of the national economy. The second one is to distribute the steadily increasing national economy fairly so that the advantages of the socialist system can be fully reflected, and the people can benefit more. In essence, the first area of focus is about increasing the wealth of the nation, while the second one is about making sure that the benefits of this increased wealth are distributed fairly. It is essential to expand the middle-income class and gradually form a more balanced income distribution pattern with a larger middle-income class and fewer people in extreme income ranges. We should prioritize supporting disadvantaged groups and focus on alleviating rural poverty. To address these two key areas of focus, the Chinese government has established three primary reform goals for advancing and improving the basic distribution system during the "13th Five-Year Plan" period. These goals include improving the initial distribution system, strengthening the mechanism for redistributing income, and standardizing the order of income distribution.

3.1. *Improve the initial distribution system*

On May 16, 2016, during the 13th meeting of the Central Leading Group for Finance and Economics, Xi Jinping emphasized the following points:

- It is important to promote the work ethic and encourage people to create a better life through labor.
- The income distribution system must be improved, with a focus on distribution according to work as the main principle, while multiple distribution methods coexist. It is necessary to combine distribution

[13] See Xi Jinping. (2016). Speech at the special study seminar for provincial and ministerial level leading cadres to learn and implement the spirit of the fifth plenary session of the 18th CPC Central Committee. *People's Daily*, May 10, 2016.

according to work with distribution according to production factors and manage the relationship between government, enterprises, and residents.

- To strengthen human capital, it is necessary to increase investment in education and improve the quality of education. This will involve establishing a modern vocational education system.
- The role of entrepreneurs must be fully utilized. Enterprises must be supported in addressing difficulties and obtaining investment returns.
- To strengthen property rights protection, a modern property rights system should be established, and state-owned asset ownership, operation rights, and enterprise legal person property rights should be protected, as well as non-public economic property rights and intellectual property rights. This will help ensure that people's property is secure and their rights are respected, thus enhancing their sense of property security.

Firstly, to increase workers' income, the core focus of all income policies in China should be enhancing their ability to earn from labor, which is their primary source of wealth creation. Since 2012, China's total labor force has started to decline, and economic growth will gradually rely on the second demographic dividend, which refers to the benefits that come from a well-educated and skilled workforce. Compared to developed countries where the majority of the labor force has intermediate to high education levels, China's labor force primarily has education levels at or below junior high school. This labor force structure not only cannot guarantee the long-term sustainable income growth of most low-income and low-skilled workers but also cannot meet the huge demand for skilled and technical personnel during the economic transformation and upgrading phase. This is the most pressing challenge that impacts China's ability to adjust to its current economic conditions and address the problem of population aging and the challenges it poses for economic development. Therefore, only by accelerating the reform of the labor force training system, with an emphasis on the education system, can China lay a solid foundation for its labor force and talent, which is a crucial element in achieving China's second centenary goal. To achieve this goal, three areas require attention:

(a) To enhance laborers' human capital value and increase their income-earning abilities, it is important to adjust and guide the investment structure toward science and technology, education, health, and public services. This will help promote China's transition from a country with a large population to a country with strong human resources, accelerating urbanization and expanding domestic investment and consumption demand. This will create conditions for China to develop a second demographic dividend, relying on scientific and technological progress, labor skills improvement, and management innovation, and promoting China's economic growth from external to internal. By achieving this transition, China will become an economic power rather than just an economic giant. These measures will not only promote the development of a society that benefits both the economy and the environment but also alleviate the pressures of population growth, resource depletion, and environmental conflicts, while addressing China's aging population problem with increased productivity and stronger international competitiveness. To achieve synergistic effects, China's population development and economic development should mutually promote and coordinate with each other, resulting in a win–win outcome.

(b) To reform the vocational education system, various investments and educational institutions should be actively introduced to encourage the integration of production and education. The vocational training system should be improved for all workers, with enterprises making full and effective use of employee education and training funds to ensure the shortest possible paid training time for workers. To improve vocational education, more financial investment should be allocated, particularly toward secondary vocational education, which should gradually become free of charge. In addition, it is necessary to establish and improve a system that provides free vocational education and training for migrant workers. The social vocational skills training, assessment, and certification system should also be improved. Vocational skills appraisal fees should be standardized to increase the economic benefits and social status of skilled talents.

(c) Higher education institutions and their teaching and research programs should be divided into different categories, in order to meet the needs of a diverse society and industry that require a range of talents at different levels. Currently, China has only 15 scientists and engineers per 10,000 people on average, which is significantly behind the level of developed countries and among the lowest in the world. To put it in perspective, Israel, a leading country in this field, has 140 scientists and technicians and 135 engineers per 10,000 people on average.

The shortage of high-tech talents in China has become a bottleneck in transforming the economic development mode. To address this, it is necessary to not only accelerate the scale of talent training but also adjust the professional settings of higher education institutions. Additionally, to construct an innovative country, it is important to not only strengthen the team of basic researchers but also train a large number of engineers and R&D personnel with professional expertise, practical skills, and solid foundations. These talents should be aligned with the development requirements of China's strategic emerging industries. To enhance the cohesive integration of talent education, training, and utilization, collaboration between industry, universities, and research institutions is crucial. This will enable talents to leverage their professional strengths and innovative thinking, leading to personal development, economic growth, and social progress, ultimately achieving the goal of developing a symbiotic relationship between personal development and economic growth.

Secondly, the system of distribution according to work (wage system) must be strengthened in the initial distribution, so that workers receive fair and legitimate wages. It is essential to establish a fundamental distribution system that pays workers according to their labor and to protect their legitimate income through institutional, legal, and regulatory means. This is the basic tenet that the socialist system should follow and is a necessary condition for protecting labor interests and stimulating work enthusiasm.

(a) To promote the implementation of a collective bargaining system for enterprise wages, a set of standardized operational measures have been jointly issued by the National People's Congress, the trade unions, and the labor security departments. Through conducting wage collective bargaining and signing collective wage agreements, a mechanism for determining employee wages, growth level, and protection can be reasonably established.
(b) In order to safeguard the labor interests of workers the minimum wage system must be strictly implemented. Enterprises must pay workers in full and on time in accordance with the requirements of the minimum wage system and are not allowed to reduce the actual minimum wage by any means. If it is necessary to pay all or part of the employees' wages according to the minimum wage standard due to production or operation reasons, it should be conducted through collective wage

bargaining and the opinions of enterprise employees or employee representatives should be sought. At the same time, it should be reported to the labor security department. Labor unions and labor security departments should regularly investigate the wage level and payment status of local enterprises, and timely correct, control, and punish any illegal or irregular problems that arise. This will gradually create an atmosphere that respects the interests of workers in society. Workers in various economic and social organizations should learn and master relevant laws and regulations and learn to use legal means to protect their legitimate rights related to labor and wages.

(c) Establishing a mechanism for normal wage growth for employees is essential in promoting the synchronized growth of labor compensation and economic development.

In recent years, wages in our country have experienced significant increases, yet the wage growth rate still lags behind the GDP growth rate. In the distribution of national income, the proportion of wages relative to capital and government income has been declining. Only by developing wage growth policies that gradually match national economic development can we boost residents' consumer demand.

The government should include considerations of wage growth in its broader plans for national economic and social development. By doing this, it emphasizes the importance of ensuring that wages grow consistently with the economy. Additionally, the government should implement a "target responsibility system" for employment and social security, which means setting specific goals and assigning responsibilities to relevant agencies or departments to achieve those goals in areas like job creation and social welfare programs. This approach ensures that there is a focused effort to address wage growth, employment, and social security issues. Promoting collective wage negotiation systems is important, and the National People's Congress, labor unions, and labor security departments should establish standardized procedures for their implementation. By forming a team of wage negotiation guidance officers and providing guidelines for enterprise wage growth, human resource market wage guidance, and industry labor cost information, enterprises can more effectively determine employee wage growth levels through collective wage negotiations and agreements. This will encourage companies to establish wage determination mechanisms that meet market economy requirements, ultimately raising the wage levels of ordinary employees.

The government needs to establish a set of standards for measuring the correlation between labor wages and inflation. By considering factors such as economic growth, the urban consumer price index, and average wage growth for employees, timely adjustments to wage standards can be made to prevent wage growth from falling below the rate of increase in the urban consumer price index. Every year, the government should set aside a portion of tax revenue for a labor income stability fund, saving funds during normal years and distributing them in years with high inflation. By assessing the relationship between worker wage income and enterprise income growth or decline, taking into account the varying levels of price fluctuations for goods and labor services across different enterprises, worker living standards can be safeguarded.

The third is to strengthen the factor market system, which allocates resources such as labor, capital, and natural resources. Emphasize the crucial role of market mechanisms in determining the allocation of modern resources and adhere to a distribution principle based on each resource's contribution.

(a) Developing various factor markets to ensure efficient supply and demand channels for resources. It is crucial to respect the principles of scientific research and shift the government's role from managing R&D to providing innovative services. The classification reform of public institutions should be accelerated. Administrative levels for schools, research institutes, hospitals, and other units should be gradually eliminated. Furthermore, suitable public institutions should be encouraged to transform into enterprises or social organizations. Leading innovators should be empowered with greater control over human, financial, and material resources. They should also have the freedom to choose the most effective path or approach to developing a particular technology. State-owned and private enterprises should be encouraged to implement employee stock ownership systems, which allow employees to become partial owners of the company they work for. This can help to increase their involvement in decision-making processes and incentivize them to contribute to the success of the company. Employee stock ownership systems can also help increase the transfer of knowledge, technology, and management throughout the organization, which can improve overall resource distribution channels. An open, transparent, and healthy capital market should be actively fostered, and the proportion of direct financing should be increased. Conditions should be established for implementing a stock issuance registration system, a multi-level equity financing market should be developed, and the reform of the Growth Enterprise Market and the New Third Board should be advanced. Additionally, the development of regional equity markets should be regulated.

(b) The salary system for managers and employees of state-owned enterprises needs to be reformed. This involves accelerating the classification management of industries and integrating personnel system reform within the enterprise, where managers have the ability to move up or down and employees have opportunities for mobility and income adjustments. The proportion of basic annual salary, performance-based annual salary, and term incentive income should be adjusted to make the income structure of employees and managers more reasonable, including their labor income, risk income, and welfare income. This will optimize the incentive and restraint functions of the salary system. To achieve this, it is important to study the relationship between implicit and explicit incentives and to properly balance the economic functions, social responsibilities, and political tasks of state-owned enterprises. This will help to address the dilemmas among the compensation of managers, the development of enterprises, and national functions.

Fourthly, conditions should be created to increase residents' property income.

(a) The supervision of the market system should be strengthened to provide legal protection for residents' property income. Any investment involves certain risks, and besides strengthening risk prevention awareness, it is also important to have standardized government regulations to prevent risks. A sound market order is crucial to protecting residents' property income. Currently, residents' property income growth is overly reliant on the capital and real estate markets. Therefore, the government should innovate the financial management system to create a favorable investment environment for residents to obtain property income. The first step is to create an open and transparent market environment, strengthen the regulation of existing investment and financing channels, and standardize transaction methods. The second step is to impose severe penalties on illegal and irregular activities such as insider trading, maintain the order of the securities market, and strengthen the governance structure. The third step is to improve the protection mechanism for the interests of small and medium investors and establish a civil compensation mechanism such as group litigation. Only when the capital market achieves healthy, standardized, and mature development can residents participate in market transactions fairly, justly, and openly. Finally, in addition to ensure that the Property Law is followed, it is also important to create laws that support and encourage residents to invest. Some principal clauses in the current laws also need to be refined with expediency through judicial interpretations and other means to enhance the operability of the law.

(b) The dividend system of joint-stock enterprises, especially listed companies should be improved. The investment returns for investors should increase. Dividend distribution is a company's return to its shareholders' investments and is their basic right. In a well-functioning market economy, cash dividends are the main form of distribution for listed companies. These dividends become the main source of property income for most residents, so listed companies generally strive to maintain the stability of cash dividends to attract investors to buy and hold their stocks. Currently, most listed companies in China do not have clear dividend policies, and the problem of insufficient cash dividends is very serious. Shareholders bear the risk but do not receive corresponding investment returns and rewards, and some listed companies have not paid any cash dividends to shareholders for more than a decade. Due to the absence of stable and continuous dividend policies, Chinese investors have turned to the secondary market to make profits from stock price differentials, leading to a strong speculative atmosphere in the stock market, which has seriously affected the healthy development of China's securities market and even the orderly operation of the national macroeconomy. To ensure the investment rights and interests of shareholders and enable investors to receive more property income in the form of dividends, China should accelerate the adoption of legislation requiring listed companies to pay cash dividends and eliminate the unfair and unreasonable phenomenon of companies only considering retaining profits and ignoring shareholder interests. At the same time, it is necessary to enhance the transparency of listed companies' dividend policies, and attention to listed companies should not be limited to annual or semi-annual reports but should be comprehensive in terms of information disclosure. Only by strictly implementing relevant regulations can the interests of the majority of small and medium-sized investors be protected and individual investors can secure stable income from their investments.

(c) Employee stock ownership systems need to be promoted and enterprise innovation incentive mechanisms need to be reformed. In modern market economies, it is common for employees to participate in the distribution of surplus value through stock ownership. Employee stock ownership systems are a form of equity arrangement that combines labor property rights with labor value, transforming enterprise employees from ordinary labor–capital relations to "beneficiaries" of the enterprise. Employees obtain a certain number of shares in the enterprise for free or at a low price, based on their labor property rights, and participate in the distribution of enterprise profits. Private small and medium-sized enterprises should be actively encouraged to promote employee stock ownership models, and effective implementation methods should be explored in mixed ownership enterprises to enable more workers to share enterprise profits and obtain property income. This will help establish a close community of interests between capital owners and labor owners, and improve the basic distribution system of "distribution according to work" while allowing for multiple distribution methods to coexist in China.

3.2. *Strengthen the mechanism for redistributing income*

The income redistribution system is crucial for social equity. In China, the idea of "not fearing poverty but fearing inequality" has always been present. We must continue to develop while doing our best to promote social equity and justice. We need to strive for progress within our means, ensuring that all individuals have access to education, employment, healthcare, elderly care, and housing, and continuously make new advancements in these areas.[14]

---

[14]Party Literature Research Center of the CPC Central Committee (Ed.) (2014). *Selected Important Documents since the 18th CPC National Congress*, Vol. I. Central Party Literature Press, p. 553.

At the Fifth Plenary Session of the 18th Communist Party of China Central Committee, Xi Jinping emphasized the need to increase the supply of public services and address the most pressing and immediate concerns of the people. This includes improving the ability to build and share public services and increasing transfer payments to former revolutionary strongholds, ethnic minority areas, border areas, and impoverished areas. The government will implement poverty alleviation projects, including targeted poverty alleviation, support for poor families, and exploring asset income support systems for the poor. They will also establish a comprehensive care service system for left-behind children, women, and elderly people in rural areas. Additionally, the government will establish a more fair and sustainable social security system, implement a universal insurance plan, establish a uniform basic pension insurance system for all employees across the country, transfer some state-owned capital to supplement the social security fund, and fully implement the major illness insurance system for urban and rural residents.

Firstly, the poverty alleviation campaign should be fully implemented to achieve common prosperity. China has been recognized by the United Nations as the developing country that has the best poverty reduction efforts. However, due to its large population and long-standing issues of imbalanced development, despite the rapid decrease in the proportion of impoverished people, there are still many living in absolute poverty. Poverty alleviation remains the most difficult and pressing issue in building a moderately prosperous society in all respects. On October 17, 2014, China established its first "Poverty Alleviation Day" and Xi Jinping stated: "Building a moderately prosperous society in all respects is a challenging task, particularly in poverty-stricken areas. To achieve this, it is necessary for the entire Party and society to work together to form a strong force for poverty alleviation and development. Party committees, governments, and leading cadres at all levels should pay special attention and care to poverty-stricken areas and populations. They should fulfill their leadership responsibilities, innovate ideas and methods, increase support, and adapt measures to local conditions. Focusing on targeted efforts and giving full play to the dynamic role of cadres and the masses in poverty-stricken areas is essential. Poverty reduction and development efforts must be carried out effectively and with determination, especially in the face of new challenges or changing circumstances. The goal is to increase the pace of poverty reduction and promote greater prosperity in areas and among populations that are experiencing poverty."[15] During a symposium with leading comrades of Party committees from certain provinces and cities in Guizhou on June 18, 2015, Xi Jinping emphasized, "Eliminating poverty, improving people's livelihoods, and achieving common prosperity are essential requirements of socialism and an important mission of our Party." At the fifth plenary session of the 18th Central Committee of the Communist Party of China, Xi Jinping set up poverty alleviation goals and called for practical and effective measures to guarantee the basic needs of impoverished rural populations such as food and clothing, and to ensure their access to compulsory education, basic medical care, and housing security.

(a) Create new innovative poverty alleviation and development methods. Based on the causes of poverty and the needs of poverty alleviation, targeted and precise support should be provided to the impoverished population. This can be achieved through developing characteristic industries, creating job opportunities, relocating poverty-stricken populations, protecting the ecology, providing education and training, and implementing medical insurance and assistance. These efforts aim to lift approximately 50 million registered poor people out of poverty. For other poor populations who have completely or partially lost their labor ability, a social security policy safety net should be implemented to help them escape poverty. Moreover, it is necessary to explore methods of supporting impoverished individuals in generating income from their assets, such as land leasing, supporting fund stock options, and rural land rights investment. This can enable them to participate more fully in the benefits derived from those assets.
(b) Development of poverty-stricken areas should be supported and accelerated. Efforts to alleviate poverty are prioritized in areas such as former revolutionary strongholds, ethnic minority communities, border regions, and areas with high levels of poverty. Increased support will be directed toward these regions, with a focus on building their capacity for self-sustenance. The objective is to ensure that rural residents in poverty-stricken areas achieve a higher per capita disposable income growth rate than the national average and to bring basic public services in key areas up to levels similar to the national average.

[15] Forge a strong partnership for development-oriented poverty alleviation through collaborative efforts across the party and society. *People's Daily*, October 18, 2014.

(c) The policy support for poverty alleviation will be strengthened. The central and provincial governments will increase financial support for poverty alleviation, and policy-based, developmental, commercial, and cooperative financial institutions will work together to integrate various poverty alleviation resources and expand funding sources. The focus will be on providing land for poverty alleviation and development, and special indicators for new construction land plans will be allocated to counties that are struggling with poverty. Efforts will be increased to improve land usage in areas affected by poverty, and impoverished counties will be permitted to utilize urban and rural construction land within their province for development purposes. Compensation in the form of collective equity will be provided for original residents affected by the use of collective land for water and electricity development and mineral resource exploitation in poverty-stricken areas. To ensure that poverty-stricken areas can benefit more from development, the mechanism for sharing the benefits of resource development will be improved. Technology-based poverty alleviation will be enhanced, and talent support programs for poverty-stricken areas and local talent training plans will be implemented.

Secondly, a comprehensive and classified personal income tax system should be established. Due to the lack of fundamental systems such as the rule of law and social supervision, and a lack of personal income and property information systems, China has not been able to establish a comprehensive and classified personal income tax system. Therefore, during the 13th Five-Year Plan period, efforts were made to establish such a system in accordance with the requirements of the "Four Comprehensives" strategic layout.

(a) To weaken the accumulation effect of wealth among high-income groups, implementing inheritance and gift taxes is necessary. Currently, real estate and vehicles have become the main part of personal property in China. It is important to create a tax system that is focused on taxing property, particularly real estate. This tax system should include various types of taxes, such as land use tax, vehicle tax, vehicle purchase tax, inheritance tax, and gift tax. By doing so, this tax system can help regulate income distribution and promote fairness in society. As the economy develops and personal property increases and accumulates, it becomes necessary to implement inheritance and gift taxes as a means of regulating personal income from property transfers. China currently has tens of thousands of billionaires and countless millionaires, and it is necessary to regulate these high-income groups through inheritance and gift taxes. To address the current situation of low tax awareness and underdeveloped tax collection and management in China, a comprehensive approach is necessary for implementing an inheritance tax system. This system would involve the "tax first, distribution later" procedure, where the inheritor or administrator is responsible for paying the tax. The inheritance tax should incorporate an appropriate threshold or minimum taxable inheritance, along with a progressive tax rate that rises in tandem with the size of the inheritance. Moreover, a gift tax should be implemented to deter individuals from transferring their assets as gifts to evade the inheritance tax.

(b) Imposing a social security tax and establishing a reliable and stable funding mechanism for the social security fund to ensure the basic right to live. The social security system can help stabilize the economy during times of economic uncertainty by adjusting income disparities through changes in contribution rates and government spending. The social security system automatically adjusts income disparities by applying higher tax rates on higher income earners and lower tax rates for lower income earners, which helps narrow income gaps and serves as a safety net for society. The social security tax is more legally binding and regulated than current social security fees. It ensures a reliable funding source for social security, extends social security coverage, and compensates for the shortcomings of personal income tax, consumption tax, and property tax in terms of addressing income inequality. Currently, urban enterprises, institutions, and individuals in China are already paying basic social security fees, such as basic pension and medical insurance, making it feasible to introduce a social security tax on top of these existing fees. Taxpayers include various forms of enterprises, institutions, and their employees, as well as individual business owners. The taxable object is the taxpayer's wages and salaries or production and business income, namely the total amount of employee wages issued by enterprises and institutions, the salary income obtained by employees, and the net income of private entrepreneurs and individual business owners. The tax rate is based on a proportional tax rate form and is determined separately for the three categories of pension, unemployment, and medical insurance. These rates are then divided into portions that enterprises and individuals should pay.

Thirdly, an equal basic public service system should be established and promoted. In recent years, the income levels of urban and rural residents in China have been constantly improving, and they have been enjoying increasing amounts and improving the quality of public services. However, due to the lag in social development compared to economic development in China over the years, the gap in the level of public service enjoyed by different social groups has relatively widened. Therefore, the following measures should be taken:

(a) Providing financial support. To achieve equal access to basic public services throughout China, a coordinated plan is needed. Based on each region's level of development, a transfer payment system that unifies financial and administrative rights should be established between the central and local governments, as well as between developed and underdeveloped regions. To ensure a reasonable allocation of basic public services, the system should categorize the responsibilities by level of government and distribute them proportionally. The central government will be responsible for defining the scope of basic public services, setting service standards, providing financial transfers, and overseeing service evaluation. Meanwhile, local governments will be responsible for service planning, organization, and implementation.
(b) Opening-up the market and improving regulation to increase the supply of non-basic public services and products. Efforts will be made to accelerate the development of non-basic public services in areas such as healthcare, elderly care, culture, and sports, diversifying service products, improving service quality, and providing personalized service solutions. New technologies and business models will be actively applied to promote the integration of online and offline services, allowing people to enjoy efficient, convenient, and high-quality services.
(c) Actively innovating the way public services are provided and promoting diversification in the supply of services. When the government is able to procure or buy services from private companies or organizations, it will no longer directly provide these services itself. Instead, it will collaborate with social capital, such as private companies or

non-profit organizations, to provide these services. The government will actively seek to involve social capital in the provision of services, such as through partnerships and joint ventures. The goal is to diversify the provision of public services and increase efficiency through the involvement of multiple actors. A list of public services that the government can purchase will be created and made available to the public. The government will also implement various methods such as franchising, targeted outsourcing, strategic partnerships, and competitive evaluation to introduce competition and encourage the participation of private businesses and organizations in providing these services. Additionally, new institutional mechanisms will be created to improve the way public welfare services are managed and to facilitate the transformation of public institutions engaged in production and business activities into enterprises.

Fourthly, accelerate the establishment of a basic pension system that connects urban and rural areas and gradually increase the guarantee standards. In the absence of a sound rural pension system, China's aging population is increasing, and the problem of "getting old before getting rich" and the urban–rural divide in pension systems needs to be urgently resolved. For this purpose, the following measures should be taken:

(a) Improving the social insurance system. During the "13th Five-Year Plan" period, the following measures will be taken: fully implementing the nationwide pooling of basic pension insurance for urban employees; promoting the reform of pension insurance system for different types of public institutions and civil servants; increasing the participation rate of migrant workers in pension insurance; improving the social pension insurance system for urban residents and new rural areas; establishing a mechanism for determining and adjusting pension benefits for all types of personnel; developing enterprise annuities and occupational annuities to complement commercial insurance; expanding the channels for financing the social security fund and establishing an investment and operation system for the social insurance fund.

Within ten years, we aim to promote a new rural social pension insurance system, reduce the gap in social pension income between urban and rural residents, gradually achieve the integration of urban and rural pension systems, and create conditions for protecting the basic livelihoods of elderly rural laborers and promoting urbanization. It is essential to ensure that all rural residents have social pension protection and to classify and design a step-by-step implementation plan based on the development level of different regions, different rural pension systems for different populations, and the current situation of rural pension protection in different regions. This will establish a rural pension protection system that is compatible with the economic growth level of the region. Within the same region, different population groups have different social pension systems, protection levels, and demands due to different employment and lifestyles. Therefore, we can adopt a phased approach to promote pension insurance for different population groups. In impoverished rural areas, pension insurance must be implemented through the government's non-payment-based social assistance pension funds, establishing a social security system based on relief and living assistance. In subsistence-oriented rural areas, where the basic living needs of farmers have been met, basic pension protection should be provided, while actively promoting the pilot of new pension insurance systems. Affluent rural areas are mainly concentrated in the southeast coastal areas and the suburbs of large cities, where the income level of farmers is high and the demand for social security is also relatively high. Therefore, we can implement an integrated urban–rural pension insurance system.

(b) Improving the national medical security system. This will involve increasing funding and improving treatment levels for basic medical insurance for urban residents and new rural cooperative medical care. The basic medical insurance system for urban and rural residents will be integrated, and there will be steady progress toward the coordination of employee medical insurance, basic medical insurance for urban residents, and new rural cooperative medical care outpatient services. A system for major illness insurance for urban and rural residents will be established, and the medical assistance system for urban and rural areas will be improved. Patients in unified regions and across provinces will have their medical expenses paid immediately. In addition, there will be a gradual increase in the per capita funding for basic public health services and an improvement in the level of basic public health services.
(c) Improving assistance and support for disadvantaged groups. The government aims to improve the living conditions of low-income urban

and rural residents by increasing the minimum living security level and subsidies for entitled groups. This will be achieved by improving the linkage mechanism between the basic living security standard and the rise in prices. The government will also establish and improve subsidy systems for economically disadvantaged elderly people who are of advanced age, living alone, or incapacitated. Additionally, the government will improve the basic living security system for orphans and promote centralized care for them. Other disadvantaged children will receive living assistance, while financially disadvantaged disabled people will be given a living allowance and severely disabled individuals will receive a nursing allowance.

3.3. *Standardize the order of income distribution*

Standardizing the income distribution order is an important part of improving the basic distribution system in China, and it is a reflection of socialist fairness and justice. In the future, China will accelerate the improvement of relevant laws and regulations, strengthen law enforcement supervision, intensify the fight against corruption, and vigorously rectify and standardize the income distribution order.

(a) Income outside of salaries will be strictly regulated. The government will implement strict regulations on subsidies, allowances, and bonuses given by government agencies and institutions, and develop guidelines for the implementation of reform subsidies. It also calls for better management of revenue generation in public institutions, specifically in the allocation of funds for research projects and development, as well as stricter regulations on official entertainment expenses and expenses related to official duties. The government also proposes stricter control over the consumption of government officials and executives in state-owned or state-controlled enterprises, including measures such as regulating the use of official vehicles, controlling the expenses for official entertainment, inspections, and training, and subjecting official expenses to democratic supervision by employees, with all relevant account records to be made publicly available.
(b) Crack down on and eliminate illegal income. By prioritizing sectors such as state-owned enterprise restructuring, land transfer, mineral exploitation, and construction projects, enhance oversight and administration to effectively close loopholes associated with the acquisition

of unlawful income. Vigorously combat economic offenses including smuggling, tax evasion, insider trading, market manipulation, counterfeiting, fraud, and deceptive loans and foreign exchange practices. Adopt stringent measures to investigate and address instances of corruption, bribery, and bribe acceptance. Implement measures to combat corporate bribery, bolster anti-money laundering endeavors, and intensify monitoring of capital outflows.

(c) Establish a comprehensive personal income and property information system and improve the system for income investigation and detection. This includes promoting the digitization, monetization, and electronic payment of salaries, accelerating the development of modern payment and settlement systems, implementing real-name registration for financial accounts, promoting card-based consumption, and standardizing cash management. Information resources from relevant departments such as public security, civil affairs, social security, housing, banking, taxation, and industry and commerce will be integrated to establish a comprehensive social credit system and income information monitoring system, as well as improve the personal income tax information management system. A unified system for investigating the income and expenditure of urban and rural households will also be established.

3.4. *Guide and leverage the role of social and non-governmental forces in the third distribution*

Encouraging and mobilizing social charity donations, and utilizing the third-party distribution role of civil organizations, are effective means to alleviate poverty, narrow the wealth gap, achieve social fairness and justice, and enhance national and social cohesion. Although China's charitable sector has made significant progress in recent years, there are still significant disparities between regions, industries, and organizations. This situation is directly related to the late start, low level of social participation, and small organizational scale of China's charitable donations. At present, the establishment and development of charitable organizations in China face many legal and regulatory constraints.

In the future, the Chinese government aims to reform and improve the approval system and admission standards for the third-party distribution subject (civil organizations), and encourage the establishment of civil organizations that provide social welfare, gradually forming a broad subject market for third-party distribution. It is necessary to develop and promulgate relevant laws and regulations that clearly define the legal status of civil organizations, determine their legal and legitimate status, and define their rights and obligations, in order to incorporate charitable causes into the legal system. The current Law on Public Welfare Donations and Regulations on Foundation Management in China needs further improvement. The operation of charitable donation funds should be subject to government and social supervision, including a series of regulatory mechanisms such as donation registration, news release, relevant inquiries, supervision, evaluation, and audit. Government departments should work together to make the development of civil organizations more transparent and credible and stimulate the enthusiasm and initiative of the whole society toward charitable causes.

Chapter 7

The Realization of Common Prosperity for All People

The notion of realizing common prosperity for all people is one of the core values and essential goals of socialism, as espoused by the founder of Marxism. Since the establishment of the first socialist state in the Soviet Union, each socialist nation has considered the gradual attainment of common prosperity for all citizens as a fundamental value and goal. Despite the heightened challenges encountered in the development of socialism on the global stage following the collapse of the Eastern Bloc, none of the current socialist states have relinquished their aspirations of achieving the objective of common prosperity.

1. The Formation and Development of the Idea of Achieving Common Prosperity

1.1. *Expositions on the idea of common prosperity by classic Marxist writers*

The notion of achieving common prosperity, rooted in a robust theoretical framework, was first proposed and elaborated upon by Marx and Engels, the revolutionary and constructional leaders of the working class. Drawing on the essence of earlier ideas, they developed the materialist conception of history and the theory of surplus value, achieving a transformation from utopian socialism to scientific socialism. Under the guidance of Marx and Engels, the concept of common prosperity has become one of the essential components of scientific socialism, transitioning from an abstract ideology to a practical and empirical reality.

The concept of common prosperity put forth by Marx and Engels mainly consists of three key elements.

First, the concept of common prosperity, accompanied by comprehensive freedom for human development, is destined to be realized in future societies, according to the works of Marx and Engels. Grounded in their critique of the capitalist system, the two scholars provided vivid descriptions of what future societies would entail. In *The Communist Manifesto*, they famously proclaimed that "in communist society, the accumulation of capital will no longer be the central goal, but rather the expansion, enrichment, and advancement of workers' lives will become the primary objective."[1] Marx further emphasized that in future societies, "the development of social productive forces will progress so rapidly that production will be aimed exclusively at ensuring the prosperity of all."[2] Engels echoed this view, stating that "through socialized production, not only can we ensure that all members of society enjoy an affluent and increasingly abundant standard of living, but we can also guarantee the full freedom of development and use of their physical and intellectual faculties."[3]

The second aspect of the common prosperity notion is that the high development of productive forces is a prerequisite for achieving common prosperity. Marx pointed out that without the development of productive forces, "there will only be the universalization of poverty and extreme destitution,"[4] while Engels emphasized that "when people cannot guarantee themselves full and adequate food, clothing, housing, and other basic necessities, they cannot be truly liberated."[5]

Third, the socialist system serves as the institutional foundation for achieving common prosperity. Marx pointed out in his *Economic and Philosophic Manuscripts of 1844* that only "communism is the positive transcendence of private property as human self-estrangement, and therefore the real appropriation of the human essence by and for man"[6]; Engels also emphasized that the difference between socialism and capitalism lies in "organizing production on the basis of the complete communal

---

[1] *Collected Works of Marx and Engels*, Vol. 2. People's Publishing House, 2009, p. 46.

[2] *Ibid.*, Vol. 8, p. 200.

[3] *Ibid.*, Vol. 3, pp. 563–564.

[4] *Ibid.*, Vol. 1, p. 588.

[5] *Ibid.*, p. 527.

[6] *Ibid.*, p. 185.

ownership of the means of production (initially, in the form of state ownership)."[7]

In 1917, under Lenin's leadership, the Russian proletariat carried out the October Revolution and established the world's first socialist country, providing the conditions and possibilities for Marx and Engels' socialist theory to become a reality. In the subsequent process of socialist construction, Lenin inherited the idea of common prosperity from Marx and Engels, initiating the exploration of the idea from theory to practice. Lenin emphasized that socialist production is intended to "guarantee the full well-being and free development of all members of society," and that "in this new and better society, there should be no poverty or wealth, and everyone should work. The fruits of collective labor should not be enjoyed by a small group of the wealthy, but by all laborers. Machines and other technological improvements should be used to ease everyone's labor, not to make a few people rich and leave millions of people in poverty. This new and better society is called a socialist society."[8] Lenin regarded productivity as a powerful driving force for social development, believing that "ultimately, labor productivity is the most important and fundamental thing that enables the new social system to triumph."[9]

Inheriting the idea of common prosperity from Marx, Engels, and Lenin, Stalin continued to explore how to achieve common prosperity for the masses in the Soviet Union during the socialist revolution and construction. In February 1933, Stalin pointed out, "Our current task is to make all members of collective farms live a prosperous life."[10] He believed that labor productivity was the fundamental factor in defeating capitalism. "Socialism can only be victorious on the basis of high labor productivity, on the basis of higher labor productivity than the capitalist system, on the basis of abundant products and various consumer goods, and on the basis of all members of society living a prosperous and cultured life."[11]

---

[7] *Ibid.*, Vol. 10. People's Publishing House, 2009, p. 588.

[8] *Lenin's Selected Works on Socialism*. People's Publishing House, 2009, p. 381.

[9] *Ibid.*, p. 151.

[10] *Complete Works of J. V. Stalin*, Vol. 13. People's Publishing House, 1956, p. 220.

[11] *Ibid.*, 1985, p. 62.

1.2. *Mao Zedong's exploration of the path to common prosperity*

In late December 1953, the Central Committee of the Communist Party of China passed *CCCPC's Decisions on Developing Agricultural Production Cooperatives*, which for the first time included the concept of "common prosperity" in a central Party document since the founding of the People's Republic of China. The Decisions stated that "to further increase agricultural productivity, the fundamental task of the Party's work in the rural areas is to educate and promote the farmers to gradually unite and organize themselves, implement socialist transformation of agriculture step by step, and transform agriculture from small-scale individual economy to advanced large-scale cooperative economy, so as to steadily overcome the contradictions between the development of the two economic sectors of industry and agriculture, and to enable the farmers to completely get rid of poverty and achieve common prosperity and general prosperity in life."[12] The Decisions were presided over and the drafting and revision were done with the participation of Mao Zedong, who not only proposed the concept of "common prosperity" for the first time but also explored the practical path to achieve it.

Mao Zedong placed great emphasis on the significance of the socialist path as the bright avenue for the rapid development of production and the prosperity of the entire farming community. He asserted that to attain socialism, it was essential to focus on the advancement of agriculture and industry, vigorously promote productive forces, and address the problem of farmers as a crucial aspect of consolidating the socialist system. In Mao's words, "The most pressing issue is educating the farmers. Without the socialization of agriculture, there can be no solid foundation for socialism."[13] During the land reform process, Mao underscored the importance of offering new prospects to the farmers, fostering productivity, increasing income, and promoting shared prosperity. Without such efforts, he believed that the impoverished population would lose faith in the Communist Party's leadership. Mao stressed that the farmers must be guided to follow the socialist path and work toward common prosperity. This would entail uplifting the less fortunate and enhancing the economic

---

[12] Party Literature Research Center of the CPC Central Committee (Ed.). (1993). *Selected Important Documents of the People's Republic of China*, Vol. 4. Central Party Literature Press, p. 661.

[13] *Selected Works of Mao Zedong*, Vol. 4. People's Publishing House, 1991, p. 1477.

well-being of all farmers, surpassing the current standard of wealth enjoyed by the prosperous farming community.[14]

Mao Zedong placed great emphasis on the important role of industrialization in achieving common prosperity. Early on in the establishment of the People's Republic of China, and during the initial stages of economic recovery, Mao put forward the overall policy of "one central task and three major improvements," and also determined the strategy of prioritizing the development of heavy industry. Throughout the process of socialist transformation, he repeatedly stressed that although the newly established China was a large country, it was neither wealthy nor strong.[15] "Our goal," Mao stated, "is to make our country much more developed, much wealthier, and much stronger than it is now." He also pointed out that only through industrialization could China achieve wealth and strength. "There can be no talk of strength and wealth in an agricultural country," Mao argued, "and we cannot build strength and wealth on an agricultural foundation." Mao Zedong paid special attention to the issue of "common prosperity" for farmers. He stated, "To consolidate the alliance between workers and peasants, we must lead the peasants to take the socialist road and ensure that the rural masses become prosperous together. The poor must become rich, and all the peasants must become prosperous. The degree of prosperity must be much greater than that of the rich peasants today."[16] Mao also made it clear that China needed to transform from a backward agricultural country into a modern industrialized one. "Only by developing modern industry, establishing an independent, democratic, united, and prosperous new China, can we liberate China's social productive forces[17] and win the support of the Chinese people,"[18] Mao declared. The innovative and practical idea of achieving common prosperity, as creatively formulated by Mao Zedong, was not only consistent with the basic principles of Marxism but also developed and adapted to the realities of China's socialist construction. It represents an important achievement in the Sinicization of Marxism and is a crucial foundation of the theory of socialism with Chinese characteristics for achieving common prosperity.

---

[14]Party Literature Research Center of the CPC Central Committee (1993), *Op. cit.*, p. 308.

[15]*Collected Works of Mao Zedong*, Vol. 6. People's Publishing House, 1999, p. 495.

[16]Party Literature Research Center of the CPC Central Committee (Ed.). (2013). *Chronology of Mao Zedong*, Vol. 2. Central Party Literature Press, 2013, p. 449.

[17]*Collected Works of Mao Zedong*, Vol. 7. People's Publishing House, 1999, p. 117.

[18]*Selected Works of Mao Zedong*, Vol. 3. People's Publishing House, 1991, p. 1477.

1.3. *Deng Xiaoping's crucial role in advancing the path to common prosperity in China*

The second generation of the central leadership of the Communist Party of China, with Deng Xiaoping as its core, based its strategies on the reality of China's national conditions, and clarified the essence of socialism. In this context, it put forth many constructive new approaches for achieving common prosperity, creatively inheriting and developing the previous ideas on the subject.

From the beginning of the Reform and Opening-up program to the Southern Tour in 1992, Deng Xiaoping summarized the experiences and lessons since the founding of the People's Republic of China, and further clarified the essence of socialism. He emphasized that "there is no poverty in socialism. The characteristic of socialism is not poverty, but wealth, and this wealth is the common prosperity of the people." He also stated that "the essence of socialism is to liberate the economy from its straitjacket, raise productivity, eliminate exploitation and economic polarization, and ultimately achieve common prosperity."[19]

Deng Xiaoping emphasized that only by following the socialist path can China achieve common prosperity. He firmly believed that "without socialism, China has no future."[20] He explicitly stated that "socialism has two very important aspects: one is the predominance of public ownership, and the other is the eradication of polarization."[21] Only by adhering to public ownership as the mainstay can true common prosperity be achieved. In March 1985, Deng Xiaoping pointed out, "One that takes public ownership as the mainstay and the other one that aspires to realize common prosperity — these are the fundamental principles of socialism that we must adhere to."[22] In 1990, he further emphasized, "Only socialism can create cohesion, solve everyone's difficulties, avoid polarization, and gradually achieve common prosperity."[23]

Building on the foundation of adhering to the socialist path, Deng Xiaoping placed great emphasis on the crucial role of productivity in the pursuit of common prosperity. He emphasized that "the primary socialist

---

[19] *Selected Works of Deng Xiaoping*, Vol. 3. People's Publishing House, 1993, p. 265, 373.

[20] *Ibid.*, p. 311.

[21] *Ibid.*, p. 138.

[22] *Ibid.*, p. 111.

[23] *Ibid.*, p. 357.

principle is to tap the society's productive potential, followed by achieving common prosperity."[24] In March 1978, during the National Science Conference, Deng pointed out that "under the conditions of proletarian dictatorship, without modernization, improvement in scientific and technological levels, and development of social productive forces, national strength cannot be strengthened and people's material and cultural lives cannot be improved. Our socialist political and economic systems cannot be fully consolidated."[25] In November 1979, he further emphasized that China's modernization was indeed a new revolution, and "the aim of our revolution is to release and develop the productive forces. Leaving aside the development of productive forces, national prosperity, and the improvement of people's lives, the revolution would be futile."[26]

It can be said that Deng Xiaoping's emphasis on the development of productive forces was a correct judgment based on China's actual national conditions, which resolved the problems that we had hoped to solve since the founding of the People's Republic of China but had failed to address properly. Deng once pointed out that "for a long period in the past, we neglected the need to develop productive forces during the socialist stage."[27] He further stressed that "if there were any shortcomings since the founding of our nation, it is that we somewhat ignored the development of productive forces." According to him, "the main task during the socialist period is to develop productive forces, continuously increase the social material wealth, improve people's livelihood day by day, and create the material conditions for entering into communism."[28]

Realizing common prosperity was one of the key driving forces behind Deng Xiaoping's great reform and opening-up plan. Deng believed that in order to achieve common prosperity in China, it was necessary to carry out reforms and opening-up. He pointed out succinctly, "All our reforms are aimed at one goal, which is to remove obstacles to the development of social productivity."[29] After the Third Plenary Session of the Party's 11th Central Committee, Deng Xiaoping repeatedly proposed allowing some regions and some people to become rich first. He believed

---

[24] *Ibid.*, p. 172.

[25] *Ibid.*, Vol. 2, 1994, p. 86.

[26] *Ibid.*, p. 231.

[27] *Ibid.*, Vol. 3, 1993, p. 157.

[28] *Ibid.*, p. 63, 171.

[29] *Ibid.*, p. 134.

that this was an effective path for China to achieve common prosperity at the present stage, and that only by solving development problems could problems arising from development be addressed. Deng stressed frequently that common prosperity did not mean synchronous or equal prosperity but required a gradual shift from non-equilibrium to equilibrium. "To follow the socialist road means to gradually achieve common prosperity,"[30] he said. It was Deng Xiaoping's recognition of this that led to his proposal of many constructive new approaches to achieving common prosperity.

To elaborate, in terms of economic policy, Deng Xiaoping proposed the encouragement of certain individuals and regions to become wealthy first, with the "purpose of achieving common prosperity faster."[31] In terms of strategic steps, Deng put forward two major development strategies. After the implementation of opening-up to the outside world, due to the relatively favorable conditions of the coastal areas, they could take the lead in development. For this reason, policies should be tilted toward the coastal areas, and other regions should follow this overall situation. When development reaches a certain level, it is required that the coastal areas put forth more effort to help develop the inland regions, which is also part of the overall situation.[32]

In the progressive development toward modernization and common prosperity, Deng Xiaoping proposed the "Three-Step Development Strategy." The first step was to double the Gross National Product from 1981 to 1990, ensuring basic food and clothing needs for the people. The second step was to double the Gross National Product again from 1991 to the end of the 20th century, achieving a moderately prosperous society. The third step was to reach the level of moderately developed countries in terms of per capita Gross National Product by the mid-21st century, achieving relative affluence for the people and realizing modernization at a fundamental level.

From the practice of reform and opening-up, the "Three-Step Development Strategy" and the "Two Overall Situations" proposed by Deng Xiaoping are key steps on the path toward common prosperity and are strategic measures that are in line with the basic national conditions of the primary stage of socialism in China. Practices have proven that Deng's

---

[30] *Ibid.*, p. 373.

[31] *Ibid.*, p. 172.

[32] *Ibid.*, pp. 277–278.

understanding of common prosperity, especially the common prosperity of socialism with Chinese characteristics, is very profound and visionary. His idea of common prosperity is a product of the combination of the basic principles of Marxism and the characteristics of contemporary Chinese practice and times. It is a continuation and development of Mao Zedong's Thoughts in new historical conditions. At the same time, it also combines the ideal socialist goals with the reality of social productive forces, and the realization of fairness with the improvement of efficiency, making it a great achievement of adapting Marxism to Chinese conditions. It constantly leads and promotes the development of the idea of common prosperity under socialism with Chinese characteristics.

2. New Developments in the Idea of Achieving Common Prosperity since the 18th CPC National Congress

2.1. *Xi Jinping's new interpretation of the idea of achieving common prosperity*

Since the founding of the People's Republic of China, the Communist Party of China has based itself on China's realities, combining the basic principles of Marxism with the practice of socialist construction, continuously innovating and developing the idea of common prosperity. As a result, the Party's grasp of the concept of common prosperity has become increasingly mature, while the people's understanding of it has become more comprehensive and in-depth.

Since the 18th CPC National Congress, the Party Central Committee with Comrade Xi Jinping at the core has further developed the idea of socialist common prosperity. The Committee has done so in line with the requirements of the times and practice, building upon the ideas of previous generations. At the National Conference on Development-driven Poverty Alleviation held on November 27–28, 2015, Xi Jinping underscored the critical importance of eradicating poverty, improving people's livelihoods, and gradually achieving common prosperity, which he emphasized as essential requirements of socialism and a critical mission of the Party. Building a moderately prosperous society in all respects was established as the Party's solemn commitment to the people of the country. The battle cry for poverty alleviation had been sounded, and the Party was determined to win this battle and ensure that all impoverished areas and populations enter into a moderately prosperous society together by 2020.[33] This strengthened the link between the idea of common prosperity and the comprehensive building of a moderately prosperous society.

In addition, Xi has closely intertwined the concept of common prosperity with development-oriented poverty alleviation efforts. As early as the end of 2012, during an inspection in Fuping County, he astutely recognized that achieving a moderately prosperous society in China's rural areas, particularly in impoverished regions, is the most challenging and demanding task. Xi has emphasized that without ensuring prosperity in these areas, the goal of building a moderately prosperous society cannot be achieved.[34] During his inspection work in Yunnan in January 2015, he further stressed that development-oriented poverty alleviation is central to achieving the first centenary goal and represents the most onerous task. Xi has called for more precise targeting, more powerful measures, and more effective action to carry out targeted poverty alleviation and eradication, with project arrangements and fund usage being more precise to provide genuine benefits to impoverished individuals.[35]

In April 2015, during the 22nd collective study session of the Political Bureau of the CPC Central Committee, Xi Jinping emphasized that the most arduous and demanding task in building a moderately prosperous society in all respects lies in rural areas, especially in impoverished regions. He called for concerted efforts to make major breakthroughs in coordinating urban–rural relations, particularly in breaking down the dual structure, promoting equal exchange of urban and rural factors, and pursuing a balanced allocation of public resources. By injecting new impetus into rural development, the aim is to enable farmers to participate in the process of reform and development on an equal footing, and to share the benefits of these initiatives.[36] During his investigation in Guizhou in

---

[33]The charge of the poverty alleviation battle has been sounded: The whole party and the nation are working hard towards our target. *Peoples' Daily*, November 29, 2015.

[34]In reference to Keeping the safety and well-being of the people in mind, bringing warmth to every household on behalf of the party and government. *People's Daily*, December 31, 2012.

[35]Resolutely winning the battle of poverty alleviation and accelerating the economic and social development of ethnic regions. *People's Daily*, January 22, 2015.

[36]In reference to The establishment of a sound urban-rural integrated development system to enable farmers to share the fruits of reform and development. *People's Daily*, May 2, 2015.

June 2015, Xi Jinping reiterated the importance of relying on industry to drive growth and necessary policy incentives to encourage entrepreneurship and job creation, with the goal of increasing the income of both urban and rural residents. To address the issues most concerning to the people, such as education, healthcare, social security, and food safety, he emphasized the need for solid and incremental progress. Through promoting employment and entrepreneurship, developing social programs, and waging an all-out battle against poverty, the goal is to continuously chart a course where the welfare of the people and economic development are mutually reinforcing.[37]

Upon further analysis of Xi Jinping's discourse, it becomes evident that his notion of common prosperity encompasses two fundamental pillars: a fundamental stance of placing people at the central focus of development and a pragmatic focus on the realistic issues currently facing China. As highlighted in the "Recommendations," Xi maintains that development must serve the people, rely on the people, and ultimately be shared by the people. To this end, effective institutional arrangements must be put in place to ensure that all individuals have a greater sense of achievement and satisfaction in contributing to and benefiting from China's ongoing development, thereby promoting unity and driving progress toward the ultimate goal of common prosperity.[38]

The development ideology of placing the people at the center, a fundamental tenet of Marxist political economics, has been consistently emphasized by Xi Jinping. His numerous calls to listen to the voices of the people, respond to their needs and aspirations, and enhance their sense of achievement reflect his deep commitment to this principle. At the opening ceremony of the Asia-Pacific Economic Cooperation (APEC) CEO Summit on November 9, 2014, Xi underscored the importance of all reforms being directed toward enhancing people's well-being, promoting social fairness and justice, and enabling ordinary citizens to lead better lives.[39]

---

[37]To discern the situation clearly, adapt to trends, give full play to advantages, and make use of dialectical thinking to plan development. *People's Daily*, June 19, 2015.

[38]Party Literature Research Center of the CPC Central Committee (Ed.). (2016). *Selected Important Documents since the 18th CPC National Congress*, Vol. II. Central Party Literature Press, p. 793.

[39]Xi Jinping. (2014). Pursuing sustainable development in a concerted effort to build an Asia-Pacific community with a shared dream. *People's Daily*, November 10, 2014.

Xi Jinping's concept of common prosperity has always been guided by a problem-oriented approach. As a developing country, China once had the largest number of people living in absolute poverty in the world. How to make the country prosperous and achieve common prosperity on that basis has always been a core issue of concern for successive Chinese leaders and the people. The period of the 13th Five-Year Plan is the decisive stage for China to comprehensively build a moderately prosperous society and achieve its first centenary goal. Currently, China has entered a new stage of economic development, facing new situations, problems, and challenges, and has entered an important stage on the road to common prosperity. To this end, Xi pointed out in the *Explanation on the Formulation of the 13th Five-Year Plan for National Economic and Social Development by the Central Committee of the Communist Party of China* that, "As the concluding plan for building a moderately prosperous society in all respects, the 13th Five-Year Plan must firmly address the weaknesses that still exist, and make greater efforts to address these weaknesses. Planning for economic and social development in the 13th Five-Year Plan period must focus on the great task of addressing weaknesses."[40] It can be seen that an important aspect of Xi Jinping's concept of common prosperity is to address the shortcomings of rural areas, primarily by precisely targeting poverty alleviation to address the shortcomings of poor rural populations, and then gradually addressing the overall development shortcomings of rural areas, thus achieving integrated urban–rural development and comprehensive prosperity, ultimately achieving common prosperity.

The concept of common prosperity aims to eliminate polarization and the gulf between the rich and the poor. However, its connotation is not simply about achieving average or simultaneous prosperity, but gradually realizing universal prosperity for all people based on the development of productivity and ensuring that everyone shares the fruits of development. Since the beginning of the 21st century, the Central Committee of the CPC has clearly stated that by 2020, it aims to "comprehensively build a higher level of well-being for over a billion people," thus opening a new era for common prosperity in China.

At the 18th CPC National Congress, it was emphasized that to achieve common prosperity, we must adhere to economic development as the central task, adhere to the basic socialist economic system and distribution

[40]Party Literature Research Center of the CPC Central Committee (2016), *Op. cit.*, p. 775.

system, adjust the pattern of national income distribution, increase the redistribution and regulation of income, focus on solving the problem of large income disparities, and handle the relationship between efficiency and fairness properly. "Common prosperity is the fundamental principle of socialism with Chinese characteristics, so we must ensure that the fruits of development benefit all people more fairly and steadily advance towards common prosperity."[41]

2.2. *Expanding the paths of achieving common prosperity*

Xi Jinping regards development-oriented poverty alleviation as an essential requirement for building a moderately prosperous society in all respects and for upholding the socialist path and the road to common prosperity. He emphasized that doing well in the work of development-oriented poverty alleviation, supporting disadvantaged groups to lift themselves out of poverty and become prosperous, and helping them overcome difficulties, are important manifestations of the fundamental purposes of the Party's wholehearted service to the people, and a significant responsibility of the Party and the government to ensure that development achievements benefit the people more fairly.

On October 16, 2015, at the National Conference on Development-driven Poverty Alleviation, Xi Jinping emphasized that since the reform and opening-up, we have successfully embarked on a unique path of development-oriented poverty alleviation in China, which has lifted more than 700 million rural poor people out of poverty and laid a solid foundation for building a moderately prosperous society in all respects. At the same time, the current situation of poverty alleviation in China remains daunting. As of the end of 2014, there were still more than 70 million rural poor people in the country. "During the 13th Five-Year Plan period, the goal of poverty alleviation was to ensure that by 2020, rural poor people would have access to adequate food, clothing, compulsory education, basic medical care, and safe housing. At the same time, the per capita disposable income of rural residents in poverty-stricken areas should increase faster than the national average, and the key indicators of basic

[41] Party Literature Research Center of the CPC Central Committee (Ed.). (2014). *Selected Important Documents since the 18th CPC National Congress*, Vol. I. Central Party Literature Press, pp. 78–79.

public services in poverty-stricken areas should be close to the national average level."[42]

The concept of targeted poverty alleviation was first proposed by Xi Jinping during his inspection tour of Xiangxi in Hunan Province in November 2013. Essentially, it is an extension and development of the idea of achieving common prosperity. The approach of targeted poverty alleviation involves precise and targeted measures to address the root causes of poverty. It emphasizes the need to identify and help impoverished families in a genuine and practical manner, and to eradicate the causes of poverty through appropriate measures that are tailored to local conditions. The ultimate goal is to help those in poverty find their own path to prosperity in a realistic and sustainable way.

Xi Jinping's concept of targeted poverty alleviation encompasses two main aspects: material assistance and spiritual support. The key to material assistance lies in precision, as he emphasized at the 2015 High-Level Forum on Poverty Reduction and Development. In the context of poverty alleviation, he stressed the importance of implementing precise strategies, leveraging the advantages of China's institutional framework, and paying attention to six precision factors: precise identification of recipients, precise project design, precise use of funds, precise measures reaching households, precise deployment of officials to villages, and precise evaluation of poverty reduction outcomes.[43]

To be specific, "six precision measures" refer to the precise identification and positioning of impoverished individuals throughout the poverty alleviation process. Currently, the nationwide method for identifying impoverished individuals is based on democratic evaluation and the establishment of a poverty alleviation registry under the total quota control system at the grassroots level. Once impoverished individuals are identified and registered, the root causes of poverty, such as illness, lack of funds, lack of technical expertise, and labor shortages, are analyzed. This allows for targeted project assistance based on the specific "poverty roots" of each household. Project assistance must be supported with adequate funding and tailored to the circumstances of each impoverished household. Additionally, a large number of supporting projects and measures of

---

[42] The charge of the poverty alleviation battle has been sounded: The whole party and the nation are working hard towards our target. *Peoples' Daily*, November 29, 2015.

[43] Converging consensus and deepening cooperation for poverty reduction. *Xinhua News Agency*, October 16, 2015.

precise poverty alleviation must be implemented at the village level, where the capacity of the village-level organization is one of the critical factors that influence the effectiveness of precise poverty alleviation efforts.

Therefore, in the process of implementing targeted poverty alleviation, it is imperative to enhance the efficacy of rural primary organizations so as to execute development-oriented poverty alleviation efforts with greater precision. It is also essential to synergize the construction of grassroots organizations with the development-oriented poverty alleviation, with a particular focus on the establishment of village-level organizations centered around the village party. Furthermore, rigorous scientific assessments and evaluations of the poverty alleviation outcomes are necessary to avert falsification and ensure that impoverished populations are not prematurely declared as lifted out of poverty.

Expanding upon the foundation of implementing precise poverty alleviation, President Xi Jinping further underscored the principle of classification and phased implementation. It is imperative to uphold a targeted approach, with policies tailored to specific individuals, regions, reasons for poverty, and types of poverty. To this end, we must support the development of production and employment opportunities for certain groups, resettle and relocate others, address poverty through ecological conservation for yet another, provide education and training for those in need, and establish a safety net through the implementation of the minimum living allowance policy. To mobilize the entire society, we must encourage and support diverse forms of participation in poverty alleviation.

The concept of spiritual poverty alleviation is a strategic focus of the targeted poverty alleviation ideology. To overcome poverty, one must first have the courage and confidence to combat it. It is crucial to help impoverished groups fully recognize their strengths and the importance of their subjective initiative, and to display the determination and perseverance necessary to overcome obstacles. Only by being mentally resilient can one become impervious to poverty. In this regard, during his visit to Hunan in November 2013, Xi noted that "the path to overcoming poverty and achieving prosperity lies in having a resolute determination. With unwavering aspirations and steadfast confidence, no obstacles are insurmountable."

Xi Jinping places significant importance on the education of children in poverty-stricken families, as education is an essential means of ameliorating spiritual poverty. During a discussion with key officials from Heze City and its counties, Xi emphasized the need to grasp education as the fundamental strategy for poverty alleviation and wealth creation, asserting that education must never be neglected and that children from impoverished families should receive quality compulsory education. He emphasized the importance of ensuring that no child is left behind at the starting line.[44] In April 2015, at the 11th meeting of the Central Comprehensively Deepening Reforms Commission, it was stated that "developing rural education, providing fair and quality education to every rural child, and preventing intergenerational poverty transmission"[45] were crucial objectives. Subsequently, the State Council issued the *Rural Teacher Support Plan (2015–2020)*, which provided a blueprint for the development of rural education over the coming years.

The strategy of integrating urban and rural development is an integral component of Xi Jinping's economic strategy and a key step toward achieving common prosperity. It is of paramount importance in enhancing the economic vitality of rural areas and ensuring that farmers have equal participation in the reform and development process and share in the fruits of progress. On April 30, 2015, during the 22nd collective study session of the Political Bureau of the CPC Central Committee, Xi stressed that promoting the integration of urban and rural development is an inevitable requirement for the development of industrialization, urbanization, and modernization of agriculture to a certain stage and an important sign of national modernization. Since the reform and opening-up, rural social programs have seen significant improvement, and remarkable progress has been made in coordinating urban and rural development and adjusting urban–rural relations. At the same time, the contradiction of imbalanced and uncoordinated urban–rural development in China remains prominent, and the urgency and significance of accelerating the integration of urban and rural development is increasingly evident.[46]

Xi Jinping emphasized the importance of taking into account China's unique national conditions and the current reality of the dual structure of imbalanced and uncoordinated urban–rural development when implementing specific measures for integrated urban–rural development. This

[44] Xi Jinping on poverty alleviation: Excerpts from important discourses Since the 18th CPC National Congress. Dangjian Official Website, December 1, 2015.

[45] Profoundly grasp the key position of comprehensively deepening reforms and consciously apply the reform spirit to plan and promote work. *People's Daily*, April 2, 2015.

[46] Establishing a sound integrated urban-rural development system and mechanism to enable the masses of farmers to share the fruits of reform and development. *People's Daily*, May 2, 2015.

involves considering China's natural resources, historical and cultural traditions, and institutional systems, while also following universal laws and avoiding dogmatism. In doing so, we must learn from international advanced experiences while avoiding mere duplication. To achieve integrated urban–rural development, it is necessary to coordinate and plan industry and agriculture, cities and rural areas as a whole. This will promote the integration and common development of urban and rural areas, particularly in terms of planning, resource allocation, industrial development, public services, and ecological protection. The focus must be on establishing a system mechanism for urban–rural integration, which will facilitate the formation of a new type of urban–rural relationship that promotes industry through agriculture, integrates cities and rural areas, mutually benefits industry and agriculture, and integrates urban and rural areas. The ultimate goal is to achieve the equalization of basic rights and interests, equal provision of public services, balanced income distribution, rational allocation of resources, and integration of industrial development for both urban and rural residents. These ideas and measures are integral to promoting coordinated urban–rural development, filling in the gaps in rural development, and ultimately realizing the goal of building a moderately prosperous society in all respects and achieving common prosperity in China under new historical circumstances.

3. Adhering to the Path toward Common Prosperity for All with Chinese Characteristics

The intellectual achievements and practical experiences of the aforementioned ideology within the Party have established a unique path toward socialist common prosperity with Chinese characteristics. This path is still in the process of exploration, just as socialism itself is constantly evolving. However, its fundamental principles and distinguishing characteristics have already taken shape.

3.1. *The importance of upholding and enriching the people-centered approach in achieving common prosperity for all*

Committing to a people-centered approach and pursuing their interests is a reflection of the class nature and the fundamental stance of Marxist political economics. From this perspective, the concept of common prosperity that our Party has formed in practice is a product of the integration of Marxist theory and Chinese practice in the new era, which has upheld and enriched the people-centered ideology in this new historical stage. In this regard, Xi Jinping pointed out during the 28th collective study session of the Political Bureau of the CPC Central Committee that "we must adhere to promoting the well-being of the people, facilitating comprehensive human development, and steadily advancing towards common prosperity as the starting point and foothold of economic development."[47]

Socialism with Chinese characteristics combines the principles of placing the people at the center and upholding the fundamental interests of the nation. In this context, the pursuit of common prosperity is not only an internal requirement and inevitable outcome of adhering to this socialist model but also a manifestation of the people's pivotal role in the country's development. As early as November 15, 2012, during a press conference of the Standing Committee of the Political Bureau of the 18th CPC Central Committee, with both Chinese and foreign journalists present, Xi Jinping stressed the importance of the people's yearning for a better life as the driving force behind the Party's pursuit of common prosperity. He emphasized the need for the Party to unite and lead the entire nation in continuing to emancipate the mind, uphold reform and opening-up, liberate and develop social productive forces, strive to solve the difficulties faced by the people in their production and life, and resolutely follow the path of common prosperity.[48]

The fundamental importance of placing the people at the center of all our efforts and using their well-being as the standard by which we measure success is evident in the Communist Party of China's emphasis on the concept of common prosperity. As Xi Jinping emphasized at a symposium commemorating the 120th anniversary of Mao Zedong's birth, "The ultimate test of the effectiveness of all our work is whether the people have truly benefited, whether their lives have truly improved, and whether their rights and interests have truly been safeguarded."[49] We must redouble our efforts to ensure that the fruits of development are shared more fairly and widely among all our citizens, as we steadily work toward the goal of

---

[47]Based on China's realities and development practices, advance Marxist political economics in contemporary China. *People's Daily*, November 25, 2015.

[48]Peoples' aspirations for a better life are our striving goals. *People's Daily*, November 16, 2012.

[49]Party Literature Research Center of the CPC Central Committee (2014), *Op. cit.*, p. 698.

common prosperity. The precision-targeted poverty alleviation campaign is an important component of Xi's vision for common prosperity, and a reflection of his deep commitment to putting the people first. As he has said, "Effective development-oriented poverty alleviation work, supporting underprivileged communities to achieve poverty eradication and prosperity, providing them with assistance and solving their difficulties, are important manifestations of our Party's fundamental purpose of wholeheartedly serving the people and a significant responsibility of the Party, and the government. This approach enables development achievements to benefit more people and be distributed more equitably."[50]

In the process of pursuing common prosperity, we must adhere to the principle of "everything for the people, everything relying on the people." The term "people" here does not refer to an abstract concept, but to the 1.3 billion Chinese people who are striving forward on the road to common prosperity. They are the fundamental force in building socialism with Chinese characteristics and promoting China's development. Xi Jinping emphasized that, when carrying out the work of development-oriented poverty alleviation, we should effectively strengthen social cohesion and mobilize and consolidate the broadest possible social forces to participate. "As long as the people's yearning for a happy life has not yet been realized, we must work tirelessly to unite and lead the people to struggle together."[51] During the 13th Five-Year Plan period, the principle of prioritizing the people's position will be upheld as the primary guideline for development, embodying the guiding ideology of promoting comprehensive human development. We aim to improve the public service system, including employment, education, culture, social security, medical care, and housing, and gradually raise the level of equalization of basic public services. All of these fully embody the Party's philosophy of pursuing development for the people, relying on the people, and taking the people as the mainstay to advance towards the path of common prosperity.

As China moves towards the goal of building a moderately prosperous society in all respects, President Xi Jinping places great emphasis on the enhancement of people's abilities. In September 2013, in his video message to commemorate the first anniversary of the United Nations'

---

[50] *Be A Secretary of the County Committee Like Jiao Yulu*. Central Party Literature Press, 2015. p. 19.

[51] Xi Jinping visits and extends his greetings to cadres and people of all ethnic groups in inner Mongolia on the eve of the spring festival. *Peoples' Daily*, January 30, 2014.

Global Education First Initiative (GEFI), he highlighted China's commitment to "developing universal education and lifelong education, building a learning society, ensuring every child has access to education, and striving to provide better and more equitable education opportunities for the 1.3 billion Chinese people, enabling them to develop themselves, contribute to society, and benefit the people."[52]

3.2. *Combining prosperity for some and prosperity for all is essential for achieving common prosperity for all people*

The strategy of "letting some regions and groups become prosperous first and then helping others catch up" refers to the organic combination of achieving common prosperity for both the early developers and the latecomers. In 1978, Deng Xiaoping stated at the closing ceremony of the Central Committee Working Conference, "In terms of economic policy, I believe that we should allow some regions, enterprises, and workers and peasants to earn more income and live a better life because of their hard work and outstanding achievements. When some people's living standards improve, they will inevitably produce tremendous demonstration power, influencing their neighbors and driving people in other regions and units to learn from them. This will make the entire national economy continue to develop in a wave-like manner, enabling people of all ethnic groups in the country to become prosperous at a fairly quick speed."[53]

One key issue that must be addressed through various means, proposals, and methods is how to prevent polarization and achieve common prosperity more quickly and effectively on the basis of the initial affluence of a certain part of the population. Since the reform and opening-up, China's economy has grown rapidly, and people's income has steadily increased. However, it cannot be denied that the widening income gap has become increasingly prominent. In fact, in 1985, during a meeting with foreign guests, Deng Xiaoping talked about the criteria for evaluating the success or failure of the reform and opening-up, saying, "If it leads to polarization, the reform has failed."[54] In 1992, at one of the important

[52]President Xi Jinping delivers video congratulatory message for the first anniversary of the UN Global Education First Initiative (GEFI). *People's Daily*, September 27, 2013.
[53]*Selected Works of Deng Xiaoping*, Vol. 2. People's Publishing House, 2009, p. 152.
[54]*Ibid.*, Vol. 3, p. 139.

talks delivered during his Inspection Tour of the South, Deng Xiaoping again mentioned the issue of the widening income gap, saying that "when and on what basis to address and solve this problem needs to be studied."[55]

Eliminating poverty and achieving common prosperity is an inevitable requirement of the socialist path with Chinese characteristics and a great mission passed down by generations of the CPC members. From the era of wars when people were put in charge, to the land reform that enabled peasants to have their own land, from the partial affluence achieved through reform and opening-up to the policy of "the prosperous areas should help the less developed areas," and finally to the goal of taking the difficult masses in impoverished areas and the entire nation toward a moderately prosperous society, and realizing the Chinese dream in the hearts of every individual by lifting them out of poverty and hardships to live a better life — all these great missions have always been interconnected and carried forward by the Chinese people.

While implementing the practice of "letting some regions and groups become prosperous first and then helping others catch up, to ultimately achieve common prosperity for all," the widening gap between the rich and the poor has generated a significant adverse impact on achieving the goal, causing confusion among the people and constant questioning of the correctness of the policy of achieving moderate prosperity before overall prosperity. As the development of reform and opening-up has progressed to the present day, we are faced with the severe challenge of constantly expanding income disparities. We need to adequately address people's concerns about this phenomenon from a theoretical perspective, and adjust and divert the potential trend towards deterioration in practice. Xi's vision of achieving common prosperity with the people at the center leads the great practice of building a moderately prosperous society in all aspects and upholding socialism with Chinese characteristics. It puts forward specific measures such as targeted poverty alleviation, urban–rural integrated development, etc. These measures can significantly improve the living standards of the impoverished population and achieve common prosperity at an early date. "By 2020, the aim is to achieve a stable eradication of extreme poverty by ensuring that impoverished rural populations have no worries about food, clothing, compulsory education, basic medical care, and housing security. At the same time, the growth rate of per capita disposable income of farmers in poverty-stricken areas will be

[55] *Ibid.*, p. 374.

higher than the national average, and the basic public service indicators in major areas will be close to the national average level."[56]

The urban–rural integrated development strategy is also an important means to achieve common prosperity in the new era. To this end, our Party emphasizes the need to continue to promote the construction of a new countryside, coordinate, and develop it with the new type of urbanization, and form a dual-wheel drive. We must adhere to the driving force of reform, continuously break the dual urban–rural structure, and improve the planning system. We must comprehensively consider the urban and rural development planning, integrate multiple plans, and effectively solve the problem of planning detachment between urban and rural areas and the emphasis on cities over the countryside. We must improve the mechanism for rural infrastructure construction, promote interconnection and sharing of urban and rural infrastructure, and innovate decision-making, investment, construction, operation, and management mechanisms for rural infrastructure and public service facilities. We should actively guide social capital to participate in the construction of rural public infrastructure. We should promote the formation of an equal basic public service system in urban and rural areas, and it is particularly important to strengthen the construction of a care service system for left-behind children, women, and the elderly in rural areas. We should accelerate the reform of the household registration system, improve the equal employment system for urban and rural workers, gradually enable agricultural migrant workers to enter, live, integrate, find employment, and start businesses in cities, and safeguard the legitimate rights and interests of migrant workers, ensuring equal employment rights for urban and rural workers.[57]

On November 17, 2012, Xi Jinping delivered a speech on the importance of upholding and developing socialism with Chinese characteristics, as well as promoting the spirit of the 18th CPC National Congress. He emphasized that "fairness and justice are inherent requirements of socialism with Chinese characteristics. Therefore, it is necessary to intensify the construction of systems that play a significant role in safeguarding social

[56]The charge of the poverty alleviation battle has been sounded: The whole party and the nation are working hard towards our target. *Peoples' Daily*, November 29, 2015.

[57]Establishing a sound integrated urban-rural development system and mechanism to enable the masses of farmers to share the fruits of reform and development. *People's Daily*, May 2, 2015.

fairness and justice, gradually establishing a social security system to promote equity." This unwavering commitment to placing the people at the center of governance and ensuring shared prosperity for all has led China toward comprehensive modernization and achieving the great rejuvenation of the Chinese nation, while paving the way for the eventual realization of common prosperity.

3.3. *Clarifying the phase goal of achieving common prosperity for all people*

The practice of socialism with Chinese characteristics is based on the leadership of the Communist Party of China, rooted in the fundamental national conditions, liberating and developing social productive forces, and promoting comprehensive human development. Its ultimate aim is to gradually achieve common prosperity for all people and build a strong, democratic, civilized, and harmonious socialist modern state. As a stage-specific goal of achieving the great rejuvenation of the Chinese nation, Xi Jinping has redefined the concept of common prosperity in the new era. In the current phase of China's strategic development, the country is at a critical juncture in its efforts to build a moderately prosperous society in all respects and achieve common prosperity. Under the guidance of Xi Jinping, the Party has raised high the banner of the Chinese Dream, inspiring the Chinese people to forge ahead on the path to common prosperity.

On November 29, 2012, during his visit to the "Road to Rejuvenation" exhibition at the National Museum of China, Xi Jinping first proposed the concept of the "Chinese Dream," stating that "realizing the great rejuvenation of the Chinese nation is the greatest dream of the Chinese people in modern times." At the closing ceremony of the 12th National People's Congress, he used the three keywords of "country's prosperity, national rejuvenation, and people's happiness" to express the profound connotation of the Chinese Dream. At this stage, the specific content of the Chinese Dream is to achieve the "Two Centenary Goals," namely to build a moderately prosperous society in all respects when the Communist Party of China celebrates its centenary and to build a modern socialist country that is prosperous, strong, democratic, culturally advanced, and harmonious when the People's Republic of China celebrates its centenary. Essentially, the inherent requirement of the Chinese Dream is consistent with the pursuit of common prosperity. The Chinese Dream aims to achieve country's prosperity, national rejuvenation, and people's happiness, which is no different in direction and essence from the ultimate social state that common prosperity pursues with abundant material and spiritual richness. The Chinese Dream is a necessary preparatory stage for common prosperity, while common prosperity is the development direction of the Chinese Dream. They complement each other and are inherently unified.

Xi Jinping's characterization of the stage goal of common prosperity as the "Chinese Dream" has significant practical significance. The Chinese Dream is not only the dream of the entire Chinese nation but also the dream of every Chinese citizen. Each individual's dream is a part of the Chinese Dream, and the realization of individual dreams will inevitably promote the realization of the Chinese Dream. Currently, China is in the critical stage of building a moderately prosperous society in all respects and needs to maximize consensus and unity. Interpreting the concept of common prosperity through the Chinese Dream can allow the idea to take root and flourish in the hearts of the people, inspiring more Chinese people to work hard to achieve their ideals, as well as the rejuvenation and prosperity of the nation. Therefore, the Chinese Dream is a bridge connecting common prosperity and contemporary people, and it is a concrete manifestation of the phased and popularized goal of common prosperity. It is of great significance for achieving the goal of building a moderately prosperous society in all respects and for the subsequent modernization of the country.

3.4. *Realizing the goal of building a moderately prosperous society in all respects is essential for achieving the common prosperity of all people*

The construction of a moderately prosperous society is a fundamental project for realizing China's dream of national rejuvenation and common prosperity. The grand goal of building a moderately prosperous society in all respects by 2020 was a major decision made based on the actual conditions of China's economic and social development at the 18th CPC National Congress. On June 5, 2014, Xi Jinping announced to international friends, "China has entered the decisive stage of building a moderately prosperous society in all respects. Achieving this goal is a crucial step towards realizing the great rejuvenation of the Chinese nation."[58] To this end, President Xi proposed the idea and policies of common prosperity, including targeted poverty alleviation, urban–rural integration, and the Chinese Dream, and outlined the specific path and fundamental measures for the final stage of building a moderately prosperous society, which realized the leap from building to completion.

The most arduous and challenging task in achieving the goal of building a moderately prosperous society in all respects lies in rural areas, particularly in poverty-stricken regions. Without rural prosperity, especially in impoverished areas, there can be no comprehensive prosperity. In July 2013, during his inspection tour in Hubei, Xi Jinping pointed out that "the difficulty in building a moderately prosperous society in all respects lies in rural areas. We must develop both industrialization, information technology, and urbanization, as well as agricultural modernization and the construction of new rural areas. We need to break down the dual urban–rural structure, promote integrated urban–rural development, and build a beautiful home where farmers can live happily."[59] In December of the same year, he emphasized at the central rural work conference that "we must see that agriculture is still the drawback of the 'Four Modernizations,' and the rural areas are still the weak point in building a moderately prosperous society in all respects."[60] In December 2014, during his inspection tour in Jiangsu, he went further, pointing out that "without agricultural modernization, without rural prosperity and strength, without farmers' secure and happy lives, national modernization will be incomplete, incomprehensive, and not insecure."[61]

The key to achieving the goal of a moderately prosperous society in all respects lies in poverty alleviation and eradication, as emphasized by Xi Jinping in January 2015 during a discussion with county party secretaries at the Central Party School. While China has only five to six years left to achieve the first centenary goal of building a moderately prosperous

---

[58] Xi Jinping. (2014). Promoting the spirit of the silk road and deepening China-Arab cooperation. *People's Daily*, June 6, 2014.

[59] Resolutely deepening reform and opening-up, steadily promoting economic and social development. *People's Daily*, July 24, 2013.

[60] Party Literature Research Center of the CPC Central Committee (2014), *Op. cit.*, p. 658.

[61] Seizing the initiative and actively adapting to the new normal of economic development to promote reform and opening-up, and modernization to a new level. *People's Daily*, December 15, 2014.

society in all respects, there are still a significant number of people living in poverty, particularly in impoverished regions. Therefore, there is an urgent need to prioritize development-oriented poverty alleviation efforts to ensure that these vulnerable populations are not left behind.[62] It is crucial to recognize that China's poverty alleviation efforts have entered the final stage, which requires greater determination, clearer thinking, more precise measures, and extraordinary efforts to achieve the target. Winning the battle against poverty has become a significant task in achieving the goal of building a moderately prosperous society in all respects.

Currently, China is in a historical period of building a moderately prosperous society in all respects and embarking on a new journey of modernization. The measures of targeted poverty alleviation and urban–rural integration guided by the idea of common prosperity are the key components in achieving the goal of building a moderately prosperous society. In turn, building a moderately prosperous society is a critical step toward achieving common prosperity. These two are mutually reinforcing and interdependent, with common prosperity providing direction and strategic guidance to the goal of building a moderately prosperous society. Therefore, it is only by upholding the concept of common prosperity to guide the construction of a moderately prosperous society that we can make it more consistent with the great practice of socialism with Chinese characteristics and truly achieve comprehensive well-being for all people.

---

[62] In reference to Learning from Jiao Yulu: The duties of a county party secretary with party, people, responsibility, and vigilance in mind. *People's Daily*, January 13, 2015.

Chapter 8

Adhering to the Direction of the Socialist Market Economy Reform

The development of socialist market economy stands as a pioneering achievement in the CPC's pursuit of building a socialist economy. It represents both a practical exploration and a theoretical innovation, reflecting the CPC's deepened understanding of the laws governing socialist construction. In his significant address commemorating the 95th anniversary of the CPC's founding, Xi Jinping emphasized, "We must maintain a focus on economic system reform and steadfastly uphold the path of reform for a socialist market economy."

1. Practical Exploration and Basic Experience in the Socialist Market Economy Reform

On December 31, 2012, when presiding over the second collective study of the Political Bureau of the 18th Central Committee, Xi Jinping pointed out, "To effectively implement the major initiatives for reform and opening-up established at the 18th National Congress of the Communist Party of China, it is essential to conduct a comprehensive review and in-depth analysis of the reform and opening-up process. This entails gaining a profound understanding of the historical necessity, discerning the underlying patterns, and embracing the significant responsibility of deepening these transformative efforts."

1.1. *Practical exploration of socialist market economy reform*

Since the publication of Mao Zedong's work *On the Ten Major Relationships* in 1956, there have been continuous explorations of economic reforms in the management system by the Party Central Committee and the central government. However, the real economic reform began at the Third Plenary Session of the 11th CPC Central Committee. The Third Plenary Session of the 11th CPC Central Committee made a strategic decision to shift the focus of the entire Party's work to economic construction and issued a mobilization order for revolutionary reform. Although this plenary session did not specifically propose goals for the reform of economic forms and systems, it has already established guidelines, basic tasks, and basic requirements for the reform. The Communiqué of the Third Plenary Session of the 11th CPC Central Committee emphasized that achieving the four modernizations necessitates a significant increase in productivity, which, in turn, requires the transformation of production relations, superstructure, and all incompatible management, activities, and ideological approaches that hinder the development of productivity. It was recognized as a comprehensive and profound revolution.[1]

From the perspective of its essence and development trend, China's economic system reform since the Third Plenary Session of the 11th Central Committee of the Communist Party of China has gradually developed toward a socialist market economy from the beginning. In the practice of reform, the CPC has gradually formed the theory of socialist market economy through continuous summary. At the end of 1978, the Third Plenary Session of the 11th Central Committee of the Communist Party of China reestablished the ideological line of emancipating the mind and seeking truth from facts, providing an important ideological foundation for reform and opening-up. In 1982, the 12th National Congress of the Communist Party of China officially recognized the important role of market regulation in the development of the national economy, proposing that "the planned economy should be given priority to, and market regulation should be supplemented." In 1984, the *Decision of the Central Committee of the Communist Party of China on Economic System Reform* adopted at the Third Plenary Session of the 12th Central Committee of the Communist Party of China clearly stated that the socialist economy is a planned commodity economy based on public ownership. In 1987, the report of the 13th National Congress of the Communist Party of China

[1]Party Literature Research Center of the CPC Central Committee (Ed.). (1987). *Selected Important Documents since the Third Plenary Session of the 11th CPC Central Committee*, Vol. I. People's Publishing House, p. 4.

further stated that the full development of the commodity economy is an insurmountable stage in China's economic development. The socialist planned commodity economy system should be an inherently unified system of planning and market. On this issue, it is necessary to clarify several basic concepts. First, the essential difference between a socialist commodity economy and a capitalist commodity economy lies in the difference in the basis of ownership. Second, planning must be based on the laws of commodity exchange and value. Third, the scope of action of both the plan and the market covers the entire society. "The new economic operation mechanism should, on the whole, be a mechanism in which the state regulates the market and the market guides enterprises."[2] All of these can be seen as a transition from a planned economy to a socialist market economy, both in theoretical understanding and in reform practice.

On June 9, 1992, Comrade Jiang Zemin clearly stated in his speech at the provincial and ministerial level cadre training class of the Central Party School of the Communist Party of China: "After more than ten years of exploration and summary of domestic and foreign experience, our understanding of the establishment of a new socialist economic system in theory and practice has become relatively mature... I think socialist market economic system can be accepted by most cadres and the masses."[3] Comrade Jiang Zemin pointed out in the report of the 14th National Congress of the Communist Party of China that reform is a great revolution. "It is not a minor repair of the original economic system, but a fundamental transformation of the economic system." Comrade Jiang Zemin officially announced, "The goal of economic system reform is to establish and improve the socialist market economic system based on adhering to public ownership and distribution according to work as the main body, supplemented by other economic components and distribution methods."[4] From then on, China's economic reform continues to advance along the goal of establishing a socialist market economy.

---

[2]Party Literature Research Center of the CPC Central Committee (Ed.). (1991). *Selected Important Documents since the 13th CPC National Congress*, Vol. I. People's Publishing House, p. 27.

[3]*Ibid.,* 1993, p. 2073.

[4]Party Literature Research Center of the CPC Central Committee (Ed). (1996). *Selected Important Documents since the 14th CPC National Congress*, Vol. I. People's Publishing House, p. 3, 11.

Building upon the progress of the socialist market economy, the 15th, 16th, 17th, and 18th National Congresses of the CPC have consistently reviewed and summarized new reform experiences, developed fresh insights, and enriched the theory of the socialist market economy. According to the report of the 15th National Congress of the CPC, constructing a socialist economy with Chinese characteristics entails, "Fostering a market economy within socialist conditions, continuously emancipating and advancing the productive forces. This objective necessitates upholding and improving the fundamental economic system of socialist public ownership as the principal component, while also fostering the common development of diverse ownership economies. It further requires the maintenance and improvement of the socialist market economic system, ensuring that the market assumes a fundamental role in resource allocation under national macroeconomic control. The Congress also emphasized the importance of adhering to and improving the distribution system based on work as the primary principle, allowing certain regions and individuals to prosper first, encouraging their subsequent progress, and gradually achieving common prosperity. Moreover, it highlighted the significance of upholding and enhancing openness and actively engaging in international economic cooperation and competition. These efforts aim to sustain, expedite, and foster the sound development of the national economy, thus enabling the people to share the benefits of economic prosperity."[5] During the 16th National Congress of the CPC, a new consensus was reached, asserting that the development of the socialist market economy must embody the principles of "two unwavering" and "one unity." According to the requirements of liberating and developing the productive forces, the 16th National Congress of the CPC put forward three basic views on upholding and improving the basic economic system with public ownership as the main body and multiple ownership economies developing together. First, it is necessary to unswervingly consolidate and develop the public ownership economy. Second, we must unswervingly encourage, support, and guide the development of the non-public sector of the economy. Third, upholding public ownership as the main body, promoting the development of the non-public sector of the economy, and integrating them into the process of socialist modernization

[5]Party Literature Research Center of the CPC Central Committee (Ed.). (2000). *Selected Important Documents since the 15th CPC National Congress*, Vol. I. People's Publishing House, p. 18.

cannot be opposed. The 17th National Congress of the CPC pointed out that to promote sound and rapid development of the national economy, "the key is to make significant progress in accelerating the transformation of the economic development mode and improving the socialist market economic system... It is necessary to deepen the understanding of the laws of the socialist market economy, better play the fundamental role of the market in resource allocation from the institutional perspective, and form a macro regulatory system conducive to scientific development."[6] The 18th National Congress of the CPC has set the goal of comprehensively building a moderately prosperous society and comprehensively deepening reform and opening-up. It emphasizes that we must use greater political courage and wisdom to seize the opportunity to deepen reform in important fields, resolutely eliminate all ideological and institutional shortcomings that hinder scientific development, and build a systematic, scientific, standardized, and effective institutional system to make various systems more mature and stereotyped. We should assign the market to the fundamental role in resource allocation to a greater extent and a wider range.

Since the 18th National Congress of the CPC, under the leadership of the Party Central Committee with Xi Jinping at its core, a series of scientific assessments and significant reform plans have been put forward for China's socialist market economy. The proposal to establish a socialist market economy system as a reform objective represents a major theoretical and practical innovation by our Party in the construction of socialism with Chinese characteristics. It addresses a longstanding challenge that has remained unresolved in other socialist countries worldwide. In the new historical period, the main issues facing China's reform efforts revolve around the incomplete soundness of the market system and its insufficient development. Specifically, the relationship between the government and the market has not been adequately clarified, and numerous constraints still limit the market's effective role in resource allocation. Therefore, it is imperative to work toward the goal of expediting the enhancement of the socialist market economic system. This involves striving to improve the institutional framework that enables the market to assume a decisive role in resource allocation while ensuring that the government functions optimally.

---

[6]Party Literature Research Center of the CPC Central Committee (Ed.). (2009). *Selected Important Documents since the 17th CPC National Congress*, Vol I. Central Party Literature Press, p. 17.

Adhering to the direction of reform toward a socialist market economy is not only a fundamental principle for economic system reform but also a crucial pillar for comprehensive reform. It requires coordinating the advancement of various institutional reforms in this direction and adapting the relevant aspects to the new requirements arising from the development of the socialist market economy.

1.2. *Basic experiences in the socialist market economy reform*

During the second collective study of the 18th Central Political Bureau, chaired by Xi Jinping on December 31, 2012, he provided a comprehensive summary of China's reform and opening-up experience spanning over 30 years. Firstly, he emphasized that reform and opening-up constitute a profound revolution, requiring steadfast adherence to the right direction and progression along the correct path. Secondly, he highlighted that reform and opening-up represent an unparalleled endeavor, necessitating the application of the correct methodology and continuous practice and exploration. Thirdly, he emphasized that reform and opening-up are systematic projects that demand comprehensive reform and the coordinated advancement of various reform initiatives. Fourthly, he stressed that stability is a prerequisite for successful reform and opening-up, and thus the unity of reform, development, and stability must be maintained. Lastly, he underscored that reform and opening-up are endeavors for the betterment of the lives of hundreds of millions of people. As such, it is crucial to uphold and respect the pioneering spirit of the people and advance under the leadership of the Party. The Third Plenary Session of the 18th CPC Central Committee summarized the basic experience of the "Four Points of Adherence" from the party's leadership, ideological line, practical subject, and scientific method. Xi Jinping's summary and the summary of the Third Plenary Session of the 18th CPC Central Committee are valuable wealth accumulated by our Party and the people of the whole country in the practice of reform and opening-up and are important guidelines for comprehensively deepening reform at a new starting point in the new historical period.

We must adhere to the leadership of the Party, the direction of reform in the socialist market economy, and the path of development with Chinese characteristics. It is crucial to understand the dual attributes of the socialist market economy. The socialist market economy encompasses both the general attributes of a market economy in terms of resource allocation and the specific attributes shaped by the socialist system. In essence, it is the integration of these general and special attributes, combining the operating mechanism of a market economy with the fundamental socialist system. The direction of reform in the socialist market economy must achieve a dialectical unity between these two aspects. As Comrade Deng Xiaoping said in a speech during his Southern Tour in 1992, "Not adhering to socialism, not carrying out reform and opening-up, not developing the economy, and not improving the people's lives can only be a dead end."[7] During the nearly 40 years of reform and opening-up, our Party has firmly grasped the correct direction of reform and opening-up, and modernization construction, always maintaining a clear political mind, and being able to identify and correct problems in a timely manner, so that it can continuously make new achievements. Former socialist countries such as the Soviet Union initiated reforms earlier than China, but their reform direction was misguided, leading to failure in improving and developing socialism and ultimately causing the demise of the socialist cause. It is essential to maintain a clear understanding of this matter. In his speech at the APEC Business Leaders Summit on October 7, 2013, Xi Jinping pointed out that "China, being a large country, must avoid making fundamental mistakes that could be subversive. Once such mistakes occur, they cannot be reversed or remedied. Our position is to be bold and steady, engaging in explorations and initiatives, while also being cautious and carefully considering actions."[8] Xi Jinping emphasized that "the crux of the matter lies in determining what should and should not be changed. There are aspects that cannot be changed, not only at present but also in the future."[9] This includes the fundamental principles and program of socialism with Chinese characteristics. We must strengthen our political determination, adhere to political principles and bottom lines, and always maintain confidence in the path, theory, and system of socialism with Chinese characteristics. We must never make subversive mistakes on fundamental issues.

We must adhere to the principles of emancipating the mind, seeking truth from facts, and basing our actions on reality, in order to continually

---

[7] *Selected Works of Deng Xiaoping*, Vol. 3. People's Publishing House, 1993, p. 370.

[8] *Xi Jinping: The Governance of China*. Foreign Languages Press, 2014, p. 348.

[9] *Excerpts from Xi Jinping's Discourse on Comprehensively Deepening Reform*. Central Party Literature Press, 2014, p. 15.

promote theoretical and practical innovation in the socialist market economy. Since the initiation of reform and opening-up, we have consistently followed the Marxist ideological line, emphasizing the need to liberate our thinking and derive knowledge from real-world experiences. Through continuous reflection on the vast practice of reform and opening-up and listening to the voices of the people, we have constantly generated new insights and theoretical advancements, providing essential guidance for the ongoing process of reform and opening-up. Deng Xiaoping's theory, the "Three Represents" important thought, and the scientific outlook on development represent the significant achievements and theoretical advancements resulting from the continuous innovation in China's socialist market economy practice. Under the leadership of the Party Central Committee with Xi Jinping at its core, a significant struggle with distinct historical characteristics has been undertaken, accompanied by theoretical innovations derived from new practices and practical implementations guided by new theoretical achievements. The Third Plenary Session of the 18th CPC Central Committee explicitly called for the further emancipation of the mind, the liberation and development of social productive forces, and the enhancement of social vitality. By embracing an open-minded approach, liberating and stimulating the social productive forces, and promoting innovation in economic practices, we can effectively drive healthy and sustainable economic and social development. It is the responsibility of Party cadres at all levels to take the lead in freeing their minds, breaking through ideological barriers, and challenging entrenched interests. As long as an idea or action contributes to the liberation and development of social productive forces, promotes the well-being and fundamental interests of the vast majority of people, and fosters a healthy and sustainable socioeconomic environment, it is necessary to courageously engage in both theoretical and practical innovation.

We must adhere to the people-centered development philosophy, respect the dominant position of the people, and firmly rely on the people to promote reform. The people are the masters of our country, the practical subject of reform and opening-up, and the fundamental force in promoting economic and social development. Since the reform and opening-up, our Party has always adhered to the mass line of doing everything for the masses, relying on them in every task, carrying out the principle of from the masses, to the masses. We consider the support, happiness, and satisfaction of the people as the starting point and ultimate goal in formulating various reform policies. The "three benefits" principle has served as a fundamental criterion for assessing the success of our reform efforts, enabling us to promote the development of the reform and opening-up through the innovative practices of the people. People-centered development must permeate all aspects of economic and social progress. We must align with the people's aspirations for a better life, continually safeguard and enhance the fundamental interests of the vast majority. By deepening reforms and fostering innovation, we can enhance the quality and efficiency of economic development and continuously meet the growing material and cultural needs of the people.

In the development of the socialist market economy, we have always adhered to the correct handling of the relationship between reform, development, and stability. The socialist market economy is a great pioneering cause in China, which has been continuously advanced through reform and opening-up. In the timely and orderly promotion of reform and opening-up, the key is to grasp the coordination and unity of the intensity of reform, the speed of development, and the degree of social affordability, promote reform and development on the premise of maintaining social and political stability, respect the initiative of the masses in the process of reform and development, care for the vital interests of the masses, maintain social and political stability, and form an ideological consensus and strong motivation for promoting reform throughout the society, Achieve stable and coordinated development of the socialist market economy.

2. Basic Characteristics of Socialist Market Economy

The theory of socialist market economy is the basic content of socialist political economics with Chinese characteristics. Since the Third Plenary Session of the 11th Central Committee, our party has amalgamated the foundational principles of Marxist political economics with the novel experiences of reform and opening-up, thereby forging a notable theoretical advancement within contemporary Marxist political economics. Following the 18th National Congress of the CPC, Xi Jinping has put forth a series of crucial statements on the socialist market economy, which bear significant guiding implications for comprehending the fundamental features of the socialist market economy and steadfastly adhering to the path of reform in this domain.

2.1. *The socialist market economy is based on the basic economic system*

The *Decision of the CCCPC on Major Issues Concerning Comprehensively Deepening Reform* adopted at the Third Plenary Session of the 18th Central Committee highlighted, "The basic economic system with public ownership as the mainstay and multiple ownership economies developing together is an important pillar of the socialist system with Chinese characteristics and the foundation of the socialist market economic system."[10]

Developing a market economy under socialist conditions is an unprecedented great transformation and unprecedented innovation. Before the 1980s, the market economies that existed in human history were all market economies based on private ownership. In the market-oriented reform of socialist countries, the main basis for believing that socialism and market economy cannot be combined is that market economy must be based on private ownership. In the traditional socialist concept, socialism implements a single public ownership system, which of course cannot be combined with a market economy. The conclusion can only be: to adhere to socialism, we cannot engage in a market economy, and to engage in a market economy, we must privatize. The major breakthrough in understanding the market economy lies in proposing that the socialist market economy is basically similar to capitalist society in terms of methods, but our market economy is combined with the basic socialist system.

What serves as the foundation for the amalgamation of the fundamental socialist system, particularly the basic economic system, with the market economy, and how can this integration be achieved? To address this inquiry, it is imperative not only to revisit the fundamental theories of Marxism but also to reassess the essential attributes of socialism in the Chinese context. In light of this, during the collective study of the Political Bureau of the CCCPC, Xi Jinping emphasized the need to "adhere to the direction of socialist market economy reform, apply dialectical and dual-point theories, persistently strive to harmonize the basic socialist system with the market economy, and fully leverage the strengths of both."[11] This directive not only underscores practical

---

[10] Party Literature Research Center of the CPC Central Committee (Ed.). (2014). *Selected Important Documents since the 18th CPC National Congress*, Vol. I. Central Party Literature Press, pp. 514–515.

[11] Based on China's realities and development practices, advance Marxist political economics in contemporary China. *People's Daily*, November 25, 2015.

requirements but also represents a guiding principle for fostering theoretical innovation within the realm of socialist political economics with distinct Chinese characteristics.

The conventional interpretation of Marx's view on the origins of commodity production in a market economy attributes it to the social division of labor and private ownership. However, we contend that this interpretation deviates from Marx's original intention. In the second chapter of the first volume of *Das Kapital*, Marx delves into the historical process of commodity production. He pointed out: "Commodity exchange begins at the end of a community, at the place where they come into contact with other communities or their members. However, once things become commodities externally, due to the reaction, they also become commodities in the internal life of the community."[12] Marx's term "community" here refers to the primitive commune. At this time, private ownership did not appear, how can the reason for the emergence of goods be attributed to private ownership? In fact, the fundamental reason why products exchanged between different communes become commodities, as Marx said, is that although they are all public-owned units, they are different stakeholders. Commodity production is an inevitable economic form of labor exchange between different interest entities under the conditions of social division of labor. Different interest subjects can be different private owners or different owners, including the exchange between private and private ownership, the exchange between public and private ownership, the exchange between state-owned and collective ownership within public ownership, and the differences within the same ownership.

Classic Marxist writers hold a negative attitude toward the combination of socialism and market economy. Because the new society they envisioned was based on the highly developed capitalist productive forces, and there were no differences in interests among various economic entities, thus there was no "free association" of commodity currency relations. And China's socialism is a socialism with Chinese characteristics established in a specific environment on the basis of backward productive forces. The basic economic system of socialism with Chinese characteristics is based on public ownership as the main body and the common development of various forms of ownership. In this society, there must be differences in interests between different forms of ownership and within public ownership. As different stakeholders, the exchange of labor

[12]*Collected Works of Marx and Engels*, Vol. 5. People's Publishing House, 2009, p. 107.

between them is inevitably a commodity exchange, and the economic activities linked by commodity exchange are also necessarily market economies. Therefore, the combination of market economy and socialism is actually the combination of market economy and socialism with Chinese characteristics. Under the conditions of socialism with Chinese characteristics, the combination of market economy and socialist basic economic system is manifested in two aspects. The first is the combination of different ownership economies under the condition of public ownership as the main body. The second is the combination of different forms of implementation within public ownership. The former combination is mainly achieved through the development of a mixed ownership economy formed by multiple ownership economies; The latter combination is mainly achieved through the reform of the property rights system of state-owned enterprises, vigorously developing a mixed public ownership economy formed by multiple internal property rights of enterprises with mutual participation of state-owned capital, collective capital, and non-public capital. Based on this, the "Decision" passed at the Third Plenary Session of the 18th Central Committee of the Communist Party of China pointed out that the mixed ownership economy is an important form of realizing the basic economic system. At the same time, the dominant position of public ownership cannot be shaken, and the dominant position of the state-owned economy cannot be shaken. This is an institutional guarantee to ensure that all ethnic groups in China share the fruits of development, and also an important guarantee to consolidate the Party's ruling position and adhere to China's socialist system.

According to this requirement, the direction of China's market-oriented reform must be unwavering. The market-oriented reform must develop diverse forms of ownership, but it cannot implement complete privatization. State-owned enterprises must deepen reform, but the purpose of the reform is not to weaken or "de-nationalize," but to establish a Modern Property Rights System that meets the requirements of the market economy, transform state-owned asset management into state-owned capital management, and achieve the preservation and appreciation of state-owned capital in a dynamic manner. Through reform, we will firmly grasp the control of the national economy in our own hands, and on this basis, we will further let the non-public sector of the economy continue to develop and grow. We will open up the entry barriers for industries and open up all areas that do not explicitly prohibit the entry of the non-public sector of the economy, including infrastructure construction and the public sector, so that all labor, knowledge, technology, management, and capital can burst into vitality. Let all sources of creating social wealth flow fully and let development achievements benefit all people more and more fairly.

2.2. *The socialist market economy is centered around correctly handling the relationship between the government and the market*

In his explanation of the "Decision" passed at the Third Plenary Session of the 18th CPC Central Committee of China, Xi Jinping pointed out that making the market play a decisive role in resource allocation and better playing the role of the government is a major theoretical viewpoint proposed in this plenary session decision and a major innovative achievement in Marxist political economics.

Properly handling the relationship between the government and the market poses a theoretical challenge that Western countries confront when developing modern market economies. Similarly, it constitutes a pivotal concern in China's reform of its socialist market economy system. How can this intricate issue be addressed? When considering the respective roles of the market and the government, it is essential to recognize that their functions are not mutually exclusive, but rather interconnected. The market's decisive role in resource allocation cannot be detached from or positioned in opposition to the government's role. Likewise, attempts to enhance the government's effectiveness should not aim to supplant or undermine the market's indispensable role in resource allocation.

Some people believe that the market determines resource allocation is the basic viewpoint of Western economics, and to play a decisive role in resource allocation, it is to guide China's economic system reform according to the theories of Western economics. This understanding is one-sided and incorrect. The market determines the allocation of resources is the general law of market economy, which is the law of value. Engels pointed out that "the law of value is the basic law of commodity production."[13] Marx has already made a penetrating analysis of the decisive role of the law of value in resource allocation, and the analysis is more comprehensive and profound than that of Western economics. Western economics

[13] *Ibid.*, Vol. 9, p. 329.

analyzes the surface of the market, while Marx analyzes the intrinsic relationships within the market. Marx's theory that the market determines resource allocation can be briefly summarized as follows: firstly, by determining the value of the same commodity based on the requirements of social necessary labor time, the difference between individual values and social values is formed, promoting the competition of survival of the fittest in the same department to compete for excess profits, and concentrating resource allocation toward advantageous enterprises; secondly, by fluctuating prices around value, the difference between price and value is formed, regulating the distribution of social resources among different departments; thirdly, promoting the continuous transfer of social resources from departments with low profit margins to departments with high profit margins through the averaging of profit margins, and promoting the rationalization and advancement of industrial structure; Fourthly, the role of the second meaning of social necessary labor time determined by value ("not only does it use necessary labor time for each commodity, but also only a necessary proportion of labor time is used for different types of commodities in the total social labor time."[14]) is to establish the allocation of social resources on the basis of the law of proportional distribution of social labor, thus achieving the rational allocation of social resources and the overall improvement of social and economic benefits. According to Marx's analysis, the process of market determining resource allocation is essentially a process that plays a decisive role in resource allocation through the interaction of competition, price, and supply and demand. According to Xi Jinping, "the most efficient form of resource allocation is through the market. The allocation of resources by the market is a fundamental principle of market economies. The essence of a market economy lies in the market-determined allocation of resources. A well-functioning socialist market economy system must adhere to this principle."[15]

To leverage the decisive role of the market in resource allocation is not to adopt the policy proposition of neoliberal markets being omnipotent and denying government regulation. The market is not omnipotent, and the allocation of resources in the market itself has spontaneity, blindness, and lag. Even developed Western countries, given the negative effects of a free market economy, have long abandoned the concept of market omnipotence and have proposed and implemented government

---

[14]*Ibid.*, Vol. 7, p. 716.

[15]Party Literature Research Center of the CPC Central Committee (2014), *Op. cit.*, p. 499.

intervention and regulation. After World War II, capitalist countries such as France, Japan, and South Korea implemented economic planning, and Germany implemented "social market economy," all of which were using the "visible hand" to guide the "invisible hand," and using the role of the government to make up for market failure. Therefore, the market plays a decisive role in resource allocation, not all of it. As a socialist country, through effective government governance and scientific macroeconomic regulation, it is an inherent requirement for China's socialist market economy system to combine the "visible hand" and the "invisible hand" more reasonably, perfectly, and effectively. Xi Jinping emphasized that China implements a socialist market economy system, and in the process of resource allocation determined by the market, we still need to adhere to the superiority of our socialist system and the positive role of the Party and government.

As an envoy of people's power and a manager of socioeconomic activities, the most important function of the Chinese government is to guide the direction of market and socioeconomic development from the overall and long-term interests of society, allocate important resources from the macro level and overall development, promote overall economic balance, provide public goods and services, ensure public safety, strengthen social construction and environmental protection, ensure fair competition, and strengthen market supervision, maintain market order, promote social fairness and justice, and gradually realize common prosperity. At present, China's market economy is in a special historical development period. On the one hand, there is a serious surplus of outdated production capacity, and on the other hand, there is a serious shortage of public goods that the people need. And these problems are difficult to solve solely by relying on the market. The government should take the initiative to eliminate backward production capacity, develop emerging industries, and increase new effective supply so as to achieve stable economic growth under the New Normal. However, government intervention in the market economy is ultimately a subjective behavior of people. Although this "visible hand" is indispensable, it also has limitations in information acquisition and cognitive abilities, and even leads to "rent-seeking" behavior. Therefore, it is necessary to deepen the reform of the government itself, scientifically limit the scope and methods of the government's role and standardize the rule of law.

To properly handle the relationship between the government and the market and deepen economic system reform, we must start from two aspects. On the one hand, we must promote reforms in related fields around more respect for market laws and enhancing market vitality, further streamline administration and delegate power, significantly reduce the direct allocation of resources by the government, accelerate the improvement of the modern market system, and truly enable the market to play a decisive role in resource allocation. On the other hand, it is necessary to promote reforms in related fields around better playing the role of the government and improving government efficiency, effectively transforming government functions, deepening financial and tax system reform, improving the macroeconomic regulation system, optimizing government organizational structure, and better integrating the role of the government and the role of the market.

2.3. *The socialist market economy aims to achieve shared development*

Shared development is the essential requirement of socialism with Chinese characteristics and the fundamental goal of the development of socialist market economy. China is a developing country, and development is the absolute principle. Achieving rapid economic development through a market economy is an inevitable choice in the primary stage of socialism in China. However, the main solution of a market economy is the issue of development motivation, which is difficult to solve the issues of fairness and sharing of development achievements. Even Western scholars do not deny this. As Samuelson clearly pointed out in his book *Economics*, "We must not be overly obsessed with the beauty of market mechanisms — think they are perfect themselves." "Defenders and critics of price mechanisms should recognize that efficient market systems can generate great inequality."[16] Only under socialist conditions can the superiority of market economies be combined with the superiority of socialist systems; only by implementing a socialist market economy can we ensure both the high efficiency of economic development and the sharing of the achievements of economic development among the people. Marx and Engels have repeatedly pointed out that only in the future society can "everyone enjoy the welfare created by everyone together,"[17] and

[16]Paul Samuelson. *Economics (Part 1)*. China Development Press, 1995, p. 78, 83.
[17]*Collected Works of Marx and Engels*, Vol. 1. People's Publishing House, 2009, p. 689.

"production will be aimed at the prosperity of all people."[18] Deng Xiaoping also repeatedly stressed that "one public ownership is the mainstay, and one common prosperity is the fundamental principle of socialism that we must adhere to"[19]; The prosperity of socialism is the common prosperity of the whole people, that is, shared development.

Since the reform and opening-up, in the process of the continuous development of the socialist market economy, the CPC Central Committee has formed a series of major strategic ideas around shared development, including taking the road of common prosperity, developing for the people, relying on the people for development, and sharing the fruits of development with the people. Since the 18th CPC National Congress in 2012, Xi Jinping has further deepened and expanded the ideological connotation of shared development. He proposed that putting people first and doing everything for the well-being of the people is an unshakable goal of China's economic development. Continuously improving the people's living standards on the basis of economic development is the fundamental goal of all work of the Party and the state. The ultimate test of the effectiveness of all our work depends on whether the people have truly benefited and whether their lives have truly improved. This is the essential requirement of adhering to the principle of remaining loyal to the Party and faithful to the people, and it is an important guarantee for the continuous development of the Party and the people's cause.[20]

Xi Jinping's series of important speeches on shared development were elevated to the ballast and ultimate goal of the five major development concepts in the "Recommendations" of the Fifth Plenary Session of the 18th CPC Central Committee. Obviously, among the five development concepts, we should innovate to solve the problem of development impetus, coordinate to solve the problem of unbalanced development, green to solve the problem of harmony between man and nature, open to solve the problem of internal and external linkage of development and share to solve the problem of common prosperity. So, for whom to innovate? For whom to coordinate? For whom is harmony with nature? For whom? Ultimately, it is all for everyone in China to share the fruits of development.

[18] *Ibid.*, Vol. 8, p. 200.

[19] *Ibid.*, p. 172.

[20] Planning for poverty alleviation and development in the thirteenth five-year plan period to ensure rural poor will be lifted out of poverty as scheduled by 2020. *People's Daily*, June 20, 2015.

Xi Jinping's shared development ideology further clarifies the essential requirements and fundamental objectives of the development of socialist market economy and is a further enhancement and important development of the Marxist political economics and our party's development concept.

In short, developing a socialist market economy is a great cause for billions of people in China. Only by having a clear understanding of the basic characteristics of a socialist market economy can we ensure the correct direction of economic system reform and smoothly achieve the "two centennial goals" of building a moderately prosperous society in all respects and the great rejuvenation of the Chinese nation.

3. The Laws and Mechanisms of Socialist Market Economy

On July 8, 2014, Xi Jinping pointed out at the Economic Situation Symposium that "Party committees and governments at all levels should learn and use political economics well, consciously understand and better follow the laws of economic development, continuously improve the ability and level to promote reform and opening-up, lead economic and social development, and improve the quality and efficiency of economic and social development."[21]

3.1. *Basic economic laws of socialist market economy*

Socialism and market economy are an organic unity, and as an organic whole, they must have their own basic economic laws. They reflect the most essential relationship of socialist market economy, determine the essence and basic characteristics of socialist market economy development, and determine all major aspects and processes of socialist market economy development.

Deng Xiaoping pointed out that "the essence of socialism is to liberate the productive forces, develop them, eliminate exploitation, eliminate polarization, and finally achieve common prosperity."[22] This scientific conclusion of Deng Xiaoping not only reflects the dialectical unity of productive forces and relations of production but also reflects the

---

[21] Better understanding and following the laws of economic development to promote the sustainable and healthy development of China's economy. *People's Daily*, July 9, 2014.

[22] *Selected Works of Deng Xiaoping*, Vol. 3. People's Publishing House, 1993, p. 373.

dialectical unity of the purpose of socialist production and the means to achieve the goal. Deng Xiaoping believed that planned economy is not an essential feature of socialism. He pointed out that "whether there is more planning or more market is not the essential difference between socialism and capitalism. A planned economy is not equal to socialism, as capitalism also has plans; a market economy is not equal to capitalism, as socialism also has markets. Both plans and market are economic means."[23] This fundamentally relieves the ideological constraints of planned economy being equal to socialism and market economy being equal to capitalism. To liberate and develop the productive forces as soon as possible and achieve the goal of common prosperity, we must develop the socialist market economy. Develop the socialist market economy, constantly liberate and develop the social productive forces, and ultimately achieve common prosperity. This is the basic economic law of socialist market economy.

In the socialist market economy, the working people are the true subjects of the development of the market economy. The underlying rationale for the existence of the Chinese market economy stems from the essential fact that the independent economic interests of the general public, along with the resulting independent economic activities, and serve as the driving force and wellspring of social and economic progress. This serves as the internal impetus for the continuous enhancement of social and economic efficiency. The people, through their pursuit of a more prosperous and civilized life, wholeheartedly demonstrate their intellect and creativity, constantly infusing society and the economy with vitality. This dynamic force lies at the core of China's economic prosperity and modernization. The primary objective of economic development is to achieve common prosperity for all individuals, allowing them to realize their self-worth and foster comprehensive and unrestricted personal growth through employment and entrepreneurship.

The purpose of developing a socialist market economy is to continuously improve and meet people's needs for material and cultural life. In general, production plays a decisive role in consumption, but the ultimate goal of human society's production is to meet people's consumption needs. After the original consumption needs are met, new consumption needs will arise, requiring the production of updated products. The continuous pursuit of consumer demand by people requires the continuous

---

[23] *Ibid.*

development of social production. In socialist society, Engels once pointed out that "through socialized production, it is not only possible to ensure that all members of society have a prosperous and increasingly abundant material life, but also to ensure that their physical and intellectual abilities are fully and freely developed and utilized."[24] Lenin also believed that for the purpose of socialist production, it is not enough to only mention "to meet social needs" and "to ensure the welfare of all members of society." Instead, it should mention "the highest welfare and comprehensive and coordinated improvement of material life,"[25] or "to ensure the full welfare and free comprehensive development of all members of society."[26] Xi highlighted, "Common prosperity represents a fundamental objective of Marxism and has been a longstanding aspiration among the Chinese people. In line with the ideas of Marx and Engels, a communist society aims to eliminate class conflicts and disparities, urban–rural divides, and the distinction between mental and manual labor. It strives to establish a system of distribution based on individual abilities and needs, ensuring genuine social sharing and the free and comprehensive development of all individuals. However, realizing this vision requires a lengthy historical process. China, currently in the primary stage of socialism, will remain in this stage for a significant period. While we must respect the limitations imposed by this stage, it does not imply inaction or a lack of effort in progressively achieving common prosperity. Instead, we should strive to make feasible advancements within the existing conditions. Through a step-by-step approach, we can implement development centered on the people, accumulating small victories that lead to significant achievements, and continuously progress toward the goal of common prosperity for all."[27] "The people, as the main drivers of development, stand to gain the most from its fruits. Guided by a development philosophy that prioritizes the well-being of the people and the promotion of comprehensive human development, we must place enhancing people's welfare and advancing their holistic growth at the forefront of our development endeavors."[28]

---

[24] *Collected Works of Marx and Engels*, Vol. 3. People's Publishing House, 2009, pp. 563–564.

[25] *The Complete Works of Lenin*, Vol. 6. People's Publishing House, 1986, p. 188.

[26] *Ibid.*, p. 413.

[27] *General Secretary Xi Jinping Important Speech Series* (2016 Edition). Learning Publishing House and People's Publishing House, 2016, p. 129.

[28] *Ibid.*, p. 128.

The means to achieve the goal of socialist production is to continuously liberate and develop social productive forces. The market economy is by far the most effective mode of production for liberating and developing productive forces in human society. The market economy can save economic resources and labor consumption, mobilize people to work diligently from their concern for their own interests, continuously improve work efficiency and economic benefits, and continuously promote social and technological progress on this basis. The tremendous achievements of China's reform and opening-up have fully demonstrated the insurmountable and irreplaceable historical role of the market economy in the development of modern economy and society. Only by developing a socialist market economy can we continuously liberate and develop productive forces. This is the historic conclusion drawn from China's reform and opening-up process, and it is a fundamental principle that we must unwaveringly adhere to.

3.2. *The main tasks of advancing the socialist market economy reform*

To advance the socialist market economy reform, we must continue to deepen the reform of state-owned enterprises. State-owned enterprises are the backbone of China's national economy. The reform of state-owned enterprises has always been the central link and top priority of China's economic system reform. The main problems existing in state-owned enterprises are, at the macro level, the unreasonable structure and layout, and at the micro level, the mismatch between the property organization and management mechanisms of enterprises and the requirements of the market economy. Therefore, we need to continue to adjust the layout and structure of the state-owned economy and reform the state-owned asset management system. The core of state-owned enterprise reform is to establish a modern enterprise system that allows state-owned enterprises to become genuine market participants in competition. At the same time, it should be fully recognized that under the new conditions of China's accession to the World Trade Organization and full participation in economic globalization, China's state-owned enterprises must move from the domestic to the international arena and compete with monopolistic companies on a global scale. This is the second leap achieved in the reform and development of state-owned enterprises in China. The system and operational rules of China's state-owned enterprises, especially large state-owned enterprises, should be in line with international prevailing rules, and compete equally with foreign enterprises in the international market. Their technical level and management level should reach the international level at that time, and their products can enter the international market and occupy a considerable share. From production to sales, from products to capital, cross-border operations can be achieved, and more and more large multinational corporations are ranked at the forefront of the world. This is a very difficult mission and must be achieved through hard work. We must further emancipate our minds, accelerate reform, and double innovation.

To advance the socialist market economy reform, we must accelerate the process of magnetization and establish a sound, unified, open, and competitive modern market system. The market system is the carrier of market mechanism operation, and the establishment of a unified, open, and orderly competitive market system is the foundation for exerting the decisive role of the market in resource allocation. Since the reform and opening-up, China's market system has been continuously developing, and significant progress has been made in both the commodity market and the factor of production market. The market's ability to allocate resources has also been continuously improving. However, so far, China's market system is not yet perfect, and the openness, fairness of competition, and transparency of operation of the market need to be improved. The price relationship between some basic industries and service industries has not been straightened out, especially since the development of factor markets is relatively lagging behind, which is difficult to meet the requirements of achieving stable and healthy socioeconomic development in China under the new conditions. Therefore, firstly, it is necessary to continuously cultivate and improve the market system. The operation of modern market economy objectively requires that all production factors enter the market and accept the effective allocation of market mechanisms. Otherwise, the market is vacant, the operation is not smooth, and resource allocation is ineffective. Labor and capital, as two important factors of production, can only enter the market and flow reasonably in the market to fully exert the overall function of the market mechanism, and improve the efficiency and economic benefits of production and operation. Secondly, create an environment for equal use of production factors by various market entities, and implement negative list access management. The government lists industries, fields, businesses, etc. that are prohibited or restricted from entering, and all areas outside the list can be freely entered, which is known as "nulla poena sine lege." Here, the negative list only focuses on what the enterprise "cannot do," which provides greater space for the market to play a decisive role compared to the positive list that stipulates what the enterprise "can only do." Thirdly, deepen the reform of the circulation system and further streamline the pricing system. At the core of market-determined resource allocation lies the principle of pricing resources based on market mechanisms. Improving the institutional and mechanistic arrangements to facilitate prices primarily determined by the market is an important task in building the market system. The "Decision" passed at the Third Plenary Session of the 18th Central Committee of the Communist Party of China pointed out that everything that can be priced by the market should be handed over to the market, and the government should not interfere improperly. Forming prices through market competition, regulating supply and demand, and optimizing resource allocation are the basic characteristics of a market economy, and are also a concentrated manifestation of the decisive role played by the market in resource allocation. Maximizing the function and role of the market in determining prices does not mean that the government will not intervene at all. For example, government intervention is essential when addressing instances of unfair competition, improper monopoly, counterfeit products, fraudulent practices, and market manipulation. But this behavior is aimed at maintaining market order and enabling the market to play its role in determining prices normally, rather than replacing the role of the market.

To advance the socialist market economy reform, we must further transform government functions and establish and improve a macroeconomic regulation system. China used to have a planned economy system, and an important feature of the planned economy was that the government mainly allocated resources or the administrative allocation of resources. Therefore, in the process of transforming from a planned economy system to a socialist market economy system, it is necessary to solve the problem of how to make the market replace the government and gradually play a decisive role in resource allocation. The key to solving this problem, whether from a theoretical analysis or a practical perspective, lies in the transformation of government functions. Only with the transformation of government functions can China's state-owned enterprises become true market entities. Because in the past, under the long-term planned economy system, the government, as the representative of state-owned enterprise owners, directly intervened in the operation and management of enterprises, managing things that should not be managed. Therefore, many current problems, such as the "three major burdens" problem and the problem of duplicate construction, although manifested in enterprises, are rooted in the government. While challenges persist in the process of separating government from enterprises, such as the enterprises' dependence on the government and their reluctance to separate, the crux of the contradiction and the driving force for change ultimately rest with the government. Only when the government firmly divides and takes the initiative to divide, can the government and enterprises be separated, and state-owned enterprises become truly independent and self-reliant market competition entities. Strengthening and improving macroeconomic regulation mainly lies in government reform. The socialist market economy is an economy with government macroeconomic regulation. In fact, under market economy conditions, the driving force for economic growth and stability is a combination of market mechanism regulation and government macroeconomic regulation, but the two have different positions and perspectives. Therefore, to develop the socialist market economy, we should not only fundamentally change the resource allocation mode dominated by administrative means, but also follow the old path of economic liberalism against government intervention. Under market economy conditions, the government mainly uses economic means such as interest rates, tax rates, and exchange rates to regulate macroeconomic aggregate balance and industrial optimization. At present, the framework of China's macroeconomic regulation system has been preliminarily established and is gradually improving. In the future, we will accelerate the pace of adjustment and improvement based on the new contradictions that arise in various aspects of the macroeconomic regulation system.

To advance the socialist market economy reform, we must establish a robust credit guarantee system and expedite the development of a comprehensive market legal framework. The market economy is a credit economy. The sense of trustworthiness of market entities is the guarantee for the operation and development of the market economy. People cannot stand without faith, businesses cannot thrive without faith, and a country cannot be strong without faith. To maintain the normal operation of the market economy and ensure fair competition and a reasonable flow of resources, there must be scientific and reasonable market rules. This rule includes both laws and regulations, as well as formal and informal industry norms, international practices, and commercial credit. Therefore, it is necessary to accelerate the establishment of a credit guarantee system and the construction of a market legal system, strictly punish such malicious behaviors as counterfeiting, tax evasion, economic fraud, and debt evasion in accordance with the law, strengthen credit awareness throughout society, strengthen moral education of honesty and trustworthiness, and advocate a moral concept of unity of righteousness and profit. In the development of the socialist market economy, promoting adherence to the law and fostering integrity requires not only strengthening educational efforts but also implementing institutional constraints. This entails establishing a sustainable mechanism that incentivizes lawful conduct and discourages non-compliance. The introduction of a unified social credit code system, alongside related real-name registration mechanisms, should be accelerated. The implementation of mobile phone numbers, bank cards, and online real-name systems should also be expedited to eradicate false information both in online and offline domains. Furthermore, it is vital to establish a disciplinary framework that holds accountable those who violate laws and breach their commitments, while concurrently providing incentives to those who honor their promises and penalizing those who fail to do so.

Chapter 9

The Role of the Market and Government in the Socialist Market Economy

Exploring the government–market relationship is a key theoretical aspect of political economics. The fundamental principles of political economics suggest that the commodity economy during China's primary stage of socialism is based on the principle of dominant socialist public ownership. In addition to defending the nation and maintaining domestic security, socialist countries also carry out the political function of leading and managing the economy. The government plays a critical role in regulating the national economy and utilizes the law of value to promote economic growth and efficiency.[1] Under the conditions of a socialist market economy, the government is not only an important political organization but also plays an important role in managing and regulating the economy at the macro level.[2] However, when implementing a market economy, it's important to allow the market to play a key role in regulating the national economy. The aforementioned points provide an essential definition of the relationship between the government and the market under socialism. Since the 18th National Congress of the Communist Party of China was held in 2012, the Party Central Committee led by Comrade Xi Jinping has demonstrated great boldness in theoretical innovation. They have introduced a series of new ideas, concepts, and judgments, including the notion of "market determinism." These new proposals represent a significant improvement in the party's understanding of the laws of the market

[1]Song Tao (Ed.). (2008). *Political Economics Tutorial* (8th Edition). China Renmin University Press, Beijing, p. 259, 369.

[2]Pang Jinju, Hong Yinxing, Lin Gang, Liu Wei (Eds.). (2007). *Political Economics* (3rd Edition). Higher Education Press, p. 404.

economy and also advance our understanding of the relationship between the government and the market to a new level. This development has laid the groundwork for further theoretical exploration and innovation. It has opened up new theoretical domains for constructing political economics of socialism with Chinese characteristics.

1. The Evolution of the CPC's Understanding of the Market's Role

Over the past 30 years, the Communist Party of China has continuously bettered its understanding of the relationship between government and the market while advancing the great cause of socialist reform and opening-up. As a result, a series of historic and significant decisions have been made. In general, scholars in the field of political economics have been consistently examining and investigating the core principles and features of a socialist market economy, particularly the market's responsibility in resource allocation and the function it should play. The CPC's understanding of this issue has evolved through three main stages.

1.1. *The first stage: The market plays a fundamental role under state regulation*

The timeframe of this stage extends from the Third Plenary Session of the 12th Central Committee of the Party up to the Third Plenary Session of the 14th Central Committee, encompassing the 14th National Congress as well. During this period, the Communist Party of China held that "the market plays a fundamental role under the state regulation," placing particular emphasis on the crucial role of state regulation in conjunction with market dynamics. In 1984, the Third Plenary Session of the 12th Central Committee proposed that the socialist market economy system is a planned commodity economy. In 1987, the 13th National Congress introduced the concept of a "socialist commodity economy," which combined planned regulation with market regulation. Although the proposal of a "socialist commodity economy" signaled a shift away from a "state-led plan" and toward "state-indirect regulation," it's important to note that the concept of "state planning" still played a significant role in the Party's understanding of the market's role in resource allocation.

At the time, both the theoretical and policy communities had a vague understanding of the relationship between government and the market. After the proposal of the concept of a "socialist commodity economy," some believed that a planned economy was synonymous with socialism, while others advocated for a return to a primarily planned economy with market regulation as a secondary component. However, Deng Xiaoping's "Southern Tour" speech helped to clarify the direction of China's economic reform and steer it back on course. Subsequently, after a serious review of the past successes and failures of socialist economic construction, the 14th National Congress of the Communist Party of China proposed that "the market plays a crucial role in resource allocation in a socialist state while being under the state's macroeconomic regulation." The Third Plenary Session of the 14th Central Committee then constructed the five pillars of a socialist market economy, which included establishing a modern corporate system, a nationally unified open market system, a robust macroeconomic regulation system, a system for reasonable individual income distribution, and a tiered social security system.

1.2. *The second stage: The market plays a fundamental role in resource allocation*

The timeframe of this stage extends from the Third Plenary Session of the 12th Central Committee to the 18th National Congress of the Communist Party of China. During this period, the party further advanced its comprehension of the market's function in resource allocation and formulated the idea that "the market plays a fundamental role in resource allocation." This proposition highlights the crucial role of the market in resource allocation while acknowledging the significance of macroeconomic regulation by the government in promoting economic and social progress. Overall, this marks a significant step forward in the party's understanding of the relationship between the market and the government.

After operating within the socialist market economy framework for years, as established at the 14th National Congress and the Third Plenary Session of the 14th Central Committee, deeper issues and conflicts gradually surfaced. Addressing these challenges became a major theoretical and practical concern. Several questions arose during this stage, including whether macroeconomic regulation was a prerequisite for resource allocation or an essential aspect of the market economy. Furthermore, did the government's macroeconomic regulation influence resource allocation, or did resources play a role in the market under government guidance? Was the government or the market responsible for resource allocation? Were they government-led or market-led? These questions couldn't be reasonably answered with the previous statement that "the market plays a fundamental role under state regulation," as it didn't reflect reality. As a result, the 16th National Congress proposed to "allow the market to play a more fundamental role in resource allocation." At the 17th Congress, it was suggested to "improve the market's fundamental role in resource allocation through institutional means." Finally, at the 18th Congress, the emphasis was placed on "allowing the market to play a more extensive and broader crucial role in resource allocation." During this learning phase, the party expanded the concept of the socialist market economy to emphasize the market's fundamental role in resource allocation on a larger scale and broader scope. This significantly improved the party's understanding of the market's function.

1.3. *The third stage: The market plays a decisive role in resource allocation*

In November 2013, during the Third Plenary Session of the 18th CPC Central Committee, it was proposed that "the reform of the economic system is at the forefront of wide-ranging and profound changes. The key challenge is to skillfully balance the relationship between government and market, empowering the market to have a decisive impact on resource allocation, while also optimizing the government's role."[3] The transition from the market's previous "fundamental" role to a more "decisive" one, along with the emphasis on enhancing government functions, signifies a fresh perspective in the CPC's approach to the socialist market economy. This change demonstrates a renewed understanding of the government–market relationship and represents a significant advancement in acknowledging the market's role in resource allocation.

The 18th CPC Central Committee's Third Plenary Session not only offered ground-breaking perspectives on the market's decisive role but

[3] Party Literature Research Center of the CPC Central Committee (Ed.). (2014). *Selected Important Documents since the 18th CPC National Congress*, Vol. I. Central Party Literature Press, p. 513.

also distinctly defined the government's functions concerning its relationship with the market. The government is responsible for macroeconomic regulation, market supervision, public services, social management, and environmental protection. In addition, whenever feasible, the government should transfer some of its responsibilities, powers, and decision-making capabilities to the market and non-governmental entities. This allows for greater freedom for various market participants, unleashes their full potential, and fosters the development and engagement of a wide range of social organizations. In a modern market economy, issues such as monopolies, public goods, and information asymmetry can lead to "market failures." In response, the government should actively address these problems and effectively carry out its responsibilities in all relevant areas. Managing the relationship between the government and the market can be summarized in two key points: first, emphasize the market's decisive role in resource allocation, and second, clearly define government functions to better leverage its role. By accomplishing these two key points, the main issue of China's economic system reform—the relationship between government and market—will be effectively resolved.

An analysis of the CPC's evolving understanding of the market's decisive role in resource allocation reveals that recognizing the market's function has always been a crucial aspect of China's reform and opening-up process. The CPC's understanding of implementing a socialist market economy has continually evolved and broadened with the progression of practice. The shift from viewing the market economy as an economic management method to a regulatory tool, and finally as an economic system, as well as the transition from the market's "fundamental" role to a "decisive" one in resource allocation, demonstrates the party's continuous adaptation of its theoretical ideas in response to evolving practical experiences. This evolving theoretical understanding of the market's role in the economy is in line with the scientific method and philosophical concepts of historical materialism and dialectical materialism of Marxism. Overall, the CPC's continuous inheritance, innovation, and development in understanding the market's decisive role has led to the emergence of new theoretical concepts and ideas, which have contributed to the construction of a political economics of socialism with Chinese characteristics. This also highlights the CPC's important characteristic of consistently being able to innovate and develop new theoretical ideas.

2. The General Law of the Market's Decisive Role

Xi Jinping emphasized that "economic system reform remains a key focus of advancing comprehensive reforms, and the core issue of economic system reform is still how to handle the relationship between government and the market."[4] Currently, China's socialist market economy has established its basic framework, and the market now plays a significantly strengthened role in resource allocation. In order to effectively utilize the market's decisive role in resource allocation, it is crucial to fully leverage the crucial effects of price mechanisms, competition mechanisms, and benefit mechanisms. It is vital to uphold free competition in the market and abide by the general laws and basic mechanisms of a market economy.

Generally, there are two methods for resource allocation: planned mechanisms and market mechanisms. Planned mechanisms rely mainly on centralized decision-making as the primary means of resource allocation. However, in modern economic societies, information is always scattered and constantly changing. Therefore, any planned administrative agency cannot fully obtain this dispersed economic information. As a result, under the planned economic system, there will inevitably be a mismatch of resources and low efficiency. In contrast, the market mechanism operates on the basis of price mechanisms or supply and demand mechanisms, competition mechanisms, and incentive mechanisms. It maximizes the freedom of information and decentralizes decision-making, achieving optimal resource allocation, economic prosperity, and national strength, ultimately realizing the goal of becoming an economically strong country.

2.1. *The price mechanism in the decisive role of the market*

To empower the market to play a decisive role in resource allocation, the price mechanism assumes paramount significance. While modern economic theory often distinguishes the "price mechanism" and the "supply and demand mechanism" as two separate market mechanisms, they are inherently interconnected in operation. Consequently, it becomes imperative to elucidate the fusion of these two mechanisms. Specifically, in a modern market economy, the price mechanism operates primarily in the following ways:

---

[4]Party Literature Research Center of the CPC Central Committee (2014), *Op. cit.*, p. 498.

First, the price mechanism is an important tool for achieving free competition. In a market economy with many buyers and sellers, producers of the same product must gain a competitive advantage based on price to capture a larger market share. In a competitive market, for the same product with similar quality and performance, the lower the price, the greater the market demand, and the greater the market share of the product. In order to expand their market share and maintain a competitive edge, producers usually adopt the method of lowering the price. The most effective and important way to lower the price is to reduce production costs, which requires producers to continuously adopt new technologies and introduce new processes to improve management, increase labor productivity, and optimize resource allocation. The result is a reduction in labor costs and an improvement in resource allocation efficiency within enterprises, which contributes to economic prosperity and development.

Second, the price mechanism is an important means of guiding production decisions. The price mechanism plays a crucial role in determining the average profit rate and guiding the allocation of social labor among sectors. The price ratio, which is determined by the price mechanism, serves as a key selection criterion for businesses when deciding which goods or services to produce and how much labor and resources to allocate to each sector. In the process of market economy operation, if the demand for a certain product increases, the supplier will raise the sales price of that product in the short term to increase profits. If the product remains in short supply, society will expand production of that product on a large scale to achieve economies of scale. Conversely, when producers face an oversupply of products and experience low prices or profits, they may respond to market signals by reallocating capital and production factors to products with higher prices and greater profitability. The law of supply and demand is the most important general principle that determines the market's decisive role in modern market economies. In this system, prices are determined by the interplay of supply and demand, with prices adjusting in response to changes in either factor.

Third, the price mechanism serves as an important tool for macroeconomic regulation. The fact that the market plays a decisive role in resource allocation does not mean that the government should do nothing. On the contrary, the government must play a greater role in compensating for market failures and strengthening macroeconomic regulation. In a market economy, the overall price level is an important indicator of social total supply and demand and is also an important basis for national macroeconomic regulation. When the price of a certain commodity changes and indicates a gap in supply and demand, the government can take action. It can use various macroeconomic tools such as interest rates, tax rates, and wages to encourage or induce an expansion or contraction of the production scale of this commodity. By doing so, it guides social resources into or out of this production sector, thus adjusting the overall supply and demand of the commodity. This approach helps to balance overall price levels and increase social productivity, ultimately leading to greater wealth and prosperity for society as a whole.

2.2. *The competitive mechanism in the decisive role of the market*

The competitive mechanism is one of the most important mechanisms in modern market economies and plays a crucial role in determining the value of goods. It is an external, coercive force that drives competition among producers to achieve their economic interests, to secure better sales outlets, and to gain better purchasing conditions for their goods. This competition involves a variety of factors, including the quantity, quality, and variety of goods produced. The fundamental reason why competitive mechanism works is that it enforces the law of "survival of the fittest" in the competition, which is clearly an important way to promote the optimal allocation of resources and economic prosperity.

Competition, as an inherent mechanism of market economy, is mainly determined by two factors. The first factor is the existence of different economic interests between the two parties involved in the competition. The foundation of the market economy is the existence of numerous independent economic entities. All activities of different interest entities are driven by their own interests. Driven by the pursuit of maximizing economic benefits, they will compete fiercely with similar economic entities to achieve an efficient allocation of resources. The second factor is the contradiction between individual labor time and socially necessary labor time that causes competition. Under market economy conditions, different producers who produce the same goods have different technological conditions, labor intensity and skill levels, and management levels, leading to different individual labor costs. However, the value of commodities on the market is determined by the socially necessary labor time, which results in a contradiction between individual labor time and socially necessary labor time, leading to competition among producers in the market. This competition in turn encourages producers to improve production conditions, strengthen management, and increase labor productivity, thereby promoting the overall strength of the economy under the role of the competitive mechanism. There are mainly three types of market competition[5]:

The first type of competition in the market is competition among sellers, or competition among suppliers of the same product. Multiple suppliers offering the same product compete against each other. The supplier that offers the product at the lowest price while maintaining the same level of quality gains a competitive advantage over other sellers. As a result, sellers compete with each other to capture market share and customers, and this competition leads to a reduction in the price of the product they supply. The reduction in the price of the product inevitably weakens the profit margins of the producers. To attain the necessary average profit rate across the entire industry or sector within the given production costs, suppliers must optimize their organizational management processes and techniques and also adopt new technologies and skills to enhance production efficiency and effectiveness. These measures are essential for winning a place in the fierce market competition.

The second type of competition is competition among buyers, also known as buyer competition. In fact, under market economy conditions, not only is there fierce competition among suppliers of goods, but also among demanders, which is an important precondition for the functioning of price and competition mechanisms. In cases where a particular commodity is scarce in the market, buyers will compete to purchase it, which in turn will raise the price of the commodity supplied. This is an important internal mechanism of the law of supply and demand, which states that "supply and demand determine price, and price adjusts supply and demand." Based on this, through the transmission and guidance of price signals, more social resources can be induced to participate in the production of the commodity, thus facilitating the increase of overall economic prosperity. This is an important path for a country to achieve economic strength.

The third type of competition is between buyers and sellers of a commodity. Buyers want to purchase goods at the lowest possible price, while

---

[5] See A.J. Isaacson *et al.* (1996). *Understanding the Market Economy*. Commercial Press.

sellers want to sell them at the highest possible price. The outcome of this competition is determined by the intensity of competition among buyers and sellers. In particular, when competition among buyers is more intense, the situation of "supply shortage" arises, resulting in an increase in the price of the commodity. This price increase acts as an incentive for more producers to invest social resources in the production of the commodity. Conversely, if competition among sellers is more intense, then the commodity is in a state of "supply surplus," resulting in a price decrease and prompting some producers to withdraw social resources from this field and invest in commodities with higher profits, ultimately optimizing resource allocation and significantly increasing the overall wealth of society.

2.3. *The incentive mechanism in the decisive role of the market*

In a market economy, the operation of the incentive mechanism is an essential internal mechanism that stimulates individuals' initiative and creativity, promotes the prosperity and strength of an economy, and serves as a critical market mechanism for a country to achieve economic power. This mechanism refers to the organic connection between the responsibilities, rights, and economic benefits of market transaction participants.[6] In fact, in any economy, the primary issue is how to balance the relationship between individual interests and social interests and guide individual pursuit of self-interest toward the same path as the overall goal of social and economic development. The effective operation of the incentive mechanism ensures that individuals' pursuit of self-interest contributes to the economic and social development of a country, ultimately achieving the strategic goal of economic power.

Undoubtedly, analyzing the incentive mechanism from the perspective of price and competition mechanisms reveals that the incentive mechanism is in fact the fundamental reason for the functioning of these mechanisms. "Supply and demand determine prices, and prices adjust supply and demand." Why does the price mechanism have such an effect? This is because price relationships reflect economic interest relationships among people. Changes in prices not only lead to the flow and

---

[6]See Li Xingshan (Ed.). (2004). *Theory and Practice of Socialist Market Economy*. The Central Party School Press, p. 143.

reconfiguration of resources but also inevitably result in the redistribution of economic interests among various market participants, ultimately achieving the optimal allocation of social resources.

Certainly, the incentive mechanism is what allows the market to attain a "natural order" that balances individual interests and ensures harmony between individual interests and social interests. The market mechanism, known as the "invisible hand," effectively directs the interests, motivations, and behaviors of various parties involved in the exchange, leading people to pursue their own interests while greatly promoting social interests. As a result, a country's economy is ultimately propelled toward prosperity and strength. In essence, the incentive mechanism is the fundamental basis for the functioning of a market economy as it drives individuals to pursue their self-interest, which, in turn, allows the market to operate efficiently.

3. Practical Issues Arising from the Market Mechanism Playing a Decisive Role

Since the 18th National Congress of the Communist Party of China was held, Xi Jinping has delivered a series of important speeches on how to build and develop a socialist market economy, which profoundly addresses a range of major theoretical and practical issues facing the development of the Party and the state under new historical conditions. These speeches are characterized by a strong awareness of problems, a clear problem orientation, a scientific and practical attitude, and a firm Marxist belief and sense of responsibility. Currently, China's socialist market economic system is undergoing a phase of improvement and development. However, the functioning of essential components such as the price mechanism, competition mechanism, and incentive mechanism, which are integral to the construction of a socialist market economy, are not yet fully optimized. There are still problems such as inconsistent market rules, inadequate competition fairness, and misplaced government functions. The theoretical innovation of "making the market play a decisive role in resource allocation" is aimed at solving these problems and fully unleashing the underlying strength, endogenous driving force, and creativity of economic development.

There are three main issues that need to be addressed in order for the market system to function effectively. The first is the need to improve the market system and ensure effective operation of the price mechanism. One of the fundamental principles of a market economy is that "supply and demand determine prices, and prices adjust supply and demand." To ensure optimal resource allocation and achieve Pareto efficiency, a well-functioning market system is necessary. Developing a socialist market economy requires creating a platform for the price mechanism to fully operate, actively improving the modern market system, allowing enterprises to operate independently and compete fairly, enabling consumers to choose and consume freely, and facilitating the free flow and equal exchange of goods and factors. A research team from the China International Economic Exchange Center has noted that while significant progress has been made in building the market system since the establishment of the socialist market economy, there is still a considerable gap between the expected goals of establishing a unified, open, and orderly market system and the current state. The price mechanism is not operating efficiently in some key areas, and further advanced reforms of pricing mechanisms, especially in areas such as water, oil, natural gas, electricity, transportation, and telecommunications, are needed. The development and cultivation of factor markets are necessary conditions for market resource allocation, but the reform of important factor markets in China is still inadequate. There is no unified urban–rural construction land market, the market-oriented mechanism for technology innovation needs improvement, the price system for resource-based products has not been established, the ecological compensation mechanism needs further improvement, and the development of information and labor markets is insufficient. Lastly, a further strengthening of the guiding role of price signals in resource allocation is needed.[7]

Take the financial system as an example. Finance is the lifeblood of economic activities, and a robust and stable financial system is deemed as a fundamental characteristic of a thriving economic power. However, China's financial system still lacks robustness due to factors such as an underdeveloped capital market, insufficient openness in the financial industry, and the accumulation of risks in local government debt. From the perspective of the price mechanism, interest rates are a price signal that reflects the scarcity of capital. Nevertheless, the degree of interest rate liberalization in China still requires further progress. On July 20, 2013, China began to fully lift the control of lending rates for financial

---

[7]See China Center for International Economic Exchanges Research Group. (2013). *Building an Upgraded Version of China's Economy*. People's Publishing House.

institutions and officially launched mechanisms such as centralized quotation and publication of loan base rates to establish a sound market-oriented pricing and self-discipline mechanism for interest rates. This milestone reform marks a significant step forward in China's interest rate liberalization process. Yet, it should be noted that the most important aspect of interest rate liberalization is the liberalization of deposit rates, which has not yet been introduced. In terms of market system construction, there are still many areas that need improvement, such as the development of multilevel capital markets, the establishment of small and medium-sized financial institutions, and so on. Therefore, in the capital market, there is still a need to further improve the market system construction and enhance the smooth operation of the price mechanism. However, there is still a gap to be bridged in achieving the goal of allowing the market to play a decisive role.

The second issue is the lack of fair market rules and inefficient operation of the competition mechanism. To a certain extent, a market economy is an economy based on competition. Only through fierce competition between buyers and buyers, sellers and sellers, and buyers and sellers, can optimal allocation of resources be achieved, ultimately leading to the maximization of individual interests and national wealth. Currently, there is no clear and specific list of areas that companies or individuals are not allowed to enter in the market, and there is also no clear and specific list of areas that companies or individuals are allowed to enter the market. As a result, there is confusion and uncertainty about what businesses or individuals can and cannot do in the market. Various illegal preferential policies persist, and various market barriers that hinder fair competition continue to emerge. The high and inefficient threshold for industrial and commercial registration and inappropriate exercise of government power also pose significant obstacles. There are evident institutional barriers in the distribution field, and a fully established rule of law commercial environment is still lacking. The market-oriented mechanism for survival of the fittest and orderly exit is also inadequate, and some industries with excess production capacity cannot implement orderly exit. The frequent occurrence of government bailouts of bankruptcies creates a significant reliance on the government by enterprises, who shift responsibility for decision-making mistakes onto society.[8]

---

[8] See Wang Yiming (Ed.). (2013). *The Benefits of Reform: Driving Economic Growth and Dynamism*. People's Publishing House.

A fundamental prerequisite for the competition mechanism to function is to ensure fairness for all economic entities in market competition. Here, fairness refers mainly to equal starting points and equal rules. In market competition, different economic entities often find it difficult to obtain equal market access conditions, especially in the fields of telecommunications, electricity, petroleum, railways, finance, and insurance, which are mostly controlled by state-owned capital and state-owned enterprises. Private capital entering these competitive fields also faces many restrictions and obstacles, which clearly contradict the required equal starting points and equal rules for the competition mechanism to function effectively.

The Chinese government places great emphasis on the development of the non-public sector and has implemented several policy measures, including the *36 Opinions on Encouraging and Supporting the Development of Non-public Economy* and the *New 36 Opinions on Encouraging and Guiding the Growth of Private Investment in a Sustainable Manner*. However, despite the government's efforts to promote fair competition and market access, there are still various forms of unfair and non-transparent practices that exist in China's market economy. Moreover, local protectionism and market segmentation are prevalent in China's market economy practice. Some regions, with a focus on protecting local commercial profits or ensuring local employment, tend to establish standards and entry barriers that favor local enterprises in the legislative process or misuse administrative power to restrict foreign enterprises and products from entering. In essence, this hinders the sales of foreign products locally and creates unfair competition among different economic entities. For example, in the areas of beer production and cigarette sales, local protectionism is evident, leading to significant discrepancies in entry barriers among different economic entities and resulting in the failure of the competition mechanism in the socialist economic system.

The third issue is excessive and disorderly government intervention, and the need for further development of the incentive mechanism. China's current situation highlights the significant issues of the government's "absence," "improper involvement," and "overstepping," which are still prevalent." Although the State Council has implemented administrative approval system reforms for many years, which has resulted in the simplification of permitting process. However, there are still many projects that require the government to delegate more power and streamline the permitting process further. The complicated permitting process acts as a barrier, limiting economic and social activities, and making it hard to move quickly and efficiently. Some approval processes are ridiculous or nonsensical, such as requiring approval from relevant government departments for the size of a keel structure on a fisherman's boat. Some companies need to go through ten, dozens, or even hundreds of departments and get dozens or even hundreds of official seals just to complete one project, which undoubtedly greatly increases enterprise costs and results in a misallocation of resources. In addition, the numerous qualifications and certifications have greatly raised the barriers to employment and entrepreneurship. According to statistics, there are currently more than 100 personal qualifications licensed by State Council departments, and more than 200 types of qualification certificates issued by government departments at all levels. The excessive government intervention in the market has caused inefficiencies and even waste in resource allocation, hampered the entrepreneurial and innovative vitality of market entities, and hindered the operation of the incentive mechanism.

In addition, the market economy is essentially a credit economy, and the social credit system is an important institutional arrangement of the market economy and also an important institutional guarantee for the market to play a decisive role. Currently, China has not yet formed a credit system covering the entire society. The lack of social integrity awareness and the weak personal credit concept have made dishonesty a systematic problem. Due to the lag in the construction of the credit system, phenomena such as financial distortion, tax evasion, contract breach, commercial fraud, malicious arrears and evasion of bank debts, and counterfeit production and sales are rampant, seriously disrupting the normal market order. To promote the decisive role of the market in resource allocation, foster economic prowess, and reform the market supervision system, it is necessary to make up for the shortcoming of credit construction, establish an incentive and restraint mechanism of "rewarding integrity and punishing dishonesty" as soon as possible, create an atmosphere of honesty and trustworthiness, and ensure a full utilization of the interest mechanism on the basis of efficient operation of the incentive and restraint mechanism in China's market economy.

4. Policy Measures That Aim to Enhance the Decisive Role of the Market in Resource Allocation

In his speech, Xi Jinping pointed out that "economic development entails enhancing the efficiency of resource allocation, especially scarce resources. The goal is to produce as many products as possible and maximize profits with minimal resource input."[9] China is currently in a prime position to build a moderately prosperous society and make the transition from an economic giant to an economic powerhouse. This is a strategic opportunity that shouldn't be missed. To seize this historical opportunity, we need to act fast and focus on improving the modern market system. This includes establishing open and transparent market rules, balancing the government's role with that of the market, and ensuring the smooth operation of the price, competition, and incentive mechanisms. By allowing the market to play a decisive role in resource allocation, we can improve the efficiency of resource allocation and promote the high-quality development of the Chinese economy in a stable and sustainable manner.

4.1. *Accelerate the improvement of the modern market system*

Under the conditions of the modern market economy, building a unified, open, and orderly competitive market system is not only a prerequisite for leveraging the price mechanism but also a foundation for enabling the market to play a decisive role in resource allocation. To effectively improve the modern market system, we must focus on developing tangible markets like commerce, labor, and land, as well as refining intangible markets such as capital, information, and technology. In accordance with the arrangements of the Third Plenary Session of the 18th CPC Central Committee, we must continue our efforts to accelerate the improvement of the modern market system and fully harness the role of the price mechanism.

Firstly, the government should further improve the construction of the commodity market system. The Third Plenary Session of the 18th Party Congress called for establishing fair, open, and transparent market rules and improving a unified and open national market. Key measures for policymakers involve promoting negative list management, streamlining business registration, reforming domestic trade systems, fostering a rule-of-law business environment, and breaking administrative monopolies and regional barriers. At the same time, policymakers should reform the market supervision system by implementing a unified approach, eliminating regulations and practices that hinder a national market and fair

[9]Party Literature Research Center of the CPC Central Committee (2014), *Op. cit.*, p. 499.

competition, opposing local protectionism, and countering monopolies and unfair competition. Additionally, policymakers should refine the mechanism for market-determined pricing. They should allow the market to form prices wherever possible, avoiding undue government intervention and emphasizing the role of the market in setting prices.

Secondly, policymakers should further enhance the development of the financial market system. Given that China's market economy history is relatively short, the price mechanism in the financial market construction has not reached optimal efficiency. This is evident in the incomplete marketization of capital prices (interest rates, exchange rates, etc.), restricted access for private capital entering the financial industry, and the need for ongoing improvements in the equity and governance structure of listed companies, as well as investor rights protection. Policymakers should continue to improve the modern financial market system, expand the openness of the financial industry to both domestic and foreign markets, encourage financial innovation, strengthen the multi-level capital market system, refine the market-oriented formation mechanism of the RMB exchange rate, accelerate the marketization of interest rates, and actively and prudently implement marketization of deposit interest rates. At the same time, further efforts should be made to enhance financial infrastructure construction, ensuring the safe, efficient operation, and overall stability of the financial market.

Thirdly, policymakers should further improve the construction of the labor market system. After more than 30 years of reform and practice, China's employment system has largely become market-oriented. However, it still faces challenges such as accommodating a large number of new job seekers, addressing structural unemployment during the transition, and managing the employment of a significant surplus of rural labor. The urbanization of the population lags behind land urbanization, and restrictions on the free movement of people hinder the unification of the national labor market. Additionally, the system faces issues arising from an aging population, such as a declining labor force and a rising dependency ratio. Therefore, it is essential to integrate urban and rural labor markets by advancing the reform of the household registration system. Policymakers should comprehensively lift restrictions on settling in towns and small cities, gradually ease restrictions on settling in medium-sized cities, reasonably set conditions for settling in large cities, and strictly control the population size of mega-cities. This will promote the settlement of eligible rural migrants in urban areas, allowing them to enjoy equal rights and benefits with urban residents.[10]

Fourthly, policymakers should establish a unified urban–rural construction land market. Currently, China's land market is primarily focused on urban land, with the pricing mechanism mainly functioning within the urban land market. The rural land market has not been officially recognized by law. During rapid urbanization, significant contradictions have arisen between urban and rural land use. The acquisition or expropriation of rural land does not provide reasonable compensation to farmers, and the marketization of rural land contractual management rights has not been achieved. The channels for rural collective construction land circulation are limited, resulting in rural construction land being circulated through hidden and non-public means to some extent. Additionally, rural land entering the market independently has become more noticeable. Therefore, to further leverage the guiding role of the pricing mechanism in the urban–rural construction land market, it is essential to allow rural collective business construction land to be transferred, leased, or used as equity, implementing equal market access, rights, and pricing as state-owned land.

Fifthly, it is necessary for policymakers to further perfect the innovation market system. Free and fair competition in the market economy encourages innovation. Only through innovation and competition can the entire economy maintain strong vitality and international competitiveness. If administrative guidance dominates technological innovation, enterprises cannot become the main body of technological innovation, and the problem of technological innovation being isolated from market demand cannot be eradicated. The Third Plenary Session of the 18th CPC Central Committee proposed to "further the reform of the scientific and technological system" by establishing a collaborative innovation mechanism among industry, academia, and research, continuously strengthening the main role of enterprises in technological innovation and building a national innovation system. At the same time, it is necessary to strengthen the application and protection of intellectual property rights and improve the incentive mechanism for technological innovation. To promote innovation, it is essential to break the dominance of administrative guidance and departmental segmentation. It is necessary to establish a mechanism

---

[10]See *National Plan for New Model Urbanization (2014–2020)*. People's Publishing House, 2014.

mainly determined by the market for technology innovation project selection, fund allocation, and achievement evaluation. This approach will allow for the development of the technology market and promote the capitalization and industrialization of scientific and technological achievements.

4.2. *Further enhance the role of government*

The market functions based on certain rules, and these rules can influence the efficiency and methods of operation. Since the reform and opening-up, China has made significant progress in establishing and constructing market rules, such as improving the pricing mechanism based on supply and demand, increasing the degree of market openness, and promoting active diversification of market players. The non-public sector has also seen considerable development, and the legal and regulatory systems related to the market, as well as the social credit system, have been continuously improved and emphasized. However, there are still many issues that need to be addressed, which requires better utilization of the government's role.

This approach involves the formulation of a comprehensive list that outlines industries, fields, and business activities subject to government prohibition or restrictions. Conversely, any ventures falling outside the scope of this list are granted unrestricted entry, adhering to the principle of "nulla poena sine lege." This reform of the market access management system has significant implications for the construction of China's socialist market economy. The negative list only specifies what companies "cannot do," as opposed to the positive list that outlines what companies "can do," thereby providing more room for the market to play its role and reflecting the important shift in the mindset of the Communist Party of China in its relationship with the market. In essence, the negative list significantly reduces the range of areas subject to government approval, provides relatively clear guidelines, and contributes substantially to the reform of the government's approval system, the improvement of government efficiency, and the reduction of discretionary power and corresponding rent-seeking space. Under the revised negative list approach, the concept of "encouraged projects" has been eliminated. Instead, businesses are encouraged to rely on their own competitive capabilities and respond to market demand when making development and investment decisions. In the past, when the government explicitly encouraged specific projects or industries, certain companies would seek preferential policy support, exploiting the associated policies. This practice was deemed detrimental to fair competition and contributed to overcapacity issues in certain sectors.

Secondly, the nationwide unified market supervision should be implemented. With a large population and a vast market, China is still in an important period of development, where optimizing resource allocation and unlocking growth potential are of immense importance. However, in order to achieve this, there needs to be a nationwide unified and fair competitive market system. In recent years, there have been many instances of "local policies" and unwritten rules that prioritize local interests, divide markets, and restrict fair competition. Some of these practices are seen as effective measures to promote local economic development. While these practices may seem beneficial to local development in the short term, they distort resource allocation, violate principles of fair competition, and fuel excessive competition among localities, which is detrimental to both local and overall long-term development. Therefore, we must follow the requirements of the Third Plenary Session of the 18th Central Committee of the Communist Party of China, strictly prohibit and punish all illegal preferential policies, oppose local protectionism, and combat all forms of monopolies and unfair competition.

Thirdly, the construction of the social credit system should be further developed. The construction of the credit system has always been a weakness of China's economic and social development. Counterfeiting, fraud, deception, and default have imposed a high cost on the economy. The Third Plenary Session of the 18th Central Committee of the Communist Party of China proposed establishing and improving the social credit system. By gradually perfecting the credit records of individuals and organizations through the credit system, it can serve as an important credit reference for their economic activities such as production, investment, circulation, and consumption. On this basis, a credit reward and punishment mechanism can be established, and the norms of performing contracts and keeping promises can be fostered to improve the overall credit level of society. While reducing administrative approval, it is also necessary to simplify admission procedures. The *Decision of the Central Committee of the Communist Party of China on Several Major Issues Concerning Comprehensively Furthering Reform* passed by the Third Plenary Session of the 18th CPC Central Committee proposed promoting the facilitation of the industrial and commercial registration system, reducing qualification certification projects, changing from "permitting after examination and approval" to "permitting before examination and approval," and gradually changing from the system of registered capital contribution to that of subscribed capital contribution. These measures have a positive effect on reducing the burden on enterprises, lowering admission thresholds, and improving the transparency of the admission process. Furthermore, it is essential to accelerate the construction of a legal business environment, form a commercial system that is in line with international standards, improve institutional and procedural rules, and ensure that all entities, including the government, act in accordance with the law and regulations, enhance the transparency of administrative operations, reduce arbitrary interventions, and enhance accountability.

Fourthly, it is necessary to improve the market-oriented exit mechanism based on survival of the fittest. The market system has both ups and downs, and a major flaw in China's market system operation is the lack of well-functioning market exit mechanisms. Currently, China's economy is facing a severe overcapacity problem. Unlike past cases of overcapacity, this round of overcapacity occurs when most important products have reached or approached historical demand peaks, and therefore has the characteristic of long-term excess. While a certain degree of overcapacity is normal in a market economy, the emergence of severe overcapacity is often due to the lack of effective market-oriented exit mechanisms. On one hand, the market must play an irreplaceable and positive role in selecting winners and losers. It is not the government's role to determine which enterprises will succeed or fail. In addressing issues such as corporate bankruptcy and mergers and acquisitions, the principle of enterprise autonomy should be upheld, and the government should avoid interfering in corporate affairs. Cross-regional and cross-ownership mergers and acquisitions should be encouraged to prevent local protectionism. On the other hand, the government should focus on creating the necessary external conditions for corporate exit and restructuring, such as improving the social security system, creating job opportunities, providing vocational training, and providing necessary financial support for mergers and acquisitions.

4.3. *Further improving the relationship between the government and the market*

In modern market economy conditions, the market is the "invisible hand" that plays a decisive role in resource allocation, while the government is the "visible hand" that primarily addresses "market failure." Whether it is to enable the market to play a decisive role in resource allocation or to better utilize the government's role, it is essential to coordinate and cooperate between the "two hands" of the government and the market and not prioritize one over the other. Only by fully utilizing the roles of these "two hands" can the pricing mechanism, competition mechanism, and incentive mechanism run smoothly.

First, further simplify administration and delegate power, and transform the functions of the government. To make good use of the visible hand of the government, it is not only necessary to cancel and delegate power but also to improve and strengthen government management to effectively govern affairs. Only by refraining from intervening in certain areas can the government focus on major issues, plan for the long term, and consider the overall situation while exercising less control over micro-level matters and more over macro-level affairs. On the basis of activating the invisible hand of the market and social vitality, the government should improve its macro-management, enhance governance capacity, improve efficiency, and build a modern government. In fact, by delegating power, the government can concentrate more on regulating areas that have a strong impact on the people and may pose significant risks to economic and social development, creating a fair and competitive environment for various market entities. Innovation in providing public services can also be achieved by delegating power, providing the people with more effective and high-quality public services. Furthermore, by delegating power, necessary administrative approval procedures can be streamlined, rent-seeking can be reduced, corruption can be prevented, and modern and scientific management systems can be established.

Second, clarify the boundary between the government and the market, and leverage the strengths of the government. The Third Plenary Sessions of the 18th Central Committee of the Communist Party of China has already provided a clear explanation of this issue. The government should undertake five functions, namely, macroeconomic regulation, public services, market supervision, social management, and environmental protection. All other functions that can be delegated should be delegated to the market and society to the greatest extent possible, to give more autonomy to market entities, unleash their vitality, stimulate the initiative of various social organizations, and overcome "market failures" such as monopoly and information asymmetry that arise in modern market economies.

It goes without saying that the roles of the government and the market are not mutually exclusive but rather complementary. The objective is not solely to enhance the market's role while diminishing the government's role, but rather to foster coordinated efforts, leverage complementary strengths, achieve organic integration, and engage in joint action. In this context, it becomes imperative to establish clear delineations between the responsibilities of the government and the functioning of the market. When the market can effectively operate, the government should simplify administration, delegate authority, provide support, and loosen restrictions, while avoiding interference. On the other hand, where the market fails to function efficiently, the government should proactively fill the gap, by firmly and effectively regulating areas within its mandate to avoid potential problems. In addition, adopting the negative list management approach can help clarify what the market cannot do, allowing market entities to make decisions on what can be done based on market changes. It is important to find the optimal balance between market functions and government actions, leveraging the strengths of both to better reflect the unique advantages of the socialist market economy.

Chapter 10

Accelerating the Implementation of the Innovation-Driven Development Strategy

Innovation is an inexhaustible driving force for economic and social development. The report of the 18th CPC National Congress states that, when implementing the innovation-driven development strategy, technological innovation is the strategic support for improving social productivity and comprehensive national strength. It must be placed in a core position in the overall development of the country. The *Decision of the CCCPC on Some Major Issues Concerning Comprehensively Deepening the Reform*, adopted at the Third Plenary Session of the 18th CPC Central Committee, deployed the reform of scientific and technological system as an important content of comprehensively deepening the reform. The Fifth Plenary Session of the 18th CPC Central Committee put forward innovation-driven development as the first of the "Five Development Concepts," emphasizing the need to place innovation at the core of national development, and made in-depth arrangements for implementing the innovation-driven development strategy. The second part of *The 13th Five-Year Plan for National Economic and Social Development of the People's Republic of China* comprehensively coordinated the implementation of the innovation-driven development strategy. In May 2016, the CPC Central Committee and the State Council issued the *National Innovation-Driven Development Strategy Outline*, clarifying the goals, directions, and key tasks of innovation-driven development in the next 30 years. Xi Jinping's strategic thinking on innovation-driven development and a series of strategic deployments issued by the CPC Central Committee are the guiding documents for promoting innovation work in the new era and the action guidelines for building an innovative country.

1. The Significance of Implementing the Innovation-Driven Development Strategy

American scholar Michael Porter has identified four stages of national advantage development: factor-driven, investment-driven, innovation-driven, and wealth-driven. Innovation-driven development implies that a country or region's competitive advantage no longer depends heavily on natural resources, labor quantity, and capital investment but rather on technological progress and innovation capabilities. Since the 1980s, especially with the development of information and communication technology (ICT), many countries have transitioned from factor-driven and investment-driven stages to innovation-driven stages in their economic development.

Over 30 years of reform and opening-up, our economy has experienced rapid growth and expansion primarily through inputs of production factors such as resources, capital, and labor. However, the conditions for such development have undergone significant changes today, making it impossible to rely solely on these input factors as we have in the past. Not only are the original conditions no longer present, but the environmental burden is also increasingly difficult to bear. China's total economic output has jumped to the second largest in the world, while its social productivity, comprehensive national strength, and scientific and technological capabilities have reached a new level. However, the problems of imbalanced, uncoordinated, and unsustainable development in China are still prominent, with increasing pressure on population, resources, and the environment. Modernization in China involves more than a billion people, and continuing to rely on a resource-driven approach is unsustainable. Therefore, innovation-driven development is not only a necessity imposed by the current situation, but also a crucial element in the rejuvenation of the nation and a reflection of the global trend of competition. We must accelerate the transition from resource-driven to innovation-driven development and leverage technological innovation to support and lead this transformation. The strength of a nation ultimately depends on its innovation capabilities. Throughout modern history, technological innovation has been a powerful force driving the transfer of the world's economic center of gravity. Therefore, innovation-driven development is a significant strategic initiative that is globally oriented and future-focused, with great importance for achieving the goal of building a moderately prosperous society in all respects by 2020 and the great rejuvenation of the Chinese nation.

As China's economy has grown rapidly over the past decades, the focus on scale expansion must shift toward improving quality and efficiency, which necessitates a shift toward innovation-driven development. The supporting factors that have fueled China's economic development are changing, and the increasing costs of labor and the strengthening of various resource and environmental constraints make the previous model of investment-driven, scale expansion, and export-oriented development increasingly unsustainable. The only way out is through innovation-driven development, which includes upgrading and transforming industries, improving value chains, and enhancing product-added value, all of which will lead to sustainable development through the improvement of quality and efficiency. China is known as the world's manufacturing powerhouse, with over 220 industrial products ranking first in the world in 2014 and industrial exports ranking first globally. Additionally, 56 Chinese manufacturing companies were included in the Fortune 500 list, which is the second-highest number of any country. However, despite these impressive statistics, most Chinese manufacturing enterprises are at the bottom of the value chain, with weak links in research and development, design, branding, supply chain management, and marketing. Thus, strictly speaking, China is a production and processing giant rather than a manufacturing powerhouse. Currently, the development model of Chinese manufacturing is facing significant challenges and needs to break out of the current situation through technological innovation. The difficulties of the Chinese manufacturing industry are mainly manifested in two aspects. First, the low-tech development model has come to an end. The foundation of this model is cheap labor, which has been gradually eroded by rising labor costs, diminishing population dividends, and an aging population trend. The era of low-cost labor is coming to an end, which has resulted in many companies shifting to China's central and western regions, and some have even moved to neighboring countries. Moreover, the global financial crisis caused a decline in demand worldwide, and the rise of trade protectionism in some countries, including the United States, has put pressure on China's manufacturing industry, which heavily relies on foreign demand. Second, the main body of the Chinese manufacturing industry, namely small and medium-sized private enterprises, is facing an increasingly difficult domestic operating environment. These enterprises have inherent disadvantages and low starting points, and most of them are labor-intensive and low value-added processing enterprises. Currently, they face difficulties in obtaining loans, rising labor costs, and the influence of imperfect competition rules. However, the core of the manufacturing industry is not just manufacturing itself but instead relies on independent core technologies supported by product research and development and design. By integrating through global procurement, manufacturers can obtain high value-added products. According to the "smiling curve"[1] analysis, the high value-added links in the value chain are the research and development, procurement, product design, brand marketing, logistics management, and finance. In contrast, the traditional manufacturing enterprises in the middle of the curve, such as processing, assembly, and manufacturing, have low value-added and profit margins. China has consumed a significant amount of non-renewable resources and faced environmental pollution, bearing the stigma of "dumping," while the majority of profits have gone into the hands of other countries. Only by strengthening innovation and driving technological advancement can China change this situation and achieve industrial upgrading based on independent innovation. By combining technology innovation with economic development, China can provide a sustained power source for economic and social development.

To effectively solve the conflicts between the economy and population, environment, and resources, we must rely on innovation to drive progress. Since the implementation of reform and opening-up policies, the demographic dividend has played a significant role in China's economic and social development. We relied on low labor costs to promote the growth of labor-intensive industries, but the demographic dividend has disappeared, labor costs have increased, and the aging population is accelerating, leading to an increase in the cost of economic and social development. According to the National Bureau of Statistics' annual statistical report for 2015, the number of people aged 60 and over in China had reached 222 million, accounting for 16.1% of the country's total population. Of these, those aged 65 and over accounted for 10.5% of the total population, reaching 144 million. Currently, China is the only country in the world with a population of over 100 million elderly people. The number of elderly people in China, which has already surpassed the total population of countries such as Brazil, Russia, and Japan, is equivalent to the total population of Indonesia. If it were considered as a country's

[1]The concept of "Smiling Curve" was proposed by Stan Shih, the founder of Acer Inc., in his book *The Acer Way: Innovation, Growth, Globalization* published in 2005. It is used to illustrate the changes in the value-added structure of the IT industry's value chain since the 1960s, CITIC Press, Beijing.

total population, it would rank fourth in the world. According to the United Nations' forecast data, the total number of elderly people aged 65 and over in China will increase from 24 million in 1950 to 331 million in 2050. As China's resources are scarce, its development faces enormous resource and environmental pressures. Whether it is energy, minerals, land, or water resources, China's per capita ownership is much lower than the world average. The per capita ownership of water and arable land resources is only one-fourth and one-third of the world average, respectively, and the per capita ownership of 45 major mineral resources is less than half of the world average. The per capita recoverable reserves of oil and gas are only 6% of the world average. The transition from element-driven to innovation-driven economic development can promote the transition from extensive resource utilization to intensive resource utilization, and promote resource conservation and optimal allocation. At the same time, as we accelerate the stages of industrialization, informatization, urbanization, and agricultural modernization, the transition to innovation-driven economic development can effectively reduce the resource and energy consumption of each unit of GDP and lower the intensity of pollutant and greenhouse gas emissions. This is not only beneficial to alleviate domestic ecological pressures but also helps China gain more initiative in international climate change negotiations.

To win development opportunities and initiative, it is necessary to rely on innovation-driven development. The fundamental key to seizing the initiative in development and seizing the opportunities for future development is to rely on the power of science and technology. According to international experience, countries in the middle- to high-income stage may face a series of challenges such as economic growth slowdown and social conflict intensification, and some countries may fall into the "middle-income trap" as a result. Implementing innovation-driven development is beneficial for seeking development opportunities in the context of development levels approaching those of technologically advanced countries and narrowing space for low-cost technology imitation, avoiding falling into the "middle-income trap." In recent years, during the process of dealing with the international financial crisis, countries, especially developed economies, have attached greater importance to implementing national innovation strategies. Worldwide, productivity, production methods, lifestyles, and the pattern of economic and social development are undergoing profound changes. Currently, the new technological and industrial revolution has begun to show its initial signs, and some important scientific and technological fields are showing signs of revolutionary breakthroughs. The deep integration of knowledge innovation, technology innovation, and industrial innovation has given rise to a new generation of technological groups and new points of industrial growth, and the world will enter an era of intensive innovation and rapid development of emerging industries. In the new international competitive landscape, developed countries and their multinational corporations control the market and resources through technology, forming a highly monopolistic position in the world market, especially in high-tech markets. Currently, China's dependence on foreign technology is over 50%, with some industries even higher, while generally developed countries are below 30%, and the United States and Japan are even lower than 5%. China's self-sufficiency in core and key technologies is low, and over 60% of equipment investment, accounting for about 40% of fixed asset investment, relies on imports. Key equipment with high technological content is almost entirely dependent on imports. Heavy reliance on imports in contrast to insufficient digestion and absorption for re-innovation have caused many Chinese enterprises to be stuck in a stage of always catching up. In recent years, the R&D intensity of China's top 500 manufacturing companies has remained at around 2%, far below the average level of 3–5% for the world's top 500. Most of China's high-tech industries are created by foreign-invested enterprises. Processing trade accounts for over 60% of China's high-tech product exports, while the proportion of software and chip exports with high technological content is less than 10%. Another undeniable reality is that three-capital enterprises account for about 60% of the main business income of high-tech industries. Looking at the distribution of enterprise classification for high-tech product exports, foreign-invested enterprises account for more than 50% of the share of high-tech product exports. Therefore, China can only gain development opportunities and initiative by constantly strengthening innovation-driven development and enhancing independent innovation capabilities, otherwise, the development gap would continue to widen, even threatening the overall national security.

2. Innovation Is the Driving Force behind Economic Growth

China's current innovation capacity is relatively weak and the overall level of technological development is not high. The ability of technology to support economic and social development is insufficient and its contribution to economic growth falls far below that of developed countries, making it the "Achilles' heel" of China's large economy. The new round of technological revolution has brought about even fiercer competition in technology. Without significant innovation in technology, a transformation in development momentum cannot be achieved, and we will be at a disadvantage in global economic competition. Therefore, it is imperative that we prioritize innovation as the leading force for development and place it at the core of our national development strategy. We must accelerate the implementation of strategies to drive development, continuously advance innovation in various aspects such as theoretical, institutional, technological, and cultural innovation, and ensure that innovation is integrated into all aspects of the work of the Party and the country, so that it can become a prevailing trend throughout the society.

2.1. *Innovation as the primary driving force for development*

On March 5, 2015, Xi Jinping proposed that innovation is the primary driving force for development during his participation in the deliberations of the Shanghai delegation to the Third Session of the 12th National People's Congress. He emphasized that grasping innovation is grasping development and seeking innovation is seeking the future. To adapt to and lead the new normal of economic development in China, it is crucial to rely on technological innovation to transform development momentum. The idea, that both the absence and lacking of innovation would render a country fall behind in development, is a continuation and development of the concept that "science and technology are the primary productive forces" and a brilliant summation and significant judgment on the development momentum of China's economy in the new normal.

Since the 16th century, technological revolutions in human society have triggered a series of industrial transformations, driving the rise and fall of great powers, the shift of the world economic center, and adjustments to the international competitive landscape. The technological innovation of the 18th century, represented by steam engines and power machinery, brought about the first industrial revolution, propelling the United Kingdom to become the world's number one power. In the mid-19th century, the electrification technological innovation represented by electric motors and internal combustion engines ushered in the second industrial revolution, enabling Germany to rise to become a world industrial power, and the United States to become the world's top economic power by the end of the 19th century. In the 20th century, the technological revolution represented by electronics and information technology drove the third industrial revolution, propelling the industrial maturity of the United States, Germany, France, the United Kingdom, and other countries. Japan seized this opportunity and achieved economic take-off. It is evident that technological innovation largely determines the changes in the global economic and political power balance, and thus determines the future and destiny of each country and nation.

The Party has always attached great importance to innovation. In the early days following the founding of the People's Republic of China, Chairman Mao Zedong called on the whole nation to "march towards science"; in 1963, he further emphasized that we must fight and win the battle of science and technology, without which no improvement would be achieved in productive forces. Since initiating the reform and opening-up policy, Deng Xiaoping's famous saying that "science and technology are the primary productive forces" is well-known to every household. The 14th CPC National Congress report included "innovation" for the first time. Afterward, Jiang Zemin pointed out in his speeches at the 10th Academy Conference of the Chinese Academy of Sciences and the 5th Academy Conference of the Chinese Academy of Engineering that "I have repeatedly said that innovation is the soul of a nation and the inexhaustible driving force for a country's prosperity and development. The essence of science is innovation, which requires constant discovery and invention." "The ability to innovate and the ability to carry out innovation are the decisive factors for economic and technological competition in the world today. All scientific discoveries and technological breakthroughs in history are the result of innovation."[2] The National Science and Technology Conference in 2006 proposed the major strategic goal of enhancing independent innovation capability and building an innovative country. The report of the 17th CPC National Congress clearly stated that enhancing independent innovation capability and building an innovative country is the core of the national development strategy. Since the 18th CPC National Congress, the central government has consistently attached great importance to innovation. Xi Jinping re-emphasized that "innovation is the soul of a nation's progress, the inexhaustible driving force for a country's prosperity and development, and also the deepest

[2]Party Literature Research Center of the CPC Central Committee (Ed.). (2001). *Selected Important Documents since the 15th CPC National Congress*, Vol. II. People's Publishing House, p. 1274.

national endowment of the Chinese nation. In fierce international competition, only innovators advance, only innovators are strong, and only innovators win."[3] In essence, the competition for comprehensive national power ultimately boils down to a competition for innovation. The driving force behind the long-term development of the world economy comes from innovation. Throughout the history of human development, innovation has always been an important force driving a country or a nation forward, and also an important force driving the whole human society forward. Summing up the historical experience, we will find that the vitality and creativity released by institutional and mechanism changes and the new industries and products created by technological progress are the fundamental factors for the world economy to overcome major crises and achieve recovery.

2.2. *Strengthening the leading role of technological innovation in comprehensive innovation*

Innovation takes many forms, including theoretical innovation, institutional innovation, technological innovation, and cultural innovation. Theoretical innovation serves as the guide and inspiration for all types of innovation, driving social development and transformation. The past 30 years of China's reform and opening-up have been a practical demonstration of ongoing theoretical innovation. The theories of the nature of socialism, the primary stage of socialism, socialist market economy, reform and opening-up, the Scientific Outlook on Development, the Five-Sphere Integrated Plan, the "Four Comprehensives" strategic layout, and the five development concepts have all significantly contributed to the thriving development of socialism with Chinese characteristics. Institutional innovation provides the guarantee for sustainable innovation, serving as the key driving force behind the vitality of various innovative subjects, and promoting long-term economic growth and social progress. A series of institutional innovations have become the original driving force for China's economic and social development since the reform and opening-up. Examples include the household contract responsibility system, the reform of state-owned enterprises, the socialist market economy

[3] Xi Jinping. (2013). Speech at the 100th anniversary celebration of the western returned scholars association. *People's Daily*, October 22, 2013.

system, the basic economic system of public ownership as the mainstay and the various ownership forms developing side by side, and the distribution system with the principle of distribution according to work as the mainstay and the coexistence of various distribution methods. Cultural innovation is an essential foundation for the sustained vitality and cohesion of a nation and serves as the inexhaustible spiritual driving force for all types of innovative activities.

In comprehensive innovation, the position and role of technological innovation are particularly prominent. Xi Jinping pointed out that "whoever holds the bull's nose of technological innovation and plays the first move of technological innovation well, will be able to seize the initiative and win the advantage."[4] Technological innovation is the core of national competitiveness and plays a leading role in comprehensive innovation. To implement the innovation-driven development strategy, we must firmly grasp technological innovation as the key. Only by firmly holding onto the "bull's nose" of technological innovation and breaking free from the embarrassment of China's core key technologies being controlled by others can China truly become a world technology and economic power.

The implementation of the innovation-driven development strategy proposed at the 18th CPC National Congress aims to promote comprehensive innovation with scientific and technological innovation at its core. The technological revolution will inevitably lead to an industrial revolution. However, scientific and technological innovations and their outcomes should not be limited to funding, forms, or publications but should be oriented toward the main battlefield of economic and social development, translated into the primary driving force for economic and social development, and translated into people's well-being. Scientific and technological achievements can only realize their innovative value and drive development when they are combined with national needs, people's demands, and market requirements, and complete the "three-level jump" from scientific research to experimental development and then to promotion and application. Therefore, we must adhere to the industrialization orientation, strengthen the research on common basic technologies in industries, make efforts to break through the core technologies that

---

[4] Being a vanguard of national reform and opening-up and continuously improving the core competitiveness of cities. *People's Daily*, May 25, 2014.

constrain the optimization and upgrading of industries, and provide strong support for transforming the economic development mode and adjusting the industrial structure. The focus should be on cultivating leading industries with core competitiveness, deploying innovation chains around industrial chains, developing strategic emerging industries with high technological content, strong market competitiveness, great driving effects, and good economic benefits, and truly integrating scientific and technological innovations into industrial development. We must also adhere to the leading role of enterprises in innovation, give full play to the decisive role of the market in resource allocation, and the advantages of the socialist system, enhance the contribution of scientific and technological progress to economic growth, form new sources of growth power, and promote sustainable and healthy economic development.

In the process of advancing the reform of the scientific and technological system, we must not abandon the important tool of the socialist system to concentrate our efforts on major tasks. Many of China's major scientific and technological achievements have been made possible by this tool. We must let the market play a decisive role in resource allocation while also strengthening the role of the government, enhancing overall coordination, vigorously promoting collaborative innovation, and concentrating our efforts on major tasks, focusing on major, cutting-edge, and fundamental areas to form a strong force for promoting independent innovation. Genuine core technology cannot be bought, and we must take the path of independent innovation. Only by mastering core technology can we truly control the initiative for competition and development, and fundamentally ensure the country's economic security, national defense, and other security. We cannot always rely on other people's technological achievements to improve our own technological level, nor can we become technical dependents of other countries, always following behind others. However, independent innovation is not about closing the door and doing innovation. Against the backdrop of deepening economic globalization, innovation resources are flowing faster worldwide, and the economic and technological links between countries are becoming closer. No country can solve all innovation problems in isolation by relying solely on its own strength. We must deepen international exchanges and cooperation, fully utilize global innovation resources, promote independent innovation at a higher starting point, and work together with the international scientific and technological community to make a due contribution to addressing global challenges.

3. Removing Institutional and Systemic Barriers to Innovation-Driven Development

Adopted in 2015, the *Several Opinions of the CPC Central Committee and the State Council on Deepening the Reform of Systems and Mechanisms to Accelerate the Implementation of Innovation-driven Development Strategies* emphasized that the implementation of the innovation-driven development strategy aims to enable the market to play a decisive role in resource allocation and better leverage the role of the government, by removing all ideological barriers and institutional obstacles that constrain innovation, and by stimulating the innovation vitality and potential of the entire society. This strategy aims to enhance the efficiency and effectiveness of labor, information, knowledge, technology, management, and capital, to strengthen the connection between science and technology and economic development, between innovation achievements and industrial application, between innovation projects and real production forces, and between innovative labor and income. By increasing the contribution of scientific and technological progress to economic development, the strategy aims to create a policy and institutional environment that promotes mass entrepreneurship and innovation. The concept of "dual-wheel drive" proposed in the *Outline of the National Strategy for Innovation-Driven Development* aims to coordinate and sustain scientific and technological innovation and institutional innovation, while promoting the reform of the system and mechanism in three areas: science and technology, economy, and government governance so as to maximize the release of innovation vitality.

3.1. *Promoting technological innovation calls for comprehensive innovation that includes the reform of systems and mechanisms*

Xi Jinping pointed out, "If we compare technological innovation to a new engine for China's development, then reform is the indispensable ignition system for lighting up this new engine."[5] For many years, China has faced the problem of a disconnect between its scientific and economic development, where there is a chronic issue of insufficient and ineffective

---

[5]Party Literature Research Center of the CPC Central Committee (Ed.). (2016). *Selected Important Documents since the 18th CPC National Congress*, Vol. II. Central Party Literature Press, p. 25.

conversion of scientific achievements into practical productivity. One of the key reasons for this is the existence of many institutional and systemic barriers in the innovation chain, resulting in inadequate connections between different stages of innovation and transformation. “Just like a relay race, the first runner has completed their leg, but the next runner has no one to pass the baton to, or they don’t know which way to run. To solve this problem, it is necessary to deepen the reform of the scientific and technological system. We need to manage the relationship between government and market, promote the deep integration of science and technology with economic and social development, and open up a pathway from a strong technological foundation to a strong industry, a strong economy, and a strong nation. By unleashing the power of innovation through reform, we can accelerate the establishment of a sound national innovation system and allow all sources of innovation to fully flow.”[6] Since the 18th CPC National Congress was held in 2012, reform measures to deepen the implementation of the innovation-driven development strategy have emerged continuously. The programs include the *Program for Deepening the Reform of the Administration of Central Finance Science and Technology Plans (Special Funds, Funds, etc.)*, the *Several Opinions of the CPC Central Committee and the State Council on Deepening the Reform of Systems and Mechanisms to Accelerate the Implementation of Innovation-Driven Development Strategies*, the *National Innovation-Driven Development Strategy Outline*, the *Implementation Plan for Deepening Science and Technology System Reform*, the *Guiding Opinions on Developing Mass Entrepreneurship and Innovation through the Development of Maker Spaces*, and the Law of the People’s Republic of China on Promoting the Transformation of Scientific and Technological Achievements. These top-level designs on innovation-driven development have been increasingly perfected, and many reform measures are being implemented in depth. The establishment of the Central Comprehensively Deepening Reforms Commission and six special groups has improved the efficiency of reform decision-making and will solve the long-standing problem of multiple departments, interdepartmental disputes, and mutual constraints that have plagued reforms. The introduction of a series of convenient measures such as the negative list, post-approval, and easy

---

[6] *Ibid.*

business registration has provided a good policy environment for the flow of market resources. Innovative entrepreneurship represented by "Internet +" is surging, and a large number of young geeks, makers, and even entrepreneurs are emerging.

3.2. *Strengthening the dominant position of enterprises in technological innovation*

The Fifth Plenary Session of the 18th CPC Central Committee has further emphasized the need to strengthen the dominant position of enterprises in innovation, which carries significant implications. The technical innovation capability of enterprises is not only an issue for the enterprises themselves but also a matter of the overall strength of the country in participating in global competition. When enterprises are strong, the country is strong. The competitive advantage of enterprises ultimately determines the competitive advantage of the nation. Entrepreneurs are often the driving force behind technical innovation, and knowledge and technical innovation can only be truly transformed into large-scale production and economic benefits through enterprises. Only when enterprises truly lead the entire technical innovation chain can the possibility of market success for technical innovation be maximized, the efficiency of innovation be highest, and the economic development strength of the country be truly enhanced.

To further strengthen the leading role and dominant position of enterprises in technological innovation, it is necessary to enable the market to become a true force in allocating innovation resources, allowing enterprises to become the decision-makers, research and development investors, research organizers, and result converters of technological innovation. This shift from "innovation is expected of me" to "I will innovate" can facilitate the rapid convergence of various innovation elements to enterprises, transforming innovation achievements into productive forces more quickly. It is crucial to enhance the application and protection of intellectual property rights and maintain a fair competitive market environment. Different innovation entities should leverage their respective advantages: large enterprises should take advantage of their resource aggregation and core technology capabilities, enhancing the overall industrial innovation capacity; small and medium-sized enterprises should capitalize on their unique strengths in adapting to rapid technological and business model changes, nurturing emerging industries through market selection; research institutes should increase investment in basic research, provide incentives for scientific research, and improve assessment mechanisms. Moreover, the government should take on its responsibilities in areas that are vital to national welfare, industrial development, and public welfare. The government must play an active role in enhancing support and coordination, establishing overall technological directions and strategies, and leveraging national-level initiatives such as major scientific and technological projects and major engineering programs to capture commanding heights. To this end, first, it is imperative to promote the marketization reform of production factors, accelerate the reform of resource pricing mechanism and industrial organization adjustment, improve the pricing mechanism and tax system that reflects scarcity and environmental impact, build pressure mechanisms that promote corporate technological innovation, and create market-driven mechanisms that encourage innovation. Furthermore, the government should improve the market competition environment, establish fair market access rules, eliminate industry monopolies and market segmentation, construct a fair, just, open, and unified market environment, and develop a supportive policy system for innovation that is accessible to all types of enterprises. We should continue to deepen the reform of state-owned enterprises, improve the performance appraisal system and the selection and appointment mechanism of state-owned enterprise executives, and integrate innovation investment and innovation performance into the assessment system. The protection of intellectual property rights must also be enhanced to encourage enterprise innovation enthusiasm and to ensure effective protection of innovative products, technologies, and patents. Third, demand policies must be adjusted and formulated to provide a market space for innovative products. The government should focus on implementing policies that reduce the cost and risk of enterprise innovation, such as the practical implementation of the pre-tax deduction policy for research and development expenses and strengthen innovation demand policies in various ways. Government procurement policies should also be further refined to incentivize innovation. Fourth, the optimization of the industrial environment, increasing industrial concentration, reducing administrative monopolies, and promoting cluster innovation mechanisms should also be prioritized. Ultimately, the government must optimize its functions, clarify its role and position, and create a favorable external environment for enterprise technological innovation.

3.3. *Strengthening basic research to inject long-term momentum into innovation development*

Basic research is the cornerstone of innovation, and major breakthroughs in this field typically have a profound impact on technological advancement. Basic research has become an increasingly important source of invention and innovation. Whether in classical physics, electronic theory, quantum theory, information technology, biotechnology, or nanotechnology, each significant advance in basic research provides a huge impetus for economic development. In modern times, scientific and technological innovations rooted in basic research have greatly liberated social productivity, enhanced productive efficiency, and facilitated rapid economic and social development. If modern science and technology can be likened to a long river, then basic research is its source.

The first strategy is to increase investment in basic research and optimize its funding models. Basic research is the source of technological innovation and the foundation of a country's scientific and economic progress. However, it is characterized by long research cycles, high risks, and unpredictable outcomes. Therefore, the government should assume a more important role in research investment to address the problem of inadequate social funding for basic research as a public good, encourage greater social attention to basic research, and build a solid foundation for the strategic goal of building an innovative country. In addition to increasing competitive project funding, support for talents in basic research should also be strengthened. This includes increased funding for national key laboratories and research institutions to update equipment, creating a relaxed and free research environment. This will ensure that researchers have the autonomy to conduct original and exploratory research activities and deliver more high-quality results. Moreover, while increasing financial investment in basic research, strong companies and civil society forces should also be encouraged to conduct basic research. The government should guide enterprises to fully recognize the supporting role of basic research in technological competitiveness and, at the same time, actively improve the macro-environment and strengthen intellectual property protection to enhance the awareness of independent innovation in enterprises. Supporting enterprises in establishing key laboratories or cooperating with scientific research institutes to establish laboratories can promote enterprises to become the main body of technological innovation, providing strategic support for their long-term development and laying a market-oriented micro-foundation for the implementation of the innovation-driven development strategy.

Second, it is essential to reinforce the strategic deployment of basic research, create a favorable scientific research environment, and optimize the evaluation system. In the future, a series of key research projects related to national development strategies should be designed, encouraging free exploration in line with national strategic needs, and optimizing the evaluation system by placing greater emphasis on the quality of basic research. The construction of scientific research platforms should be strengthened, and the management model of basic research programs reformed, with increased support for original and breakthrough innovation projects. The top-level design of research platform construction should be aimed at meeting major strategic scientific and technological needs. The objective should be to improve originality and innovation capabilities, by more effectively coordinating projects, talents, and scientific research bases. It is necessary to strengthen the sharing of data and collaborative technology research in basic research, in order to improve the systematic and holistic nature of basic research. A scientific evaluation method for basic research achievements should be established, emphasizing the assessment of originality and innovation, the development of scientific research ethics, and the eradication of low-level duplication in basic research. For a long time, China's scientific research projects have tended to focus excessively on the likelihood of achieving research goals, resulting in applicants being more inclined to pursue projects with a high probability of success. In contrast, projects that involve original and major innovations, and higher risks, are usually less recognized by evaluation experts. It is important to improve the evaluation standards for project innovation, introduce peer review comprehensively, shift the focus from the quantity of results to their quality and original value, and prioritize originality in the project proposal process, thus encouraging research that emphasizes originality and innovation. The spirit of scientific exploration and innovation should be promoted, and a scientific research environment that rejects impatience and tolerates failure should be cultivated, creating a society-wide culture that reveres innovation, respects knowledge, and values science. In this way, experts engaged in basic research can devote themselves to research with greater creativity, take bold steps forward, and achieve more high-quality and influential original breakthroughs.

The third strategy for scientific and technological development emphasizes the importance of basic research as well as the cultivation of talent in this field. Compared to developed countries, China's emphasis on talent cultivation in the field of basic research is relatively low. Universities and research institutes are the basis for cultivating talent, but in recent years, the number of graduates in applied majors such as business management, marketing, law, and finance has increased, while disciplines related to basic research have not received sufficient attention. The proportion of students in science, technology, engineering, and mathematics (STEM) fields has decreased, and combined with limited investment in basic research, China lacks world-class leading talents in this area. If basic research is the source of technological innovation, then talent is the foundation of technological innovation. Active measures should be taken to attract high-level talent to engage in basic research activities. We should increase support for basic disciplines, promote the development of STEM colleges and related disciplines, encourage high-level talent to apply for STEM fields, and improve the quantity and quality of basic talent in natural sciences. We should encourage undergraduate and graduate students to participate in basic research, provide them with sufficient research funding and excellent research environments, and stimulate their curiosity and exploration of the unknown world, enabling them to pioneer innovation in the field of basic science. We should also support young talents to independently carry out basic research, explore cutting-edge scientific fields, and produce high-impact original results. According to the law of talent development in science and technology, the middle-aged period is generally the peak age for scientists to achieve breakthrough innovations. Based on the age distribution of Nobel Prize winners, most scientists achieve breakthrough innovations between the ages of 30 and 40 years (many during their doctoral studies). We should vigorously cultivate and utilize high-level young and middle-aged scientific and technological talents, adhere to the principle of flexible ways of screening talents under strict selection, and increase support for young talents. This will allow China to gain greater control in cutting-edge scientific and technological fields.

3.4. *Vigorously promoting the transformation and industrialization of scientific and technological achievements*

To achieve the transformation and industrialization of scientific and technological achievements, it is necessary not only to give full play to the leading role of enterprises in technological innovation, but also to better leverage the role of government and realize the efficient operation of the national innovation system. A significant part of Silicon Valley's success can be attributed to its largest risk investor: the government. The history of Silicon Valley can be seen as the best demonstration of the benefits of military-to-civilian technology transfer, as well as a perfect case of overall government intervention. The initial impetus for radio and electronic engineering came largely from the military during the two World Wars; the development of computers was heavily funded by the governments of the United Kingdom and the United States; the National Aeronautics and Space Agency (NASA) was the primary user of the first integrated circuits; the Defense Advanced Research Projects Agency (DARPA) of the United States Department of Defense created the Internet; and the World Wide Web was invented by the European Organization for Nuclear Research (CERN), which is a research center funded by multiple European countries.

To promote the transformation and industrialization of scientific and technological achievements, it is necessary to implement laws and regulations that govern such activities. In China, the Intellectual Property Law and the Promotion of Science and Technology Achievements Transformation Law are two important pieces of legislation that protect scientific and technological achievements and promote their commercialization. As economic and social development progresses, it is essential to revise and update these laws to effectively safeguard research activities, stimulate the creativity of researchers, and raise the overall level of social productivity. The United States has seen remarkable success in the transformation of scientific and technological achievements, largely due to the establishment of a robust legal framework for technology transfer. The Bayh–Dole Act, enacted in 1980, explicitly stated that patents resulting from the use of federal funds for university research belonged to the universities rather than the federal government. Universities could then transfer new technologies to companies and enterprises, with the revenue generated from such transfers remaining with the universities, and the inventors could share in patent licensing revenues. Subsequent legislation in the United States such as the Technology Innovation Act, Small Business Innovation Development Act, and Federal Technology Transfer Act, among others, further inspired universities, federal laboratories, and businesses to actively participate in technology transfer and commercialization activities, and also helped numerous prestigious universities in the

United States develop comprehensive patent policies. China's newly revised Promotion of Science and Technology Achievements Transformation Law has been in effect since October 1, 2015. However, besides improving relevant laws and regulations, it is also crucial to promote policies and regulations, promotion plans and key promotion projects, typical promotion cases, and experiences related to scientific and technological achievements transformation. By clarifying the ownership of intellectual property rights for scientific research achievements that are government-funded, researchers' creativity can be stimulated, and legal protection can gradually become an important component of the national innovation system.

Next, it is crucial to improve the pilot platforms for transforming scientific and technological achievements. Drawing on the experience of developed countries like the United States, the investment ratio for research and development, pilot testing, and product commercialization is typically 1:10:100, while in China, it stands at a mere 1:1:10. Currently, there is a lack of pilot bases in Chinese universities and research institutions, with most technological achievements remaining in the experimental stage or even just at the conceptual level, far from practical application. Companies, on the demand side of technology, are often reluctant to invest in or introduce such technological achievements due to potential technical risks. In many cases, research institutions blindly attempt to commercialize their achievements without conducting sufficient pilot testing or comprehensive engineering research. This approach can lead to failed transformation. Alternatively, when laboratory results have been achieved after a certain level of research, investment in engineering research and pilot testing is often abandoned due to the high costs involved. Consequently, when such achievements are combined with enterprises, additional development may be necessary, resulting in a delay in the transforming process and making it difficult to realize technological achievements. To address these issues, the government should implement policies that encourage the establishment of pilot platforms for research institutions and enterprises. First, financial support should be consolidated to establish a certain number of pilot platforms, utilizing funds that were previously distributed for the purpose of promoting technological achievements. The government should also actively attract private sector investment to promote the industrialization of pilot testing services. Second, an assessment of pilot testing should be added to the completion criteria for research projects, with the establishment of a profit-sharing mechanism for pilot testing achievements, thus motivating and incentivizing researchers to pay attention to pilot testing. Third, it is also important to provide incentives for pilot testing professionals.

Furthermore, there is a need to enhance the platform for sharing scientific and technological achievements. This can be achieved by establishing a comprehensive database and information-sharing platform, which can truly play a pivotal role in promoting information sharing. There is also a need to strengthen the basic infrastructure for intellectual property information retrieval and establish a patent database that is more user-friendly for the general public. The review process for intellectual property rights should be expedited to reduce the cost of review. The establishment of a national information infrastructure network can promote the public disclosure of enterprise intellectual property information, foster the development of existing technology investigation institutions, and establish an intangible asset evaluation system. To improve the utilization rate of intellectual property, enterprises can be encouraged to contribute their unused patents to a database that can be accessed by the public, which will significantly increase the utilization rate of scientific and technological achievements through information platforms and patent transfer platforms. At the national level, a nationwide technology transfer organization should be established to cover the entire country. This organization, in the form of a technology management association, should consolidate the technology transfer offices of various universities and research institutes into a national organization with technology transfer and industrialization as its core objectives. This will facilitate extensive cooperation and communication between various organizations. The United States has well-known national technology transfer centers, such as the National Technology Transfer Center (NTTC) and the Federal Laboratory Consortium for Technology Transfer (FLC). The NTTC's main task is to use its large and advanced computer network to quickly transfer technology with industrial application prospects from over 700 federally funded national laboratories, universities, and private research institutions to society and industry, turning them into productivity as soon as possible. The aim of the FLC is to accelerate the penetration of federally-funded research results into the national economy.

Finally, it is imperative to develop entrepreneurial universities for promoting the transformation of scientific and technological achievements. The concept of an "entrepreneurial university" was proposed by the famous American educationist Burton Clark, who studied many characteristic universities in Europe and America. He predicted that entrepreneurial universities would play an increasingly important role in the knowledge-based economy society and even become the core institutions for future social development. The goal of building entrepreneurial universities is to guide the transformation of university development and promote the prosperity of scientific and technological entrepreneurship. The mission of universities has shifted from the transmission of knowledge (education) to the creation of knowledge (research) and the commercial application of the new knowledge created (entrepreneurship or innovation). The research-oriented university (a model adopted by Humboldt University in Germany), which emerged as a special institution at the end of the 19th century, combined teaching and research activities that were previously developed separately in universities and scientific associations. Similarly, the entrepreneurial university combines the mission of promoting economic and social development with the missions of teaching and research. Entrepreneurial universities have four pillars: (1) academic leaders who can formulate and implement their own strategic ideas; (2) organizational capabilities to transform results through granting patents, issuing licenses, and incubation; (3) management personnel, faculty, and students who generally have an entrepreneurial spirit; and (4) the ability to legally control university resources, including physical property and research intellectual property.[7] Entrepreneurial universities have a strong culture of innovation, with professors, researchers, and students actively promoting the commercialization of research results. The technology transfer office is responsible for identifying technologies that can be commercialized from university research and selling them to industrialized companies. To become an "entrepreneur," a university must have a considerable degree of independence and autonomy, being both independent of government departments and industrial sectors while also maintaining close ties and interactions with these sectors. Entrepreneurial universities advocate for the application of knowledge in practical settings, and to achieve this goal, many countries have different institutional arrangements. For example, in the United States, ownership of intellectual property can be shared between inventors and universities, while in countries such as Sweden, the intellectual property belongs entirely to the inventors. In order to purchase patent ownership and commercialize it,

[7]Henry Etzkowitz. (2005). *The Triple Helix: University-Industry-Government Innovation and Entrepreneurship.* Orient Press, p. 31.

universities have established holding companies and have to some extent taken on corporate characteristics. Another type of entrepreneurial university is a new type of entrepreneurial university established on the basis of science parks, research centers, or some companies. For example, the Blekinge Institute of Technology was developed on the basis of the software center of the Karlskrona/Ronneby Science Park in Sweden. This university model is different from other universities, where the primary activity is knowledge-based economic activities, followed by university research work. The formation and development of the high-tech industry model in the United States show that the transformation of some university research institutes is crucial. Since the 1990s, a major feature of the US high-tech industry has been the shift of everyone's attention from large-scale R&D to R&BD (research and business development, the commercialization of R&D results). With this transformation, many universities have begun to transform from research universities to entrepreneurial universities, with Stanford University being the most typical and successful example.

Compared to Stanford University in the United States, whose technology transfer rate reaches 60–70%, the current technology transfer rate of Chinese universities is low. Nonetheless, a major issue has been overlooked: regardless of whether it is in natural sciences, engineering, or social sciences, the education provided in universities corresponds directly to the modern knowledge system, which differs from the knowledge required for industrial development. The university knowledge system is more advanced and ahead of its time. However, in terms of actual industrial development, what is needed is more suitable technology that corresponds to the market competition strategy, namely technology that can solve problems and meet the requirements of enterprise competition or operational strategies, rather than the most advanced technology. It should be noted that universities play a role in knowledge creation and talent development within the R&D organizational system. Universities need stable and basic financial support to explore freely and cultivate innovative talents. But currently, most research funding and scientist income come from projects. Over-emphasizing the technology transfer rate of university research projects may lead to universities becoming increasingly utilitarian. For universities, research institutes, and public basic service institutions, it is necessary to provide them with the ability to independently determine research directions and allocate resources, in order to lay a knowledge foundation for industrial technology innovation.

Therefore, to resolve the contradiction between university supply and industry demand, it is necessary to further clarify the positioning of various types of universities and develop a group of entrepreneurial universities. The main difference between entrepreneurial universities and research universities is that entrepreneurial universities closely integrate basic research, applied research, teaching, and industrial innovation, and capitalize on knowledge, forming a virtuous circle between knowledge and industry, thereby promoting regional and national economic development.

3.5. *Implementing the strategy of prioritizing talent development*

Talent is the foundation of innovation, and innovation-driven essentially means talent-driven. Whoever possesses first-class innovative talent possesses the advantage and dominant position in technological innovation. Without a strong talent team as a backing, independent innovation is like water without a source or a tree without roots. In essence, the competition for comprehensive national power ultimately boils down to a competition for talent. The characteristics and functions of talent resources as the first resource for economic and social development are more evident, and talent competition has become the core of comprehensive national strength competition. Whoever can cultivate and attract more outstanding talent can occupy an advantageous position in the competition.

China possesses a significant pool of human resources and is home to the world's largest scientific and technological teams. In 2015, the number of R&D personnel in China reached 3.95 million, ranking first globally. However, China currently faces several prominent challenges in the field of talent development. These include the low level and inadequate structure of R&D personnel, a shortage of world-class scientific and technological experts, insufficient leading and top-notch talent, a gap between the training of engineering and technical personnel and production and innovation practices, a need to improve talent policies, and the need for further reforms in education. Therefore, there is a pressing need to innovate the mechanisms for utilizing, training, and attracting talent.

First and foremost, it is crucial to effectively leverage and mobilize talent by establishing a more dynamic talent management mechanism, enhancing the evaluation system, eliminating institutional barriers that hinder talent flow, utilization, and effectiveness, and harmonizing the construction of talent teams across different domains, including high-level innovative talent, young scientific and technological talent, and practical technical talent. By doing so, we can provide the utmost support and assistance to scientists and technologists in their pursuit of innovation and entrepreneurship. Moreover, we should empower innovative leaders with greater control over financial, human, and technological resources, as well as decision-making authority on technological paths. The voice of entrepreneurs must also be amplified in the national innovation decision-making system. Ultimately, it is imperative to actively cultivate world-class scientists, scientific and technological pioneers, outstanding engineers, and high-performing innovation teams, as it is commonly said that "it is easy to assemble an army of one thousand soldiers, but difficult to find a good general."

Secondly, there is a need to deepen education reform and advance quality education by innovating teaching methods and enhancing the quality of talent cultivation, in order to create an environment conducive to the growth of innovative talent. It is essential to cultivate a society-wide culture that encourages bold, courageous, and inclusive innovation, while valuing not only success but also embracing failure. Individualized talent development must be promoted by advocating academic freedom and independent thinking, emphasizing critical thinking skills in students, and discouraging herd mentality. Discovering, nurturing, and respecting individualized behaviors among students will facilitate their comprehensive and free development. Encouraging questioning and innovation and inspiring students to put forth innovative academic perspectives are also paramount. Building a platform for intellectual exchange among different schools of thought will allow teachers and students to interact freely and equally in academic discussions, creating a fertile ground for innovative sparks. Moreover, creating a soil conducive to the development of young students' personal interests and strengths, cultivating the courage to question and explore, and fully promoting their initiative, enthusiasm, and creativity in learning and research, are essential in providing a relaxed environment for the cultivation of innovative talent and promoting their all-round development. Finally, it is important to deepen education and teaching mode reform and promote flexibility in the teaching process. While ensuring strict standards for teaching quality and curriculum assessment, more attention should be paid to enhancing flexibility in the teaching process. Drawing on the experience of advanced countries in higher education, continuous innovation in terms of years of study, professional and course offerings, study modes, teaching methods, and assessment methods should be encouraged. Teachers should also be encouraged to adopt new methods and innovative teaching techniques. By strengthening personalized and innovative education for students, a flexible environment for their all-round development can be created.

The third goal is to actively recruit outstanding talent from abroad, selecting the best and brightest from around the world and implementing more proactive policies for attracting innovative talent. Through the gathering of distinguished individuals with global perspectives and exceptional competencies, who occupy prominent positions in industry and technology, a culture can be cultivated that embraces talent from across the world. This approach facilitates the consolidation of resources for talent acquisition while optimizing institutional and functional arrangements. At the national level, we should establish overseas talent liaison stations to keep abreast of the latest developments among foreign talents and gather information on them. We should also steadily advance the opening-up of the human resources market and encourage domestic HR service organizations that meet the requirements to collaborate with their foreign counterparts, gradually improving the efficiency of talent acquisition. After professional talent recruitment agencies have evaluated and recognized them, we can offer high salaries, bonuses, or research funding to attract these outstanding scientists and technicians to work or visit China. It is essential to fully trust and empower these talents, supporting them in deep participation in national projects and conducting scientific research. Furthermore, we should continuously improve supporting policies for talent acquisition, including addressing issues related to employment, social security, household registration, and education for children. It is also viable to further utilize local talents by establishing research and development bases overseas or using the high-tech talents of foreign companies through acquisition or merger.

It is recommended to relax the conditions and implement relevant measures for high-tech talents from abroad to apply for visas and residency in China. Policies should be formulated for the management of permanent residency for foreigners, and legislation should be accelerated to regulate and relax the conditions for technical talents to obtain permanent residency permits. High-end foreign talents holding permanent residency permits should be given the same treatment as Chinese citizens in innovative activities such as starting high-tech enterprises.

Convenience should be granted for work permits for qualified foreign talents, as well as visas and residency permits for them and their accompanying family members. Age restrictions for work permits for qualified foreign high-level scientific and technological innovation talents can be lifted under certain conditions. In addition, professional agencies can be established to manage foreign visas, residency, and immigration affairs in a unified manner, standardize the approval of residency and naturalization applications, and provide comprehensive residency and household registration security for foreign high-end talent in China.

Chapter 11

Actively Adapt, Lead, and Grasp China's New Normal for Economic Development

Analyzing and studying the stages and key tasks of China's economy holds significant importance within the realm of political economics, particularly in the context of socialism with Chinese characteristics. In the process of amalgamating the fundamental principles of Marxism with the realities of China, our Party has consistently propelled theoretical innovation through practical application, thereby enriching and advancing Marxist political economics. During his visit to Henan Province in May 2014, Xi Jinping introduced the notion of the "new normal." Subsequently, in November 2014, at the opening ceremony of the APEC Business Leaders Summit, he presented a comprehensive elucidation of the principal characteristics, developmental opportunities, and the comprehensive deepening reform of China's new normal for economic development. Further expounding on this matter, Xi Jinping emphasized, at the Central Economic Work Conference held in December 2014, the imperative nature of "understanding the new normal, adapting to the new normal, and leading the new normal" as the fundamental logic driving China's current and future economic development.[1] The proposition of "China's New Normal for Economic Development" not only represents a novel assertion, achievement, and category within the domain of Marxist political economics, but it also equips us with a fresh theoretical instrument and framework to analyze and examine the forthcoming developmental trends of China's economy.

[1]Central economic work conference held in Beijing. *People's Daily*, December 12, 2014.

1. New Stage, New Normal: China's Evolving Economic Development

Xi Jinping emphasized the necessity of "a scientific understanding of the current situation, an accurate assessment of future trends, and a historical and dialectical comprehension of the stage characteristics of China's economic development."[2] Despite more than three decades of rapid economic growth, China's economy has now transitioned to medium- to high-speed growth. In 2015, China's total GDP reached 68.6 trillion yuan, accounting for over 15% of the global economy. From various perspectives such as economic volume, structure, efficiency, and impact, China has undeniably emerged as a formidable economic power. Nevertheless, it is important to acknowledge that the "13th Five-Year Plan" period will confront a range of risks and challenges. These include the diminishing demographic dividend, the potential "middle-income trap," and profound adjustments in the international economic landscape. Consequently, China's economy is entering a new stage of development and transitioning into a "new normal" of economic progress.

Firstly, China has successfully ascended as a major economic power and finds itself at a significant turning point in its journey toward achieving this status. From an assessment of our nation's current situation, the "new normal" economy can be regarded as representative of an economy befitting a major country. Notably, historical data reveals this remarkable transformation. In 1978, China's GDP amounted to a mere $218.4 billion, positioning it as the 10th largest economy globally. However, by 2015, China's GDP had soared to 68.6 trillion yuan, surpassing $10 trillion and firmly securing the second rank on the world stage. In certain economically advanced provinces and cities along China's eastern coast, the economic aggregate and per capita GDP have approached or even surpassed those of moderately developed nations. When juxtaposed with the GDP figure of 1.3 trillion yuan in 2010, it is projected that by the conclusion of the "13th Five-Year Plan," our economic aggregate will exceed 80 trillion yuan, marking a significant milestone in our economic scale.

According to United Nations, at the end of 2014, China's output of more than 200 industrial products such as steel, coal, cement, and cotton cloth ranked first in the world, and China's position as a major manufacturing country was basically established. Through a horizontal comparison

---

[2] *Ibid.*

of comprehensive indicators such as economic aggregate, per capita GDP of some provinces and cities, and manufacturing output value, it can be seen that China's Reform and Opening-up over the past 30 years have created a "growth miracle" in the history of the world economy, and has become a veritable economic power. This is an important feature of China's economy entering a new stage.

Nevertheless, it is crucial to recognize that a large economy alone does not guarantee strong international competitiveness. Historically, in 1830, before First Opium War, China's GDP accounted for 29% of the world economy, ranking first in the world. In contrast, Britain's GDP accounted for only 9.5% of the world economy during the same period, but its industrial structure is completely different from that of China. At this time, British steel production continued to increase, and machine manufacturing developed rapidly, starting to export steam engines and various technical equipment to various countries in Western Europe, while China's total GDP mainly came from agricultural products and handicrafts. The turning point arrived in 1840 when Britain, armed with powerful ships and cannons made possible by the Industrial Revolution, forcefully opened China's doors. Subsequently, China regressed into a weak and impoverished semi-colonial and semi-feudal nation. Therefore, as we stand at the threshold of a new historical phase in our journey toward economic prowess, we must prioritize the optimization of our industrial structure and the enhancement of economic quality. Only by doing so can we genuinely augment national competitiveness and propel China's economy to loftier heights.

Secondly, the "Lewis turning point"[3] has accelerated and the constraints on factor resources have intensified. The "Lewis turning point" concept elucidates the phenomenon observed in developing countries characterized by a dual economic structure. Initially, surplus labor is abundant, allowing for a continuous supply of labor to meet industrialization needs without causing significant wage increases. However, a critical moment arrives when industrialization absorbs all available surplus labor. At this juncture, in order to continue absorbing surplus labor, wage levels must rise. Failing to increase wages would result in agricultural laborers

---

[3] William Arthur Lewis conducted groundbreaking research on the economic development of developing countries, a contribution that earned him the prestigious Nobel Prize in Economics in 1979. The "Lewis turning point" is named after him.

remaining outside the industrial sector. This pivotal stage is known as the "Lewis turning point."

Since the initiation of China's Reform and Opening-up policy, the sustained and rapid economic growth of the country has been significantly driven by the continuous release of population dividends. This has been primarily attributed to China's advantageous position in terms of low production costs and wages for domestic labor, which has attracted offshore manufacturing outsourcing. However, this comparative advantage is gradually diminishing due to changes in China's population structure. According to statistics, in 2012, the working-age population (aged 15–59 years) was recorded at 937.27 million, reflecting a decrease of 3.45 million compared to the previous year's end. Concurrently, the proportion of the elderly population continues to rise, with 193.9 million individuals aged 60 and above, accounting for 14.3% of the total population. This indicates a 0.59 percentage point increase from the preceding year's end. The emergence of an inflection point in China's population dividend has brought forth three significant consequences. Firstly, the cost of labor has escalated, leading to a gradual weakening of the comparative advantage associated with labor costs. Secondly, the rise in the elderly population has resulted in an increased population dependency ratio, leading to a decline in savings rates and an upward pressure on funding costs. Thirdly, the reduction in the total labor force population has caused labor shortages, such as the "shortage of migrant workers."[4] These three consequences directly contribute to a decrease in China's potential economic growth rate.

Since 2010, based on the caliber of permanent residents, that is, considering the factors of labor migration from rural to urban areas, the decrease in the rural working-age population has been approaching the increase in the urban working-age population year by year (the point where the two are equal is the moment when China as a whole stops increasing the working-age population), and the labor market is gradually responding to this, On the one hand, there is a continuous "shortage of migrant workers" phenomenon throughout the country, and on the other hand, the wages of migrant workers are increasing year on year. By definition, this is the characteristic manifestation of the arrival of the "Lewis turning point." In essence, the arrival of the "Lewis turning point" means the disappearance of the traditional demographic dividend.

[4]See Wang Yiming (Ed.). (2013). *The Benefits of Reform: Driving Economic Growth and Dynamism*. People's Publishing House.

However, looking ahead, it is crucial to proactively generate new demographic dividends by bolstering the human capital of the working-age population and transitioning toward a nation that excels in human capital rather than sheer population size.

In addition, the increasing supply constraints on factor resources also indicate that China's economy has entered a new stage of development. Over the past 30 years, China's economic growth model of excessive reliance on investment and external demand has made the constraints of energy, resources, and the environment increasingly evident. According to statistics, at present, China's average consumption intensity of five major resources, including freshwater, primary energy, steel, cement, and commonly used nonferrous metals, is about 90% higher than the world average, making it one of the countries with the highest GDP energy consumption in the world. The external dependence on important mineral resources such as iron ore, copper concentrate, and bauxite exceeded 50%. In 2015, China's oil external dependence exceeded 60%, and the import pressure is increasing. It can be said that the marginal supply increment of factors has been difficult to support the traditional high-speed development path of the economy, which has objectively prompted the Chinese economy to gradually fall back to a new stable growth range.

Third, entering the ranks of middle-income countries faces the risk of a "middle-income trap." By the end of 2015, China's per capita GDP approached $8000, and according to the World Bank's standards, it had entered the ranks of upper and middle-income countries, and its economic development had entered a new historical stage. Some countries in Latin America and Southeast Asia have long entered the ranks of middle-income countries. However, as most countries are climbing toward high-income economies, economic growth still relies on strategies, models, and methods for developing from low-income economies to middle-income economies. Further economic growth is locked in by the original growth mechanism, and per capita national income struggles to surpass the lower threshold for high income, resulting in these countries consistently hovering at the middle-income level. This is the "middle-income trap." Standing at the new starting point of development, we must be fully aware of the risks and challenges currently facing us, strive to achieve the "new normal" and smoothly overcome the "middle-income trap." These risks include the following: First, technological innovation capabilities need to be further improved. "Inadequate technological innovation capabilities leading to low input output efficiency" is the primary basic characteristic of some economies falling into the "middle-income trap." On the whole, China's technological innovation capability is low, and the level of industrial technology needs to be further improved. In recent years, China has achieved remarkable results in building an innovative country, with major breakthroughs in manned spaceflight, lunar exploration projects, and high-speed railways. However, the mastery of original inventions and key core technologies is still far from sufficient. The second is the slow progress of economic restructuring. "The excessive dependence of the economy on external demand leads to unstable economic development" is one of the basic characteristics of some countries and regions falling into the "middle-income trap." Judging from the actual situation of China's economic operation, China's long-term economic growth model driven by external demand has undergone significant adjustments, supported by a series of strong policies aimed at expanding domestic demand. However, it is worth pointing out that existing research shows that from 2000 to 2013, the consumption rate in China's economic growth has been showing a downward trend, while the investment rate has always been at a high level. Third, the fairness of income distribution needs to be improved. Before the reform and opening-up, China gave priority to the development of heavy industry at the expense of agriculture. Purchase agricultural products at low prices, accumulate funds for industry, and subsidize cities in order to achieve industrialization and form a skewed income distribution for urban residents. Since the reform and opening-up, although the government has taken a series of measures to narrow the income gap between urban and rural residents, due to the significant economic and social development gap between urban and rural areas in China, the income level of urban and rural residents has been continuously widening. The unfairness of income distribution also leads to the entrenchment of social interests and the reduction of social mobility, causing dissatisfaction among the masses and social conflicts.

Fourth, there are many systematic and institutional obstacles, and the comprehensive deepening of reform has entered a critical period. A notable challenge lies in the persistent lack of separation between the government and enterprises, capital, society, and affairs within China's economic landscape. The fiscal and tax system exhibits significant shortcomings, including an irrational tax structure, as well as a mismatch between financial resources and powers held by the central and local governments. The modern financial system requires substantial improvements to enhance its effectiveness. Additionally, there are several emerging contradictions within the ownership structure and income distribution system that need to be addressed. Overall, China's comprehensive deepening of reform has entered a critical period and deep water zone. Although breakthroughs have been made in some areas of reform through more than 30 years of Reform and Opening-up, market-oriented reform has not been completely completed, and many areas are still not in place. Key supporting reforms, such as those related to the land system, registered residence system, social security system, and investment and financing system with a focus on new urbanization, are still in their early stages and require further comprehensive deepening. In addition, government departments still intervene more in microeconomic activities, and administrative approval methods still occupy a significant position in resource allocation. In the new normal where the market plays a decisive role, government functions need to be repositioned and adjusted, and institutional mechanisms need to be straightened out to achieve administrative process reengineering.

Fifth, the world economic landscape has undergone profound adjustments, and global governance has entered a new stage. Since the 2008 global financial crisis, the world economic growth has hit two bottoms. Growth differentiation among various economies has intensified, and political, economic, and geopolitical factors are intertwined and have deepened their impact on the world economy. The world economy is still in a period of deep adjustment after the global financial crisis. Currently, the world economy may have many unstable and uncertain phases, and the recovery path remains tortuous. The probability of a significant recovery is small, making China's external economic environment more complex. Developed countries are collectively caught in the "Japanese disease." The main manifestations are: First, entering the liquidity trap. Interest rates in the United States, Europe, and Japan are generally very low, at around 1% or even lower. Countries have adopted unconventional monetary policies, such as the Bank of Japan expanding bond purchases. The second is the deep debt crisis. European countries have just emerged from the European debt crisis, and it will still take a long time for their economies to regain momentum. The overall debt ratios of Japan and the United States are even higher than those of countries in the European debt crisis. The high level of government debt has greatly weakened the government's ability to stimulate the economy. The third is the aging of the population. The phenomenon of population aging in Japan and Europe is becoming increasingly serious. The majority of population born during the "baby boom" era in the United States is now retired, and the pressure of aging will also increase in the future. To a large extent, this will cause global demand to shrink and weaken China's external demand. Emerging economies collectively enter a period of adjustment. Some countries have experienced capital outflows, inflation, and a slowdown in economic growth. The economies of emerging economies have differentiated with differences in economic autonomy. With the continuous decline in energy and resource prices, countries such as Russia and Brazil that rely excessively on resource and energy prices have seen a significant decline in their economic growth rate. Although India has been less affected by international trade, its fragile financial system has been severely impacted by international capital flight. On the whole, this may make global competition more intense and trigger the rise of trade protectionism.

2. New Normal: The Path to Comprehensive Economic Optimization and Upgrading

The term "new normal" was initially coined by foreign financial institutions to describe the process of global economic recovery following a crisis. Among Chinese leaders, Xi Jinping was the first to adopt the term "new normal" to assess and depict economic performance. He also placed a primary focus on the trajectory of economic growth rate, specifically the transition "from high-speed growth to medium-high growth." On November 10, 2014, during the opening ceremony of the APEC CEO Summit, Xi Jinping emphasized, "China's economy has embarked upon a new phase characterized by several significant features. Firstly, there is a shift from a period of high-speed growth to one marked by medium-to-high-speed growth. Secondly, ongoing efforts are being made to optimize and upgrade the economic structure. This entails the increasing dominance of the tertiary industry and consumer demand, the reduction of the urban–rural gap, a rising proportion of residents' income, and a broader distribution of development benefits. Thirdly, the country is undergoing a transition from a factor-driven, investment-focused economy to one propelled by innovation."[5] These are the three major features of the "new normal," namely the transformation of growth pace, the optimization of economic structure, and the shift in driving forces. In December 2014,

[5]Xi Jinping. Pursuing sustainable development in a concerted effort to build an Asia-Pacific community with a shared dream — speech at the opening ceremony of the APEC CEO summit. *People's Daily*, November 10, 2014.

Xi Jinping provided a more comprehensive elaboration on the concept of the "new normal" during the Central Economic Work Conference. He proposed, "China's economy was evolving into a more advanced and complex form, characterized by a more rational division of labor and a more reasonable economic structure. The shift was marked by a transition from high-speed growth to a medium-high growth trajectory. Furthermore, the focus was shifting from simply expanding the scale and speed of economic development to a more concentrated effort on improving its quality and efficiency. The approach to economic development was being transformed from incremental expansion to a more profound adjustment of existing resources while optimizing new additions. The driving forces behind economic development were also transitioning from traditional growth points to new ones."[6] In summary, the "new normal" in China encompasses four key features: a shift in the growth rate, a change in the mode of development, optimization of the economic structure, and a shift in the driving forces of development.

During the Central Economic Work Conference, Xi Jinping proposed nine distinct trend characteristics of China's "new normal" for economic development.

- *Consumer Demand*: The era of imitative wave exhaust consumption has largely concluded, with personalized and diversified consumption gradually becoming the prevailing trend.
- *Investment Demand*: While traditional industries have reached a saturation point, numerous investment opportunities have emerged in areas such as infrastructure connectivity, new technologies, new products, new formats, and new business models.
- *Exports and Balance of Payments*: With global aggregate demand currently sluggish, efforts to cultivate new comparative advantages are necessary to sustain the supportive role of exports in economic development.
- *Production Capacity and Industrial Organization*: The supply capacity of traditional industries has surpassed demand significantly. Emerging industries, service industries, and small and micro enterprises have gained prominence. The miniaturization, intelligence, and specialization of production are emerging as new characteristics of industrial organization.

[6]Central economic work conference held in Beijing. *People's Daily*, December 12, 2014.

- *Relative Advantages of Production Factors*: Previously, low labor costs were the primary advantage. However, with an aging population, economic growth will increasingly rely on the quality of human capital and technological progress.
- *Market Competition Characteristics*: Formerly driven by quantity expansion and price competition, market competition is gradually shifting toward quality-based and differentiation-based competition.
- *Resource and Environmental Constraints*: In the past, there was relatively more leeway regarding energy resources and the ecological environment. Today, it is essential to meet people's expectations for a sound ecological environment and foster a new path of green and low-carbon circular development.
- *Accumulation and Resolution of Economic Risks*: Addressing both the symptoms and root causes of economic risks is crucial. The application of appropriate measures and the establishment of effective institutional mechanisms for risk resolution are necessary.
- *Resource Allocation Patterns and Macroeconomic Regulation Methods*: The marginal effects of comprehensive stimulus policies have diminished significantly. It is imperative to grasp the new changes in the overall supply–demand relationship comprehensively and conduct macroeconomic regulation in a scientifically informed manner.

It is worth noting that there are many misconceptions about the new normal economy in society at present. Some people see the economic downturn as the new normal for China's economic development. In fact, the downward pressure on the economy comes from both external and internal sources, is not without remedy, and is not a "free fall." At present, China's industrialization and urbanization have not been completed, and its economic development has ample room for maneuver, ample space, and good resilience. The economic slowdown is only a short-term pressure. In addition, China is currently able to maintain a growth rate of about 6.5%, which is still high among the world's major economies. Some people see deflation as the new normal for China's economic development. In fact, deflation is the main risk in our country's current economic operation, but we have not fallen into deflation, and deflation is a short-term economic fluctuation problem. There is still a lot of room for our fiscal and monetary policies, and if the policies are appropriate, the situation of deflation can be completely avoided. Some people see overcapacity as the new normal for China's economic development. From a practical point of view, with the continuous improvement of China's market economy system and the in-depth promotion of international production capacity and equipment cooperation, the risk of overcapacity will be effectively resolved in the future and for some time to come.

Some people hold the misconception that GDP can be disregarded in the context of the "new normal." However, this perspective is flawed. China is still a developing nation, and the key to addressing various challenges lies in continued economic development. Consider the consequences if GDP were neglected — how could we ensure employment opportunities and improve people's livelihoods? It is important to understand that, within China's "new normal" for economic development, the objective is not to pursue GDP growth at any cost, but rather to foster environmentally sustainable, inclusive, and socially beneficial GDP. While it is necessary to accept a certain degree of decline in economic growth, strategic focus should be maintained and strengthened in order to align with the goals of China's new economic development paradigm.[7]

The understanding, adaptation, and leadership of China's "new normal" for economic development serve as the guiding principles during the "13th Five-Year Plan" period. The evolving economic landscape in China presents both challenges and opportunities. By effectively harnessing these changes and trends, it is possible to achieve comprehensive optimization and upgrading of the country's economy. This is evident in the following areas:

First, the economic growth rate has shifted from high to medium-high. The transformation of the growth rate is a basic feature of China's New Normal for Economic Development of China's economy. From the second quarter of 2010 to the first half of 2016, China's economic growth rate has slowed for 23 consecutive quarters. In fact, a moderate decline in economic growth is a common rule after the economy reaches the level of middle-income countries. From an international perspective, after World War II, a number of successful catch-up countries such as Japan, South Korea, and Germany experienced rapid economic growth in the 1960s and 1970s, and without exception, their growth rate fell, with an average range of 30–40%. At this stage, these countries begin to transition from high growth to medium to high growth, and then to medium to low growth.

---

[7]Deepening reform, bringing advantage into play, and innovating ideas to ensure sustainable and healthy economic development, social harmony, and stability. *People's Daily*, May 11, 2014.

As a middle-income country, China's economic growth has entered a medium to high-speed stage from its original high speed. We need to find a "golden balance" between necessity and possibility, between transformation and upgrading, and maintaining a reasonable growth rate, so as to maintain growth within a reasonable range and ensure relatively full employment. This can leave space and time for promoting China's economic quality and efficiency, stability, and long-term development. However, it should also be noted that although China's economic growth has slowed somewhat, the growth rate of around 6.5% is still relatively high globally, not only much higher than that of developed countries but also significantly higher than that of major developing countries. In 2014, the US economy grew by 2.4%, the eurozone by 0.9%, and Japan's economic growth rate was zero. Therefore, we need to maintain strategic focus, strengthen confidence, and continue to promote the transformation and upgrading of China's economy.

The second is to transform the development mode from extensive growth based on scale and speed to intensive growth based on quality and efficiency. The transformation of development mode is a basic requirement of the new normal of China's economy. Over the past 30 years of reform and opening-up, China's economic development and construction have achieved remarkable achievements, and problems such as imbalance, uncoordinated, and unsustainable development have been continuously improved. In recent years, we have made continuous efforts to improve the means of performance evaluation, improve economic quality and efficiency, move toward quality-based differentiated market competition, promote green and sustainable development, and pay more attention to ensuring and improving people's living standards, providing important support for the transformation of the economic development mode to quality efficient and intensive growth. The original market competition mainly relies on quantity expansion and disorderly competition in prices, the continuous strengthening of resource and environmental constraints on economic growth, the environmental carrying capacity has reached or approached the upper limit, the mismatch between investment and consumption, the large income distribution gap, the weak foundation of agricultural development, uncoordinated urban and rural regional development, the coexistence of total employment pressure and structural contradictions, and other issues have gradually been improved. During the transition period of the growth stage, the slowdown in the growth rate is easy to attract attention. However, speed changes are quite superficial, and more importantly, the structural and developmental quality changes behind speed are of greater importance. Over the past 30 years of reform and opening-up, China's economic development has maintained an average annual growth rate of nearly 10%, which is a leap in quantity. From a research perspective, it is important to recognize that even if China's economy experiences a further decrease in its potential growth rate and overall growth rate, successful completion of the transformation of economic growth drivers and a focus on quality-based economic growth can yield significant results. While the previous era of rapid growth may not be replicated, the overall value generated by this transition and the outcomes achieved through a slowdown in growth can surpass the effects of past high-speed growth. By prioritizing sustainable and high-quality economic development, the goals of economic progress can still be attained.

The third is the transformation of the industrial structure from mid- to low-end to mid- to high-end. Upgrading the industrial structure is the main direction of the new normal of China's economy. From the current situation, developing countries have long been at the low end of their industrial structure. On the one hand, it has formed a huge gap between them and developed countries in traditional industries; On the other hand, the industrial cliff of high-tech industries and modern service industries is emerging, which means that developed countries highlight the huge contrast with developing countries and, to a considerable extent, suppress the development of the latter with their large bodies and high levels of high-tech industries and modern service industries. As a large country with a large population, land area, and industry, China must constantly promote its industrial structure from the low-end to the medium to high-end, in order to lay a solid material foundation for achieving long-term sustainable economic growth and long-term social stability. Since the reform and opening-up, China's industrial structure is mainly located at the middle and lower tiers of the global value chain, with relatively low comparative benefits. In 2013, the added value of China's tertiary industry accounted for 46.1% of GDP, surpassing the secondary industry for the first time; In 2015, this proportion climbed to 50.5%, which is a very good sign of structural optimization. With the vigorous development of strategic emerging industries, advanced manufacturing industries, and the accelerated implementation of measures to gradually resolve the risk of overcapacity, China's industry is gradually improving its position in the global value chain, and the "Chinese Efficiency" are gradually emerging.

The fourth is the transition from factor-driven and investment-driven growth to innovation-driven growth. This shift in growth momentum constitutes the core essence of China's economic transformation. Over the past three decades, China has followed a development path characterized by high investment, high consumption, high pollution, and low efficiency. However, the sustainability of the high-speed growth model reliant on factors and investment has reached its limits. In response to the global wave of technological innovation and industrial revolution, and with enterprises increasingly embracing transformation and innovation, the driving force behind China's economic growth is gradually evolving. In recent years, the national investment in science and technology has witnessed continuous growth, which has in turn stimulated the investments made by enterprises and society as a whole. The overall social expenditure on research and development (R&D) has experienced annual increases of over 20%, surpassing the growth rates of developed countries. China's economy is gradually transitioning into an innovation-driven new normal, forging a unique "Chinese quality" and achieving a shift from the pursuit of high growth rates to a focus on high-quality growth. The first step in abandoning the old growth model and embracing the new normal is the innovation-driven growth. China is in the process of addressing deep-rooted contradictions and accumulated problems stemming from more than three decades of rapid economic development. It is adapting to the new characteristics and requirements of medium to high-speed and high-level development. Concurrently, there is a shift in how local officials evaluate their performance, moving away from an overemphasis on growth rates and factor-driven development. Efforts are being made to stimulate the innovative vigor of the entire society, align China's economic development with the "three major principles"[8] of economic, natural, and social laws, and facilitate a transformation from factor-driven and investment-driven growth to innovation-driven growth. This transformation is being pursued primarily through reforms and fostering a culture of innovation.

Fifth, there is a transformation in resource allocation from the market playing a fundamental role to a decisive role. This shift in resource

---

[8]On July 29, 2014, during the Political Bureau meeting of the Central Committee, President Xi Jinping put forth the proposition that development should adhere to the principles of scientific development based on economic laws, sustainable development based on natural laws, and inclusive development based on social laws.

allocation patterns serves as a crucial mechanism in China's new normal for economic development. Market-determined resource allocation is a fundamental principle of a market economy. At its core, a market economy is based on the principle that the market determines resource allocation. The primary concern in all economic activities revolves around how to allocate resources in the most efficient manner. Resource allocation refers to the utilization of various production factors for the production of different goods and the distribution of these goods among the owners of the production factors. Different resource allocation methods will lead to different allocation efficiency. Economic development is about improving the allocation efficiency of resources, especially scarce resources, and investing as few resources as possible in producing as many products as possible to achieve the greatest possible benefits. Both theory and practice have proven that market allocation of resources is the most efficient form. The market determines the allocation of resources by allowing market economic laws such as the laws of value, competition, and supply and demand to play a decisive role in the allocation of resources in economic activities. In the past, we emphasized the fundamental role of the market in resource allocation under the conditions of a socialist market economy. Obviously, government carries out more economic functions and has management authority. From past practice, China's economic system is basically a government-led imperfect market economy. There are many problems, such as the obviously unreasonable allocation of resources, and the vulnerability to serious corruption issues. The Decision of the Central Committee of the Communist Party of China on Several Major Issues Concerning Comprehensively Deepening Reform was adopted at the Third Plenary Session of the 18th CPC Central Committee, and it proposes to make the market play a decisive role in the allocation of resources. The Fourth Plenary Session of the 18th CPC Central Committee proposes that the socialist market economy is essentially a legal economy, indicating that our Party has reached a new level of understanding of the laws of the market economy. Under the new normal, in which the market plays a decisive role, the government does not engage in strong stimulus. It mainly transfers the decision-making power of resource allocation to the market through changing functions, streamlining administration, delegating power, reducing taxes, and transferring profits, continuously enhancing the endogenous power of the economy, and compensating for "market failure" through interval regulation, targeted regulation, and other methods.

Sixth, the transformation of economic well-being from an unbalanced type to an inclusive and shared type. The transformation of economic well-being is the result of the development of China's new normal. The report of the 18th National Congress of the Communist Party of China proposes that ensuring and improving people's living standards should be given a more prominent position. Under the new normal, the Chinese government has combined economic development with ensuring and improving people's well-being in accordance with the requirements of "stabilizing growth, promoting reform, adjusting the structure, and benefiting people's well-being." Financial expenditures in key areas of people's well-being such as education, medical care, and housing security, continuously increased employment, and the improvement of people's well-being. From pursuing high economic growth to pursuing people's wealth, a new picture of life is unfolding in China. In recent years, the income of rural residents in China has increased faster than that of urban residents, and the trend of narrowing the urban–rural income gap has begun to manifest. The proportion of residents' income in national income has increased, and new progress has been made in the reform of the income distribution system. With the coordinated advancement of China's new industrialization, informatization, urbanization, and agricultural modernization, a new phenomenon has emerged in the construction of new rural areas in the urban–rural relationship. The urban–rural dual structure is accelerating its transformation to a unitary structure, and a new type of urban–rural relationship between industry, agriculture, and rural areas, featuring industry-promoting agriculture, city-leading rural areas, mutual benefit between industry and agriculture, and urban–rural integration, is accelerating the formation. In addition, there are more than 70 million poor people in China. Under the new normal, with the continuous development of new situations in poverty alleviation and development work, the battle to win the poverty alleviation campaign of building a moderately prosperous society in all respects is being sounded. Under the new normal, the gradual shift toward inclusive and shared economic well-being will be a long-term trend.

3. New Normal, New Mindset

Achieving the new normal cannot be left to chance; it demands strenuous efforts. In line with the strategic guidelines set forth by the Fifth Plenary Session of the 18th CPC Central Committee, adapting to and leading the new normal necessitates fresh thinking, innovative concepts, and novel methodologies. We must maintain a balance between progress and stability, strategically reshape the economic structure, and strive for tangible and sustainable growth. By approaching the challenges with a steady mindset, prudently addressing uncertainties, and taking decisive actions, we can effectively embrace and guide the new normal.

The first aspect entails upholding the overarching principle of seeking progress while maintaining stability, emphasizing strategic focus and a steady mindset. Seeking progress while maintaining stability encapsulates the accumulated development experience, the ability to respond to evolving domestic and international circumstances, the necessity of comprehensive reform, and the manifestation of the Party Central Committee's leadership in economic affairs. Stability refers to the steady state of affairs, while progress pertains to the evolving state of affairs. The integration of seeking progress while maintaining stability represents the dialectical unity of these two states and necessitates an approach that embraces gradual development. Stability serves as the prerequisite and foundation for achieving steady growth and macroeconomic stability, while progress entails transforming the mode of economic development and pursuing higher-quality economic growth, constituting the direction and objective. In the context of the new normal characterized by shifting economic growth, mode transformation, structural adjustment, and changes in driving forces, it is crucial to adopt an objective and composed perspective and maintain a steadfast mindset. We should refrain from fixating solely on speed and being anxious about changing approaches. Instead, we need to acknowledge that a shift toward improved quality and efficiency is both a rule and a trend. Furthermore, it is essential to promote the transformation of the economy from traditional extensive development to one characterized by high efficiency, low costs, and sustainable growth. This should be done strategically and in conjunction with maintaining stable economic operations.

Adhering to the principle of seeking progress while maintaining stability means highlighting the theme of comprehensively deepening reform in the process of accelerating the transformation of the economic development mode, and better integrating stable growth, price control, structural adjustment, benefiting the people's living standards, emphasizing reform, and promoting harmony. Stability and progress are unified and mutually conditional, and stability can lead to more scientific development and more lasting progress. In economic work, it is necessary to correctly handle the relationship between stability, progress, and reform, assess the situation, plan for future actions, and achieve calm and calm, orderly movement, and effective reform. To accurately grasp the balance between reform, development, and stability is to consciously unify the intensity of reform, development speed, and social affordability. Accurately grasping the balance between short-term goals and long-term development requires both planning for top-level design and focusing on immediate practice. To accurately grasp the combination of economic and social development and improvement of people's lives, it is necessary to promote economic growth and simultaneous improvement of residents' income, so that the results of reform and development can benefit all the people. To seek progress while maintaining stability, we must adhere to the principle of maintaining stability in macro policies, maintaining flexibility in micro policies, and maintaining a solid foundation in social policies. To maintain a stable macroeconomic policy, we must adhere to a proactive fiscal policy and a prudent monetary policy, and firmly promote economic restructuring. The purpose of stabilizing policies is to stabilize market expectations. Focus on targeted regulation, not relying on short-term stimulus policies to stimulate economic growth but relying on reform and the market to promote development. To make micro policies active, it is necessary to act in accordance with the laws of the market economy, take problem-solving as the guide, promptly implement various policies and measures that have been introduced, and enhance the endogenous power of market entities. Social policies should be considered as a fundamental safeguard, aiming to continually enhance people's well-being, innovate social governance, and prioritize the improvement of basic living conditions. This entails bolstering social security and establishing a safety net to ensure social stability. Seeking progress while maintaining stability serves as the overarching policy for achieving scientific development. Throughout history, it has been observed that stability not only fosters scientific development but also facilitates long-lasting progress.

The second is to attach great importance to preventing various risks and maintaining a reasonable economic development speed. Currently, the conditions for economic development at home and abroad will undergo significant changes. To maintain the overall stability of the economy, on the one hand, it is necessary to scientifically distinguish between structural and cyclical factors and their different impacts on economic growth. For cyclical factors, we can take some short-term and temporary measures to address them, while structural factors require us to further promote the transformation and upgrading of the economic structure in order to bring about healthy and sustainable economic development. On the other hand, it is necessary to adhere to "the bottom line management and interval regulation," neither blindly and hastily implement strong stimulus economic plans, nor passively and conservatively watch the economic development imbalance and decline. Instead, it is necessary to scientifically determine the reasonable range of economic operation based on the economic development potential and current reality, not only maintaining the lowest limit of stable growth and employment promotion, but also grasping the upper limit of inflation prevention, and always keeping the economic operation in a reasonable range. Macroeconomic policies have remained basically stable, providing a good economic environment for transforming the development model, adjusting the economic structure, promoting reform and innovation, and creating an upgraded version of the Chinese economy.

At the same time, we should adeptly employ a bottom-line mindset, preparing for the worst while striving for the best outcomes. Being prepared for potential dangers enables us to navigate challenges without succumbing to panic and to maintain control. Embracing a bottom-line approach represents our scientifically grounded strategy for navigating the complexities of the current situation and our guiding philosophy for adapting to the new normal. To proactively adapt and maintain control, we must possess a clear understanding of various potential economic and social risks in this new normal phase, including real estate risks, local government debt risks, and financial risks. Leveraging the predictive power of bottom-line thinking, we can enhance our awareness of challenges and risks, and respond proactively to the various risks and challenges that may arise within the economic and social landscape. Furthermore, under the new normal, our focus should not solely be on total GDP. It remains imperative to sustain a reasonable pace of economic development. Ensuring the continued growth of a vast economy like China is of utmost importance, as reversing a state of inertial decline would prove arduous and costly. Development serves as the fundamental cornerstone for effectively addressing all issues within our country, leaving no space for hesitation or indecision. Hence, maintaining a reasonable pace of economic development is even more essential under the "new normal." Naturally, achieving sustainable economic growth necessitates relying on reforms to optimize and upgrade the economic structure.

Thirdly, we aim to promote the optimization and upgrading of China's economic structure, striving for substantial and value-added growth.

From the perspective of global value chains, China has long been at the lower end of the value chain. Thomas Friedman, in his book *The World Is Flat*, astutely illustrates the impact of globalization, wherein products are distributed globally, labor and capital flow freely, and barriers to factor movement diminish. The international division of labor has shifted from an inter-industry division to an intra-product division. Rather than a single country undertaking all stages of production for a product, different countries specialize in different parts of the production chain, contributing a specific component or service. The added value of different industrial chains varies, but the distribution of their value chains is mostly represented by a "Smile Curve." For example, the production process of the iPhone 5 produced by Apple in the United States is jointly completed by the United States, Japan, Germany, South Korea, and China. Although Apple's own profit margin is high, China's Foxconn, which provides original equipment manufacturer (OEM) services for Apple's phones, contributes only 3.6% to the value of each iPhone. On the whole, China's total trade volume is large, but in fact, the benefits obtained from the global division of labor system are very small. As a world processing factory, China has long been locked in the low end of the global value chain and is at a disadvantage in the global production and benefit distribution chain. Within various industries, industrial deepening and innovation lag behind, manifested in the low proportion of high value-added and high-tech products, low technological level, and the long-term dominance of OEM in the value chain, making China's industrial value-added rate, profitability, core technology, and product grade comprehensively lag behind the world's advanced level.

China needs to accelerate the adjustment and optimization of its five major structures: industrial structure, demand structure, urban–rural structure, spatial structure, and income distribution structure. The transition toward a new normal economy is characterized by the gradual dominance of the tertiary industry and consumer demand, the narrowing of the urban–rural regional gap, and the emphasis on optimizing and upgrading the economic structure. China's rapid economic growth has come at a significant cost, manifested in low efficiency, structural imbalances, overcapacity, and environmental pollution. The diminishing growth drivers, such as external demand and population dividends, have necessitated the transformation of China's economic growth drivers and the pursuit of "Chinese quality" to achieve a slowdown in growth rate and an enhancement in growth quality. Substantial and genuine growth serves as a profound reflection on past developmental shortcomings and guides our future endeavors. In the new normal economy, achieving genuine and substantial growth entails improving assessment methods, enhancing economic quality and efficiency, promoting green and sustainable development, and prioritizing the well-being and livelihood of the population.

The fourth is to adhere to the concept of ecological civilization and strive to build a beautiful China. Nature serves as the life-support system for the entire human race. It has nurtured our ancestors in the distant past and will continue to sustain future generations. In the grand scheme of things, we are temporary occupants of the universe and caretakers of resources and the environment. It is our obligation to pass on to the next generation the invaluable assets for life's existence, including water, atmosphere, forests, soil, and organisms. Integrating the principles of ecological civilization into economic development is not only conducive to the present well-being of people but also a responsibility we bear for the future. In granting future generations the right to rational utilization of natural resources, we must not deprive them, or subsequent generations, of their entitlement to meet their needs in order to fulfill our own. Furthermore, we should not burden future generations with the consequences of our excessive exploitation and utilization of resources. It is essential to prioritize intergenerational fairness in ecological matters, whereby we not only focus on the well-being of the present generation but also consider the interests of future generations. We must avoid benefiting from the legacy of our ancestors while sacrificing the future generations' well-being.

The 18th National Congress of the Communist Party of China underscored the pivotal role of ecological civilization, emphasizing its "integration across various domains, including economic, political, cultural, and social realms."[9] The objective is to "strive for the construction of a beautiful China and attain sustainable development for the Chinese nation." The Third Plenary Session of the 18th CPC Central Committee highlighted the institutional construction and institutional mechanism innovation of ecological civilization, which is both a clear understanding and accurate judgment of the stage of China's economic development. It also points out the direction for integrating the concept of ecological civilization into economic development under the new normal and achieving

[9]Party Literature Research Center of the CPC Central Committee (Ed.). (2014). *Selected Important Documents since the 18th CPC National Congress*, Vol. I. Central Party Literature Press, pp. 30–31.

equal emphasis on economic development and ecological protection. We must truly turn the beautiful words written on paper into the great rivers and mountains of the country. In recent years, the severe reality of resources, ecology, and environment in China has warned us that it is urgent to transform production methods and handle the relationship between economic development and environmental protection. Under the new normal, it is necessary to integrate the concept of ecological civilization into economic development, including both golden mountains and silver mountains, as well as green waters and green mountains. Green waters and green mountains are the largest and longest mountains of gold and silver. To develop the economy, we must operate within the limits of resource and environmental carrying capacity, without compromising ecological integrity or causing irreversible harm to the environment. The concept of ecological civilization must be integrated into economic construction, including all aspects and the entire process of political, cultural, and social construction, to ensure the protection of the resource base, the sustained and healthy development of the economy and society, and the sustainable development and long-term stability of the Chinese nation.

4. Strategic Choices to Adapt to and Lead the New Normal

At present, China's economy is in a critical period of transformation of growth momentum, not only enduring tremendous downward pressure from the economy, but also experiencing profound changes in the new stage of economic development. At the same time, it is also facing unprecedented historical opportunities. We should be good at seeking breakthroughs from changes and opportunities, maintaining and enhancing strategic focus, enhancing our reform and innovation capabilities, and enhancing development confidence. We should adopt stronger and more promising policies and measures to smoothly achieve the goal of building a moderately prosperous society in all respects by 2020.

The first is to improve macroeconomic control policies and maintain stable economic growth. Maintaining a stable growth rate is crucial for China's economic development. There is ample room for optimizing fiscal and financial policies, with a particular emphasis on enhancing macroeconomic control measures to support stable economic growth. It is essential to effectively utilize fiscal, financial, and industrial policies to bolster the steady progress of the real economy. By adhering to proven strategies that rely on macroeconomic regulation and innovation to stabilize and stimulate growth, we can further refine and enhance interval-based and targeted regulatory policies. Macroeconomic regulation is a dynamic process that focuses on addressing long-term growth challenges. Its objective is not only to prevent the economy from deviating from a reasonable range, but also to enhance the sustainability of economic development by activating potential, optimizing structures, and unleashing long-term growth potential. To achieve this, we need to expedite capital turnover, optimize credit structures, increase the proportion of direct financing, reduce social financing costs, and channel more liquidity toward the real economy. Furthermore, it is crucial to strengthen targeted regulatory efforts by prioritizing key areas such as major infrastructure projects, central-western region's railway networks, intercity transportation systems, water conservation initiatives, housing programs, urban transportation networks, underground utilities, energy efficiency, and environmental protection measures.

The second is to give play to the traction role of economic system reform and enhance the endogenous driving force of economic development. Only by giving full play to the traction role of economic system reform can we better actively adapt to and lead the new normal of China's economy. First, continue to transform government functions. We should further reduce administrative approval, strive to delegate power to the market and society, further innovate the way government provides public services, actively promote government procurement of services from social forces, and better play the decisive role of the market in resource allocation. The second is to comprehensively promote the strategic adjustment of the state-owned economy. Give full play to the important role of state-owned enterprises in promoting industrial upgrading, participating in international competition, and enhancing comprehensive national strength. For industries such as railways, petroleum, electric power, and civil aviation, it is necessary to effectively separate natural monopolies from competition. Third, deepen the reform of the fiscal and tax system. We should further rationalize the financial distribution relationship between governments at all levels, optimize income distribution and financial allocation, and achieve the matching of central and local financial powers. Optimize the structure of transfer payments, increase the scale and proportion of general transfer payments, reduce the merging of some special transfer payment projects, and accelerate the formation of a unified and transparent financial transfer payment system. Fourth, promote the reform of the financial system. We should steadily promote market-oriented reform of interest rates so that they can sensitively reflect the supply and demand of funds. Strengthen the corporate governance of financial institutions, promote the construction of a modern financial enterprise system, and improve the financial organization system. Fifth, deepen the reform of resource product prices. We should deepen price reform in accordance with the principle of "factor marketization" and further rationalize the price adjustment system to promote structural adjustment and resource protection. Priority should be given to price reform of water, electricity, natural gas, and refined oil, and price leverage should be used to promote the conservation and effective use of land resources, water resources, and energy resources.

The third is to promote economic structural adjustment and create a competitive advantage in China's economy. Structural reform is the highlight of the reform during the 13th Five Year Plan period, and it is also the key to testing whether China's economy can transform and upgrade. At the 2014 Central Economic Work Conference, it was proposed to actively identify and cultivate new growth points, which requires structural reform to promote, and efforts should be made in demand structure, investment structure, urban and rural structure, regional structure, industrial structure, distribution structure, and other aspects. Here are several points to note: First, focus on cultivating new economic growth points. This includes both cultivating new consumption growth points and forming new regional growth poles. Coordinate the strategic combination of "Four Regions" and "Three Initiatives"[10] to optimize the regional economic layout. Second, strive to optimize the investment structure. Deepen the reform of state-owned enterprises, further relax market access, implement various policies and measures to promote private investment, and create a fair investment environment to stimulate the vitality of private investment. Develop long-term major projects such as shantytowns renovation, railways, water conservancy, energy, and ecological and environmental protection that span a five-year plan. The third is to promote the construction of a new type of urbanization centered on people, mainly by implementing the development plan for the new type of urbanization, and the key is to solve the problem of "three a hundred million." To prevent "empty cities" and "ghost cities," and constantly optimize the spatial

[10]The term "Four Regions" refers to the western, northeastern, central, and eastern regions. The term "Three Initiatives" refers to the Belt and Road Initiative, coordinated development of the Beijing-Tianjin-Hebei region, and development of the Yangtze Economic Belt.

pattern of economic development through the healthy development of new urbanization. Fourth, accelerate and improve the development level of the service industry. Driven by market demand, we will further optimize the industrial layout, adhere to the principle of placing equal emphasis on both productive and living services, and develop both modern and traditional services. Furthermore, we will refine the detailed implementation guidelines to facilitate the rapid development of the service industry, comprehensively elevating its scale and overall performance.

Fourth, accelerate the implementation of the innovation-driven development strategy and create a new engine for China's economy. Innovation is the foundation of national prosperity and the soul of progress, and it is the strategic core of actively adapting to and leading the new normal of the economy. Encourage enterprises to establish research and development institutions based on market demand, guide enterprises to increase investment in research and development, improve the mechanism for organizing technological research and development, product innovation, and transformation of scientific and technological achievements, strengthen the connection between innovation and the market, and support enterprises in promoting the industrialization of major scientific and technological achievements. Adhere to giving priority to motivating innovators in various reform policies, emancipate the mind, improve mechanisms, provide scientific and technological personnel with reasonable benefits and spiritual encouragement, innovate talent cultivation, use, and introduction models, and fully stimulate the innovative vitality of the entire society. Vigorously promote mass entrepreneurship and innovation initiatives and make mass entrepreneurship and innovation initiatives a breath of the times, a social trend, and a value orientation. We should actively promote scientific and technological innovation and institutional innovation, continue to vigorously support new industries that have formed certain advantages, such as high-speed rail, nuclear power, photovoltaic, shipbuilding, regional aircraft and other industries to continue to grow bigger and stronger, strive to develop powerful industries and technologies, and accelerate the implementation of "Made in China 2025" and "Internet plus" action plans. To be good at planning and promoting innovation from a global perspective, in the new global competitive landscape, Chinese enterprises must plan and promote innovation from a global perspective, learn to integrate global resources, and improve their innovation capabilities by learning from and competing with experts.

The fifth is to deepen the process of opening-up to the outside world and create a high-level open economy. In 2014, China's actual outward investment exceeded the scale of utilizing foreign capital, and China has become a net exporter of capital. Under the new normal, China should continue to deepen the process of opening-up to the outside world and move toward a new stage of development at a higher level. First, innovate the opening-up model, deepen coastal opening up, expand opening up, and create a new regional opening-up model featuring division of labor, collaboration, complementary advantages, and balanced coordination. Second, accelerate the implementation of the going global strategy, promote international cooperation in production capacity and equipment manufacturing, and superimpose industrial exports on the basis of expanding product imports and exports. We will not only focus on consumer goods but also investment goods and attach greater importance to promoting high-end manufacturing industries such as high-speed rail and nuclear power to go global. Third, accelerate the transformation and upgrading of processing trade, adhere to the principle of attaching equal importance to both export and import, and form a new competitive advantage in export with technology, brand, quality, and service as the core. Fourth, accelerate the construction of economic cooperation platforms such as the China–South Korea Free Trade Area, the China–ASEAN Free Trade Area, and the Shanghai Free Trade Area, and continuously improve China's position in international organizations such as the World Trade Organization and the World Bank. Fifth, implement the marine power strategy, promote land and sea coordination, improve the ability to develop marine resources, promote the transformation of the marine economy into a quality and efficiency-oriented economy, and protect the marine ecological environment. Sixth, we should accelerate the promotion of the vision and action of the "Belt and Road," accelerate the construction of connectivity, customs clearance and international logistics channels, and constantly optimize the new pattern of opening up.

The sixth is to ensure and improve people's living standards and promote inclusive development of China's economy. Ensuring and improving people's living standards is the starting point and foothold for actively adapting to and leading the new normal of the economy. It is essential to adhere to the fundamental principle of safeguarding the minimum living standards, prioritize key areas, enhance institutional frameworks, shape public opinion, provide timely support, and place greater emphasis on ensuring the basic livelihoods of the population, particularly those with low incomes, in order to foster overall societal stability. Continue to increase policy support for agriculture, rural areas, and farmers and vigorously implement targeted poverty alleviation policies. In accordance with the strategic deployment of the Central Economic Work Conference, we will accelerate the transformation of the agricultural development mode and solve the "three rural" issues. We will further improve the basic conditions for running schools with weak compulsory education in poverty-stricken areas, and support social capital and social forces in starting education. We should strengthen poverty alleviation efforts, adhere to the main and leading role of government investment in poverty alleviation and development, attract social forces to participate in poverty alleviation and development, and implement targeted poverty alleviation strategies. We should continue to deepen the reform of the income distribution system, optimize the income distribution structure, mobilize the enthusiasm of all parties, promote the transformation of the economic development model, maintain social fairness, justice, harmony, and stability, achieve the sharing of development achievements by the people, and lay a solid foundation for building a moderately prosperous society in all respects. To reinforce ecological protection and pollution control, it is imperative to enhance the institutional mechanisms for promoting ecological civilization. Special attention should be given to combating smog, with concerted efforts aimed at achieving the standard of clear skies during events such as "APEC Blue" and "Parade Blue," making it a regular occurrence.

Chapter 12

The Theory and Practice of Supply-Side Structural Reform

Analyzing the laws governing macroeconomic operations in a socialist system, uncovering the tensions between total social supply and demand under socialism, and exploring methods to maintain a balance between them in both volume and structure are essential research tasks in the field of political economics. Since the 18th National Congress of the Communist Party of China, the Party Central Committee, led by Comrade Xi Jinping, has been addressing the complex international situation and the challenging domestic tasks of reform, development, and stability. They have confronted the problems and conflicting factors in China's economy and proposed to focus on these measures:

1. Strengthening structural reform
2. Moderately expanding total demand
3. Reducing overcapacity
4. De-stocking
5. Deleveraging
6. Lowering costs
7. Overcoming shortcomings

These measures are designed to enhance the quality and efficiency of the supply system, boost the effectiveness of investments, and stimulate new growth drivers. Moreover, they seek to transform and upgrade traditional competitive advantages, reinforce the driving forces for long-term growth, and foster overall progress in China's social productivity.[1]

[1]The central economic work conference took place in Beijing. *People's Daily*, December 22, 2015.

The introduction of "supply-side structural reform" is a significant milestone in the political economics of socialism with Chinese characteristics. This concept not only expands the theoretical framework of socialist macroeconomic management but also provides a clear direction for China's economic policy in the coming years.

1. The Significant Importance of Advancing Supply-Side Structural Reform

Xi Jinping pointed out, "To stabilize economic growth, we must pay more attention to supply-side structural reform."[2] Supply-side reform is relative to demand-side management and mainly focuses on improving the quality and efficiency of economic growth, enhancing the long-term innovative capacity of enterprises, and emphasizing the long-term and sustainable development of the economy. To ensure stable and moderately rapid growth in China's future economy, it is essential to concentrate on both demand management and structural reform, with an emphasis on supply-side innovation. This approach will be vital for fostering the healthy and sustainable growth of China's economy. Various obstacles to the free flow of production factors and commodities nationwide, a large amount of excess capacity, and structural problems in the economy cannot be solved by demand-side management. However, focusing more on supply-side structural reform can lay the foundation for stable and relatively rapid economic growth. Therefore, intensifying supply-side structural reform is a fresh approach for the central government to manage the economy effectively under the new normal.

First, supply-side structural reform is a key factor driving the new normal. The new normal encompasses a myriad of prominent issues and problems. Although the Chinese economy seemingly grapples with the issue of sluggish growth, its fundamental causes can be traced back to structural factors, specifically the presence of surplus capacity and inefficiencies within the supply chain. Therefore, to solve the current economic difficulties, it is necessary to focus on promoting supply-side structural reform. The key to supply-side reform is to advance the structural adjustment of supply, which involves innovating supply structures to facilitate the upgrading and adjustment of demand structure. The economic development history of countries around the world has shown that

---

[2] *Ibid.*

the most dramatic changes in industrial structure occur when transitioning from an upper-middle-income country to a high-income country. Currently, China's supply-demand relationship is facing a noticeable structural imbalance, and the "supply-demand mismatch" has become the biggest obstacle to China's sustained economic growth. In addition, excess production capacity has become a major burden on China's economic transformation, while the supply system in China is generally characterized by an oversupply of low- and mid-end products and an insufficient supply of high-end products. Therefore, emphasizing supply-side reform means focusing on the production and supply side, adjusting the supply structure, and seeking paths to truly stimulate domestic demand and create new driving forces for economic development.

Second, supply-side structural reform fosters the long-term sustainable development of the economy. Economic structural reform is a task that requires a long-term commitment. The shift from emphasizing demand-side management to supply-side structural reform reflects the transition of economic thinking from focusing on short-term economic growth to emphasizing sustainable development and improving the quality and efficiency of economic growth. A developing country like China must balance short-term economic stability with long-term sustainable development. By replacing the Keynesian model, which mainly focuses on short-term demand management, with a more innovative approach that prioritizes the creation of effective institutions and policies to support sustainable economic growth in the medium and long term, we can improve the supply-side environment and mechanisms that facilitate production and supply in the economy. By providing efficient and effective economic institutions and creating an open market environment, it is possible to stimulate innovation, entrepreneurship, and creativity among small businesses and individuals. This, in turn, can help to create new sources of economic growth and development that will help to maintain the stability of the Chinese economy in the long term. Previously, the "Troika" of investment, consumption, and exports was used to guide macroeconomic policies in China and it led to short-term counter-cyclical adjustments in macroeconomic regulation, based on the results of economic performance.[3] This time, the focus on the supply side starts from the very beginning of economic activity and examines the issues from the perspectives

[3] See Jia Kang. (2014). New supply: The Chinese innovation in economic theory. *Review of Economic Research*, Issue 1, 35–37.

of industries and enterprises. This approach emphasizes the need for long-term transformation and upgrading, rather than just short-term fixes. Third, with the help of supply-side structural reform, the decisive role of the market in resource allocation can be utilized better.

Supply-side structural reform is essentially about properly handling the relationship between the government and the market, giving full play to the decisive role of the market in resource allocation, and better leveraging the role of the government. Previously, there was an overemphasis on the role of the government in macroeconomic regulation, particularly from the demand side, resulting in excessive intervention by the "visible hand." Going forward, with the promotion of supply-side structural reform, more weight will be given to the roles of enterprises and individuals. The primary responsibility of the government is to formulate laws, regulations, standards, and policies, providing enterprises and the market with relatively stable expectations, and enhancing their enthusiasm and creativity. By streamlining administration and delegating power, the government can transfer authority to the market and enterprises, invigorating the market and encouraging enterprises to produce. This macroeconomic regulation aims to activate microeconomic vitality by reducing taxes, reforming finance, and helping enterprises lower costs, which benefits their development capabilities and increases effective supply. The main players in supply-side structural reform are not the government and officials but enterprises and entrepreneurs. Entrepreneurship is the soul of economic development, and to activate it, a fair, just, and open competitive environment must be created for all enterprises. Nevertheless, attaining this objective poses a considerable challenge for China, as it represents the most formidable aspect of supply-side structural reform to overcome.

2. Transition from Demand Management to Supply Reform

China's economy has undergone a change since 2013, with the major economic indicators showing different trends and not moving in a synchronized manner. Economic growth has been slowing down, consumer price index (CPI) has remained at a low level, household incomes have increased while corporate profit margins have declined, consumption has risen while investment has fallen, and so on. Compared to classical economic theories, the current situation in China is neither traditional "stagflation" nor standard "deflation." Despite the implementation of intensified monetary policies at the macroeconomic level, the results have been disappointing, with the initial rapid growth of investment followed by a slowdown, and signs of fatigue in the old economy. However, the new economy based on the "Internet+" model, which refers to the integration of the Internet and traditional industries, has flourished. Meanwhile, the economic situation in Northeast China has worsened, but some previously disadvantaged western provinces have experienced remarkable progress. This has led to a mixed picture of both positive and negative developments. In short, China's economy is becoming more diverse in terms of its structure. To better adapt to the changing economic landscape, China needs to improve its supply-side environment and mechanisms while recognizing that there is still room for improvement in traditional demand management. This can be achieved by reforming institutional supply, stimulating the innovation and entrepreneurship of microeconomic entities, and strengthening new driving forces for long-term economic development.

2.1. *China's past macroeconomic focus: Demand-side management*

In a market economy, supply and demand are interdependent forces that coexist in a contradictory unity. While they may appear to be in opposition, they work together to determine prices and allocate resources. In theory, in any given period, both the supply side and the demand side should be given equal importance. However, in certain situations, such as when external conditions or policy objectives change, macroeconomic management may prioritize one side over the other. For instance, since the 1998 Asian financial crisis, China has generally focused on managing demand-side factors in its macroeconomic regulation.

The theoretical basis for demand-side management comes from the national income equilibrium analysis in Keynesian theory. In simple terms, Keynes believed that economic growth mainly originated from the driving forces of investment, consumption, and net exports, often referred to as the "Troika." It can be expressed in a formula as[4]:

$$Y = C + I + G + NX$$

[4]See Gao Hongye (Ed.). (2014). *Western Economics* (6th Edition). China Renmin University Press, Beijing.

Among them, Y represents total output, C stands for consumption, I stands for investment, G represents government expenditure, and NX represents net exports.

When the economy experiences a downturn, demand-side management theory believes that this is mainly due to insufficient effective demand. Therefore, the solution is to do everything possible to increase effective demand. At the policy level, the main tools of demand-side management are the coordination and cooperation of fiscal policy and monetary policy. Monetary policy focuses on overall regulation, while fiscal policy focuses on structural adjustment. Depending on the situation, there are four policy combinations: tight fiscal-tight monetary, tight fiscal-loose monetary, loose fiscal-tight monetary, and loose fiscal-loose monetary.

Since the beginning of reform and opening-up, China has attached great importance to demand-side management while promoting the transition from a planned economy to a market economy. A notable illustration of this approach is evident in the coastal regions, which heavily relied on the "three-plus-one" trading-mix strategy during the early stages of reform. This strategy involved engaging in the processing of imported materials, manufacturing products based on provided samples, assembling parts supplied by external sources, and participating in compensation trade. These measures effectively tapped into the demands of the international market. Domestically, due to a lack of infrastructure, the country relied on multiple rounds of infrastructure construction mainly funded by government investment. After the 1998 Asian financial crisis and the 2008 international financial crisis, the combination of "proactive fiscal policy" and "prudent monetary policy" was adopted successively. It must be pointed out that the term "prudent monetary policy" is more of a strategic concept or a theoretical framework, rather than a strict set of guidelines that must be followed in practice. For many years, whether at the central or local level, the government has primarily focused on investment and exports to drive economic growth. It can be said that demand-side management has become the most widely used and effective method that the Chinese government has employed in promoting economic growth in the past.

Demand-side management has played a significant role in promoting China's economic growth. In 1998, China was the first country to recover from the Asian financial crisis, and in 2008, China quickly bounced back from the global financial crisis and helped to stimulate the recovery of other countries' economies. China's rapid economic growth has led to remarkable changes in urban construction and infrastructure. By 2015,

China's GDP had exceeded 67 trillion yuan, ranking second in the world in terms of total output. This achievement was driven in part using demand-side management, which played an indispensable role in China's economic success.

However, over time, the side effects of demand-side management have become increasingly apparent. After the 2008 global financial crisis, the economies of the United States and Europe experienced a significant downturn. As a result, China's external demand began to decline, which had previously provided substantial support for economic growth. This decline continued over time and became a major challenge for China's economy. Due to various structural problems, China's economy has entered a period of decline, with the growth rate dropping from double digits to single digits. Since 2015, China's economy has been in a prolonged downturn, with key indicators such as GDP, CPI, and producer price index (PPI) showing persistently weak performance for many consecutive months. Overall, China's economy has faced a challenging period, experiencing declines in economic growth, industrial product prices, corporate profits, and fiscal revenue growth, while the probability of economic risks has increased. To maintain economic stability, the government has taken steps such as increasing investment, lowering interest rates, and adjusting reserve requirements to stabilize the economy's downward trend. However, the effectiveness of demand-side management has declined over time, and its costs have become more apparent compared to the past. In the present phase of China's economic development, the nation faces the challenge of addressing multiple factors simultaneously. These include managing a deceleration in economic growth, undertaking arduous structural adjustments, and managing the repercussions of previous economic stimulus policies. Consequently, the imperative for transformation and upgrading has become more pressing than ever before. However, the traditional Keynesian approach to solving medium- and long-term economic problems has limitations. The fundamental solution lies in structural reform, which must be transformed in a timely manner to focus on supply-side structural reform.

2.2. *Shifting from demand management to supply-side reform*

To promote sustainable economic growth, it is important to strengthen supply-side structural reform while moderately expanding total demand in the present and future. From a supply-side perspective, long-term economic growth is supported by five key factors: labor, land and natural resources, capital, innovation, and institutions. These factors can be represented by the following formula:

$$Y = F\,(L1, L2, C, I1, I2)$$

The symbol Y represents the total output, while F is a function that depends on five factors from the supply-side perspective: labor (L1), land and natural resources (L2), capital (C), innovation (I1), and institutions (I2). In other words, economic growth from a supply-side perspective depends on the quality and quantity of these five essential factors: labor, land and natural resources, capital, innovation, and institutions.

The primary difference between demand-side management and supply-side management lies in their underlying theoretical assumptions. Demand-side management is grounded in the assumption of perfect competition, where the supply side is presumed to be already operating in a favorable or optimal state. Therefore, the policy focus is on adjusting effective demand to achieve macroeconomic stability. However, the premise of supply-side reform is rooted in the assumption of imperfect competition. In this scenario, the supply side faces a range of serious problems, including monopolies, insufficient innovation, and inadequate institutional mechanisms. Therefore, addressing these structural issues is critical for promoting sustainable economic growth through supply-side reform.

The second key difference between demand-side management and supply-side reform relates to their respective application periods. Demand-side management is typically employed as a short-term tool for making adjustments and timely decisions within the economic cycle. In contrast, supply-side reform is a long-term strategy aimed at achieving more profound and lasting structural changes. As such, supply-side reform is better suited for addressing the underlying causes of economic problems, whereas demand-side management is geared towards managing the symptoms.

The third key difference between demand-side management and supply-side reform lies in the policy tools employed. Demand-side management relies primarily on fiscal and monetary policies to effect short-term adjustments, while supply-side reform focuses on implementing institutional changes to promote long-term structural transformation. This involves reducing government regulation, lowering taxes, and trimming welfare programs, all aimed at stimulating social vitality and promoting market-oriented reforms of state-owned enterprises.

Supply-side reform should not be seen as a simple substitute for demand-side management. Rather, it is a distinct approach that should be chosen based on different periods, situations, and conditions. Short-term macro adjustments should be made based on specific circumstances and can focus on either supply or demand. However, in the long term, supply and demand are interdependent and must be addressed together despite their contradictory aspects. It is important to prioritize the appropriate phase for each strategy. While the economy faces both cyclical and structural challenges, the current main challenge has become a structural problem. Therefore, it is necessary to focus on strengthening supply-side structural reform while also expanding demand moderately and adjusting demand structures. The ultimate goal should be to improve the supply structure and achieve a balance between supply and demand that is sustainable and beneficial for the economy.

2.3. *Since the reform and opening-up, China's economic reform has focused on institutional supply and structural adjustment*

In the past 30 years, China's economy has grown at an average annual rate of almost 10% over the past three decades, lifting the country from the tenth largest to the second-largest economy in the world and increasing its share of the global economy from less than 2% to about 13%. In 2010, China's per capita GDP crossed the $4,000 mark, officially entering the category of middle-income countries. Since then, China's per capita GDP has continued to rise steadily, reaching $5,000 in 2011, $6,000 in 2012, $6,767 in 2013, $7,485 in 2014, and almost touching $8,000 in 2015. The long-term high-speed growth of China's large-scale economy is a rare feat in human economic history and is often referred to as the "Chinese miracle." This achievement was mainly accomplished by prioritizing economic revival, managing demand while focusing on institutional supply and structural adjustments from the perspective of total supply, which facilitated the transition from a planned to a market economy. In 1984, the Third Plenary Session of the 12th Central Committee of the Communist Party of China passed the *Decision of the Central Committee of the Communist Party of China on the Reform of the Economic System*, clarifying the direction, nature, tasks, and basic principles and policies of economic system reform, and stating that "the reform is to establish a socialist economic system that is full of vitality." In November 1993, the

Third Plenary Session of the 14th Central Committee of the Communist Party of China passed the *Decision of the Central Committee of the Communist Party of China on Some Issues Concerning the Establishment of a Socialist Market Economic System*, which proposed the overall approach to establishing a socialist market economic system. Looking back, this major institutional change from the supply side is the real and strongest driving force behind China's economic growth. In 2001, China's decisive and courageous decision to join the World Trade Organization (WTO) and actively engage in international trade and globalization marked a significant achievement in institutional reform, paving the way for nearly two decades of high-speed economic growth. While demand management has certainly played an important role in China's economic take-off, the main driving force behind the country's remarkable economic growth has been the great institutional change from a planned economy system to a market economy system.

2.4. *Supply-side reforms are urgently needed in China's factor market to address the existing constraints and inhibitions*

Although China has made significant progress in establishing a socialist market economy, a fully perfect, complete, and standardized market economy system has yet to be fully developed. The relationship between the government and the market remains unclear, and there are still many improper government regulations and interventions in the market. Supply-side factors that hinder long-term economic growth, such as "supply-side constraints" and "supply-side suppression"; exist. These are the fundamental reasons for promoting supply-side reforms.

The first reason is the decline of demographic dividend and the increase in labor costs. China has the largest population in the world and since the reform and opening-up, the massive transfer of rural population, represented by migrant workers, to cities and industries has been one of the main contributing factors to China's economic development. However, according to academic estimates, around 2011, the "Lewis turning point" of labor force transfer had already appeared in China, and the contribution of labor force transfer, which is characterized by quantity, to the Chinese economy has been declining. The continuous occurrence of labor shortages, difficulties in recruitment, and significant wage increases for the labor force in recent years are clear evidence of this trend. At the same time, China's population structure has shown a clear trend toward aging. Some studies have shown that in the next decade, China will enter an aging society, and the speed of aging will exceed that of Japan and exceed the speed of China's economic development. Looking at the history of global population and national strength, changes in population size and structure have a long-term decisive effect on national strength and destiny. Therefore, China's population policy, which has been aimed at controlling population size since the 1970s, has reached a critical point where adjustments are necessary.

The second reason is the rigid land management system and excessive consumption of natural resources. Due to various reasons, there are significant supply constraints in the management of land and related natural resources in China. With the development of urbanization, a large amount of rural land (including collective construction land and homesteads, etc.) near cities has been converted into urban development land through various means, which is a natural part of urbanization. However, the overly rigid current land management system has resulted in a significant amount of rural land being converted into urban land, with interests being heavily skewed in favor of local governments and real estate developers, leading to numerous social conflicts and mass incidents. In response, voices advocating for "protecting the countryside" and "protecting farmers" emerged, blocking market and business forces from spreading to the countryside. This delay in rural development amidst the modernization wave has widened the already significant urban–rural gap in China, making it difficult to bridge. The challenges associated with natural resource management in China are highly related to the significant interest adjustments required among the various stakeholders involved in the land system. This is just one example of lagging institutional supply, where the institutional framework governing natural resource management has not kept pace with the needs and challenges of the current situation. In addition to land, various other natural resources in China are facing issues such as missing pricing mechanisms and extensive use driven by the government's strong economic development motivations. These issues have caused serious problems in recent years, including strong public opposition to water, soil, and air pollution, as well as excessive consumption of resources and energy.

The third reason is that financial repression is prevalent and there is inadequate support for the real economy. China is one of the wealthiest countries in the world, with ample foreign exchange reserves and domestic savings. However, the efficiency of capital utilization and the degree to which capital is nourished by economic activity in China's financial sector lags far behind. In fact, the supply constraints and restraints in China's financial sector are among the most severe in the world. This is reflected in several ways: first, interest rate liberalization has only progressed two-thirds of the way. Second, financial market entities are unequal in size, with a disproportionate share of state-owned enterprises and insufficient involvement of private and foreign capital. In addition, large banks dominate at the expense of small and medium-sized financial institutions. Third, the capital market structure is unbalanced, with the main board market dominating and other markets such as the innovation board, the new third board, and the over-the-counter equity trading market being underdeveloped. These factors have hindered small and medium-sized enterprises, which have been major contributors to China's economic growth and employment, from obtaining reasonable financing support. As a result, the real economy, including agriculture, rural areas, and farmers, has been unable to receive adequate financial support for upgrading and development despite policy initiatives.

The fourth reason is the inflexible nature of the science and education system and the insufficient emphasis on innovation-driven growth. It is widely acknowledged that the current driving force for economic growth in China must shift toward innovation. As early as the 16th National Congress of the Communist Party of China, the goal of building an innovative country was proposed. However, the progress towards this goal has been slow, as the scientific research papers and patent applications by Chinese researchers rank among the top in the world, yet the conversion rate of scientific achievements into actual products and industries is less than 10%. The main reason for this is the lack of an effective system and mechanism to stimulate innovation among researchers and enterprises. Specifically, there are four reasons: first, the incentive mechanism for scientific achievements is falling behind; second, intellectual property protection is inadequate; Third, the improvement of human resources is hindered by outdated and inflexible systems and mechanisms that violate regulations, leading to a lack of innovative talent; fourth is the obstruction caused by narrow sector interests, which has become particularly evident since 2016 in various difficulties encountered during the integration of the internet with traditional industries.

The fifth reason is the inadequacy of government management and reform, which has resulted in institutional supply falling behind the pace of development. The government is the main player in China's monopolistic supply system. The country's impressive economic and social growth since the reform and opening-up is closely tied to the government's adjustment of management concepts, transformation of methods, and continuous optimization of institutional mechanisms. However, as the reform enters a more challenging stage, various interest entanglements become increasingly complex, and the current government lags in a series of institutional reforms that aim to improve supply. This is mainly evidenced by: Firstly, inadequate key functions. Under market economy conditions, the government's primary roles are market supervision, public services, and social management, but they are far from adequate. The repeated calls for "multiple regulations integration" have made little substantive progress, and the 2015 stock market crash that shook domestic and international markets is a prime example. Secondly, insufficient reform in key areas, such as land, finance, state-owned enterprises, income distribution, and population strategy adjustment, which have yet to meet social expectations. Thirdly, the government's means of supporting economic development are outdated, still relying on replacing the market and using "politics" instead of "economics." Subsidies and preferential policies are used instead of solid market environments and infrastructure construction. Lastly, there is a need to improve the quality and effectiveness of "streamlining administration, delegating powers, and optimizing services," as practical barriers to mass entrepreneurship and innovation remain relatively high.

Furthermore, there are various other constraints related to the market environment and institutional mechanisms, including the absence of a level playing field, significant income inequality among residents, uneven regional development, an incomplete social security system, and a pressing need to enhance social fairness and justice. All these factors underscore the fact that China's journey toward establishing a fully-fledged market economy system is still incomplete, with the pivotal role of market mechanisms in resource allocation yet to be fully recognized.

3. The Overall Ideas and Directions of the Supply-Side Structural Reform

In November 2015, during the 11th meeting of the Central Leading Group for Finance and Economics, Xi Jinping first proposed promoting the structural reform of China's economy. This proposal garnered significant attention from all sectors. The term "structural reform" is familiar to many of us. Following the 2008 financial crisis, discussions on structural reform became widespread, not only in emerging economies but also in developed countries such as the United States, Europe, and Japan. Institutions like the World Bank and the International Monetary Fund also needed to implement structural reforms. At that time, there were many discussions in China about structural reform, with different perspectives. Some believed it meant changing the relationship between government and the market, while others thought it meant transforming the economic development mode from external to internal, restructuring investment and consumption, changing the industrial structure, reforming the ownership structure, and so on. Regardless of the interpretation, structural reform represents a significant and crucial reform. Currently, China's structural reform of the economy mainly focuses on a significant adjustment from "demand management" to "supply-side management." This interpretation is based on the expression of the Fifth Plenary Session of the 18th Central Committee of the Communist Party of China on "releasing new demands and creating new supplies," and the spirit of General Secretary Xi Jinping's speeches.

3.1. *The key focus of supply-side reform is institutional innovation*

As China's economy enters a new stage of transformation and upgrading, it's become clear that certain institutional systems have fallen far behind, highlighting the urgent need for innovative institutional supply. In summary, there's a need to fully leverage the decisive role of the market in allocating resources while also improving the role of the government. Despite implementing a socialist market economy system for over 20 years, China's economy can still only be considered "half-baked." Significant supply constraints remain in critical areas such as land, labor, capital, and innovation, which hinder economic growth. Moreover, the current institutional and production structures are unable to meet the new demands arising from China's burgeoning middle-income families. This situation poses a risk to China's potential economic growth rate and the goal of building a moderately prosperous society. It's in this context that the Fifth Plenary Session of the 18th CPC Central Committee emphasized the need to "release new demand and create new supply."

Institutional innovation is critical for improving the management of the economy and society. This requires significant changes to the government's approach, especially in terms of deepening administrative approval system reform. This reform aims to regulate and enhance the government's role as a "visible hand" by strictly enforcing integrity, efficiency, transparency, fairness, and openness. By doing so, it can optimize the market environment for legal operations, fair competition, and high-level rule of law, while also strengthening the government's oversight and regulation of the market and providing better public goods and services. The ongoing administrative approval system reform faces numerous systemic and fundamental challenges, requiring determination, courage, and professional technical solutions to advance the reform. There is still considerable room for improvement in this area, and it is essential to clarify the boundaries of government power and prioritize reducing government intervention. This involves fostering a culture of self-improvement in administrative practices, while also fulfilling the government's basic responsibilities for macroeconomic regulation, market supervision, public services, social management, and environmental protection. By taking a more hands-off approach, the government can better regulate and optimize the market environment for legal operations, fair competition, and high-level rule of law.

Another critical area of focus is advancing the reform of the fiscal and taxation system. This involves establishing a stable economic relationship and a standardized government financial management system between the government and citizens, as well as between the central and local governments. Fiscal policy is the foundation and an essential pillar of national governance. While great strides have been made in recent years to reform the fiscal and taxation system, the current economic downturn and slowing fiscal revenue growth require further comprehensive reforms. Going forward, these reforms should not only coordinate with other initiatives but also prioritize addressing critical issues such as real estate tax, personal income tax reform, central and local power reform, local revenue system restructuring, budget management system construction, and public–private partnerships (PPP). Each of these complex areas requires careful attention and innovative solutions to enhance the modernization of the national governance system and capacity. By addressing these challenges, fiscal and taxation reform can serve as a critical driver of institutional innovation in China.

In addition to ensuring effective governance and sound financial management, it's crucial to actively promote the reform of state-owned enterprises, income distribution, and social security systems. These reforms can create a level-playing field for market competition and promote social fairness and justice. Given China's current conditions, the top priority of the supply-side structural reform is a comprehensive reform of the factor market. This reform aims to leverage the decisive role of the market in resource allocation, unlocking the full potential of economic and social vitality.

3.2. *The reform of factor markets is a critical component of the supply-side structural reform*

In the long run, the quantity and quality of factors play a critical role in determining a country's economic growth efficiency. However, in China's context, all five key factors, namely land, labor, capital, technology, and resources, currently grapple with institutional obsolescence and are not sufficiently adapted to the requirements of a market-oriented economy. Consequently, it becomes imperative to undertake further reforms in these areas.

Firstly, there is an urgent need to adjust the population policy by shifting from population control to implementing a human capital strategy. People are the most fundamental factor in economic growth. With the disappearance of China's demographic dividend and the approaching challenge of an aging society, it is necessary to promptly and decisively adjust China's population policy. In particular, this adjustment should entail a comprehensive "two-child policy" as announced during the Fifth Plenum of the 18th Communist Party Congress. This policy should be dynamically implemented, continuously optimized, and closely monitored to ensure effective outcomes. Moreover, the population control that was centered on family planning should transition to a population strategy that prioritizes eugenics and improving the quality of the population. This should further evolve into a human capital strategy that focuses on education and innovation. In addition, it is crucial to promote population mobility and attract immigrants as an integral part of China's population policy. Lastly, reforms related to household registration and social security systems should be promptly improved to create a unified national labor market.

Secondly, it is important to carefully promote land system reform and establish a unified land circulation system for both urban and rural areas.

The land system is a foundational system of the country and is an essential aspect of supply management. Currently, the focus of land system reform is mainly on rural land. We should actively implement the spirit of the *Decision of the Central Committee of the Communist Party of China on Some Major Issues Concerning Comprehensively Deepening the Reform* passed during the Third Plenary Session of the 18th CPC Central Committee. This involves defining the scope and methods for rural collective-operated construction land entering the market, establishing and improving market trading rules and service regulatory systems, and drawing lessons from Chongqing's experience in using the "land ticket" system to share the benefits of urbanization with farmers far from the city center within the framework of "balancing occupation and compensation." We need to comprehensively promote the registration, circulation, transfer, and leasing system for the use rights of contracted rural land and protect the legitimate rights and interests of farmers. We should explore multiple forms of ensuring housing security for farmers in different areas. When establishing a unified urban–rural land property framework and circulation system, we should consider the experience of land system reform in the Shenzhen Special Economic Zone, which used the "state-owned platform, integration and classification, equitable rights, gradual unification" approach, and create a land value-added income distribution mechanism that considers the interests of the country, units, and individuals. In the context of land requisition, we should strictly define the scope of public interest land, standardize procedures, and disclose information. We should establish reasonable, standardized, and diverse compensation, livelihood protection, and production guidance mechanisms for farmers whose land is requisitioned.

Thirdly, we need to deepen financial reform and comprehensively remove the "financial repression." Finance is the core of modern economy. Currently, China's financial market suffers from structural imbalances, incomplete functions, and other forms of "financial repression" that hinder its development. Therefore, we need to comprehensively push forward financial reform to address these issues. First, we should further deepen the reform of financial institutions, especially state-owned commercial banks, by appropriately reducing the state's shareholding and increasing the shareholding of social capital. Second, we should accelerate the development of private banks and actively develop many community banks and village banks to form a well-structured and complementary banking ecosystem. Third, we need to vigorously develop a multi-level capital market, actively explore various property rights trading markets and "big asset management companies" covering the entire country, in addition to continuing to improve the main board, small and medium-sized enterprise board, and Growth Enterprise Market (GEM) markets. Fourth, we should fully liberalize interest rate controls on deposits and loans and realize market-oriented pricing. Fifth, we need to reform the financial regulatory system, strengthen the unified leadership and coordination among different regulatory departments, reasonably define the central and local financial regulatory responsibilities, and implement regional and layered supervision. Lastly, we should actively promote the internationalization of the Renminbi.

Fourthly, we need to comprehensively implement an innovation-driven strategy, with the goal of building an innovative country. Innovation is the first of the "five concepts" proposed at the Fifth Plenary Session of the 18th Central Committee of the Communist Party of China. Its importance for today's China cannot be overstated. The most urgent task at hand is to promote scientific and industrial innovation and strive to achieve integration between technology and the economy. In the field of high-end "unobtainable technology," we must rely on original and independent innovation to advance with difficulty. For mid- to high-end technology, we need to rely on a combination of comprehensive openness and the "importation, assimilation, absorption, and re-innovation" approach, along with integrated innovation, to ultimately build an "innovative country." At the same time, we must reform the scientific and technological management system, methods of transforming scientific research achievements, and accelerate higher education reform to cultivate more innovative talent. We must strengthen intellectual property protection and provide high incentives for innovation.

Fifthly, to improve the current situation for enterprises and create a business environment that allows them to reach their full potential, there are several steps that can be taken. First, we should establish a "negative list" that sets a high standard for a rule-of-law business environment. This will enable enterprises to have the freedom to pursue their goals without unnecessary bureaucratic obstacles. We can take inspiration from free trade zones and streamline administration, delegate power, reduce access controls, reform supervision methods, optimize services, and promote standardized administrative approval procedures nationwide. We can also establish a nationwide credit information system that covers all legal entities and individuals and enforce uniform market supervision rules to minimize social transaction costs and create a favorable operating environment for enterprises. Second, we should lower the social security contribution rates and accelerate the implementation of a nationwide unified basic endowment insurance system. This will allow us to establish a nationwide unified social security system that can be combined with the incorporation of state-owned assets. This will help reduce the financial burden on enterprises and ensure that they have the resources they need to thrive. Third, we should reduce or eliminate unnecessary fees and charges that burden enterprises, especially non-tax burdens, in order to reduce their overall burdens. We can achieve this by furthering fiscal and taxation reforms, implementing structural tax reductions, and severing the interest linkage between administrative approval and fees. We should establish a system and mechanism for the classification and reconstruction of fee management, incorporate fees and funds of quasi-tax nature into the general public budget, and enhance cost accounting and information disclosure in budgetary funds. We should also lower the level of burden imposed by industry associations and intermediary organizations providing services by breaking monopolies and enhancing competition. Finally, we should effectively eliminate the burden imposed on enterprises by "dishonest brokers" and rental agencies by combining anti-corruption and clean governance efforts.

3.3. *The supply-side structural reform needs to overcome five major challenges in the near future to achieve its goals*

Xi Jinping pointed out that we must "increase the intensity of structural reform, correct the distortion of factor allocation, expand effective supply, improve the adaptability and flexibility of supply structure, and increase total factor productivity."[5] To promote the supply-side structural reform, our strategy should prioritize a sustained effort, balance progress with stability, and adapt to changing conditions. We must also use targeted tactics to reduce overcapacity, clear inventory, decrease debt, lower costs, and strengthen vulnerable areas. In the short term, the supply-side structural reform should continue to make progress while maintaining stability, and adjust the pace and intensity as needed. Our focus should be on the five key areas of reducing overcapacity, clearing inventory, decreasing debt, lowering costs, and strengthening vulnerable sectors.

---

[5]The central economic work conference took place in Beijing. *People's Daily*, December 22, 2015.

The first area of focus is to actively and prudently resolve overcapacity. We need a comprehensive policy system that follows the principles of enterprise-led, government promotion, market guidance, and legal disposal. To deal with overcapacity, we must take a differentiated and orderly approach based on local conditions, while balancing social stability and structural reform. We should also create favorable conditions for implementing a market-oriented bankruptcy process, accelerate the handling of bankruptcy and liquidation cases, and introduce policies such as financial and tax support, non-performing asset disposal, re-employment and livelihood security for the unemployed, and special awards and subsidies. Additionally, the capital market should support corporate mergers and acquisitions, with the goal of achieving more mergers and acquisitions and fewer bankruptcies and liquidations. We must also be diligent in worker placement and strictly control capacity growth to prevent new overcapacity.

The second area of focus is helping enterprises reduce costs. We need to launch a comprehensive campaign that uses a range of measures to reduce costs for the real economy. This includes reducing institutional transaction costs, transforming government functions, streamlining administration, and regulating intermediary services. We should also aim to reduce the tax and fee burden on enterprises, standardize tax collection, and create a fair tax environment. To further support the manufacturing industry, we can explore reducing the value-added tax rate. In addition, we should study ways to simplify and consolidate social insurance, reduce financial costs for enterprises, and promote the normalization of interest rates to benefit the real economy. We must also work to lower electricity prices, promote market-oriented electricity price reform, and improve the linkage mechanism between coal and electricity prices. Finally, we need to reduce logistics costs and drive the reform of the circulation system.

The third area of focus is to resolve the inventory of real estate. It is necessary to accelerate the urbanization rate of the registered population and further the housing system reform and stabilize the real estate market by increasing effective demand, clearing inventory, and establishing a smooth supply-demand channel. The reform of the household registration system should be implemented, allowing non-registered population such as migrant workers to settle in the employment areas, creating their expectations and demand for buying or long-term renting houses in those areas. To advance the housing system reform, we should clarify the direction by focusing on meeting the housing needs of new urban residents and establishing a system that combines both purchasing and renting options. Public rental housing should be expanded to the non-registered population. We should promote the development of the housing rental market by encouraging individuals and institutional investors to purchase commercial housing and use it for rentals. Additionally, we should encourage the growth of specialized enterprises that focus on the housing rental business. Real estate development companies should adjust their marketing strategies in accordance with market laws and consider reducing the prices of commercial housing to stimulate demand. Additionally, promoting industry mergers and reorganization can increase the concentration of the industry. It is also important to abolish outdated restrictive measures.

The fourth area of focus is expanding effective supply. We need to win the battle against poverty by targeting poverty alleviation and eradication efforts toward the registered poor population. This requires increasing investment in funds, policies, and practical measures to improve the quality of poverty alleviation. We also need to support enterprise technological transformation and equipment upgrades, reduce enterprise debt burdens, and innovate financial support methods to enhance the investment capacity of enterprise technological transformation. To promote growth and development, we must cultivate and develop new industries, accelerate innovation in technology, products, and business models, and address shortcomings in both hard and soft infrastructure to improve investment effectiveness and accuracy. This includes promoting the formation of market-oriented and sustainable investment mechanisms and operational mechanisms. Additionally, we need to increase investment in people to help workers adapt to the changing market environment. We must continue to promote agricultural production and ensure the effective supply of agricultural products, guarantee food security, and ensure stable income growth for farmers. To support agricultural development, we must strengthen the basic construction of agricultural modernization, including implementing strategies such as grain reserves and grain storage technology. We should also focus on protecting and improving the comprehensive production capacity of agriculture and the quality of agricultural products by allocating targeted funds and implementing relevant policies.

The fifth area of focus aims to prevent and mitigate financial risks. Credit defaults must be dealt with in accordance with the law. We must effectively address local government debt risks and carry out the replacement of outstanding local government debt. Additionally, we need to improve the management of government debt at all levels and the issuance of local government bonds. To achieve these goals, comprehensive supervision must be strengthened, various financing activities should be regulated, and special efforts should be made to address financial risks. Illegal fundraising should be resolutely curbed, and we must enhance risk monitoring and early warning systems, handle risk cases properly, and firmly maintain the bottom line of preventing systemic and regional risks.

In summary, prioritizing the supply-side structural reform is not only a response to the challenges posed by the evolving international economic landscape but also driven by the critical issues and challenges confronting China's economic growth. The goal of the reform is to better leverage the role of the government and further enhance the decisive role of the market in allocating resources, improving the quality and efficiency of China's supply system, and contributing to the comprehensive construction of a moderately prosperous society and the realization of the Chinese dream of national rejuvenation.

4. Several Misconceptions About the Supply-Side Structural Reform

Xi Jinping pointed out that the economic growth in China is affected by prominent problems that include not only the overall quantity but also structural issues. These problems have arisen due to the three overlapping periods, namely the period of accelerated transformation of China's economic development, the period of major changes in the global economic and trade situation, and the period of major changes in the domestic economic and social development situation.[6] Since the Party's Central Committee proposed the active promotion of the supply-side structural reform, all sectors of society have been carefully studying its core principles and objectives, which align with relevant economic theories and are widely supported. However, there have been some misinterpretations and misconceptions about supply-side structural reform. For instance, some people think that it is an all-encompassing reform that completely abandons demand-side management in favor of supply-side management. Others even believe that promoting supply-side structural reform is a step

[6]Party Literature Research Center of the CPC Central Committee (Ed.). (2016). *Selected Works of General Secretary Xi Jinping's Important Speeches and Articles*. Central Party Literature Press, p. 307.

back to the old days of the planned economy. It is crucial to clarify these mistaken notions.

4.1. *Supply-side structural reform focuses on critical areas rather than encompassing the entire structure*

Structural reform is a global issue that has been relevant not only to developing countries or emerging economies but also to developed nations since the international financial crisis. In fact, developed countries have also faced significant "systemic structural problems" (or institutional defects). Structural reform aims to address structural problems and institutional defects by reforming corresponding system mechanisms and improving regulatory systems. There are generally two situations that require structural reform. The first is when there are major structural problems in economic development, and institutional innovations are needed to fundamentally solve these issues. This is a standard concept in development economics. The second situation is when there are significant institutional defects in the economic system, especially in the fiscal and financial systems, which can be compensated for by strengthening regulation and improving supervision to make up for the loopholes in the existing system.

Based on these two scenarios, it can be concluded that structural reform is not an all-encompassing overhaul of the entire system, but rather a targeted reform focused on critical areas. It plays a crucial role in shaping the entire system and neglecting it could lead to considerable setbacks or even failure in China's economic development and social progress. Presently, China's economy is grappling with substantial structural and institutional challenges, demanding comprehensive and profound reforms to be implemented.

The supply-side structural reform indicates that the main challenge of the current reform lies in the supply side, as the negative impacts of the planned economy system's intervention in the supply chain have not been fully addressed. Certain key areas are particularly affected by these issues. For instance, the finance sector's interest rate controls, administrative monopolies in specific industries, and the long-standing restrictions on private capital entering the service sector. Furthermore, "plot ratio controls" in long-term housing construction and government monopoly in land supply contribute to regulatory constraints. These constraints hinder the effective supply's growth, ultimately affecting demand growth (as monopoly prices suppress it). At the same time, they also generate enormous rent-seeking opportunities and lead to severe corruption issues. In essence, China's structural and institutional challenges are mainly rooted in the supply side, and the supply system's imperfections can also cause demand-side problems. Therefore, supply-side structural reform targets structural problems on the supply side, with a focus on key supply systems. For instance, state-owned enterprise reform and household registration system reform are supply-side reforms. The land, financial, and tax systems, including corporate and property taxes, are also supply-side reforms, representing the primary areas of reform during the "13th Five-Year Plan" period. In the context of China's new normal economic conditions, China's structural reform primarily involves furthering the supply-side reform, eliminating the remnants of the planned economy system, establishing a well-developed socialist market economy system, and accelerating economic transformation and upgrading.

4.2. *Supply-side management complements demand-side management, emphasizing their mutual interaction rather than a simple replacement*

In China, demand management has been the primary approach for macroeconomic regulation for a considerable period of time,[7] but there are aspects of it that need reform. Current macroeconomic policies in China primarily focus on investment to increase investment demand, which emphasizes policies that increase supply. However, this approach has led to serious overcapacity problems in some competitive industries and a shortage of supply in the public service sector. The reform of demand management aims to reduce the direct intervention of the government in the micro-economy and shift the focus of macro policies from excessive emphasis on investment to promoting employment, expanding consumption, and increasing public services. In contrast, Western developed countries advocate that macroeconomic policies should focus on long-term issues and supply-side policies that promote human capital accumulation and innovation. However, increasing long-term supply requires

---

[7]See Wang Xiaoguang. (2015). Two major issues that urgently need to be clarified about the supply-side reform. *People's Forum*, Issue 23.

institutional innovation and efficient institutions to promote productivity growth. Supply and demand are interdependent and can influence each other, so it's important to focus on both. However, it's crucial to prioritize and allocate resources accordingly to achieve the desired outcomes. Since the international financial crisis, more people have realized that structural reforms are essential for addressing the root causes of economic challenges. To achieve a more balanced approach to economic management, moderate demand management policies should be implemented alongside greater efforts to improve the supply side. This includes improving the total factor productivity of the economy and making the supply system more adaptable to changes in the structure of demand. Currently, both cyclical and structural contradictions exist in the economic cycle, but the main contradiction has transformed into structural problems. Therefore, we need to strongly promote reforms that improve the supply-side structure of the economy, making it better equipped to meet changes in demand. We must shift our focus from maintaining a basic balance of supply and demand to achieving a higher level of balance, where the economy is more dynamic and efficient. Certainly, ensuring a stable macroenvironment is imperative when promoting supply-side structural reform. It is crucial to avoid overly expansionary or contractionary demand policies, as they can potentially disrupt overall economic stability and yield adverse consequences.

4.3. *The supply-side structural reform aims to better utilize the role of the government rather than to introduce a new "planned economy"*

There is a misconception that promoting supply-side structural reform is similar to establishing a new "planned economy." However, this is not the case. The goal of supply-side structural reform is to fully utilize the market's decisive role in resource allocation by improving market mechanisms and correcting distortions caused by excessive reliance on administrative allocation of resources in the past. To achieve this, policies and institutional arrangements that cause distortions need to be adjusted, which will stimulate the vitality of market entities and better unleash the decisive role of the market in resource allocation. This is the improvement and advancement of the socialist market economy under the new economic situation and is not a return to the old path of the planned economy.

In the past, the market faced various structural challenges due to the insufficient role of market mechanisms and excessive government intervention. For instance, unprofitable "zombie enterprises" were still receiving loans and subsidies in some regions.

The direction and requirements of the supply-side structural reform were proposed at the Fifth Plenary Session of the 18th Communist Party of China Central Committee. It aims to promote modernization in agriculture, accelerate the building of a manufacturing powerhouse, speed up the development of the service sector, improve the level of infrastructure network, and foster new drivers of growth. The reform also emphasizes innovation-driven development, promotes the integration of industry, education, and research, and strengthens incentives for innovation and the application of innovation achievements. In addition, it supports the development of new drivers of growth, encourages the optimization and upgrading of traditional industries through technological progress, activates a large stock of assets, and promotes green development and the development of the real economy. However, the state's industrial policies only provide guidance, and investment projects should be identified, selected, and chosen by entrepreneurs and various investment entities in the market. The role of the government is to create favorable conditions for businesses to thrive by promoting competition, supporting corporate and industry restructuring, and helping small and micro enterprises. However, the government's objective is not to replace the market but rather to facilitate its efficient functioning.

4.4. *The goal of supply-side structural reform is to improve and innovate macroeconomic regulation, not replace it*

Supply-side structural reform and macroeconomic control are not the same, but combining them can effectively boost China's potential economic growth rate. This integration is an important aspect of macroeconomic innovation and a significant achievement of the political economics of socialism with Chinese characteristics.

In summary, by combining the efforts of supply-side structural reform and macroeconomic control, the effectiveness of controlling the economy on a larger scale can be improved. In other words, the government can better manage economic growth and development by implementing both supply-side structural reform and macroeconomic control measures. It is seen as an important innovation in macroeconomic management. The reform can optimize the macroeconomic control environment and enable the use of more market-based and economic-based means in macroeconomic control. The integration of the two can also promote the optimization of economic structure and institutional innovation, which are the main factors determining the potential economic growth rate. The current government's adoption of the "short-term + long-term" approach in macroeconomic control signifies its acknowledgment of the prevailing new normal economic conditions. This approach emphasizes the significance of taking a long-term perspective and addressing structural and institutional concerns to improve the economy's potential growth rate. By making changes to the way the economy is structured and by introducing new systems and policies, it is possible to increase the potential rate of growth for the Chinese economy, while also ensuring that this growth is sustainable in the long term. Structural change and institutional innovation serve as the foundation for economic development. Particularly, as China's economy has transitioned into the new normal, these elements become even more crucial. By focusing on structural change and institutional innovation, China aims to achieve "dual high" development, characterized by high quality and high efficiency. This approach is vital for the long-term success and stability of the economy.

Chapter 13

Development of Agriculture, Farmers, and Rural Areas

The largest social group in China is farmers, and the issue of farmers has always been a fundamental problem in China's modernization process. The Central Rural Work Conference held on December 23–24, 2013, emphasized that "If China wants to be strong, agriculture must be strong; if China wants to be beautiful, rural areas must be beautiful; if China wants to be wealthy, farmers must be wealthy. China can achieve a more proactive approach to all work, as well as guarantee the country's overall stability and security, by prioritizing the development of agriculture and rural areas, fostering a stable and harmonious rural society, and ensuring the prosperity and well-being of farmers."[1] In December 2012, during his visit to Fuping County in Hebei Province to inspect poverty alleviation and development work, President Xi Jinping highlighted the challenges of achieving a comprehensive construction of a moderately prosperous society in all aspects by 2020. He emphasized that, "The most difficult task lies in rural areas, particularly impoverished areas. A society cannot be considered fully prosperous or moderately prosperous if there is a lack of prosperity in rural areas, especially in impoverished areas. The central government attaches great importance to poverty alleviation and development projects. At all levels, party committees and governments should recognize their responsibility and mission in poverty alleviation and development work. This includes establishing plans, allocating funding, setting goals, implementing measures, and conducting inspections. Let us join hands to help our rural compatriots lift themselves out of poverty and

[1] Central rural work conference took place in Beijing. *People's Daily*, December 25, 2013.

improve their living standards."[2] These statements summarize China's decades of experience in development and provide strategic guidance for addressing issues related to farmers, rural areas, and overall modernization. China prioritizes agriculture, rural areas, and farmers' issues, with the primary task of agricultural development being the assurance of food security. Achieving this requires educating farmers, transforming traditional agriculture, and building a new socialist countryside, all of which are the major tasks that China needs to accomplish.

1. Prioritizing the Development of Agriculture, Farmers, and Rural Areas

As the economy grows and national income per capita increases, the proportion of industry in the gross national product also tends to increase, while the proportion of agriculture in the gross national product decreases. Despite this trend, agriculture remains the foundation of the national economy. This is because agriculture plays a critical role in ensuring human survival. As the saying goes, "Food is the most important necessity for human beings." While people can survive without coal or electricity, they cannot survive without food. Agriculture is the only sector that produces food, and the development of agriculture directly impacts the ability to solve the problems of hunger and malnutrition, ensuring a stable food supply and ultimately guaranteeing the stability of the nation. Another important aspect of agriculture is its role in guaranteeing national food security. With the development of international trade, food supply can now rely on imports. However, relying on other countries for staple food and survival can make a country vulnerable to restrictions imposed by exporting countries. After World War II, the United States employed the use of the "food weapon" as a tool to manipulate the economies of other countries. Most nations view food as a fundamental or strategic commodity, equivalent to military weaponry. Thus, they strive for a certain level of self-sufficiency in their food supply to prevent reliance on other countries and potential vulnerabilities. The third important aspect of agriculture is that the development speed of agriculture limits the development speed of other industries, especially the industrial sector, in the national

[2]Always keep in mind the well-being of the people and warm the hearts of thousands of households with the care of the party and government. *People's Daily*, December 31, 2012.

economy. In other words, agriculture is a foundation industry that supports the development of other sectors of the national economy. Furthermore, the pace of development in other industries, particularly the industrial sector, is constrained by the rate of development in agriculture. This is because improvements in labor productivity in agriculture serve as the foundation for labor transfer from agriculture to other industries. As a result, the continuous enhancement of agricultural productivity not only supports the development of other industrial sectors in the economy but also sets limits on their growth rate, particularly that of the industrial sector. The fourth important aspect of agriculture is that agriculture plays a significant role in providing raw materials, labor, capital, foreign exchange, and product sales markets for other industries and sectors. In China, labor-intensive products are competitive in the international market due to the low cost of agricultural labor. This is why some foreign companies choose to establish factories in China. The fifth important aspect of agriculture is its role in providing a good ecological environment. Agriculture serves as a green resource for the country, supplying natural landscapes and maintaining ecological balance, while also supporting the development of sightseeing tourism and holiday leisure. As the economy develops, the importance of agriculture in fulfilling these roles only grows.

The Chinese Communist Party has always attached great importance to the development of agriculture and rural areas. There are classic theories and effective practices on agriculture and urban–rural issues. Mao Zedong proposed the ideology of promoting both industry and agriculture, emphasizing that the development of industry must be carried out simultaneously with the development of agriculture. Mao stated, "We have always placed great importance on both agriculture and light industry. Our unwavering focus on agriculture has ensured the necessary supply of grain and raw materials for the development of industry.[3] Neglecting food production can be extremely dangerous. Failure to prioritize it may lead to social unrest and upheaval in the future."[4] "Simultaneous development of industry and agriculture is essential. This synergy ensures the availability of raw materials and markets for the industrial sector, ultimately facilitating the accumulation of additional funds for the growth of heavy industry."[5]

---

[3] *Collected Works of Mao Zedong*, Vol. 7. People's Publishing House, Beijing, 1999, p. 24.

[4] *Ibid.*, p. 199.

[5] *Ibid.*, p. 241.

Mao also emphasized the importance of handling the relationship between the state and farmers and protecting farmers' material interests in his essay "On the Ten Major Relationships." He wrote, "Our approach towards the peasant population diverges from the Soviet model, instead aiming to strike a balance between state interests and the well-being of the farmers. Historically, our agricultural taxation has been comparatively light. We have implemented a policy to reduce the gap between agricultural and industrial product prices, aiming for exchanges at or close to equal values. Agricultural products are purchased at regular prices to ensure that farmers do not suffer any losses, with the purchase prices gradually increasing over time. In terms of supplying industrial products to farmers, we adopt a policy of thin profit, maintaining stable prices or implementing appropriate reductions. Additionally, in areas facing food shortages, slight subsidies are generally provided for food supply to farmers. Nevertheless, we acknowledge the possibility of committing various mistakes if we are not careful. Considering the significant errors made by the Soviet Union in this regard, it is imperative for us to place greater emphasis on managing the relationship between the state and the farmers."[6] In Mao Zedong's "On the People's Democratic Dictatorship," he highlighted the crucial task of educating the farmers. Given the decentralized nature of the peasant economy, the process of socializing agriculture will require substantial time and meticulous efforts, as evidenced by the Soviet experience.[7] Before the Third Plenary Session of the 11th Central Committee of the Communist Party of China, Deng Xiaoping made a series of important statements emphasizing the importance of agriculture and rural economic development. As early as 1962, Deng Xiaoping pointed out that "without good agriculture, there is no hope for industry, and the problem of clothing, food, and housing will not be solved."[8] After the Third Plenary Session of the 11th Central Committee of the Communist Party of China, the agricultural production in China developed rapidly. However, Deng Xiaoping still stressed not to take agriculture lightly,[9] stating "Agriculture is fundamental. Don't forget it."[10] "The stability of Chinese society and the development of the economy depend largely on the development of rural

---

[6] *Ibid.*, p. 30.

[7] *Ibid.*, Vol. 4, 1991, p. 1477.

[8] *Selected Works of Deng Xiaoping*, Vol. 1. People's Publishing House, 1994, p. 322.

[9] *Ibid.*, Vol. 2, 1994, p. 406.

[10] *Ibid.*, Vol. 3, 1993, p. 23.

areas[11] and the well-being of farmers."[12] Jiang Zemin also pointed out that "The continuous development of agriculture, combined with the high enthusiasm of farmers, has ensured food security for everyone, which in turn has made it easier for the government to manage national and societal affairs. This is a fundamental lesson we have learned from our governance experience."[13] In his report to the 18th National Congress of the Communist Party of China, Hu Jintao pointed out that "solving the problem of agriculture, rural areas, and farmers is the top priority for the entire party. Urban–rural integration is the fundamental way to solve the 'three rural' issues." He further proposed to "develop a new type of urban–rural relationship, featuring industry supporting agriculture, cities leading rural areas, mutual benefit between urban and rural areas, and the integration of industry and agriculture."[14] In December 2014, Xi Jinping emphasized during his research in Jiangsu Province, "Without modern agriculture, rural prosperity, and the well-being of farmers, the modernization of the country will be hindered, and the nation will be unstable. To ensure stable and sustainable development, developed regions should take the lead in promoting the synchronous development of industrialization, information technology, urbanization, and agricultural modernization."[15] In July 2015, during his visit to Jilin Province, Xi Jinping emphasized the importance of agriculture, farmers, and rural areas, stating that they should never be overlooked or neglected. He called for a continuous adherence to policies that strengthen agriculture, benefit farmers, and enrich rural areas without weakening them. He also called for efforts to improve the overall well-being in rural areas and to keep up the positive momentum in terms of people's awareness, attention, and investment in rural development.[16]

---

[11] *Ibid.*, pp. 77–78.

[12] *Ibid.*, p. 159.

[13] *Selected Works of Jiang Zemin*, Vol. 1. People's Publishing House, 2006, p. 258.

[14] Hu Jintao. (2016). Persist in moving forward along the path of socialism with Chinese characteristics and strive to build a moderately prosperous society in all aspects. *Selected Works of Hu Jintao*, Vol. 3. People's Publishing House, p. 631.

[15] Seizing the initiative and actively adapting to the new normal of economic development to promote reform and opening-up, and modernization to a new level. *People's Daily*, December 15, 2014.

[16] Maintain strategic focus, enhance confidence in development, ensure stable progress of China's Economy. *People's Daily*, July 19, 2015.

During his inspection tour of Hunan province from November 3 to 5, 2013, Xi Jinping emphasized, "Development is the fundamental solution to eradicate poverty. To help lift our fellow rural citizens out of poverty, we must consider local conditions, determine what crops and livestock to raise, where to increase income and how to improve local livelihoods. We must also make sure to provide quality compulsory education in rural areas and equip the next generation with more knowledge and skills."[17] In June 2015, during a symposium in Guizhou with the main officials of the Party committees from some provinces, autonomous regions, and municipalities, Xi Jinping emphasized the importance of precision in poverty alleviation, stating that "precision is the key to successful poverty alleviation. The key is to be precise in identifying and targeting the poor, precise in project planning and implementation, precise in the use of funds, precise in providing assistance to individual households, precise in sending officials (first secretaries) to work in villages, and precise in assessing the results of poverty alleviation efforts."[18]

2. Ensuring Food Security

Food is a strategic commodity. As a country with over a billion people, we must insist on relying on domestic production and achieve basic self-sufficiency in food. On February 16, 2012, Xi Jinping pointed out at the China–US Agricultural Symposium, "Agriculture is the basic industry on which human society depends for survival and development. China has consistently recognized the criticality of ensuring national food security, and therefore, has accorded utmost priority to developing agriculture, empowering rural areas, uplifting farmers, and addressing the food needs of its vast population of 1.3 billion. These measures are essential in effectively governing the country and fostering stability in the nation."[19] On November 28, 2013, Xi Jinping emphasized at a symposium at the Shandong Academy of Agricultural Sciences, "Ensuring food security is

---

[17]Advancing reform and opening up, promote innovation-driven development to achieve the annual economic and social development goals. *People's Daily*, November 6, 2013.

[18]Planning for poverty alleviation and development in the thirteenth five-year plan period to ensure rural poor will be lifted out of poverty as scheduled by 2020. *People's Daily*, June 20, 2015.

[19]Xi Jinping attends and addresses China–US agriculture symposium. *People's Daily*, February 18, 2012.

a perennial issue and can never be taken lightly at any time."[20] China's grain production has achieved continuous growth for many years, and the food supply is relatively abundant. However, as there are many factors that affect food security, ensuring national food security is still a challenging task. We must ensure that the Chinese people always have control over their food supply, and that the majority of Chinese food is produced domestically.

2.1. *Challenges in China's medium to long-term food security*

Agriculture is the foundation of the national economy, as it not only affects the level of economic development but also has a direct impact on national food security. Grain is a strategic material, as the Chinese government has always attached great importance to food security. With the development of the economy and the improvement of people's living standards, the total consumption of agricultural products in China has continued to increase. However, the resources that agricultural production relies on, such as land and water, are limited. Therefore, China inevitably relies on foreign agricultural resources and imports agricultural products. In recent years, the quantity and variety of agricultural products imported into China have increased year on year. Therefore, it is necessary to adjust the food security strategy according to China's national conditions. The Central Economic Work Conference held in December 2013 proposed: "To effectively ensure the national food security of a country, it is necessary to follow a food security strategy that relies on the country's own resources, is based on domestic production, ensures sufficient production capacity, imports food products appropriately, and is supported by advancements in science and technology. It is important for a country to prioritize food security by depending on its own resources and protecting key resources within the country. Additionally, it is essential to attain basic self-sufficiency in grain and absolute security in staple foods, while equally prioritizing quantity and quality. We also need to focus on the quality and safety of agricultural products and ensure proper governance and supervision throughout the entire production and sales process.

[20] Fully implementing the decisions of the third plenary session of the 18th CPC central committee is crucial to generate strong momentum for advancing reforms in all areas. *People's Daily*, November 29, 2013.

To promote sustainable development, we need to transform the mode of agricultural development by developing water-saving and circular agriculture. It is also important to enhance capacity-building for ensuring food security, strengthen agricultural infrastructure, and accelerate technological progress in agriculture."[21] China's adjustment of the food security strategy is in line with the country's development needs, and ensuring the absolute security of staple foods is crucial for achieving food security. Importing agricultural products will inevitably lower China's self-sufficiency rate in this sector. In addition to focusing on quantity, China also places great emphasis on the quality and safety of food, which is a major issue that the government is actively addressing.

2.2. *Taking measures to ensure China's food security*

To ensure food security, we need to tackle issues such as the availability of arable land, the number of farmers cultivating the land, and the funding for agriculture. The significance of land in food production cannot be overstated. As China undergoes further industrial and urban development, it becomes imperative to strike a balance between the land dedicated to these endeavors and the land reserved for agriculture. The 1.8 billion mu arable land redline is the Chinese government's limit on non-agricultural use of farmland and this limit cannot be exceeded. To address food security issues, we must also stimulate farmers' enthusiasm for grain cultivation, which means improving the comparative benefits of planting food crops. After the reform and opening-up, the rural areas implemented the household responsibility system for contracting land, and the rural economy has been booming. However, this has also brought about problems such as small-scale land management and difficulties in connecting with the larger market. Compared to working outside, planting food crops has lower comparative benefits, so young labor forces in rural areas have gone to work in cities. However, these phenomena also indicate new increases in rural productivity. The fragmentation of rural land calls for moderate-scale farming, and new agricultural management methods such as family farms, collective management, cooperative management, and enterprise management are gradually being promoted in rural areas in

[21] The central economic work conference was held in Beijing. *People's Daily*, December 14, 2013.

China. Moderate-scale land management will promote the improvement of agricultural technology and mechanization levels, as well as the comparative benefits of planting food crops, thereby ensuring national food security. Commercial capital has entered rural areas to develop modern planting and breeding industries that are suitable for corporate management and will introduce modern production elements and management models to agriculture. Funds are needed for food production, and funding is an important factor restricting rural economic development. Guaranteeing that financial institutions use rural deposits mainly for agricultural and rural policies will help solve the problem of rural capital outflow. At the same time, China encourages the development of cooperative economies in rural areas, supports the development of large-scale, specialized, and modern management, and allows cooperatives to engage in credit cooperation, which will also help solve the problem of difficult rural funding. Agriculture is a weak industry that requires the support and protection of the state. China provides direct subsidies to grain farmers and is addressing challenges in major grain-producing areas, including the imbalance between agricultural and industrial development and fiscal constraints. This is being done through improving compensation mechanisms, encouraging and supporting grain cultivation, and promoting national food security. To promote grain production and ensure food security, it is important to utilize market mechanisms and provide government support to make grain cultivation profitable for farmers. Additionally, effective management of food reserves and strategic use of domestic and international markets and resources should be prioritized, alongside increasing agricultural globalization efforts.

We should take proactive measures to accelerate the construction of China's food security guarantee system, mainly including: first, we should implement a stricter system of farmland protection. Farmland is the foundation of China's food security guarantee system. With limited per capita arable land resources, the issue of land shortage will only become more severe in the future economic development process. Therefore, reasonable development and utilization of farmland must be carried out, and the policy of strict farmland protection must be implemented to prevent the disorderly use of farmland. At the same time, in terms of implementing responsibilities, it is necessary to clarify that protecting farmland is not only the responsibility of the central government or the Ministry of Land and Resources but also the shared responsibility of local governments at all levels. Accountability systems can be established to increase efforts to protect farmland. Second, we should establish an effective long-term mechanism for grain subsidies. The problems facing agriculture, rural areas, and farmers are interconnected, and farmers are at the root of these issues. Ultimately, food security depends on the enthusiasm of farmers to plant crops. Therefore, maintaining the enthusiasm of farmers to grow crops is crucial to ensuring food security. To ensure the sustainable development of agriculture, the national grain subsidy policy must be continuous and stable. As the country's economic strength grows, the standard of grain subsidies should also increase to ensure that farmers receive corresponding income returns for growing crops. Agriculture, to a certain extent, benefits from economies of scale. Therefore, it is essential to enhance the agricultural land circulation market, promote moderate-scale production and operation in agriculture, raise farmers' income, and safeguard national food security. The state should increase the protection and purchase price of grain. Third, we need to strengthen the supervision of foreign investment penetration and control of China's agriculture. Foreign investment entering China's food sector has become an inevitable fact. Effective countermeasures should be taken to strengthen the supervision of foreign investment penetration and control of China's grain market. We should be prepared and guard against potential risks to ensure the security of China's grain market. This mainly involves strict regulation of foreign capital mergers and acquisitions of Chinese grain enterprises and entry into the grain sector.

3. Promoting Agricultural Modernization

From a global perspective, according to the level of productivity development and the history of agricultural development, agriculture can be roughly divided into three different stages. The first stage is the period of ancient agricultural development. This refers to a long historical period during which stone and iron tools were used in agriculture and eventually replaced by mechanized farming tools. During this stage, agricultural production relied mainly on human and animal power, with the use of simple iron and wooden farming tools. Traditional knowledge and direct experience accumulated over time played a significant role in agricultural technology. The second stage is the modernization period of agriculture. This refers to the historical period of agricultural development from the late 19th century to the 1940s. This stage is characterized by the dominant position of mechanized farming tools powered mainly by mechanical power in agricultural production. Agricultural technology mainly relies on the research achievements of modern natural science. Moreover, agricultural production has shifted from a self-sufficient mode to a large-scale commercial and social production mode. The third stage is the Contemporary Period of Agriculture. This period generally refers to the level of agricultural productivity achieved by economically developed countries from World War II to the present. At this stage, agriculture is characterized by high levels of mechanization, scientific advancement, and socialization.

The concepts and characteristics of contemporary agriculture have evolved alongside the progress of agricultural productivity throughout history, making it the most advanced form of agriculture in the world. Despite this evolution, there are still common international standards for contemporary agriculture during certain periods. Based on the current state of agricultural development worldwide, the fundamental characteristics of contemporary agriculture can be summarized as follows: The first feature of modern agriculture is the use of mechanized and electrified tools and equipment to replace human and animal labor. Apart from the harvesting of some vegetables and fruits by using traditional methods, developed countries have almost fully mechanized their agricultural production, with significant improvements in the technological and economic performance of agricultural machinery. In addition, highly automated and factory-like production methods have been adopted in areas such as livestock farming and vegetable greenhouses. Secondly, modern agricultural production heavily relies on scientific technology, which has replaced traditional techniques based solely on experience in the past. Understanding objective laws through science is increasingly necessary in agricultural production. Agricultural science has been widely applied in various aspects of production, resulting in ever-increasing returns. Improvements in seeds, fertilizers, pesticides, herbicides, cultivation, breeding, soil improvement, water conservancy, and the application of electronic technology, atomic energy technology, laser technology, remote sensing technology, and others in agriculture have greatly enhanced agricultural productivity. Thirdly, there is an increasing trend toward socialization in agricultural production. This is evidenced by the expansion of agricultural enterprise scale and the specialization of social division of labor in agricultural production. On the one hand, this has led to the regionalization and specialization of agricultural production through the development of regional and enterprise divisions of labor. On the other hand, many production processes in agricultural production, such as breeding improved strains, fertilization, pest control, feed processing and modulation, and agricultural product processing, are being separated from agriculture and forming a series of labor and business enterprises that serve agricultural production. As a result of these changes, the integration of agriculture, industry, and commerce has become more prominent, underscoring the growing importance of scientific management in the agricultural economy. The hallmark of modern agriculture is its unprecedented levels of productivity. Land productivity has increased significantly, and labor productivity has seen remarkable growth. In countries where agriculture has been modernized, a single agricultural laborer can now cultivate hundreds or thousands of acres of land, raise hundreds of cows or thousands of pigs, and produce tens of thousands or even millions of kilograms of grain, meat, eggs, milk, and other animal products, thereby supplying agricultural products for dozens of people at a higher level.

Ancient China was once one of the world's advanced agricultural countries. However, the prolonged existence of a feudal society spanning 3,000 years resulted in a significant lag in agricultural production compared to the global advanced standards. Since the founding of the People's Republic of China, and particularly after the reform and opening-up, agriculture has flourished, and the level of mechanization has significantly increased. Improved seeds, fertilizers, pesticides, and other inputs are widely used in China. However, the country still faces the challenging task of modernizing agriculture, rural areas, and farmers. This is a long-term process, as evidenced by the slow pace of labor transfer in some developed countries. Labor transfer is the result of two forces: the increase in labor productivity and the backwardness of rural living conditions (push factors), and employment and living standards in cities (pull factors). The transfer of labor from agriculture to non-agricultural sectors is a lengthy process. For example, it took about three centuries in the UK, about one and a half centuries in the United States, and about a century in Japan for the share of labor in agriculture to decline from 75% to 10%. France took about a century and Japan took about half a century to reduce the share of labor in agriculture from around 50% to around 10%.

In order to develop contemporary agriculture, it is necessary to transform traditional agriculture. One of the most famous theories on this topic is Schultz's theory of transforming traditional agriculture. Theodore Schultz was a renowned American economist and winner of the 1979 Nobel Prize in Economics. Since the 1950s, he has stressed the critical role of agricultural and rural development in the process of industrialization and the development of human capital in industrialization. Schultz believed that, just like industry, agriculture is a crucial sector of the economy, and its contribution to economic development is enormous. Policies that prioritize heavy industry and overlook agriculture cannot achieve good industrialization results or modernize the economy and society and can instead lead to an imbalanced and stagnant national economy and worsened livelihoods. Schultz's theory of transforming traditional agriculture is a new theory of economic growth that holds an important theoretical position. He proposed the idea of developing and transforming agriculture, investing in farmers, and providing new production factors to agriculture.

China's agriculture is gradually transitioning from traditional agriculture to modern agriculture, which will bring about a series of changes in agricultural management and organization, as well as an acceleration of the transfer of agricultural labor to urban areas. Correspondingly, China's agricultural policies also need to undergo changes. Before the reform and opening-up, the basic features of China's rural economy were the collective ownership of land and the collective management of farming under the people's commune system, and the government's unified purchase and sale of agricultural products. The collective ownership of land under the people's commune system resulted in farmers collectively farming and managing the land. The unified purchase and sale system of agricultural products involved the government purchasing agricultural products at a low price and then selling them to urban residents and industrial sectors at a unified price. Since the Third Plenary Session of the 11th Central Committee of the Communist Party of China, the main reforms in agriculture and rural areas have been the establishment of a dual-layer management system based on household land management and the combination of unified and separated management, and the reform of the agricultural product circulation system, among others. China's rural reforms have proven to be successful, and the macro effects on China's agriculture, rural areas, farmers, and the entire national economy have attracted worldwide attention. The main reason for the success of rural reforms is that they have given farmers the autonomy to manage their own land and survive in the market economy. In the 1980s, the main rural reforms were implemented through the land contract system and the increase in agricultural product prices to stimulate farmers' production enthusiasm and achieve rapid agricultural development. These reforms mainly took place within the rural areas, and thus progressed quickly. After the 1990s, reforms not only took place within rural areas but also involved improvements to the surrounding areas of rural communities, including adjustments to the urban–rural relationship and changes to the national income distribution pattern. These changes ultimately increased the overall cost of the reforms.

Since the reform and opening-up policy, the agricultural and rural economies in China have undergone tremendous changes and entered a new stage of development. The supply and demand of agricultural products have shifted from the previous shortage to surplus, and the second and third industries in rural areas have flourished. Large numbers of rural laborers have moved to cities, and the living standards of farmers have greatly improved. However, we must also acknowledge the challenges that China faces in developing modern agriculture. In recent years, it has become increasingly common for young and middle-aged rural laborers to go out to work in cities, while elderly farmers remain to tend the land, and in some places, large areas of land have been abandoned. To address this situation, China has proposed allowing voluntary land transfers, but due to factors such as the low return on investment for rural land and a lack of intermediaries for land transfers, the scale of rural land transfers is still limited. Rural areas not only have small-scale land management but also lack funding. Given the aging of the agricultural labor force, the decline of economic activity in rural areas, and the growing number of children left behind in rural communities, it has become challenging to achieve substantial progress through traditional agricultural reforms. China must accelerate the transformation of its agricultural development mode, speed up the pace of agricultural technological innovation, and move toward a path of modernizing agriculture that is characterized by high efficiency in output, product safety, resource conservation, and environmental friendliness.

Firstly, it is necessary to give farmers more comprehensive and secure land contract rights. During his inspection tour of Wuhan in Hubei Province from July 21 to 23, 2013, Xi Jinping pointed out, "As a society, it is important for us to prioritize the advancement of rural reform and the improvement of basic rural operating systems. This can be achieved by studying and understanding the intricate relationship between rural land ownership, contract rights, and management rights, while always respecting the will of farmers in land transfer. It is crucial that we prioritize the protection of basic farmland and food security, while simultaneously working towards increasing the income of farmers."[22] During the Central Rural Work Conference held on December 23–24, 2013, it was emphasized that the Party's rural work must prioritize the maintenance of the basic rural operating system. The collective ownership of rural land by farmers was specifically highlighted as the "soul" of this system. It is essential that we prioritize the upholding of household management and ensure that rural collective land is contracted by rural residents who are members of collective economic organizations. It is important to note that no other entity can replace the land contract status of rural residents. In order to achieve this, we must work toward stabilizing land contract relationships and legally safeguarding rural residents' rights to possess, use, benefit from, transfer, mortgage, and guarantee land contract rights. The separation of land contracts and management rights is a new trend in China's agricultural production relations, and it presents new requirements for improving the basic rural operating system. Therefore, we should continuously explore effective forms of realizing collective ownership of rural land, implement collective ownership, stabilize farmers' contract rights, and liberate land management rights. This will accelerate the construction of a three-dimensional, compound, and modern agricultural management system based on household operation, cooperation, and coordination as the link, and socialized services as the support. We must remember that the basic rural operating system is the cornerstone of the Party's rural policy.[23] Thus, it is imperative that we continue to explore effective forms of realizing collective ownership of rural land, improve the method of separating land ownership, contract rights, and management rights, and implement collective ownership, stabilize farmers' contract rights, and liberate land management rights.

During the initial stages of reform, farmers created the concept of "separation of two rights" — collective land ownership and household land contract management rights. Later, in some places, the "separation of three rights" was introduced, which clarified land ownership, stabilized land contract rights, and freed up management rights. In order to realize the "separation of three rights" in rural land ownership, contract management, and operational management, it is important to maintain the mainstay of contracted farmers during the land transfer process and allow them

[22]Resolutely deepening reform and opening-up, steadily promoting economic and social development. *People's Daily*, July 24, 2013.

[23]Central rural work conference took place in Beijing. *People's Daily*, December 25, 2013.

to have control over the transfer of land management rights. As a legal property right granted by law, rural land contract management rights give farmers the right to choose how they manage their land. They can manage it themselves, rent or subcontract the right to operate land to others, exchange land parcels voluntarily with other collective economic organizations, develop cooperative production with other farmers in the form of land shares, use the management rights of contracted land as collateral to obtain financing from financial institutions, and invest the management rights of contracted land as shares in agricultural industrialization. It is crucial to accelerate the process of confirming, registering, and issuing certificates for rural collective land ownership and household land contract management rights. This will provide a legal basis for protecting the collective ownership of rural land and the stable contract management rights of farmers and create a suitable institutional environment for the transfer and concentration of land management rights. Confirming, registering, and issuing certificates can also ensure accurate and precise land rights and shares.

Secondly, family farming needs to shift toward the use of advanced technology and production methods. The use of advanced technology and production methods can increase farmers' income, improve their standard of living, and achieve sustainable agricultural development. Whether it is to expand the scale of family land management or to increase land productivity, advanced scientific technology and production methods are needed, and the investment in technology and other production factors needs to be increased. During a visit to Shandong province in November 2013, Xi Jinping pointed out the importance of integrating agricultural technology, mechanization, information management, and environmental protection to build a technology system that can meet the requirements of high-yield, high-quality, high-efficiency, ecological, and safe agricultural development. In areas with well-developed land management, there has been a notable surge in farmers' demand for agricultural machinery. This increased adoption of agricultural mechanization is expected to facilitate the widespread adoption of high-quality and standardized cultivation techniques.[24] In areas where intensive farming is practiced, increasing technology and material investment can lead to significant improvements

[24]Fully implementing the decisions of the third plenary session of the 18th CPC central committee is crucial to generate strong momentum for advancing reforms in all areas. *People's Daily*, November 29, 2013.

in agricultural productivity. In order to support this, it is important for the government to increase investment in agricultural technology. In order to promote the development of agriculture and rural economies in China, it is crucial that we shift toward a more collaborative and cooperative approach to management. This involves the formation of a diversified, multi-level, and multi-form farming service system that prioritizes the development of farmer cooperation and collaboration. For small-scale farmers, market risks and natural risks can present significant challenges when it comes to survival and growth in a market economy. This is where farmer cooperatives can play a valuable role in supporting the development of agriculture and rural economies. In many developed countries, farmers have established cooperative relationships to address these challenges. However, in rural China, despite the mobilization of farmers' enthusiasm through the household land contract system, the lack of a social service system has resulted in a weak level of unified management and a low level of organization among farmers. To address this, we need to prioritize the development of farmer cooperatives and support the establishment of a strong social service system that can help farmers to overcome market risks and natural risks and achieve long-term success in the agricultural sector.

In order to transform farmers into professionals and make agriculture a profitable industry, it is crucial to provide them with the necessary training. This involves both agricultural management theory and practice, as well as training in agricultural technology. Only by equipping farmers with knowledge in these areas can we achieve modernization in agriculture. Furthermore, the migration of the rural population to urban areas for employment highlights the need for vocational skills training in rural areas. It is essential to provide rural populations with the necessary education and training to improve the quality of labor in the secondary and tertiary industries. These tasks are arduous and long-term, and it is the responsibility of the government to play a role in supporting these efforts. The government should prioritize the development of agricultural technology promotion departments to support farmers with the latest technological advancements. Local governments can also encourage schools and social organizations to provide training for farmers through the purchase of services. By investing in education and training for farmers, we can ensure that the agricultural industry continues to thrive and that rural communities have access to the necessary skills and knowledge to succeed in the modern economy.

Thirdly, the government needs to strengthen support and protection for agriculture. China has put forward policies of industrial support for agriculture and urban–rural integration, but in reality, they have not been fully implemented, and the coordinated development of industry and agriculture has not been truly achieved. In the process of industrialization, the rational allocation of resources between industry and agriculture is a primary aspect of optimal resource utilization, and the symbol of this is the coordinated development of industry and agriculture. Coordinated development of industry and agriculture is an objective requirement for economic development and a basic condition for the stable development of the national economy. International experience has shown that sustainable and healthy development of the national economy during the process of industrialization can only be achieved through coordinated growth of the agriculture and industry sectors. Neglecting or sacrificing agriculture can result in a crisis for the entire economy, making it imperative to prioritize the development of both sectors in a balanced and sustainable way. For example, in the process of industrialization, the Soviet Union ignored the development of agriculture, resulting in serious imbalances in the national economy, severe shortages of consumer goods, and a mismatch between supply and demand in the market. The growth of agricultural production was long constrained by the Soviet economic development. Since the establishment of New China, several major cyclical economic fluctuations have occurred due to the underdevelopment of agriculture, which has negatively impacted industrial development. In these instances, emphasis on agriculture has been crucial in restoring economic growth. This highlights that the cost of sacrificing agriculture is not just limited to the agricultural sector, but rather it impacts the entire national economy and society. Coordinated growth of agriculture and industry is essential not only for the prosperity of the agricultural sector, but also as an important guarantee for the steady and sustainable development of industry and the entire national economy.

Achieving sustained and coordinated development between industry and agriculture under market economy conditions can be challenging. Market forces can lead to excessive resource loss in the agricultural sector due to its inherent weaknesses. In many cases, countries tend to prioritize rapid industrialization over agriculture, leading to suppressed growth in the agricultural sector. To ensure optimal resource allocation and coordinated growth between industry and agriculture, appropriate government intervention is necessary to support and protect the agricultural sector.

The two-sector labor surplus model proposed by Fei Jinghan and Gustav Ranis illustrates the interdependent relationship between industrial and agricultural production in an ideal industrialization model. While industrialization can take on different forms in different countries, the principle that coordinated growth of industry and agriculture is necessary to ensure smooth progress in the early stages of industrialization remains unchanged. This has been demonstrated by the industrialization practices of various countries.

The development of agricultural policies during industrialization typically follows a certain pattern. Based on changes in the relationship between industry and agriculture, industrialization can be divided into three basic stages. The first stage is the phase of agriculture supporting the development of industry, also known as the agriculture to industry (ATI) stage. This stage belongs to the initial period of industrialization. Its agricultural policy is mainly to provide capital accumulation for industry through agriculture, while also taking certain measures, such as investing in the construction of farmland water conservancy and encouraging the use of new technologies, to support agricultural production. The government's support for agriculture during this stage does not refer to the usual flow of industrial surplus back to agriculture. Instead, it aims to allocate resources between industry and agriculture in a reasonable manner, and to introduce new technologies to agriculture to improve productivity. The second stage is the phase of equal development of agriculture and industry, also known as the agriculture and industry self-support (AIS) stage. This stage belongs to the middle period of industrialization. Its agricultural policy is mainly to gradually reduce the burden on agriculture while taking measures such as providing funds for agricultural production to support agriculture and prevent excessive loss of agricultural resources. The third stage is the phase of industry supporting the development of agriculture, also known as the industry to agriculture (ITA) stage. This stage belongs to the advanced period of industrialization. Its agricultural policy is mainly to increase investment in agriculture and rural areas, making industrial surplus flow back to agriculture. China must strive to achieve policies that support industrial development in agriculture and promote integration between urban and rural areas. To this end, it is crucial to prioritize and strengthen support for the agricultural sector. During the Central Rural Work Conference held from December 23 to 24, 2013, Xi Jinping emphasized the need for the entire Party to prioritize the resolution of the "three rural" issues. He also stressed the importance of adhering to policies that support industrial development in agriculture, promote urban support for rural areas, and reduce government control while increasing support for agriculture. The aim is to consistently increase support for agriculture, benefit the agricultural sector, and improve the livelihoods of farmers. It is essential to always remain focused on improving the "three rural" issues and achieving success in rural development.[25]

Fourthly, the government should encourage transferring the surplus labor from agriculture. The fundamental solution to the development of agriculture and the rural economy in China is to transfer surplus labor from agriculture to other industries. During the process of industrialization, the transfer of labor from agriculture to non-agricultural sectors is an inevitable trend. The transfer of labor from agriculture is influenced by several factors. These include the improvement of agricultural labor productivity, which serves as the foundation for such a transfer. In addition, the capacity for capital accumulation in non-agricultural sectors also plays a role, as it affects the development of these sectors and, in turn, the number of labor transfers from agriculture. The ratio of capital to labor is another factor, as capital-intensive businesses typically employ fewer workers than labor-intensive ones. Other considerations include the values of farmers and the employment policies of the government. While older farmers may prefer to stay on their land, younger farmers are more likely to leave the countryside for urban areas. The government's policies, whether they are restrictive or encouraging, can also significantly impact the transfer of labor from agriculture.

Looking at the situation of rural laborers moving to work in cities, the government's policies toward rural labor mobility have undergone several changes, from limiting it to allowing, controlling, and eventually regulating it. Before the reform and opening-up, China implemented a household registration system and employment system that divided urban and rural areas, and rural labor mobility was strictly limited. Even at the beginning of the reform and opening-up period, these restrictions remained in place. From 1984 onward, the government allowed farmers to raise funds and grow their own food, and to work and do business in cities and towns. This marked the loosening of the household registration and employment system that had been in place for 30 years, and rural labor transfer and mobility entered a period of rapid growth. After rectification and restructuring in 1989, the government improved the management of rural labor

[25] Central rural work conference took place in Beijing. *People's Daily*, December 25, 2013.

mobility and kept most of the policies and measures in place to support it. From 1992 onward, the policy toward rural labor mobility gradually changed from controlling unregulated migration to encouraging, guiding, and implementing orderly mobility under macroeconomic regulation. The employment system for rural labor mobility across regions centered on employment certificates was implemented, and the household registration system for small towns was reformed. After 2000, the government gradually lifted various unreasonable restrictions on farmers' employment in cities, actively promoted supporting reforms, and entered a new development stage of rural labor transfer and mobility. Since the 18th National Congress of the Communist Party of China was held, the country has further emphasized the urbanization of rural migrant workers and the promotion of rural labor transfer. To support the integration of rural and urban areas, it's important to reform the household registration system and ensure equal employment opportunities for both rural and urban workers. This includes enabling rural migrant workers to enter and settle in cities, protecting their rights and interests, and promoting equal employment rights for all workers.

4. Building a New Socialist Countryside

The construction of a new socialist countryside was highlighted as a significant historical task during the Fifth Plenary Session of the 16th Central Committee of the Communist Party of China. This task involves "improving production, raising living standards, promoting cultural and ethical progress, enhancing village aesthetics, and facilitating democratic management."[26] To achieve these goals, there should be coordinated development in the rural economy, politics, culture, society, and Party. During a visit to Yunnan Province in January 2015, Xi Jinping emphasized that the development of a new countryside should align with the actual conditions and development patterns of rural areas, fully reflect their unique features, preserve their appearance and natural environment, and evoke a sense of nostalgia for the countryside.[27] This provided further

[26]Party Literature Research Center of the CPC Central Committee (Ed.). (2006). *Selected Important Documents since the 16th CPC National Congress*, Vol. II. Central Party Literature Press, p. 1050.

[27]Resolutely winning the battle of poverty alleviation and accelerating the economic and social development of ethnic regions. *People's Daily*, January 22, 2015.

guidance for the advancement of the building of a new socialist countryside.

Since the establishment of the People's Republic of China, the Communist Party has repeatedly put forward the task and requirements of building a new socialist countryside. The significant historical task of building a new socialist countryside proposed by the Fifth Plenary Session of the 16th Central Committee of the Communist Party of China sets out the overall requirements of developing production, improving living standards, fostering a civilized rural culture, ensuring clean and tidy villages, and promoting democratic management. The task of building a new socialist countryside involves not only economic development but also the development of other aspects such as politics, culture, society, ecology, and the Communist Party, and all these aspects must be developed in a coordinated and unified manner. To achieve the goals of building a new socialist countryside, it is crucial to adopt various measures. Increasing national investment, carrying out industrial support for agriculture, and urban support for rural areas, and mobilizing the whole society for extensive participation are necessary methods to achieve these goals. Xi Jinping stresses the importance of preserving the unique cultural aspects of rural areas and maintaining a connection to the past while working toward the development of a new socialist countryside. Building a new socialist countryside is a continuation and development of CPC's strategic thinking on the "three rural" issues, and a strategic measure to strengthen the "three rural" work in light of new circumstances.

The construction of a socialist new countryside is a grand and systematic project and a long-term and arduous historical task. There are several major tasks that need to be completed in the construction of a socialist new countryside. First, the primary task is to develop modern agriculture. The second aspect is the development of rural public services, which is not only a crucial component of the new rural construction but also a key area in need of improvement. This involves improving rural compulsory education, promoting the new rural cooperative medical system, and undertaking major infrastructure projects such as water supply, road construction, electricity, and gas. Third, advancing the rural reform is crucial as it provides the institutional guarantee for the construction of a new countryside and serves as the driving force for agricultural and rural development. To promote the development of rural areas, it is crucial to accelerate rural reform and establish effective mechanisms for coordinating and equally developing urban and rural areas. To achieve this, a market system with reasonable resource allocation and orderly product flow should be established, along with an efficient management system with clear rights and responsibilities. Comprehensive promotion of rural finance reform and acceleration of the reform of the land expropriation system are also essential. Additionally, comprehensive reform of township institutions, rural compulsory education, and county and township financial systems should be promoted. Fourth, it is important to promote democratic political construction in rural areas. Although significant progress has been made in rural democracy management, China's transition from a feudal society to a socialist society has left limited traditions of democracy. As a result, rural democracy management has faced various challenges and issues in some regions. Only by properly addressing these challenges can rural democracy develop in a healthy and sustainable way.

During the 1970s, South Korea initiated the "Saemaul Undong" or "New Village Movement," which effectively transformed the rural areas, narrowed the urban–rural gap, and laid the foundation for the take-off of the Korean economy. China is currently promoting the construction of a new socialist countryside, and there is great interest in South Korea's experience in rural development because the situation in South Korea at that time was similar to China's current stage of economic and social development, and they faced comparable challenges. The "Saemaul Undong" movement was widely defined as a way to accelerate the development of rural modernization by participating in village construction projects and developing farmers' ethical spirit. The purpose of the movement was to improve farmers' ethical standards and living conditions and achieve the goal of "escaping poverty and moving toward prosperity" with the principles of "diligence, self-help, and cooperation." The "Saemaul Undong" was led by the government, with extensive participation from the rural masses in a top-down manner. The role of the government was to support, coordinate, serve, train, and guide. The Korean government attached great importance to the "Saemaul Undong." During the key period from 1970 to 1979, parliamentary leaders and cabinet members participated in meetings on this work, chaired by the President. The main measures taken to promote the "Saemaul Undong" were as follows: firstly, the project was implemented on a village-by-village basis. The selection and determination of projects were democratically conducted, jointly discussed by local officials (mainly township cadres) and villagers, and gradually reported to the central government. Secondly, the government provided material support. The government provided tangible support, such as cement in the first year and steel bars in the following years. Cement was provided in the first year and steel bars were provided starting from the second year. Thirdly, farmers' self-help and cooperative spirit were encouraged. The initial purpose of the "Saemaul Undong" was to guide farmers to improve their village facilities, enhance their ethical standards, and establish self-help and cooperative spirits. Fourthly, the role of grassroots organizations and village leaders was emphasized. The most basic level of government in Korea is the "Myeon" (township), which includes about 20 villages. Each township government has about 20 staff members who actively participate in new village construction work and are responsible for the distribution of cement and steel bars to one or two villages per person. At the same time, the "Saemaul Undong" required each village to select a leader, who was usually a respected person or a young person with good education and dedication, to lead the project construction in their own village. Fifthly, always place emphasis on the training programs. The Korean government believed that training village leaders was crucial and attached great importance to training programs. The training content mainly included lectures on policies and economic development issues, success stories, visits to advanced areas, group discussions, engineering technology, etc. In addition, there was also training for township cadres and training for trainers. In order to enhance the public's awareness and support for the "Saemaul Undong," the Korean government organized relevant training programs for senior officials, social elites, and village leaders. The purpose of various types of training at all levels was to boost morale, improve quality, cultivate an enterprising spirit, encourage farmers to actively participate in new village construction, increase income, and improve their quality of life. The "Saemaul Undong" serves as a useful model for China's efforts to build a new socialist countryside.

Chapter 14

Advancing People-Centered New Urbanization

After the 18th National Congress of the Communist Party of China concluded in 2012, the Chinese government has been prioritizing urbanization as a key strategy for building socialism with Chinese characteristics. Under the leadership of Comrade Xi Jinping, the government has recognized the significant opportunities presented by urbanization and has integrated urbanization efforts into "the Five-Sphere Integrated Plan." To accurately assess the new trends and characteristics of urbanization, it is important to address the problems connected with urbanization, adhere to the laws of development, seize opportunities while mitigating risks, and adopt a people-centered and coordinated approach with Chinese characteristics. This approach has greatly enriched the theoretical framework of Marxist political economics on urbanization. Urbanization is a natural historical process that accompanies industrialization growth, the agglomeration of non-agricultural industries in urban areas, and the concentration of rural population in urban areas. It is an objective trend in the development of human society, an important indicator of national modernization, and a significant practical field of political economics of socialism with Chinese characteristics. General Secretary Xi Jinping emphasized, "Addressing the issue of people is key to advancing new urbanization; the most fundamental trend of urbanization is the transfer of rural surplus labor and rural population to urban areas."[1]

[1] Party Literature Research Center of the CPC Central Committee (Ed.). (2014). *Selected Important Documents since the 18th CPC National Congress*, Vol. I. Central Party Literature Press, p. 593.

1. People-Centered New Urbanization Path as the Historical Choice

In late 2013, the Central Urbanization Work Conference underscored the critical significance of new urbanization in China's economic progress. Xi Jinping highlighted, "If millions of urban residents continue to live in an unstable situation, it will not only hinder their potential consumption demand and exacerbate the issue of dual land usage in urban and rural areas but also result in a multitude of social conflicts and risks."[2] Against the backdrop of new economic and social development, this statement eloquently elucidates why it is imperative to advance people-centered new urbanization.

Urbanization refers to the process by which people move from rural areas to urban areas, resulting in the expansion of urban areas and a series of accompanying economic and social changes. In terms of the transformation of economic structure, urbanization involves the gradual shift from agricultural activities to non-agricultural activities and the upgrading of industrial structures. From a social structure perspective, urbanization is the gradual transformation of rural populations into urban populations, as well as the diffusion of urban culture, lifestyle, and values to rural areas. In terms of spatial structure changes, urbanization is the process by which various production factors and industrial activities are concentrated in urban areas and subsequently redistributed.[3] Based on this definition, urbanization is a multifaceted process involving significant changes in a country or region's economic, social, and spatial structures—the "three major structures." This process is a complex historical evolution that requires adherence to the principles of comprehensive change in these structures. However, China's urbanization process also has unique characteristics that reflect the country's "Chinese characteristics" and the new type of urbanization path. At the core of this path is a "people-centered" approach.

The history of global economic and social development since the Industrial Revolution demonstrates that successful modernization requires a focus on urbanization alongside industrialization. In China today, urbanization, industrialization, agricultural modernization, and digitalization

---

[2] *Ibid.*

[3] See Wei Houkai (Ed.). (2014). *The Path to New Urbanization with Chinese Characteristics*. Social Sciences Academic Press, p. 2.

develop concurrently and complement each other, forming the core of evolving modernization. Industrialization takes the lead and serves as the main driving force for development; agricultural modernization is the essential foundation and basis for development; digitalization has the advantage of being a late-mover and injects new vitality into development; urbanization acts as the carrier and platform, providing development space for industrialization and digitalization, driving the acceleration of agricultural modernization, and playing an integrating role. Urbanization is a key driver for maintaining a sustainable and healthy economy, accelerating the transformation and upgradation of industrial structures, addressing issues related to agriculture, rural areas, and farmers, promoting coordinated regional development, and fostering comprehensive social progress. Advancing urbanization actively, prudently, and in an orderly manner is crucial for China's transition from a large economy to a powerful one. It holds great practical and far-reaching historical significance for building a moderately prosperous society in all aspects, accelerating the process of socialist modernization, and achieving the Chinese Dream of the great rejuvenation of the Chinese nation.

New urbanization is not only significant for China, but it can also have a positive impact on promoting global development. There is no precedent in human history for the urbanization of a developing country with a population of over 1.3 billion people. As Xi Jinping pointed out, China remains the world's largest developing country, with imbalances in industrial, urban–rural, and regional development. There is still plenty of room for us to explore new avenues of industrialization, urbanization, and regional development. This is advantageous for China as it allows us to firmly grasp the initiative of development and move toward a more balanced and prosperous society.[4] According to Xi, if we have the right urbanization goals and direction, we can unleash the potential of domestic demand, boost labor productivity, eliminate the urban–rural divide, promote social equity and common prosperity, and benefit both the global economy and environment.[5] Therefore, when addressing urbanization issues, we should not only focus on our own problems and avoid being narrow-minded. Instead, we should adopt an international perspective and

---

[4] See The political bureau of the CPC central committee holds meeting to discuss government work report. *People's Daily*, February 25, 2014.

[5] Party Literature Research Center of the CPC Central Committee (2014), *Op. cit.*, p. 590.

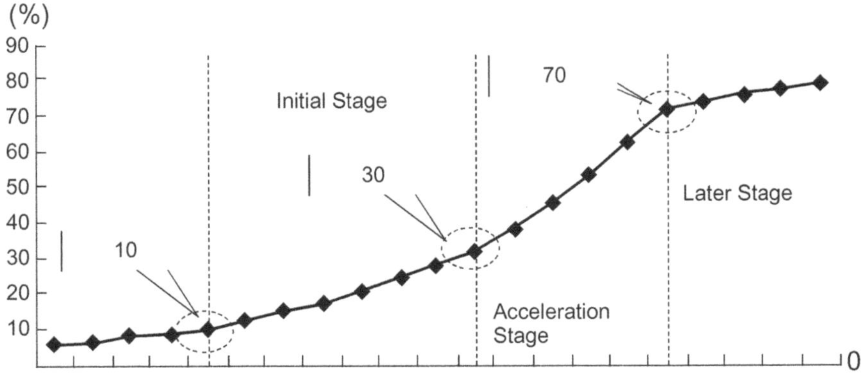

Figure 1. Urbanization curve.

global mindset, explore and learn from the experiences of other countries, and ultimately contribute to the progress of human society as a whole.

In 2011, Nobel laureate in economics Professor Joseph Stiglitz proposed that two major events would shape the course of the 21st century: the high technology of the United States and the urbanization of China. Urbanologist Northam studied the urbanization processes of various countries and developed an analytical tool called the "urbanization curve." This curve is a valuable analytical tool for determining a country's stage of urbanization (see Figure 1).

Urbanization in Western developed countries can be generally characterized by an inverted "S" curve, showing a three-stage process. The initial phase is characterized by a slow growth rate with an urbanization rate below 30%. In the second stage, the urbanization rate accelerates and ranges between 30% and 70%, which is a critical period for urbanization development. The third stage begins when the urbanization rate exceeds 70%, and it indicates the maturity stage of urbanization. Most Western developed countries have already entered this stage. Applying the "urbanization curve" to assess China's urbanization stage shows that China is in the middle to later stages of the acceleration phase.

Tracing China's urbanization process from 1949 reveals significant historical changes. In March 1949, the Second Plenary Session of the Seventh Central Committee of the Party made an explicit statement, marking the beginning of China's urbanization: "From now on, we are entering a period where the countryside transitions to the city, and the city leads the rural areas. The focus of the Party's work has shifted from rural areas to cities." However, before the reform and opening up, China's urban development had advanced slowly and experienced setbacks and periods of stagnation. By 1979, the urbanization rate was only 18.96%, with a small urban population of 195 million. Following the reform and opening up, China's urbanization began to recover and enter a rapid development stage. In 2011, the urban population reached 691 million, exceeding the rural population for the first time, and the urbanization rate rose to 51.27%. By 2015, the urbanization rate reached 56.1%, and the urban resident population increased to 770 million. Within this population, several key urban areas are experiencing rapid growth, such as the Beijing-Tianjin-Hebei, Yangtze River Delta, and Pearl River Delta regions. These areas cover only 2.8% of China's land area but are home to 18% of the population and generate 36% of the GDP. These urban centers have become critical drivers of China's rapid economic growth and participation in global economic cooperation and competition.[6]

During the 16th National Congress of the Party, it was proposed to prioritize the coordinated development of large, medium, and small cities and towns, and to adopt an urbanization model that reflects Chinese characteristics. At the 17th National Congress, the urbanization model with Chinese characteristics was identified as a fundamental component of the socialist approach in China, alongside other models, such as independent innovation, new industrialization, agricultural modernization, and political development. At the 18th National Congress, the Chinese government proposed prioritizing the new industrialization, digitalization, urbanization, and agricultural modernization models, all with Chinese characteristics. The Third Plenary Session of the 18th Central Committee later emphasized the importance of adopting a people-centered model for new urbanization, with Chinese characteristics. These developments illustrate that adopting a people-centered model for new urbanization, with Chinese characteristics, is an important historical decision.

2. China's Urbanization Calls for Increased Emphasis on the Human Aspect

What should be noted is that while urbanization in China is developing rapidly, the quality of urbanization is becoming more of a concern. According to data from the National Bureau of Statistics, there are

[6]See Xu Shaoshi. (2014). Unswervingly follow the path of new urbanization with Chinese characteristics. *China Economic and Trade Herald Journal*, Issue 7.

currently around 260 million people who are classified as agricultural transfer population (agricultural population migrated to cities) living in cities in China and who have made enormous contributions to the development of cities but have not been able to enjoy the same level of public services as urban residents with household registration. They have long been excluded from urban residency and find it difficult to integrate into urban society. Additionally, land urbanization has been happening at a faster rate than population urbanization. This has led to inefficient use of urban land, unreasonable distribution of urban space and scale, and a mismatch between urban development and the capacity of resources and the environment. As a result, cities exhibit a prominent dualistic structural conflict (in other words, inequality or socio-spatial polarization), and both urban and rural development lack distinctive features. In order to fix these issues, we must move away from traditional urbanization concepts, avoid blindly imitating foreign models and practices, stay true to China's unique circumstances, and pursue a people-centered urbanization approach that embodies Chinese characteristics.

The main problems that have arisen in China's urbanization can be classified into the following areas:

One significant issue in China's urbanization process is the limited integration of migrant workers into urban areas, resulting in a widespread phenomenon of "semi-urbanization." Xi Jinping emphasized: "Currently, there are over 200 million migrant workers and other individuals who have become permanent urban residents, but they find themselves in a state of "semi-urbanization" or "amphibious" living. These people are more suited to settle in urban areas compared to those still in rural regions, and efforts should be made to stabilize their settlement in cities."[7] Looking at the bigger picture, China's urbanization is a typical case of incomplete urbanization. This incompleteness is primarily manifested in the significant influx of migrant workers to cities for employment, the transition of agricultural residents to non-agricultural residents in urbanized suburban areas, and the substantial presence of farmers even after urban expansion. Although they reside in urban areas and are counted as urban residents, they have not genuinely integrated into the city and still exist outside the urban system, caught in an awkward position between urban and rural. Their lifestyles and consumption habits still retain the customs and

[7]Party Literature Research Center of the CPC Central Committee (2014), *Op. cit.*, p. 593.

characteristics of rural residents, resulting in a low degree of urbanization. The National Bureau of Statistics' "2015 Migrant Worker Monitoring Survey Report" reveals that in 2015, the number of migrant workers in China reached 280 million, with 170 million of them being migrant workers from other regions. Statistically, these migrant workers primarily work and reside in urban areas and are counted as urban residents by government departments. However, from a public service perspective, they still face challenges in accessing equal treatment as urban residents in terms of employment, wages and benefits, children's education, social security, and purchasing affordable housing. In fact, under China's current statistical framework, a large number of rural household registered populations are included in the urban population count, and non-local residents make up a significant proportion of the urban population. For example, according to data from the National Bureau of Statistics' *2015 National Economic and Social Development Statistical Bulletin*, China's urbanization rate reached 56.1%[8] in 2015. However, in reality, the proportion of urban household registered population was still below 40%. This clearly demonstrates that the urbanization process of China's agricultural transfer population is severely lagging, resulting in a "new dual structure" (in other words new urban-rural divide) in cities.

Another issue is that China's urbanization has been accompanied by a concerning trend of uncontrolled expansion of urban space, where the conversion of rural land to urban land is happening at a faster rate than the increase in urban population. The rapid expansion of urban land has to a large extent squeezed the space available for urbanization of the population. From 2001 to 2014, the growth rate of China's urban built-up areas and construction land area was 6.02% and 6.07%, respectively, while the growth rate of population urbanization during the same period was less than 4%. According to the *2015 China Land and Resources Bulletin* released by the Ministry of Land and Resources at the end of 2015, the total construction land area in China had reached 578 million mu, with 7.6 million mu[9] of newly added urban construction land in 2015. These data indicate that in recent years, the expansion of urban land in China has far outpaced the growth of its population, with land urbanization developing much faster than population urbanization. Additionally, several large cities have been experiencing the trend of restructuring counties,

[8] See National Bureau of Statistics' website.

[9] See Ministry of Land and Resources website.

establishing new districts, and constructing new areas, with the lax constraints of planning and interest-driven motives in the planning industry fueling this impulsive expansion of urban spaces. This expansion is characterized by a significant degree of mindlessness and disorder. Statistical data shows that the planned areas of many new urban districts in large cities span hundreds or even thousands of square kilometers. For example, the planned areas of Shanghai's Pudong New District, Tianjin's Binhai New District, and Chongqing's Liangjiang New District all exceed 1,000 square kilometers. This expansion-driven urbanization process has directly led to the loss of vast amounts of farmland for farmers, causing numerous rural residents to become landless. They are compelled to migrate to cities for work, turning into residents who straddle both urban and rural lifestyles. In fact, most construction projects tend to use high-quality farmland. Even though the country enforces strict policies to maintain a balance between the land taken for development and the land preserved for agriculture, the problematic practice of using prime land for development while providing less suitable land as compensation still exists. The rapid, sprawling growth of urban spaces in China has put significant pressure on the living and working spaces of rural populations, ultimately going against the fundamental principle of people-centered new urbanization.

The third issue is that the distribution of urban areas is not entirely reasonable, resulting in an uneven allocation of resources.[10] Xi Jinping highlighted that cities offer certain advantages in terms of promoting economic development, urban transportation, residents' living standards, and resource conservation. However, he also emphasized that excessive expansion of cities is not desirable. China's urban system includes different levels, such as municipalities under the direct administration of the central government, sub-provincial cities, large cities, prefecture-level cities, county-level cities, and towns. For a significant period, the administrative system's hierarchical distribution of resources has led to the concentration of various resource elements in municipalities under the direct administration of the central government, sub-provincial cities, provincial capital cities, and other large cities. As a result, a clear trend of "polarization" has emerged within China's urban system. Specifically, this is manifested by the expansion of large cities, the shrinking number and scale of medium and small cities, and the disorderly development of small

[10]Party Literature Research Center of the CPC Central Committee (2014), *Op. cit.*, p. 594.

towns, resulting in a lack of strong support for medium and small cities in the urban system. In particular, with the trend of widespread county-to-city conversions and the establishment of new areas, the number of large cities in China has been continuously increasing, while the development of medium-sized and small cities has fallen behind. Under this system, the capital, municipalities directly under the central government, provincial capital cities, and sub-provincial cities have gained many more development opportunities than medium and small cities. This has led to large-scale population and industry agglomeration, rapid urban expansion, high tension in resources and energy, severe traffic congestion, serious air pollution, and intensified social conflicts.[11] These problems are completely contrary to the concept of new urbanization with a people-centered approach. From the perspective of small towns, the polarization effect of large cities on the surrounding small towns, coupled with the lack of development opportunities, insufficient industrial support, inadequate infrastructure, and limited public services, have greatly impacted the quality of life and living standards of residents in small towns. As a result, they are unable to benefit from the advantages brought by new urbanization.

The fourth issue is that the process of urbanization in China has come at a high cost to the environment and natural resources, while the utilization efficiency of these resources has been low. Currently, China's urbanization is characterized by extensive expansion and superficial development, with an emphasis on outward physical growth rather than inner development. The rapid pace of urbanization has been built on the foundation of high consumption of resources and energy, resulting in significant environmental costs. For instance, in terms of water resources, according to the *2014 China Water Resources Bulletin* published by the Ministry of Water Resources, the consumption of water resources in urban areas has increased dramatically from 7.87 billion cubic meters in 1978 to nearly 60 billion cubic meters in 2014, with an annual increase of 1.38 billion cubic meters. From a nationwide perspective, currently over 400 cities in China are experiencing water shortages, with more than 200 of them suffering from severe shortages. Excessive exploitation of groundwater in many cities has led to accelerated subsidence of the ground, which has had serious negative impacts on the living and production of urban residents. From the perspective of resource utilization, although China's urban resource utilization efficiency has made significant

[11] See Wei Houkai (2014), *Op. cit.*, p. 15.

progress, with the energy consumption per unit of GDP continuously decreasing, its resource utilization efficiency is still relatively low compared to some countries like the EU, the United States, and Japan. From an environmental protection perspective, the frequent occurrence of smog in recent years in regions such as East and North China has posed a severe warning to the existing urbanization model in China, directly affecting the health and quality of life of urban residents. Considering the current situation in China, the long-standing structural challenges and inefficient economic development methods cannot be easily addressed. The pressure on energy, environment, and other aspects that constrain China's urbanization and economic development will only increase.

We must directly confront the above-mentioned issues in order to promote the new urbanization process with a people-centered approach. As pointed out by Xi Jinping, "We should concentrate on enhancing the quality of urbanization by utilizing favorable circumstances, maximizing benefits, minimizing risks, and promoting the overall healthy growth of urbanization."[12] It is essential to adopt the right guiding principles and understand that urbanization is a natural historical progression. We must take into account China's unique national conditions at the initial stage of socialism and follow the natural course of urbanization, rather than forcing growth or rushing for results. Urbanization should be a smooth and organic development process. When promoting urbanization, we need to be proactive, cautious, and practical, taking a clear direction, maintaining a steady pace, and putting in place effective measures.[13] If we veer off course in urbanization and fail to address existing issues promptly, it may become increasingly difficult to rectify the situation, leading to significant risks.[14]

3. Accelerating the Advancement of Key Initiatives for the "Three Groups of 100 Million People"

Xi Jinping emphasized the need for patience and a long-term perspective when it comes to the issue of population urbanization.[15] People move to

[12] The central economic work conference was held in Beijing. *People's Daily*, December 17, 2012.

[13] Party Literature Research Center of the CPC Central Committee (2014), *Op. cit.*, p. 591.

[14] *Ibid.*, p. 590.

[15] See Xinhua News Agency Central News Interview Center (Ed.). (2013). *Transcripts of Press Conferences at the 2013 National Two Sessions*. People's Publishing House, p. 13.

cities in search of a better life. The new type of urbanization with Chinese characteristics is not simply about relocating people from rural to urban areas; rather, it aims to achieve a series of economic and social transitions from "village" to "city." This is done through economic development, job creation, entrepreneurship encouragement, social security improvement, and enhanced public services, ultimately building inclusive and harmonious urbanization that shares its benefits. Taking into account China's present national circumstances, the three primary challenges affecting the largest portion of the population in the country's development include the disparities between urban and rural areas, the uneven development across different regions, and the internal divide within cities, often characterized by a separation between long-term residents and migrant workers. About two-thirds of the population, based on household registration, live in rural areas. A large portion of the agricultural transfer population struggles to integrate into cities, with many living in shantytowns and urban villages. Almost two-thirds of the population resides in central and western regions of China. In accordance with the central government's urbanization strategy, which focuses on improving the lives of approximately 300 million people, the promotion of people-centered urbanization must tackle the three major issues mentioned earlier. These include integrating agricultural transfer population into cities, speeding up the redevelopment of shantytowns and urban villages, and prioritizing urbanization efforts in the central and western regions of the country.

3.1. *Promoting the urbanization of about 100 million permanent agricultural transfer population*

At present, there is considerable debate among academics and policymakers regarding the urbanization of the agricultural transfer population. This is an essential and high-priority task for the development of a new, people-centered urbanization model that embodies China's unique characteristics. According to the *2013 National Monitoring Report on Migrant Workers*[16]

---

[16]The terminology surrounding the term "农民工" (nóngmín gōng), commonly translated as "migrant worker," has faced critique from numerous scholars. In this book, with the exception of direct quotations from authoritative reports that employ the original term "农民工," the concept of "农业转移人口" (nóngyè zhuǎnyí rénkǒu), translated as "agricultural transfer population," is generally employed.

published by the National Bureau of Statistics, China had a total of 268.94 million migrant workers in 2013, an increase of 6.33 million or 2.4% compared to the previous year. This figure included 166.10 million migrant workers who left their hometowns for work, growing by 2.74 million or 1.7%, and 10.284 million local migrant workers, increasing by 3.59 million or 3.6%. This substantial population has long been caught in a "dual" state between urban and rural areas, experiencing a large-scale back-and-forth movement without fully integrating into urban society, which significantly impacts the quality of China's urbanization. Actively promoting the urbanization of the agricultural transfer population is crucial to achieving a people-centered approach to new urbanization.

Firstly, it is necessary to promote the settlement of qualified agricultural transfer population in urban areas. To promote the new people-centered type of urbanization, the current priority is to facilitate the orderly attainment of household registration status for urban permanent residents who can stabilize their employment and life in the cities. Building on this, it is necessary to improve the quality of life and skills of the entire urban population. Accelerating household registration system reform is one of the major tasks in promoting the new type of urbanization. The National Conference on Urbanization has set a goal to grant urban household registration to around 100 million agricultural transfer population who have migrated to cities for long-term work and business by the year 2020. This is an important step in promoting the attainment of household registration status for the agricultural transfer population. According to statistical data, in 2012, there was approximately 72 million agricultural transfer population who had lived in their destination cities for more than 5 years, and thus had the ability to obtain urban household registration. By 2020, it is estimated that this group will increase to over 120 million people. The key to promoting the attainment of household registration status for the agricultural transfer population is to "promote the settlement of qualified agricultural transfer population in urban areas," which requires a proactive and prudent reform of the current household registration system. From the experience in China, the reform of household registration system in small cities and towns has progressed more rapidly, while the focus and difficulty of the issue lies in mega-cities such as Beijing, Shanghai, and Guangzhou. To promote the reform of the household registration system, differentiated settlement policies should be implemented according to the size of the urban population, gradually allowing qualified agricultural transfer population to settle in urban areas.

The general principle is to fully lift all the restrictions on household registration in small cities and towns, while implementing a controlled relaxation of restrictions in medium-sized cities and a reasonable relaxation of restrictions in large cities. The latter two categories of cities may set specific requirements such as the length of participation in urban social security. For mega-cities, population size needs to be strictly controlled, and a point-based system or other methods can be used to set up a step-by-step system for agricultural transfer population to obtain urban household registration.

Secondly, efforts should be made to ensure that agricultural transfer population has access to basic urban public services. The mobility of rural labor between urban and rural areas has been a long-term phenomenon. Therefore, we should follow the basic principle of "guaranteeing the basics and making gradual progress" and make efforts to actively shift the provision of basic urban public services from mainly targeting local household registration population to serving all permanent residents. This will gradually solve the problem of limited access to basic urban public services for agricultural transfer population who work and reside in cities but do not have urban household registration. The first priority is to ensure that the children of migrant workers have equal access to education. To achieve this access, compulsory education for the children of migrant workers should be incorporated into the education development plans and financial protection categories at all levels of government. Additionally, school layouts should be reasonably planned, the number of teachers should be scientifically calculated, and sufficient education funds should be allocated. As a result, the children of migrant workers should have access to compulsory education, with public schools being the primary option. The second priority is to improve the employment and entrepreneurship service system for the general public, strengthen vocational skills training for agricultural transfer population, further increase the support for employment and entrepreneurship policies, and improve their overall professional skills to make them more employable and entrepreneurial. The third priority is to expand the coverage of social security and reduce social insurance rates as appropriate. This involves actively improving the basic endowment insurance system for workers, establishing a nationally unified basic endowment insurance system for urban and rural residents, and gradually increasing the proportion of agricultural transfer population participating in urban workers' work-related injury insurance, unemployment insurance, and maternity insurance. The fourth priority is to improve basic medical and health conditions. This will involve allocating basic medical and health service resources in urban areas based on the needs of the permanent resident population and integrating agricultural transfer population and their families into the community health service system. Additionally, free public health services such as health education, maternal and child healthcare, and vaccination will be provided to all members of the agricultural transfer population. The fifth priority is to broaden the scope of housing security. This will involve improving the living conditions of agricultural transfer population through various means, such as affordable housing, public rental housing, and rental subsidies. Efforts will be made to fully integrate rural residents who settle in cities into the urban housing system and provide them with adequate housing.

Thirdly, we need to establish an effective mechanism for promoting the integration of agricultural transfer population into urban society. Promoting the integration of agricultural transfer population into urban society is the top priority for achieving a people-centered new type of urbanization. The key to its implementation lies in establishing a reasonable mechanism for cost-sharing and social participation. In terms of the cost-sharing mechanism, the government should bear the public costs of promoting the integration of agricultural transfer population into urban society, including compulsory education, employment, basic pension, basic medical care, housing security, and municipal facilities. Enterprises should ensure that migrant workers receive the same pay as urban employees for the same work. They should also increase investment in employee skill training and lawfully contribute to the social insurance funds for the agricultural transfer population, including pension, medical care, work injury, unemployment, and maternity insurance. Agricultural transfer population should actively participate in urban social insurance, vocational education, and skill training, and take on the corresponding expenses as required, in order to enhance their ability to integrate into urban society. From the perspective of social participation mechanism, it is important to facilitate the social integration of agricultural transfer population by implementing the "four integrations" process, which includes integrating them into enterprises, their children into schools, their families into communities, and their groups into society. By enhancing educational and awareness programs for the migrant agricultural population, we can boost their scientific and cultural knowledge while encouraging their involvement in community activities, development, and management. This will enrich their cultural lives, help them integrate into urban society, and allow them to better enjoy the benefits of city living.

3.2. *Speeding up the renovation of urban shantytowns and dilapidated areas for 100 million residents*

Speeding up the transformation of urban shantytowns and urban villages is vital to achieving people-centered new urbanization. The transformation of urban shantytowns and urban villages is a global challenge and a crucial task for achieving people-centered new urbanization in China. This issue is closely related to the protection and improvement of people's livelihoods, economic and social development, as well as the success and quality of new urbanization with Chinese characteristics. In China, urban shantytowns and urban villages exhibit a distinct divide between different segments of the urban population. Workers from legacy companies, urban-employed migrants, and many agricultural workers often lack basic living conditions in cities, which consequently prevent them from living in a suitable environment for development. This significantly hinders the progress of urbanization in the country. Investigations and research show that, at present, in cities and towns across the country, there are more than 40 million units of various types of shantytowns, dangerous houses, and incomplete housing without piped water, kitchens, or toilets. This affects a population of approximately 100 million people. It's worth noting that many cities also have a significant number of urban villages where thousands of migrant workers live, including a considerable number of university graduates. These people are members of the urban family, and the development of cities cannot be achieved without them. It is essential to create conditions to improve their living conditions. Practical experience has shown that the renovation of urban shantytowns and urban villages often follows a pattern of "transform one area, revitalize another," which has been welcomed by the majority of the people.

In the past, during the process of promoting the market-oriented and social development of the housing sector, we focused on the economic function of housing for quite some time. We highly valued the role of market forces but did not pay much attention to the social function of housing and overlooked the role of government support.[17] The 13th

---

[17]See Zhang Zhanbin. (2014). *Analyzing New Urbanization*. Economic Science Press, p. 78.

Five-Year Plan called for speeding up the renovation of shantytowns and building urban affordable housing. The goal was to reach a nationwide coverage rate of around 20% for affordable housing by 2015. Data from the Ministry of Housing and Urban-Rural Development shows that by the end of September 2013, a total of 6.2 million urban affordable housing units had been started for construction, and 4.1 million units had been basically completed, reaching 98% and 87% of the annual targets, respectively. In 2014, the target for urban affordable housing construction in China was to complete at least 4.8 million units and start construction of over 6 million new units, with at least 3.7 million units for shantytown renovation. These figures indicate that China is steadily implementing people-centered new urbanization.

Advancing the redevelopment of urban shantytowns and urban villages is crucial, and securing diverse funding sources is essential. The central government must continue to increase subsidies for localities, and national fiscal construction funds must also be directed toward the redevelopment of urban shantytowns and urban villages, supporting the construction of relevant supporting facilities. Local governments should also increase fiscal revenue and implement relevant tax and fee reduction policies. The most important aspect of promoting the transformation of urban shantytowns and urban villages is to innovate investment and financing mechanisms, actively improve policy-based financing, and provide more stable and cost-appropriate financial support for the redevelopment of urban shantytowns and urban villages. At the same time, it is essential to ensure the quality and safety of urban shantytown and urban village renovation projects. We must resolutely prevent companies and individuals from taking advantage of these projects to misappropriate state financial funds and deliver substandard constructions. By establishing a stable financing mechanism for urban shantytown and urban village renovation projects, we can ensure timely and effective housing supply.

Promoting the renovation of urban shantytowns and urban villages requires scientific planning. Premier Li Keqiang pointed out that we must pay attention to preventing urban diseases in places where high-rise buildings coexist with shanty towns. The Chinese government is determined to renovate over ten million households of all types of shantytowns, which not only solves the urban–rural divide within cities but also reduces the threshold for urbanization such as providing more accessible and inclusive pathways to urbanization. Renovating urban shantytowns and urban villages is a long-term and arduous task that cannot be completed in three to five years. During the process of urbanization, some decrepit and clustered houses may still emerge in the urban–rural interface (outskirts of the cities/rural–urban fringe). In order to address these issues, we need to strengthen scientific planning for the renovation of urban shantytowns and urban villages, so that these renovation projects can be coordinated with other buildings, infrastructure, and natural landscapes in the city to construct a project that benefits the people and gains their support.

To promote the renovation of urban shantytowns and villages, it is essential to advance institutional reforms. The renovation of urban shantytowns and villages should be integrated with reforms in the housing system and housing security system. These reforms should be built upon the previous and existing reforms to fully reflect social fairness and focus on future system construction and innovation. Policies and system designs should be tailored to the different situations of residents in urban shantytowns and villages, to ensure that they receive appropriate support. Several key factors should be considered to ensure the success of the renovation of urban shantytowns and villages. One factor is the reform of the housing distribution system, in which fairness must be prioritized. Additionally, the pricing mechanism for housing renovation costs and market prices must be carefully designed. Another crucial aspect is the reform of the compensation system for demolishing urban shantytowns and villages, which should ensure fair compensation for the original landowners while minimizing significant disparities in compensation amounts. In other words, the compensation amounts should be fair and consistent for all original landowners, without creating an excessively large gap between the highest and lowest amounts. Finally, it is crucial to ensure proper resettlement for the original residents of urban shantytowns and villages.

3.3. *Achieving urbanization for approximately 100 million people in the central and western regions of China*

Currently, the urbanization rate in the eastern region has exceeded 62%, while in the central and western regions, it is only around 49% and 45%, respectively, indicating a significant lag in the urbanization process in the central and western regions. To promote regional coordinated development, achieve a moderately prosperous society in all respects, enhance the well-being of all ethnic groups, consolidate national unity, safeguard national security, and advance people-centered urbanization, it is essential to accelerate the pace of urbanization and drive urban development in the central and western regions. In summary, accelerating urbanization in the central and western regions is essential for achieving broader regional goals and promoting people-centered urbanization.

First, we need to promote employment and entrepreneurship opportunities for agricultural transfer population in the central and western regions. According to data released by the National Bureau of Statistics, there were approximately 150 million rural migrant workers in the central and western regions in 2013, with around 90 million working in the same region and about 60 million working in the eastern region. Currently, a growing number of agricultural transfer population is returning to the central and western regions for local employment and entrepreneurship, with over 8 million people returning in 2013. From 2014 to 2020, through urbanization and industrial development in the central and western regions, we can create conditions that will encourage at least 40 million agricultural transfer population who are currently working in the eastern cities to settle down and seek employment or entrepreneurship in the central and western cities. At the same time, we can address the issues of stable employment, stable residence, and improved public services for about 60 million rural migrant workers who are already employed in the central and western cities, totaling around 100 million people.

Second, we need to tap into the existing potential for urbanization in the central and western regions. Especially in the central and western regions, it is important to find effective ways to tap into the existing potential for urbanization, rely on industry to provide employment opportunities for agriculture transfer population, and accelerate the pace of urbanization. This is a key task in promoting people-centered new urbanization in China. The central and western regions should follow the national plan for land use planning and promote the development of key areas in an organized manner. This will facilitate the formation of new economic hubs through the development of urban clusters and urbanization regions. At the same time, it is important to accelerate the development of small and medium-sized cities in the central and western regions and create many distinctive small towns that serve as hubs for regional development, connecting urban and rural areas and becoming important containers for absorbing agricultural transfer populations.

Third, we need to address the issue of urbanization for agricultural transfer populations. The central and western regions are significant suppliers of agricultural products and ecological protection and possess immense potential for urbanization development. Although the challenge of urbanizing agricultural transfer populations in these areas is not as pronounced as in the Pearl River Delta and Yangtze River Delta regions, the agricultural transfer populations in the central and western regions are still substantial and will face continuing pressure from population growth in the future. Therefore, it is essential to address the urbanization issue for existing agricultural transfer populations in the central and western regions in a proper manner and actively respond to the urbanization issue for new agricultural transfer populations. This is a critical aspect in achieving a people-centered new urbanization. The solution should involve reforming the rural land and household registration systems, as well as ensuring that basic public services are available to all residents in the region.

4. Balancing Interrelated Relationships in New Urbanization Development

During urbanization, it is important to pay attention to two interrelated factors: the relationship between government and the market, and the relationship between the central and local governments. The essence of the new urbanization strategy is to prioritize the fundamental interests of the people and construct a development path for new urbanization that is centered on the people, prioritizes quality, and is guided by reform and ecological considerations. Xi Jinping emphasized at the Central Conference on Urbanization that urbanization is a significant social process that impacts the whole country. Thus, it is crucial to establish and adhere to the correct principles from the start, as correcting the course becomes more difficult once we deviate from it.[18]

First, it is imperative to examine the interplay between the government and the market concerning the facilitation of urbanization. In order to promote urbanization, it is important to strike a balance between the role of the market in resource allocation and the government's responsibilities in creating an institutional environment, planning for

[18] Party Literature Research Center of the CPC Central Committee (2014), *Op. cit.*, p. 592.

development, building infrastructure, providing public services, and enhancing social governance. Both the market and the government have their respective strengths, and it is crucial to fully utilize them without bias. The healthy development of urbanization requires the coordination of both tangible and intangible measures. The government must actively guide the planning process to ensure that urbanization stays on the right track. In the first half of 2014, the *National New-Type Urbanization Plan (2014–2020)* was officially announced by the Chinese government. As the government strengthens its strategic planning, it's important to also leverage the market mechanism and improve the efficiency of resource allocation in the urbanization process. Effective measures should be taken to encourage private investment in urbanization construction projects. Competition mechanisms should also be introduced in social affairs management services, and the government should purchase services from non-governmental organizations to achieve a reasonable division of labor. Enterprises, intermediary agencies, and non-profit organizations should be fully utilized to play an important role in urbanization development.

Second, the dynamic relationship between the central and local governments deserves closer examination. The relationship between the central and local governments is an ever-evolving process that needs to be adjusted according to changes in economic, social, and historical conditions. There is no single solution that can solve everything at once. Due to the significant regional differences in China, the development of new-type urbanization requires customized approaches and region-specific measures that consider local conditions. This includes proper arrangements for the allocation of finances and taxes, such as determining a reasonable ratio of tax revenue distribution between the central and local governments, increasing national financial transfer payments, and scientifically constructing a local tax system. Another key factor is the deepening of administrative system reforms to optimize the structure of government powers, dividing legislative authority, economic management, personnel appointment and removal between the central and local governments in a balanced way and maintaining stability over a long period of time. This enhances local development autonomy, avoids competition between the central and local governments caused by granting and transferring powers, leadership and subordination relationships, and builds a collaborative and mutually beneficial relationship between the central and local governments. The central government sets overall policies and determines the strategic layout of urbanization development, while local governments implement the plan, make corresponding plans, and carry out construction and management work creatively based on practical needs.

Of course, in promoting the people-centered new-type urbanization, it is important to strike a balance between the goals and the means. Indeed, the mission of new-type urbanization is one of humanistic care, which prioritizes the well-being, dignity, and cultural values of people. The core of new-type urbanization is the urbanization of people, which respects people's choices, addresses their livelihood issues, and reflects a people-oriented approach. However, we must not forget the new-type urbanization is also about promoting economic, social, and ecological development. The Central Urbanization Work Conference has emphasized that promoting urbanization is crucial for addressing issues related to agriculture, rural areas, and farmers, as well as supporting regional coordinated development, and increasing domestic demand. It also has significant practical and historical significance in the comprehensive building of a moderately prosperous society and accelerating the promotion of socialist modernization. Setting correct and appropriate goals and directions for urbanization is crucial in paving the way for new opportunities and unlocking the huge potential of domestic demand, while simultaneously increasing labor productivity, breaking down the urban–rural divide, and promoting social equity and shared prosperity. Putting people at the center is the fundamental basis and focus of new-type urbanization. In the process of new-type urbanization, the various benefits such as economic, social, and ecological should be fully and scientifically utilized to support and prioritize the people-oriented approach. In other words, the benefits should be used to serve the needs and well-being of the people and not the other way around. By doing so, the new-type urbanization can navigate the challenges and succeed in promoting the well-being of people and the sustainable development of society.[19]

[19]See Song Jiechen. (2014). Properly handling six major relationships in the process of new urbanization. *Frontline*, Issue 4.

Chapter 15

The Development Strategy of the "Belt and Road Initiative"

The "Belt and Road Initiative" encompasses the "Silk Road Economic Belt" and the "21st Century Maritime Silk Road." This national strategy, proposed by China in the new era, has far-reaching strategic implications for the country's modernization efforts. The "Belt and Road" strategic concept caters to the shared requirements of the nations along its route and presents novel prospects for these countries to leverage their respective strengths and foster development through cooperative endeavors. As a new platform for international cooperation, the "Belt and Road" encourages countries to collaborate within a fair framework, exemplifying a spirit of peace, communication, understanding, inclusivity, cooperation, and collective benefit.

1. Belt and Road Initiative: Factors and Process of Its Formation

In 2013, during visits to Central Asia and Southeast Asia, Xi Jinping proposed the initiatives to build the Silk Road Economic Belt and the 21st Century Maritime Silk Road. The development of the "Belt and Road" is a major strategic decision made by the Party Central Committee and a crucial measure to further enhance China's global engagement. Xi Jinping used a metaphor to describe the "Belt and Road," stating that it's like adding two wings to a powerful bird (symbolizing China), enabling it to soar to fly higher and reach greater distances once the initiatives are fully realized.[1]

---

[1]Publicity Department of the CPC Central Committee (Ed.). (2016). *General Secretary Xi Jinping Important Speech Series* (2016 Edition). Learning Publishing House and People's Publishing House, Beijing, p. 266.

Over 30 years of reform and opening-up, China has achieved remarkable accomplishments that have drawn global attention. However, due to factors such as geographical location, resource endowment, and development foundations, the pace of China's integration with the global economy has been uneven — faster in the eastern regions compared to western regions, and stronger in coastal areas compared to inland regions. The "Belt and Road" will create a new phase of global integration, characterized by a "central core with two wings," encouraging westward expansion while sustaining the existing level of eastward engagement. This approach will help move inland border regions from the fringes to the forefront of global connectivity ("central core with two wings" is a metaphor to describe a balanced approach to development. The "central core" refers to the core strategy, while the "two wings" represent the two complementary directions of expansion (eastward and westward) that work together to achieve the desired outcome). Following the Silk Road spirit of peaceful cooperation, openness, shared learning, and collective benefit, China and countries along the route will strengthen their collaboration in areas such as transportation infrastructure, trade and investment, energy cooperation, regional integration, and the internationalization of the RMB.

China's economic development needs the creation of a more favorable international and regional environment. The "Belt and Road" strategy builds upon the existing level of global engagement, initiating a new pattern of integration that creates broader opportunities for China's economic development and infuses new vitality. Furthermore, it provides significant opportunities for the shared growth and prosperity of the world economy. This ambitious strategy, which addresses domestic needs while taking a global outlook, has been met with positive reactions from the international community, particularly from countries along the route. The "Belt and Road" initiative carries forward the ancient Silk Road's spirit of openness, inclusivity, and diversity while incorporating modern-day features. It continues to foster a more favorable regional and international environment for China's economic development. During the 2013 "Two Sessions," Xi Jinping emphasized while attending the Shanghai delegation's deliberation: "China's reform has entered a crucial phase and uncharted territory. To further deepen the reform, we must bolster confidence, forge consensus, coordinate plans, and promote synergy. We need the courage to break through ideological barriers and entrenched interests, tackle tough challenges, and venture into unexplored areas. We must respect market laws even more, enhance the government's role, and seek greater development opportunities by embracing openness to the fullest extent."[2]

To advance the construction of the "Belt and Road," China will take advantage of the strengths of different regions, implement a more proactive opening-up strategy, strengthen interaction and cooperation among the eastern, central, and western regions, and improve the level of economic openness across all sectors. China plans to utilize the unique advantages of various regions to deepen exchange and cooperation with neighboring countries along the Belt and Road. Xinjiang will play an important role as a window to the west and serve as a key transportation hub, commercial and logistics center, and cultural and educational center on the Silk Road Economic Belt. The provinces of Shaanxi, Gansu, Ningxia, and Qinghai will work together to build on their economic and cultural strengths, creating a new highland for inland reform and opening-up centered around Xi'an. This effort will involve accelerating development and opening-up in Lanzhou and Xining, promoting the construction of the Ningxia inland open economy pilot zone, and building channels, commercial and logistics hubs, key industries, and centers for humanistic exchange. These will all be geared toward enhancing economic ties with countries in Central Asia, South Asia, and West Asia. Inner Mongolia will take advantage of its location to connect Russia and Mongolia and strengthen the land–sea transportation cooperation among Heilongjiang, Jilin, Liaoning, and the Russian Far East. Guangxi will leverage its unique location advantages adjacent to Association of Southeast Asian Nations (ASEAN) countries to build international transportation links and strengthen economic ties with the ASEAN region. It will accelerate the opening and development of the Beibu Gulf Economic Zone and the Pearl River Delta Economic Belt, creating a new strategic hub for economic development in Southwest and Central South China. Yunnan will use its location to advance the construction of international transportation links with neighboring countries, foster economic cooperation in the Greater Mekong Subregion, and establish a hub for economic and cultural exchange with South Asia and Southeast Asia.

China plans to take full advantage of the high degree of openness, strong economic strength, and significant influence of the Yangtze River

[2] Resolutely deepening reform and opening-up, strengthen innovation-driven development. *People's Daily*, March 6, 2013.

Delta, Pearl River Delta, Western Taiwan Strait, and Bohai Rim economic zones. To accomplish this, China will make full use of the opportunities provided by open cooperation zones such as Shenzhen Qianhai, Guangzhou Nansha, Zhuhai Hengqin, and Fujian Pingtan, deepen collaboration with Hong Kong, Macao, and Taiwan, and develop the Guangdong–Hong Kong–Macao Greater Bay Area.

China intends to advance the development of the Zhejiang marine economy demonstration zone, Fujian Straits blue economy pilot zone, and Zhoushan Archipelago new area, and increase the efforts in opening up and developing the Hainan international tourism island. International hub airports in Shanghai, Guangzhou, and other cities aim to improve and enhance their capabilities and services to strengthen their position as important international transportation hubs. By expanding its openness, China is driving deep and comprehensive reforms, innovating its open economic system, increasing investment in technological innovation, and enhancing its competitiveness to actively participate in and lead international cooperation and competition.

Moreover, China intends to harness the unique advantages of overseas Chinese as well as the special administrative regions of Hong Kong and Macao to actively engage and support the "Belt and Road" initiative.

The world is undergoing complex and profound changes. The long-lasting impacts of the international financial crisis continue to manifest themselves, and the world economy is experiencing slow recovery and varying degrees of development. The international investment and trade patterns and multilateral investment and trade rules are undergoing profound adjustments, and countries are continuing to face severe development challenges. The construction of the Belt and Road Initiative responds to the trend of world multi-polarization, economic globalization, cultural diversity, and digitization. Upholding the spirit of open regional cooperation, the initiative is committed to maintaining the global free trade system and an open world economy. The initiative promotes orderly and free flow of economic factors, efficient resource allocation, and deep market integration, and encourages economic policy coordination among the countries along the Belt and Road. It aims to conduct more extensive, high-level, and in-depth regional cooperation, and jointly create an open, inclusive, balanced, and beneficial regional economic cooperation framework. The Belt and Road Initiative serves the fundamental interests of the international community, embodies the common ideals and aspirations of human society, and is an active exploration of a new model of international cooperation and global governance, which will bring a positive impact to the world's peaceful development.

The Belt and Road Initiative is committed to promoting connectivity and communication among the continents of Asia, Europe, and Africa, as well as nearby oceans. It aims to establish and strengthen partnership relationships for connectivity among countries along the routes. It seeks to construct an all-dimensional, multi-level, and composite connectivity network that can provide diverse and comprehensive services. The connectivity projects of the Belt and Road Initiative will facilitate the alignment and coupling of development strategies among countries along the routes, tap into the potential of the regional market, promote investment and consumption, create demand and employment opportunities, enhance cultural exchanges and shared learning, and foster trustful relations and respect among people of different countries, ultimately contributing to a harmonious, peaceful, and prosperous life for all.

China's economy is now highly interconnected with the world economy. To deepen this interconnectedness, China will continue to adhere to its fundamental national policy of opening-up and pursue a comprehensive approach to further open up its markets. This includes building a new all-encompassing pattern of openness and integrating deeply into the global economic system. The Belt and Road Initiative serves a dual purpose for China: expanding and deepening its economic ties with the world, and strengthening collectively beneficial cooperation among nations across Asia, Europe, and Africa. China is committed to assuming a greater role in promoting peaceful development and is ready to fulfill its responsibilities and obligations, making significant contributions to the global community.

Firstly, China's domestic economic and social reforms have entered a critical phase. The economy has entered a transitional period with growth rates shifting from double digits to single digits, which is determined by the objective laws of economic development. China's structural adjustment is currently facing a painful period as it proactively accelerates the transformation of its economic development. This includes the critical phase of supply-side structural reform, which was highlighted in the Fifth Plenum of the 18th National Congress of the Communist Party of China. To overcome development challenges and cultivate advantages, it is necessary to establish and implement a development concept that prioritizes innovation, coordination, environmental sustainability, openness, and equitable sharing. This requires the coordination of both domestic and international resources and markets, seeking new drivers and growth points for economic development. The Belt and Road Initiative not only embodies the historical changes and progress of the times, but also reflects the complexity, difficulty, and severity of the challenges it faces. Therefore, we need to proactively respond to the challenges by combining domestic development and international expansion and taking the initiative to address new obstacles.

Secondly, the global economy is expected to continue experiencing a weak recovery. Since the outbreak of the 2008 global financial crisis, the world's industrial structure has entered a period of deep adjustment. The global economy has been slow to recover, with developed economies facing the dual challenges of insufficient total demand and low long-term growth rates. In particular, the low growth in global trade has been difficult to fundamentally reverse. The new changes in the global economic situation have brought complex and profound impacts on China's participation in international economic cooperation and competition and have raised new and higher demands for improving the strategic layout of opening-up to the outside world. We need to recognize the situation, enhance our sense of urgency and mission, and continuously improve our regional layout for opening up, trade, and investment, in order to better promote economic and social development. The construction of the "Belt and Road" is not just a single policy adjustment, but a significant strategic move for China to implement all-round opening up under new historical conditions and to promote a platform of collective benefit and multi-win cooperation. We must adopt a higher position and broader vision, draw on historical experience, and apply innovative ideas and thinking to ensure that the people of countries along the route can truly feel the benefits brought by the "Belt and Road" initiative. We need to encourage active participation in the construction of the "Belt and Road," making it a new growth point for the economies of all countries involved.

Thirdly, in the context of increasingly fierce competition in the international market, China has put forward new concepts such as the new type of major power relations, the "amity, sincerity, collective benefit, and inclusiveness" principle of neighborhood diplomacy, and the Silk Road spirit of "peaceful cooperation, openness and inclusiveness, shared learning, and collective benefit." All these concepts are based on the premise of adhering to the Five Principles of Peaceful Coexistence. The construction of the "Belt and Road" initiative will strengthen the connections between China and the rest of the world, promoting all-around cooperation with more countries and regions and contributing to common prosperity. China's proactive participation in international affairs and its image as a responsible major power are fully demonstrated through its efforts, including the "Belt and Road" initiative. This shows that China is willing to assume its due responsibilities and obligations within its capacity and make greater contributions to world peace, prosperity, and stability.

Considering the current domestic and international situation, China's "Belt and Road" strategy is expected to have a considerable impact on both China's and the world's development. The initiative will establish an economic development belt extends throughout the prospective Asia–Europe international community, with China playing a central role. This will foster collaborative efforts between China and countries along the route to promote a new pattern of world economic development.

2. The Significance of the "Belt and Road" Initiative

After more than 30 years of development through reform and opening-up, China has formed a pattern of rapid economic growth in the eastern region and relatively slower development in the western region. It has entered the "new normal" of economic development, which is characterized by a slower pace of economic growth, overcapacity, and surplus foreign exchange reserves. China is highly dependent on foreign oil and gas resources and mineral resources. Its industrial and infrastructure facilities are concentrated in coastal areas, making it vulnerable to external pressures and at risk of losing key infrastructure. At present, China's border regions are in their best historical period, and neighboring countries are increasingly willing to strengthen cooperation with China. These are the domestic and international conditions of China's current economic development. Based on these realities, the "Belt and Road" initiative not only opens up new opportunities for China's economic development but also integrates China's economic growth with the development of countries along the route. This initiative aims to jointly promote the comprehensive development of the world's economic relations.

Firstly, from the perspective of promoting domestic economic development and supply-side structural reform, the "Belt and Road" initiative provides new opportunities. As one of the "two wings" of China's economic development and supply-side structural reform, the "Belt and

Road" initiative will play an important role. The State Council has clearly stated that in order to double the GDP by 2020, the annual average economic growth from 2016 to 2020 should be around 6.5%. The Chinese economy is facing significant challenges and new uncertainties. The National Development and Reform Commission, Ministry of Foreign Affairs, and Ministry of Commerce jointly released the *Vision and Actions on Jointly Building the Silk Road Economic Belt and the 21st Century Maritime Silk Road*. The document proposes leveraging Xinjiang's unique geographical advantages and its role as an important gateway to the west to deepen exchanges and cooperation with countries in Central Asia, South Asia, West Asia, and other regions. The aim is to establish important transportation hubs, commercial logistics, and cultural and educational centers along the Silk Road Economic Belt, thereby creating a core area for the economic belt. Leveraging the advantages of high openness, strong economic strength, and significant radiating effect of the Yangtze River Delta, the Pearl River Delta, the western coast of the Taiwan Straits, and the Bohai Rim Economic Zone, China aims to deepen cooperation with Hong Kong, Macao, and Taiwan. Starting from specific points and gradually expanding to larger areas, China aims to promote regional cooperation. On May 21, 2014, during the Conference on Interaction and Confidence Building Measures in Asia, President Xi Jinping stated that China will work with other countries to accelerate the construction of the Silk Road Economic Belt and the 21st Century Maritime Silk Road, launch the Asian Infrastructure Investment Bank at an early date, and participate more deeply in the regional cooperation process to advance shared progress and security in Asia. During the strengthening of the Partnership for Connectivity Dialogue on November 8, 2014, Xi Jinping pointed out that the joint construction of the Silk Road Economic Belt and the 21st Century Maritime Silk Road is closely related and complementary to the efforts to enhance connectivity. If we compare the "Belt and Road" to the two wings that drive Asia's growth, then connectivity is the lifeblood of these two wings.

The supply-side structural reform aims to reduce overcapacity, inventory, and leverage, lower costs, and make up for shortcomings. This requires enhancing the supply of high-quality goods and services, reducing ineffective supply, expanding effective supply, improving the adaptability and flexibility of the supply structure, and increasing total factor productivity, so that the supply system can better adapt to changes in demand structure. Currently, China is grappling with an excess of production capacity and inventory, necessitating the exploration of fresh solutions. Building the "Belt and Road," especially infrastructure construction, is an effective way to reduce overcapacity. While increasing demand, it is crucial to focus on reforming and improving land, labor, capital, and innovation, which are essential factors influencing economic growth. It is necessary to eliminate supply constraints and supply suppression, to meet the diverse needs of the growing middle-income households, and to release consumption potential and benefits of the reform. This will achieve the goal of "new demand and creating new supply" proposed at the Fifth Plenary Session of the 18th Central Committee.

According to economic laws, it is impossible for a country's economy to maintain high-speed growth for a long time. After achieving high growth for over a decade and creating a miracle in the world economy, China's economy has entered a period of medium- to high-speed growth, which is in line with China's actual situation and economic laws. The "new normal" of economic development refers to the new characteristics of China's economy, which include the following main features:

The first feature of the new normal is the transition from high-speed growth to medium-high-speed growth. Despite the slowdown in China's economic growth, the actual increase in economic output is still substantial. In 2013, China's economic increase for the year was equivalent to the total economic output of the entire year in 1994, ranking 17th in the world.

The second feature of the new normal is that the economic structure has been continuously optimized and upgraded, with the consumption demand of the tertiary industry gradually becoming the mainstay. The gap between urban and rural areas and regional disparities has gradually narrowed, and the proportion of residents' income has increased, with the benefits of development reaching a wider range of people.

The third feature is the shift from factor-driven and investment-driven to innovation-driven growth. The government has vigorously streamlined administration and delegated power to lower levels, which has further unleashed market vitality. The innovation-driven strategy is resolutely implemented to continuously create new supply to meet new demand. Under this new normal, there is an urgent need to develop new technologies, new industries, and new business models. The idea is to create new demand by promoting the development of new technologies, which in turn will lead to the emergence of new industries. By creating new supply with new technologies, the goal is to stimulate new demand and make innovation the primary driving force behind the country's economic development.

Under the new normal, there is a need for new driving forces for economic development. The "Belt and Road" strategy creates new opportunities for expanding supply, optimizing structures, and providing new development impetus. When it comes to expanding investments, the Asian Infrastructure Investment Bank that we have launched provides favorable financial conditions for infrastructure construction in countries along the Belt and Road, creating opportunities to showcase our manufacturing capabilities and leading position. In areas such as high-speed rail, ports, and bridges, there is a vast market for us to tap into.

Continuously achieving economic structural optimization and upgrading is an important task for the new normal. The "Belt and Road" initiative provides a wide range of opportunities for the transformation of the economic structure. The increase in personnel exchanges, service trade, the development of the tertiary industry, and the tourism industry provide a foundation for China and countries along the route to optimize and upgrade their industrial structure. China has vast territory and each region has its own unique advantages. The potential for developing the tertiary industry is enormous, especially with the advancement of urbanization and modernization of agriculture. This provides a wide range of possibilities for optimizing structure, upgrading industries, and narrowing the gap between urban and rural areas. The implementation of the "Belt and Road" strategy undoubtedly injects new vitality into promoting structural optimization.

The shift from factor-driven to innovation-driven growth is the core of the new normal and the key to whether China's economy has sustained development momentum. Innovation-driven development, in essence, means moving from quantity-driven development of factor inputs to quality-driven development. Innovation-driven development includes theoretical innovation, technological innovation, management innovation, institutional innovation, system innovation, policy innovation, cultural innovation, and action innovation, among others. The essence and goal of innovative, efficient, environmentally sustainable, and high-quality development is to achieve high economic growth without increasing or minimizing the input of material factors. To achieve this transformation, it is necessary to intensify domestic reform efforts, further unleash market vitality, and truly place innovation at the core of the country's overall development. Innovative thinking should be infused into every aspect of the Party and the nation's endeavors, acting as a guiding principle for all activities and manifesting through practical measures. At the same time, to promote innovation through opening up, favorable external conditions are also essential. The "Belt and Road" initiative is an innovative development that provides various opportunities for innovation and breakthroughs in cooperation and win-win development.

Secondly, in terms of promoting regional economic development, the "Belt and Road" initiative spans the Eurasian continent, connecting the Asia-Pacific economic circle to the east and entering the European economic circle to the west. Historically, the ancient Silk Road and Maritime Silk Road were the major channels for China's economic, trade, and cultural exchanges with Central Asia, Southeast Asia, South Asia, West Asia, East Africa, and Europe. The Belt and Road Initiative inherits and builds upon the legacy of the ancient Silk Road, responding to the needs of the times and the aspirations of countries to expedite their development. It provides a broad and inclusive platform for development, rooted in deep historical and cultural ties. By aligning the interests of China's rapidly advancing economy with those of countries along the route, the initiative seeks to foster collectively beneficial cooperation and development. The "Belt and Road" initiative is a development initiative, a cooperation initiative, and an open initiative. It emphasizes the principle of equal consultation, joint contribution, and shared benefits, and seeks to promote policy coordination, infrastructure connectivity, trade facilitation, financial integration, and people-to-people bonds among countries along the route. Accelerating the construction of the "Belt and Road" initiative will help strengthen exchanges and shared learning among different civilizations and promote world peace and development.[3]

The "Belt and Road" initiative connects the Asia-Pacific and European economic circles, which are among the most dynamic regions in the world for economic growth. The Asia-Pacific economic circle is considered to be the engine of global economic growth. Through the integration of the Southeast Asian economy, the Northeast Asian economy, and ultimately the European economy, the "Belt and Road" strategy is promoting a major trend of economic integration across the Eurasian continent. Chinese leaders have visited many countries and attended dialogues on strengthening

---

[3]Publicity Department of the CPC Central Committee (Ed.). (2016). *General Secretary Xi Jinping Important Speech Series (2016 Edition)*. Learning Publishing House and People's Publishing House, p. 267.

connectivity partnerships, holding meetings with heads of state and government on bilateral relations and regional development issues. They have elaborated on the profound connotations and positive significance of the "Belt and Road" initiative and reached a broad consensus on its co-construction.

The "Belt and Road" initiative is more than just a physical infrastructure project but rather a comprehensive and dynamic network that connects regions in multiple dimensions. It is a vibrant and collaborative open system. Many of the development strategies or initiatives proposed by various countries have points of convergence with the Belt and Road Initiative. The Belt and Road Initiative has opened up broad prospects for cooperation and development between the Asia-Pacific and European economic circles.

Finally, from the perspective of promoting global economic development, the "Belt and Road" initiative not only aims at regional economic cooperation but will also have significant implications for the peaceful development of the world economy. Xi Jinping pointed out that "major powers are the decisive force that affects world peace. It is crucial to effectively manage major power relations and build a healthy and stable framework for major power relations." Russia is China's largest neighbor and a world power with extensive shared interests. The two countries are good neighbors, partners, and friends. They have firmly established a comprehensive strategic partnership of coordination, supported each other's development and rejuvenation, firmly supported each other's core interests, and firmly supported each other's independent choice of development path and social-political system. Substantial progress has been made in practical cooperation, and international strategic coordination and cooperation have reached new heights, setting an example for peaceful coexistence and win–win cooperation. The relationship between China and the United States is one of the most important bilateral relationships in the world today and occupies a special and significant position in China's diplomatic layout. The construction of a new type of major-country relationship between China and the United States, based on mutual respect, cooperation, and a commitment to avoiding conflict and confrontation, is a universal aspiration of both countries' peoples and the international community and is the right choice in keeping with the trend of the times. The Pacific Ocean is vast enough to accommodate the development of both China and the United States. Europe is an important pole of a multipolar world and a comprehensive strategic partner of China.

We should view China–Europe relations from a strategic perspective, combine the two major forces, markets, and civilizations of China and Europe, and jointly create four major partnership relations of China–Europe peace, growth, reform, and civilization. We should enhance the global influence of the China–Europe comprehensive strategic partnership and make greater contributions to the development and prosperity of the world.[4]

With regards to global economic development, the "Belt and Road" Initiative encompasses prominent nations and economies including China, Russia, the United States, and the European Union, among others, which hold significant influence in the global economy. By translating the "Belt and Road" Initiative from mere concepts and proposals into tangible actions, and by collaboratively constructing a broad community with a shared future, it aims to foster beneficial development for all participating countries within a peaceful environment.

3. The "Belt and Road" Initiative Builds an Open System of Connectivity, Integration, and Collective Benefits

China has established various levels of opening-up policies, from the initial establishment of special economic zones, coastal open cities, economic and technological development zones, and coastal economic open areas to the opening-up of border areas, along the Yangtze River, and inland provinces and regions, forming a multi-level system of opening-up across the country. As economic globalization deepens and regional economic integration takes on new characteristics, China's opening-up has entered a new phase under the guidance of the opening-up policy at the Fifth Plenary Session of the 18th CPC Central Committee. The implementation of the Belt and Road Initiative has marked this new stage, which is characterized by new features and three transformations in the levels of openness: First, China has shifted its opening-up policy from a reactive approach, where it simply responded to changes in the global economy, to a proactive approach where it takes the initiative in shaping the global economic order. Second, China used to open up to the world without

[4]Publicity Department of the CPC Central Committee (Ed.). (2016). *General Secretary Xi Jinping Important Speech Series* (2016 Edition). Learning Publishing House and People's Publishing House, pp. 268–269.

much influence or say in the rules and institutions of the global economy. Now, China is actively building its own voice and influence in the global economic order. Third, China has shifted its opening-up policy from a narrow focus on specific policies and measures to a more comprehensive and strategic approach that takes into account the broader national interests and long-term goals.

Firstly, the opening-up in the 1980s was a transition from self-isolation to openness, characterized by actively adapting to the objective laws of open development in accordance with the trend of reform and opening up, and moving from a closed economy to an open economy. This was a huge transformation and progress, and opening up has become one of the fundamental characteristics of China's economic development. The "Belt and Road" initiative is a strategy that is being developed now, and it is based on more than 30 years of economic development in China. China is leading this initiative, and it is taking place on a regional and global scale. This strategy is taking the country's opening-up policy to a higher level. The "Belt and Road" initiative represents a shift from the adaptive opening-up of the 1980s to a leading opening-up approach. While the former followed global development trends, the latter demonstrates China's leadership in promoting regional and global economic growth. This demonstrates China's ongoing efforts to increase its level of openness. The "Belt and Road" initiative, which is being implemented today with China at the helm, marks a significant turning point in China's history, transforming its level of openness and development.

Secondly, in the past, China's opening up was mainly passive, meaning that China did not have much influence or power in the international economic arena. The new round of opening-up, symbolized by the construction of the "Belt and Road" initiative, is characterized by our efforts to increase China's institutional discourse power in global economic governance. The shift from having no voice to enhancing our voice reflects a change in our international status and role. In the early stages of opening-up in the 1980s, China was merely a participant striving to actively integrate itself into the global economy. Enhancing our institutional discourse power in global economic governance was a relatively unfamiliar concept at that time, and we lacked the ability to do so, and could only be observers. However, with the implementation of the "Belt and Road" initiative, there has been a fundamental change. With the rapid growth of China's economic, political, cultural, technological, and military strength, China cannot remain a bystander. Enhancing China's institutional discourse power in global economic governance has become an urgent and realistic issue. The Fifth Plenary Session of the 18th Central Committee of the Communist Party of China has included it in the plan for achieving the first of the "Two Centenary Goals." Our current opening-up is aimed at continuously enhancing China's institutional discourse power in global economic governance during the opening-up process. We are not only participating in the opening-up but also taking an active role in leading it and participating in the establishment of various institutional frameworks in global economic governance. The process of opening-up and the strengthening of our institutional power of discourse are intertwined.

Thirdly, in the past, China's opening up focused primarily on traditional forms of international trade, such as the import and export of goods, technology, and services. This was often achieved through the strategy of "going out" (investing overseas) and "bringing in" (attracting foreign investment). In other words, China's opening-up was largely limited to the economic aspect of international relations. The openness of the "Belt and Road" initiative goes beyond the traditional concept of opening-up, which mainly revolves around the trade of goods, technology, and services, coupled with the "going global" and "bringing in" strategies. It is proposed as a comprehensive national strategy to build a system of openness that fosters connectivity, integration, and collective benefit. We have explicitly declared that the Belt and Road Initiative is a more advanced national strategy for opening-up, which is a major strategic decision made by the Central Committee of the Communist Party of China. It is a significant measure and development strategy for implementing a new phase of opening-up. The initiative aims to upgrade the previous straightforward exchange of goods, technology, and people into a new era of interconnectivity, integration, and collective benefit. This transformation marks a shift from a shallow opening policy to a profound and all-encompassing national opening-up strategy.

Xi Jinping pointed out that the construction of the "Belt and Road" initiative is a major strategic decision made by the Central Committee of the Communist Party of China, and an important measure for implementing a new round of opening up. To successfully build the "Belt and Road" initiative, it is essential to focus on interconnectivity, integration, and collective benefit. The initiative adheres to the principle of equal consultation, joint construction, and shared benefits, with the aim of promoting policy coordination, facilities connectivity, unimpeded trade, integrated financial systems, and people-to-people bonds among countries along the route. These "five connections" represent the fundamental features of the new phase of opening-up.

Policy coordination refers to the promotion and coordination at the government level. The implementation of the Belt and Road Initiative is premised on policy coordination and communication among governments. When policies are aligned, all aspects of work can proceed smoothly without encountering obstacles. When the policy environment of each country improves, there will be great potential for development in private-sector cooperation in various industries. Therefore, the construction of the Belt and Road initiative is not a purely civil cooperation project, but rather a strategic cooperation project advocated, supported, and encouraged by governments of various countries. It is driven by government initiatives rather than private initiatives. One distinctive feature of the Belt and Road Initiative is the top-down approach to resolving policy issues at the government level and promoting the development of an open system.

The facility connectivity is a fundamental requirement for the Belt and Road Initiative. In the past, countries were primarily focused on domestic infrastructure construction, while international infrastructure connectivity did not receive sufficient development due to various factors such as policies, funds, technology, and national strength. The focus on connectivity is a key aspect of the Belt and Road Initiative's long-term development strategy, with regional connectivity among countries along the route viewed as a fundamental project. Through collaborative efforts, each country stands to benefit significantly.

Unimpeded trade is the most important aspect of the Belt and Road Initiative, as trade is the most widely accessible project in the economic interactions among countries. Unimpeded trade is meant to ensure that trade between countries along the route is as smooth and unimpeded as domestic trade. The main barriers to trade between countries are tariffs and various trade protection policies, as well as other factors such as transportation. However, the most critical issue to tackle to promote trade is the enabling environment, specifically trade policies and efficient management. The ease of trade largely reflects the level of openness and international integration among countries. Promoting trade facilitation is a common goal for all countries involved in the Belt and Road Initiative.

Financial integration is a key feature of modern economic development, representing the lifeblood of modern economies. It drives comprehensive economic growth, as trade, technology, and infrastructure development all require the support of capital. Capital is a shared element for the economic development of all countries, and it can quickly transform into various material, human, and technological elements. With access to capital, countries are better equipped to tackle a wide range of challenges. By establishing funds such as the Silk Road Fund, the Asian Infrastructure Investment Bank, and the New Development Bank of BRICS (Brazil, Russia, India, China, South Africa), funds can be effectively utilized to support the common development of countries along the route.

People-to-people bonds encompass the cultivation of understanding and trust among individuals, forged through shared interests and collective progress. These bonds serve as the underlying catalyst for the widespread support and endorsement of the Belt and Road Initiative across diverse nations. It is crucial to ensure that the countries along the route perceive the Belt and Road Initiative as a venture founded on the principles of shared benefit and cooperative gains, affording them the opportunity to actively participate in its construction and engage in collaborative endeavors. Such active involvement will foster a conducive environment encompassing politics, public opinion, commerce, and trust. Together, we can strive toward constructing an open, inclusive, balanced, and reciprocally beneficial regional economic cooperation framework.

The new round of opening-up, characterized by these "five connections," has set the basic direction for China's opening-up efforts. The Belt and Road Initiative has opened up greater opportunities for China's participation in international multilateral affairs and promoted the development of its diplomatic strategy.

Firstly, establishing a healthy and stable framework for relations with major powers is of utmost importance, as major powers are a decisive force affecting world peace. Russia is our largest neighbor and a major world power with whom we share broad common interests. The two countries have built a solid foundation for a comprehensive strategic partnership and are good neighbors, partners, and friends. We firmly support each other's development and revitalization, protect each other's core interests, and respect each other's choice of development paths and basic social systems.

Secondly, the relationship between China and the United States is one of the most important bilateral relationships in the world today and occupies a particularly significant position in China's diplomatic priorities. A new model of major-country relations between China and the United States, characterized by no conflict or confrontation, mutual respect, and win–win cooperation, is a universal aspiration of the two peoples and the international community, as well as the right choice in line with the trend of the times. The Pacific Ocean is vast enough to accommodate the development of both China and the United States. China and the United States should maintain close contacts and exchanges at all levels, expand and deepen practical cooperation in various fields, enhance people-to-people exchanges, and respect each other's differences in history, culture, social systems, development paths, and development stages. They should continue to deepen dialogue and cooperation on Asia-Pacific regional affairs and work together to address various regional and global challenges.

Finally, Europe is an important pole of the multipolar world and a comprehensive strategic partner of China. It is essential to view China–Europe relations from a strategic perspective and combine the two great powers, markets, and civilizations to create a partnership that promotes peace, growth, reform, and civilization between China and Europe. This will enhance the global influence of the comprehensive strategic partnership between China and Europe and contribute to the development and prosperity of the world.

The surrounding areas are the foundation of China's development and prosperity. The overall environment of China's surrounding areas is stable and vibrant, and has significant development advantages and potential. Neighborly relations and cooperation are the mainstream of China's relations with its neighbors. It is important to consider the big picture, emphasize strategic planning, and improve diplomatic efforts in surrounding areas. The concept of affinity, sincerity, benefit, and inclusiveness should be highlighted. Northeast Asia, Southeast Asia, and Central Asia are strategic priorities for China's surrounding diplomatic work. They are also regions where China's overseas interests are concentrated, with close contacts and strong external influence. China firmly supports the construction of the ASEAN Community and highly values friendly cooperation with Central Asian countries. We aspire to collaborate closely with Central Asian countries, aiming to foster trust, deepen cooperation, and promote common prosperity.

Developing countries around the world share common ground with China in pursuing peaceful development. Although China has achieved significant development, it still considers itself a developing country and believes in balancing its principles and interests. China will prioritize ethical considerations and will continue to work with developing countries to promote common development and establish closer connections. In simpler terms, China sees other developing countries as allies in their pursuit of peaceful development and will work with them to ensure common growth and prosperity.

China and Africa have long shared a community of common interests and a vision for a shared future. China's unwavering commitment to strengthening solidarity and cooperation with African countries is a strategic choice that has been consistently upheld. It is imperative for China and Africa to forge ahead by establishing a comprehensive strategic partnership that builds upon their illustrious tradition of genuine friendship. This entails promoting the ethos of mutual assistance, adhering to equitable and mutually advantageous cooperation, fostering an open and inclusive approach to multi-party collaboration, prioritizing cooperation on fundamental needs, and focusing on practical capacity-oriented initiatives.

4. Enhancing China's Institutional Discourse Power in Global Economic Governance

The Fifth Plenary Session of the 18th CPC Central Committee proposed developing a more advanced open economy and actively participating in global economic governance and the provision of public goods to enhance China's institutional discourse power in global economic governance. This is a new issue that requires in-depth thinking and research. Before entering the 21st century, the institutional discourse power in global economic governance was a relatively unfamiliar concept for China. As China's economic, political, cultural, technological, and military power has rapidly grown, enhancing its institutional discourse power in global economic governance has become an urgent and pressing issue. With the implementation of the "Belt and Road" initiative as a symbol, China's institutional discourse power in global economic governance has been comprehensively enhanced.

A country's discourse power refers to its language power, influence, and guidance in expressing its economic, political, cultural, technological, military, and national interests. It reflects the country's status and role in the international community. Discourse power is a complex entity, consisting of multiple factors. It is both a form of hard power and soft power, tangible and intangible. The formation of discourse power, especially institutional discourse power, cannot be achieved overnight. It is a concrete manifestation of a country's depth, breadth, intensity, as well as its role, influence, and participation in global economic activities. There are specific factors that contribute to the formation of a country's discourse power, particularly its institutional discourse power. These include two main aspects. First is hard power, which primarily consists of economic, political, technological, and military strength. Second is soft power, which mainly includes spiritual, cultural, and national cohesion. The third factor is influence, which mainly includes the affinity, influence, penetration, expansion, and challenge a country possesses during the process of communication, dialogue, and cooperation with the world. The fourth factor is self-confidence, which mainly includes the belief and confidence in one's own discourse, as well as confidence in one's own national culture.

China has been striving to enhance its institutional discourse power in global economic governance since the 18th National Congress of the Communist Party of China. The "Belt and Road" initiative, a national strategy led by China with an open approach, is expected to boost China's international status, influence, and institutional discourse power in global economic governance. The establishment and operation of the Asian Infrastructure Investment Bank (AIIB) is a complementary initiative to the Belt and Road strategy, implemented in tandem. The establishment of the AIIB is a major step taken by China to enhance its institutional discourse power in global economic governance. It is the first multilateral financial institution initiated and led by China and a successful example of a high-standard international financial institution initiated by developing countries and joined by developed countries.

The establishment and operation of the AIIB has institutionally guaranteed the enhancement of China's discourse power in the international financial field. As an institutional arrangement in the international financial field, it challenges the existing international financial system mainly led by developed countries and is also an institutional innovation in the international financial field initiated by China. The establishment of the AIIB will drive a large number of infrastructure projects in Asia. The AIIB will invest in Asian countries, promote infrastructure construction, and interconnectivity, help build a large Asian market, further unleash the potential of Asian economic development, and promote national economic growth. This, in turn, will boost and enhance the overseas market demand for Chinese goods, and promote economic and trade cooperation between China and other Asian countries. The creation of the AIIB is a significant step toward China's financial internationalization, and it will help to promote the internationalization of the Renminbi. China will play a greater role in the international financial system and gain more influence in the formulation of international economic and financial rules.

Firstly, the AIIB serves the revitalization of Asia. It is estimated that from 2010 to 2020, the total demand for infrastructure investment in developing countries in Asia is as high as $8 trillion, with an average annual investment requirement of over $700 billion. However, the existing multilateral development banks' annual investment in Asian infrastructure is only $10 billion to $20 billion. In this context, the creation of the AIIB will stimulate increased investment in infrastructure and connectivity in the region, providing long-term support for economic growth in Asia and fostering closer cooperation between neighboring countries and China. The establishment of the AIIB has accelerated the promotion of infrastructure interconnectivity in the region and facilitated regional economic cooperation, injecting new impetus into the development of the Asian economy. In his speech at the opening ceremony, President Xi Jinping pointed out that the official establishment and opening of the AIIB will effectively increase infrastructure investment in the Asian region, mobilize various resources, especially private sector funds, to invest in infrastructure construction, and promote regional interconnectivity and economic integration.[5]

Secondly, it serves South–South cooperation and North–South cooperation. One of the key highlights of the AIIB's innovation is that developing countries have a majority of voting rights and greater discourse power. This not only conforms to the development changes of the international economic landscape but also demonstrates the confidence and determination of developing countries to promote regional development in Asia together. The AIIB has 57 member countries across Asia, Oceania, Europe, Africa, and Latin America, with developing countries as its main members and a significant number of developed countries also included. This unique advantage enables it to become a bridge and link for promoting South–South cooperation and North–South cooperation.

Lastly, it serves global governance. The establishment of the AIIB not only inspires reform of the international financial system but also paves the way for new paths in global governance in the 21st century. The bank follows the principle of "openness, transparency, and merit-based selection" for the selection and management of its staff, which is explicitly stated in its agreement. This innovative approach distinguishes it from

---

[5]AIIB officially launched. January 16, 2016. Retrieved from: http://news.xinhuanet.com/english/2016-01/16/c_135008182.htm.

the existing major multilateral development banks and reflects the modern governance concept that the AIIB has consistently adhered to. As pointed out by President Xi Jinping, "the establishment and operation of the AIIB will help promote the development of a more just, reasonable and effective global economic governance system."[6] In order to accomplish this, the AIIB has learned from the best practices and experiences of established multilateral development banks in areas such as governance structures, environmental and social safeguards policies, procurement policies, and debt sustainability, and has started its operations at a high standard. It adheres to open regionalism, promoting various forms of cooperation and benign competition, such as joint financing, knowledge sharing, and capacity building, to learn from each other, complement each other's strengths, and improve the contribution of multilateral development institutions to infrastructure interconnectivity and sustainable economic development in Asia. The establishment of the AIIB has greatly expanded the global impact of the Belt and Road Initiative, and enhanced people's confidence in its construction.

The AIIB has 57 member countries, including major developed countries from Asia, Europe, Africa, Latin America, and Oceania, excluding the United States and Japan. In terms of appearance, the establishment of the AIIB has significantly boosted China's international influence. It stands out as a new initiative taken by China outside the framework of the US-led World Bank and Japan-led Asian Development Bank and has garnered some measure of diplomatic clout. Notably, it has created some distance between China and the United States and Japan, who have been skeptical of China's growing economic power. In fact, the political and economic significance of the establishment of the AIIB goes far beyond this. This shift indicates that China has transitioned from a reactive stance to a proactive approach in light of global dynamics. The following layers of significance are particularly prominent:

The first layer of significance is that China is beginning to establish global economic rules. The World Bank, the International Monetary Fund, and the World Trade Organization led by the United States have set the rules of the game for the world economy, which serve the interests of the United States and give it absolute discourse power in the world economic order, especially in the world financial order. Within this framework, Japan established the Asian Development Bank with the support of the

---

[6] *Ibid.*

United States and was able to gain a share of the benefits under US leadership. In recent years, the establishment of the European Union and the euro system has shaken the US hegemony in the global economy and finance. However, Europe is neither able nor willing to truly challenge the United States. With the continuous strengthening of China's economic strength, China will not be satisfied with being just a world factory. It is an inevitable trend for China to influence the world economic order and even formulate rules for the world economy. It is through the establishment of a regional Asian Infrastructure and Investment Bank led and controlled by China that China seeks to seek dominance over the world economy and financial order and to increase its discourse power in the fields of world economy and finance.

The second layer of significance is that China's strong foreign exchange reserves have finally found a place to be invested. China is the largest creditor nation of the United States. As of the first quarter of 2015, China's holdings of US Treasury bonds had exceeded $1.2 trillion. Given the substantial foreign exchange reserves, it is imperative to invest and manage them rather than leaving them idle in the treasury. However, China lacks its own globally prominent bank or international monetary fund, as well as renowned financial institutions like Goldman Sachs or Morgan Stanley. The United States is the world leader and buying its bonds is certainly safer. However, with the establishment of the AIIB and the Silk Road Fund, China has at least found a way out for its foreign exchange reserves of over $100 billion. In the first quarter of 2016, China had already reduced its holdings of US Treasury bonds by more than $40 billion consecutively, making Japan the largest creditor of US Treasury bonds instead of China.

The third layer of significance lies in the fact that it tightly binds the interests of many founding member countries together. When most of the countries in Asia become founding members of the AIIB, they will certainly choose the AIIB as their first option for infrastructure construction, rather than the World Bank or the Asian Development Bank. As the AIIB is controlled by China and headquartered in Beijing, it can use the yuan for lending and settlement. It is likely that when member countries seek to build high-speed rail using Chinese technology, the lending process will be highly efficient. The emotional ties and economic tools employed by the AIIB will likely produce more positive outcomes. The establishment and ongoing operation of the AIIB marks an important step for China in increasing its institutional influence in the field of international finance.

Chapter 16

Developing a More Advanced Open Economy

Opening-up to the outside world is a fundamental policy of China. After more than 30 years of reform and opening-up, China's economy is undergoing a significant transformation from "bringing in" to a dual focus on "bringing in" and "going global." Only by adhering to opening-up policies and deeply integrating into the world economy can sustainable development be achieved. Accurately grasping the new trends of global economic globalization and the new requirements of China's opening-up to the outside world, and effectively addressing the difficulties and challenges faced in our economic and social development, require us to further expand our opening-up and develop a more advanced and comprehensive open economy, which enables us to take the initiative in economic development and international competition.

1. Continuously Improving the Level of Opening Up to the Outside World

In today's world, openness is the way forward and building an open economy is in line with the objective requirements of economic development. Openness has become a major trend of the times and striving to improve the level of open economy has become a common goal for all countries.

Firstly, enhancing the level of an open economy is an objective requirement for accelerating a country's economic development. Today, a country's level of economic development cannot be simply measured by its level of openness. Instead, what is more important is the degree of openness, as it determines how comprehensively a country can access various resources and conditions from the outside world. Under today's development conditions, due to various limiting factors, a country's economic development inevitably involves advantages and disadvantages. Enhancing the degree of openness in an economy can effectively capitalize on its inherent strengths, offset its limitations, and facilitate accelerated economic growth. Conversely, nations that persistently maintain closed economic systems are bound to encounter sluggish development. Similarly, countries with a low level of openness cannot adapt to the trend of world development. This has been proven by history, as countries with higher openness levels generally have higher levels of economic development. In reality, those unable to keep pace with openness risk being marginalized in the world. Xi Jinping pointed out that "a country can only be confident in its openness when it has a strong economy, and opening up, in turn, reinforces a country's economic strength. The success of China's reform and opening up since the Third Plenary Sessions of the 11th CPC Central Committee demonstrates the pivotal role of openness in driving China's economic and social development. As China's economy becomes the second largest in the world and enters a new phase of development, it is imperative to maintain sustainable and healthy growth by adopting a global perspective, consciously balancing domestic and international issues, comprehensively planning a broad strategy for opening up, and actively engaging with the world in a proactive manner."[1]

Secondly, countries can reap various benefits for their economic development by expanding their openness. Openness not only allows access to various resources, technologies, factors, markets, and other economic development necessities, but more importantly, it provides opportunities for growth, broadens understanding of the world, updates perspectives, facilitates institutional and policy adjustments, and helps create favorable conditions for economic development by better aligning with the global community. Expanding openness not only improves the material conditions for economic development but also creates necessary conditions for enhancing the overall environment. This is a crucial aspect of continuously improving the level of an open economy. In the past, it was believed that opening-up could only address tangible factors, but that is no longer sufficient. It is important to acknowledge the significant role that institutional and policy innovation plays in enhancing the level of an open economy.

---

[1]Summarizing experience, strengthening confidence, and solidly promoting the construction of the Belt and Road to benefit the people of countries along the route. *People's Daily*, August 18, 2016.

Ultimately, countries can achieve mutual development through cooperation and by forming a community where their interests are mutually beneficial. While the trend of global economic integration is on the rise, the emphasis on national interests is also growing stronger. These two factors are both in conflict and interrelated. Countries can sustain an open economy by forming a community of shared interests through cooperation and mutual benefits. Today's world is no longer one where larger or stronger nations can bully or oppress weaker ones, so an approach to opening up that relies on such tactics will face increasing resistance. Instead, political equality and mutual economic benefit are the key trends driving international cooperation among nations. Xi Jinping emphasized that the Belt and Road initiative is an open platform that creates connections between Asia, Europe, and Africa, forming a vast community of shared interests. All countries interested in participating are welcome to join this community. China welcomes active participation from countries along the route and extends a warm welcome to friends from all five continents to join hands in this endeavor. The Belt and Road Initiative is a win–win situation that will bring tangible benefits to the people of countries along the route and create enormous opportunities for common development between China and these countries. The Belt and Road Initiative aims to create diverse opportunities and benefits for all stakeholders, without favoring any particular group. It is not designed to serve the exclusive interests of a single party, but rather to pave the way for collective progress.[2] This commitment to inclusivity represents a sincere endeavor to continually advance an open economy, as sustainable development can only be achieved within such a framework of economic openness.

The Belt and Road Initiative demonstrates China's new approach to an open economy, showcasing its innovative strategies, values, and image to the world. As a leading economic power, China recognizes the importance of contributing to the global community, not only as a shared aspiration of all nations but also as its responsibility and obligation. China not only proactively and actively opens its economy but also aims to lead the way in promoting open economic systems globally by enhancing institutional frameworks. Today, China is not merely an ordinary member participating in openness but has become a leading nation that plays a crucial

---

[2]Publicity Department of the CPC Central Committee (Ed.). (2016). *General Secretary Xi Jinping Important Speech Series* (2016 Edition). Learning Publishing House and People's Publishing House, Beijing, pp. 267–268.

role in shaping the regional and global economy. Cooperation for global economic development cannot proceed without China. The establishment of an international economic order depends on China, and the smooth operation of the global economy requires China's participation. China is now an important member of the international economic family and its role in promoting global economic growth is increasingly prominent.

China is committed to enhancing its competitiveness and influence in the global economic landscape, in order to better adapt to changes in the external environment and comprehensively improve the level of an open economy. In December 2015, the State Council issued the *Opinions on Accelerating the Implementation of the Free Trade Zone Strategy*, launching China's free trade zone strategy. This is an important part of China's new round of opening-up to the world. At the 18th Party Congress, a proposal was made to speed up the implementation of the free trade zone strategy, and this was further emphasized in the Third and Fifth Plenary Sessions with a focus on the surrounding areas. The goal is to create a network of high-standard free trade zones that face the world, in response to the new trends of economic globalization. Currently, China's economic development has entered a new phase, where opportunities and challenges coexist in foreign trade. The strategies of "bringing in" (attracting foreign investment, technology, etc.) and "going out" (promoting Chinese companies and products overseas) are facing new development situations in China's current economic phase, where foreign trade opportunities and challenges coexist. Accelerating the implementation of the free trade zone strategy is an objective requirement for China to adapt to the new trend of economic globalization, and a major choice for comprehensively deepening reform, promoting reform through opening up, and building a new system for an open economy.

Reform and opening-up are intricately interconnected, with opening-up being a form of reform and reform encompassing the act of opening up. Of course, openness, in its original sense, refers to a form of economic development. Economic development can be closed or open. However, openness and closure are not naturally formed but are constituted by a series of institutional and policy conditions of countries. When these conditions are not in place, it is necessary to achieve openness through reforms. Therefore, the statement that "reform is the only way for openness" is valid in this sense. Deng Xiaoping made insightful remarks on this relationship. Reform can further promote openness, and openness can also further promote the advancement of reforms. The main focus of

China's Belt and Road Initiative is openness, which will inevitably further promote the development of reform.

Firstly, further expanding and improving the level of openness requires domestic institutions and policies to be in place, which can be achieved through reforms. The greater the efforts made in reforms, the stronger the support for openness will be. In particular, when certain institutions and policies cannot meet the objective requirements of open development, reforms become even more significant for expanding openness.

Secondly, openness can promote the advancement of reform from an ideological perspective. Expanding and improving the level of openness will firstly affect people's attitudes and change their views on various issues, which will directly lead to further reflection on various systems and policies. Examining the existing institutions and policies to identify problems and find solutions through reform reflects how open development can have a positive impact on deepening reforms.

Finally, reform and opening-up always work together and influence each other, but the process is not always balanced or consistent. Sometimes, the primary concern is addressing reform problems, while at other times, the primary focus is on opening-up. When the main issue is to tackle reform problems, it creates a situation where reform drives opening-up. Similarly, when the main issue is to address opening-up problems, it creates a situation where opening-up drives reform. Reform and opening-up have been advancing through such a mutually reinforcing interaction.

Despite the profound and complex changes in world politics, peace and development remain the main themes of our times, and the trend toward peace, development, cooperation, and win–win outcomes is becoming even stronger. Many emerging market countries and developing countries have embarked on the fast track of development. Hundreds of millions, or even billions, of people are moving toward modernization. Multiple development hubs are gradually emerging in various regions around the world, and the balance of international power is shifting toward promoting world peace and development. Favorable conditions now exist for maintaining overall stability in the international situation and promoting common development among countries. However, the world is still far from peaceful, and humanity still faces many problems and challenges. The international financial crisis has had a profound impact, resulting in increased instability and uncertainty in global economic growth, as well as exacerbating imbalances in global development. Geopolitical factors have become more prominent, with local turbulence frequently occurring, and an increase in trends of hegemony, power politics, and new interventionism. Non-traditional security threats and global challenges are on the rise, making the task of maintaining world peace and promoting common development more challenging. Facing the deepening of multi-polarization, economic globalization, cultural diversity, and continuous social digitization in the world, humanity today is better equipped than ever before to move toward the goal of peace and development, and cooperation and win–win is the practical way to achieve this goal.

Countries should jointly promote the establishment of a new type of international relations centered on cooperation and win–win outcomes, and people from all countries should work together to maintain world peace and promote common development. Every country and its citizens should be entitled to equal dignity, fair access to development benefits, and collective security guarantees. All countries should be treated equally, irrespective of their size, strength, or wealth, and their right to choose their own development paths should be respected. Interference in other countries' internal affairs should be opposed, and international fairness and justice should be safeguarded. All countries must collaborate to safeguard global peace, foster development through peaceful means, and solidify peace through development. While pursuing their own development, each country should actively promote the shared development of others. The world should not be built on a foundation where some countries become increasingly prosperous while others remain impoverished and underdeveloped for extended periods. We must turn challenges into opportunities and use them as a driving force for cooperation. This can be achieved through the pursuit of cooperative, collective, and common security, replacing confrontation with cooperation and seeking win–win outcomes instead of monopolies.

China is an important force for maintaining world peace and promoting common development, and a reliable partner and friend that can be trusted by the international community. China will uphold the principles of peace, development, cooperation, and mutually beneficial partnerships. It will firmly grasp the main theme of adhering to peaceful development and promoting national rejuvenation, safeguard national sovereignty, security, and development interests, and create a favorable international environment for peaceful development. China will enhance friendly exchanges with people around the world, broaden the convergence of interests with countries worldwide, and make positive contributions to the noble cause of promoting global peace and development.

Choosing the path of peaceful development is a strategic decision made by China in accordance with the trend of the times and its fundamental interests as a nation. Xi Jinping pointed out that the "Two Centenary Goals" proposed at the 18th Party Congress, which include the goal of realizing the Chinese Dream of national rejuvenation, require a peaceful international environment. Without peace, neither China nor the world can achieve smooth development. Similarly, without development, neither China nor the world can achieve lasting peace. Only by adhering to the path of peaceful development and working with all countries to safeguard peace can China achieve its own goals and make greater contributions to the world. China's choice of the path of peaceful development is not a temporary expedient or a diplomatic rhetoric but a conclusion drawn from objective judgments based on history, reality, and the future. It represents the organic unity of ideological confidence and practical consciousness. China's confidence and consciousness in pursuing the path of peaceful development stem from the profound origins of Chinese civilization, the recognition of the conditions necessary to achieve development goals, and the grasp of the trend of global development. Since ancient times, the Chinese nation has actively engaged in foreign exchanges and trade, rather than aggression and expansionism. The Chinese people have adhered to patriotism focused on defending their own homes and country, rather than colonialism aimed at expanding territory. The pursuit of peace, harmony, and amity is deeply ingrained in the spiritual essence of the Chinese nation and flows through the veins of the Chinese people. Despite enduring long-term aggression and bullying from imperial powers, the Chinese people did not adopt the "might is right" logic of bandits. Rather, they became even more committed to upholding peace. The most valuable lesson that the Chinese people learned from their victory in the Chinese People's War of Resistance Against Japanese Aggression and the World Anti-Fascist War is the unwavering need to pursue the path of peaceful development.

China's path of peaceful development has been gradually formed through arduous exploration and continuous practice, especially since the founding of the People's Republic of China and the implementation of reform and opening-up policies. China's experience over the past 30 years of reform and opening-up has shown that the decision to pursue a path of peaceful development is a strategic choice rooted in China's national conditions, social system, and cultural traditions. This choice aligns with the trend of the times, serves China's core interests, benefits neighboring countries, and is in the interest of all nations around the world.

Therefore, there is no reason to deviate from this path. A prosperous and stable world presents an opportunity for China, just as China's development presents an opportunity for the world. Pursuing the path of peaceful development is beneficial for China, Asia, and the world as a whole. China adheres to the path of peaceful development, actively seeking a peaceful international environment for its own development, while also promoting world peace through its own growth. This approach allows China to better utilize global opportunities and share its own opportunities with the world, fostering positive interactions and mutual benefits between China and other countries around the world. China remains committed to its path of peaceful development and hopes that all countries around the world will join together in this pursuit. Through collective effort, we can ensure that peace always shines brightly on the planet that we all share.

2. The Free Trade Zone Strategy Is an Important Part of Building a High-Quality Open Economy

Accelerating the implementation of the Free Trade Zone Strategy is an important aspect of China's new round of opening-up to the outside world. The 17th National Congress of the Communist Party of China elevated the construction of free trade zones to a national strategy, while the 18th National Congress further proposed accelerating the implementation of this strategy. The Third Plenary Session of the 18th Central Committee of the CPC subsequently put forward the idea of accelerating the implementation of free trade zone strategy, with a focus on neighboring countries, to form a global network of free trade zones. The "Belt and Road" Initiative is closely linked to the Free Trade Zone strategy. Building a network of free trade zones around the countries along the "Belt and Road" is a crucial and important step for the future of China's Free Trade Zone strategy.

In 2013, China established the China (Shanghai) Pilot Free Trade Zone, which opened up a new mode of exploring the construction of free trade zones. After that, the China (Guangdong) Pilot Free Trade Zone, the China (Tianjin) Pilot Free Trade Zone, and the China (Fujian) Pilot Free Trade Zone were established. In 2016, seven more free trade zones were established in Liaoning, Zhejiang, Henan, Hubei, Chongqing, Sichuan, and Shaanxi provinces. The construction of China's free trade zones has progressed smoothly. China has signed and implemented a series of free trade agreements within its free trade zones and is currently negotiating multiple free trade agreements, covering Asia, Africa, North America, South America, and other regions across the world. Under the strategic framework of the "Belt and Road" initiative, the construction of free trade zones during the 13th Five-Year Plan period will be greatly accelerated.

The term "自贸区" in Chinese is associated with two different concepts: the Free Trade Area (FTA) and the Free Trade Zone (FTZ). However, the similarity in their Chinese translations often leads to confusion when it comes to understanding these concepts.

The FTA concept originates from the World Trade Organization's (WTO) provisions on "free trade zones" and was first mentioned in the 1947 General Agreement on Tariffs and Trade. According to the WTO's Article 24(8)(b), an FTA is understood as a group composed of two or more independent customs territories that eliminate tariffs and other trade-restrictive regulations on trade liberalization between them. FTA members retain their own external trade policies while essentially canceling trade restrictions among each other. There are currently several FTAs in the world, such as the European Union (EU) and North American Free Trade Agreement (NAFTA), and the China–ASEAN Free Trade Area is also a typical FTA.

FTZ, or Free Trade Zone, is a concept that originated from the World Customs Organization's (WCO) definition of "free zones." The Kyoto Convention developed by the WCO states that an FTZ is "a part of the territory of a contracting party where any goods introduced are generally regarded, insofar as import duties and taxes are concerned, as being outside the Customs territory." An FTZ is typically a small area within a country's borders that is separated by fencing or other barriers, and it is an initiative of a single sovereign nation or region. The main characteristic of an FTZ is that it typically grants duty-free or bonded status to imported goods, rather than reducing import tariffs. Many free ports and free trade zones established in various countries fall under this category, such as the Hamburg Free Port in Germany and the Colon Free Trade Zone in Panama.

More than 20 years ago, the first bonded area in mainland China was established in Waigaoqiao, Shanghai. At that time, it was translated into English as "Free Trade Zone" rather than "Bonded Area." As of the end of June 2015, there were a total of 122 customs special supervision areas in China, including bonded areas, export processing zones, bonded logistics parks, cross-border industrial zones, bonded port areas, and comprehensive bonded areas. These areas are located in 29 provinces, with 76 in the eastern region, accounting for 62.3% of the total, and 46 in the central, western, and northeastern regions, accounting for 37.7%. They have played a huge role in promoting China's foreign trade development.

In the development of economic globalization and regional integration, numerous bilateral and multilateral trade agreements have emerged, with many countries calling for a more open world economic system. Notably, there are three highly regarded free trade agreements currently gaining considerable attention: two led by the United States and one led by China and ASEAN.

The Trans-Pacific Partnership (TPP) led by the United States adopts a closed, self-centered, and exclusive approach. On the one hand, this approach has its progressiveness—it adapts to the development of international trade and investment, expands the field of standards, and promotes higher-level trade. On the other hand, because of its exclusivity, it creates new pressures on China's external environment.

The Regional Comprehensive Economic Partnership (RCEP) being promoted by China, covers the ten ASEAN countries, as well as China, Japan, South Korea, India, Australia, and New Zealand. It will become the world's largest free trade zone in terms of population, member diversity, economic development levels, and vitality. The RCEP initiated by China and ASEAN is expected to complete negotiations by the end of 2016, and by the end of 2017, there will be three of the world's largest free trade zones.

The State Council has issued a document titled *Several Opinions on Accelerating the Implementation of the Free Trade Zone Strategy*, which proposes strengthening strategic planning for "going global" and implementing a more active free trade zone strategy to expand the development of an open economy. China will cooperate with neighboring countries to develop free trade zones, promote international production capacity cooperation, actively negotiate and establish free trade zones with countries along the "Belt and Road," and build the "Belt and Road" into an open pathway for trade and commerce.

The 18th National Congress of the Communist Party of China called for speeding up the implementation of the free trade zone strategy. The goal is to transform China from a major trading nation to a trading powerhouse, by consolidating its traditional advantages in foreign trade, developing new competitive advantages, expanding its development space, and actively increasing imports. China aims to adopt a strategic mindset and a global perspective, acknowledging the interdependence between domestic and international affairs, while consistently advancing its commitment to global openness.

The short-term goal of this strategy is to accelerate the negotiation process of existing free trade zones, gradually increase the level of liberalization of established free trade zones under suitable conditions, actively promote the establishment of free trade zones with most neighboring countries and regions and increase the proportion of China's total foreign trade volume with free trade partners to reach or exceed the levels of most developed countries and emerging economies. The medium to long-term goal is to establish a global network of free trade zones, including neighboring countries and regions, countries along the "Belt and Road" initiative, and important countries across five continents. This network aims to achieve liberalization and facilitation of most of China's foreign trade and two-way investment.

The free trade zone strategy is an important platform for economic development. We need to speed up the implementation of the free trade zone strategy, utilizing the role of free trade zones to promote trade and investment, helping Chinese companies to better tap into international markets, injecting new impetus and vigor into China's economic development, and creating new opportunities for growth.

The free trade pilot zones are a significant strategic layout aimed at promoting reform through openness. In the first two batches of the four major free trade zones, Shanghai and Tianjin are two municipalities directly under the central government, while Guangdong and Fujian are two provinces that were early experimenters of economic special zones. These four free trade zones cover three major economic regions in China: the Yangtze River Economic Belt, the Pearl River Delta Economic Zone, and the Beijing-Tianjin-Hebei Integration Zone. The four free trade zones are becoming free trade bases for building the Maritime Silk Road and connecting domestic and foreign trade. In 2016, the establishment of the third batch of seven free trade pilot zones in Liaoning, Zhejiang, Henan, Hubei, Chongqing, Sichuan, and Shaanxi provinces will further advance China's strategy of shifting from a major trading country to a trading powerhouse.

The free trade zone is a pioneer in institutional innovation. The first and second batches of the four free trade pilot zones will prepare for a wider and deeper level of opening up and enhance China's competitiveness and influence in the future global economic landscape. Xi Jinping pointed out that building free trade pilot zones is a national strategy, and we must firmly grasp international rules and boldly explore and try new ideas. We should independently implement reforms and quickly form a batch of replicable and scalable new systems, accelerating the development of effective measures to facilitate investment and trade, streamline regulations, and create a normative legal environment. The first batch of successful outcomes in these areas should be tested and validated as soon as possible. We need to conduct stress tests to effectively prevent systemic risks, especially financial risks. The establishment of free trade zones is a new development and requires liberation of thinking, reform, innovation, and bold experimentation. All relevant departments should address existing issues based on the actual situation of each test zone. They should adhere to bottom-line principles and risk prevention, coordinate and plan comprehensively, vigorously promote reforms, remove obstacles, and strongly support the pioneering role of the free trade pilot zones in reform and opening-up. Additionally, they should recognize the status of these zones as trailblazers for innovation and development and work to form more replicable and scalable experiences.

During his visit to the Shanghai Free Trade Zone, Xi Jinping emphasized the importance of the zone as a major testing ground for economic and trade innovations. He called for careful cultivation, management, and promotion of the experience gained from these innovations to achieve a good outcome. Shanghai aims to take the lead in promoting scientific and technological innovation and implementing an innovation-driven development strategy, advancing toward becoming a globally influential center for scientific and technological innovations. Shanghai should leverage its leading role in cooperation and communication within the Yangtze River Delta, participate in the construction of the Silk Road Economic Belt and the 21st Century Maritime Silk Road, promote the development of the Yangtze River Economic Belt, and continue to improve the cooperation and coordination mechanism in the Yangtze River Delta region. Shanghai should strengthen special cooperation, expand the scope of cooperation, enhance regional planning connectivity and forward-looking research, and strive to promote the integrated development and leading development of the Yangtze River Delta region. At the 6th meeting of the Central Comprehensively Deepening Reforms Commission, Xi Jinping emphasized the importance of the Shanghai Free Trade Zone. He highlighted the active explorations and bold attempts made by the zone in the core area of institutional innovation since its establishment. The goal of these explorations is to form experiences that are replicable and scalable. Xi Jinping also mentioned the joint efforts of the central government, relevant departments, and the Shanghai municipal government in achieving this goal. The Shanghai Free Trade Zone has achieved significant progress in various areas, including simplifying administration and delegating power, combining regulation with service, accelerating the transformation of government functions, innovating systems and mechanisms, promoting trade and investment facilitation, and creating a market-oriented, internationalized, and legalized business environment. These achievements have allowed the zone to explore new paths and accumulate new experiences in deepening reforms and expanding opening up nationwide. In short, it has made a series of new achievements that contribute to the development of China's reform and opening up policies. At the Third Plenary Sessions of the 18th CPC Central Committee, the development of free trade zones (ports) in areas with favorable conditions was proposed, building on the success of existing pilots. The experience gained from the Shanghai Free Trade Pilot Zone represents the seeds we have cultivated in this test field. We must now spread these seeds to a wider range and achieve results quickly. Furthermore, we should promote the replicable and scalable experiences gained from the pilot in other regions and nationwide.

Accelerating the implementation of the free trade zone strategy is an important part of China's new round of opening up to the outside world. The goal is to seek regional and global economic prosperity and continuously improve people's well-being. The Asia-Pacific region is currently the most dynamic region in the world economy and the most active in terms of trade liberalization. Various bilateral and multilateral free trade negotiations are being conducted within the region. China has always been a strong promoter and participant in this process and in global free trade. Advancing bilateral and multilateral free trade negotiations, opposing trade protectionism, and "forming a network of high-standard free trade zones that faces the world" are important measures for China during the "13th Five-Year Plan" period. Currently, China has signed 14 free trade agreements with 22 countries and regions, including ASEAN, Chile, Switzerland, New Zealand, South Korea, and Australia. In addition, negotiations are ongoing with relevant countries on the RCEP, the China–Japan–South Korea Free Trade Area, and the upgrade of the China–ASEAN Free Trade Area. China is gradually building a high-level free trade zone network that is interconnected domestically and internationally and aims to promote global economic integration.

The "13th Five-Year Plan" proposes to promote negotiations on the RCEP. Since 2002, China, Japan, South Korea, Australia, New Zealand, and India each signed a 10+1 free trade agreement with the 10 ASEAN countries. On this basis, the process of East Asian regional economic integration has been accelerating and presenting a diversified development trend. In November 2012, the aforementioned 16 countries announced the initiation of RCEP negotiations. The RCEP, which accounts for 30% of the global GDP and trade volume among its member countries, is currently the largest trade agreement in Asia. The RCEP negotiations involve three major areas: trade in goods, trade in services, and investment. In addition to market access, the negotiations also cover various rule-making aspects. One of the distinctive features of the RCEP negotiations is its high degree of transparency, openness, and inclusiveness. Once concluded, the RCEP will become the world's largest free trade area, covering the most populous region with the most diverse membership, the greatest development level differences, and the most dynamic economic vitality. The leaders of participating countries have pledged to negotiate a comprehensive, high-quality, and mutually beneficial regional free trade agreement through the RCEP negotiations based on existing economic connections. This will strengthen economic cooperation, broaden and deepen economic integration, and promote regional economic growth and equitable development. At the Boao Forum for Asia Annual Conference in 2014, Premier Li Keqiang pointed out that the "Regional Comprehensive Economic Partnership" (RCEP) is the largest trade agreement negotiation in the Asian region in terms of the number of participating members and scale and involves the integration of established free trade zones. RCEP is highly inclusive and conforms to the actual industrial structure, economic model, and social traditions of Asia. It adopts a gradual approach and takes into account the different levels of development of its member countries. It is not exclusive to other regional trade arrangements. China is willing to actively promote the negotiation process with all parties. At the APEC CEO Summit, Xi Jinping pointed out that "we are willing to work with all parties to complete the negotiations on the Regional Comprehensive Economic Partnership as soon as possible and accelerate the negotiations on the China–Japan–Korea Free Trade Zone."

The proposal suggests "promoting the construction of the Asia-Pacific Free Trade Area." The Asia-Pacific Free Trade Area, like China's Belt and

Road Initiative and the Asian Infrastructure Investment Bank, aims to establish an open, inclusive, balanced, and beneficial framework for regional economic cooperation. It embodies the spirit of the Silk Road. Building an Asia-Pacific free trade area is a shared aspiration of all its members. It will deepen the development of intra-regional and global value chains, contribute to the establishment of an open economy in the region, and bring great benefits to the economic and social development of the region. It will also help achieve the United Nations' 2030 sustainable development goals. As an ideal path to end the "fragmentation" of cooperation in the Asia-Pacific region, the APEC roadmap for the realization of the Asia-Pacific Free Trade Area was adopted during the APEC Beijing Summit on November 12, 2014, which marked the official launch of the construction of the Asia-Pacific free trade zone. At the APEC CEO Summit in November 2015, Xi Jinping pointed out that over the years, the Asia-Pacific region has adhered to the principles of openness, integration, and development, and has embarked on a unique and dynamic path of regional economic cooperation. This path serves as an exemplary model for economically disparate nations to work toward integration. In 2015, APEC leaders launched the process of establishing an Asia-Pacific free trade area, taking a historic step. Currently, new regional free trade arrangements continue to emerge, causing concerns about the trend toward fragmentation. We need to accelerate the construction of the Asia-Pacific Free Trade Area and promote regional economic integration. We should participate on an equal footing, fully consult, and maximize the openness and inclusiveness of free trade arrangements to improve the level of open economy in the Asia-Pacific and uphold the multilateral trading system. We should be committed to win–win cooperation, oppose protectionism, and promote fair competition.

For more than half a century, multilateral trading systems and regional trade liberalization have been interdependent and evolving in alternation, jointly promoting the process of globalization. Currently, the progress of the WTO is difficult, and regional trade negotiations such as TPP and RCEP are becoming increasingly challenging. China is an active participant, defender, and contributor to the multilateral trading system, advocating that the WTO-led multilateral trading system is the main channel for global trade rules, and regional trade liberalization is a beneficial supplement that promotes mutual development. China has an open attitude toward the active exploration of trade and investment-related rule-making by relevant countries. At the same time, it believes that since the establishment of the current multilateral trade system in 1995, it has played an irreplaceable role in promoting global trade and investment liberalization and world economic growth. China believes that WTO members will not easily give up the multilateral trading system that benefits the global economy. All parties will work together to support the early completion of the WTO Doha Round negotiations and truly achieve the development goals jointly formulated by all members.

Xi Jinping has repeatedly expressed China's support for the multilateral trading system. In September 2013, during his meeting with the Director-General of the WTO, Roberto Azevêdo, Xi Jinping stated, "The multilateral trading system, with the World Trade Organization at its core, is the foundation of trade liberalization and facilitation ... China firmly supports the multilateral trading system and will continue to be a responsible member of the WTO, actively participating in the development of the multilateral trading system."[3] At the 9th G20 Leaders' Summit, he stated: "Expanding world trade benefits all countries and a shrinking global market is not beneficial for any country. We need to continue to be the champion of global free trade, uphold the multilateral trading system, build a mutually beneficial global value chain, and cultivate a global market. We need to continue to oppose trade and investment protectionism and promote the Doha Round negotiations. We need to promote all types of free trade agreements to be open, inclusive, transparent, and non-discriminatory, and avoid market fragmentation and trade system differentiation."[4] At the 23rd APEC Economic Leaders' Meeting, the leaders of the Asia-Pacific region issued *The 23rd APEC Economic Leaders' Declaration*, which affirmed once again the value of the multilateral trading system with the World Trade Organization at its core, and its central and primary position in international trade. "We are committed to strengthening the multilateral trading system based on rules, transparency, non-discrimination, openness, and inclusiveness. To further implement this commitment, we have decided to issue a separate statement on the occasion of the 20th anniversary of the establishment of the World Trade Organization, expressing our support for the

---

[3]Xi Jinping meets with WTO Director-General Azevêdo. *People's Daily*, September 6, 2013.

[4]Xi Jinping. (2014). Promoting innovation and development to achieve interconnected growth. *People's Daily*, November 16, 2014.

multilateral trading system and the 10th Ministerial Conference of the World Trade Organization."[5]

The concept of an inclusive economy has become a guiding principle for global economic development, while regional trade agreements are rapidly expanding like a field of blooming mushrooms after the rain. We cannot afford to be mere spectators or followers but should strive to be active participants and leaders in shaping the global economic landscape. By promoting the construction of free trade zones, China can enhance its international competitiveness and make significant contributions to the formulation of international rules, ensuring that our country's development interests are safeguarded and expanded. In the 13th Five-Year Plan period, China aims to promote trade integration at the domestic, regional, and multilateral levels. By participating in and leading free trade zones, China will exert its influence on the global economic landscape. The construction of free trade zones will enter a new era under this plan.

3. Building a Community with a Shared Future for Mankind

The open world economy requires a fair, reasonable, and sound order to maintain its operation. The development of the world economy is uneven, and countries of different sizes, strengths, levels of development, and statuses have different positions and levels of influence. These are objective factors that exist. However, in the process of economic cooperation, all countries have equal status and share a common vision of cooperation. This is what we have consistently emphasized: the need to promote win–win cooperation and safeguard the core interests of all countries. This is the major direction and trend of international cooperation today, as well as the basic premise for the smooth development of an open world economy. Under the old and unequal international economic order, sustainable development of the world economy was impossible. Where there is inequality, there will inevitably be resistance. Cooperation leads to mutual benefit, and mutual benefit leads to continued cooperation. This is the law of a virtuous cycle.

The world economic order must be jointly upheld by all countries, and each nation has its own principles and limits. China remains committed to

---

[5]APEC leaders' declaration of the 23rd APEC economic leaders' meeting. *Xinhua News Agency*, November 19, 2015.

the path of peaceful development and steadfastly advocates the concept of win–win cooperation. While we remain committed to the path of peaceful development and the principles of win–win cooperation, we must also be firm in safeguarding our core national interests. Xi Jinping pointed out, "We must adhere to the path of peaceful development, but we must never give up our legitimate rights and interests, and we must never sacrifice our core national interests. We will not compromise our core interests with any foreign country, nor will we accept any consequences that jeopardize our country's sovereignty, security, and development interests."[6]

Safeguarding the core interests of the country is a crucial mission of China's diplomacy. Throughout the more than 60 years since the founding of New China, the nation has unwaveringly maintained its commitment to protecting national independence, sovereignty, and dignity. Despite facing extreme poverty several decades ago, China demonstrated remarkable courage in defending its national interests and opposing global powers. It has never bowed down to external pressure. Now that China has become strong and powerful, it will not yield to any foreign pressure. Some people label China's defense of its legitimate national rights and interests as "domineering," "arrogant," and "hard-line," and promote the "China threat theory." However, these claims are unfounded. China always regards safeguarding national sovereignty, security, and development interests as the basic starting point and foothold of its diplomatic work. It is the responsibility of the Chinese government to safeguard its territorial sovereignty and legitimate and reasonable maritime rights and interests. We must persist in resolving disputes through peaceful and negotiation means, while also being prepared to deal with various complex situations. We will resolutely contain the destructive activities of separatist forces such as "Taiwan independence," "Tibet independence," and "East Turkestan independence" in the international arena, prevent the infiltration of international violent and terrorist activities into the country, and safeguard national sovereignty and security. We will not shy away from issues and will address differences and conflicts with relevant countries in a proper manner. At the same time, we will promote exchanges and cooperation in various fields, and expand common interests through cooperation. This will help us maintain good relations with neighboring countries and ensure regional peace and stability.

---

[6] Publicity Department of the CPC Central Committee (2016), *Op. cit.*, p. 272.

China's peaceful development will not be smooth sailing. While our intent is not to provoke conflicts, we also possess the courage to confront them if necessary. When it comes to issues that concern our fundamental interests, we must be willing to draw red lines and make our bottom line clear. As China's peaceful development continues to deepen, we will have more resources and means to safeguard our national interests, and our position in doing so will become more proactive.

Advancing the reform of the global governance system is an important part of jointly maintaining and developing an open world economy, and realizing the Chinese Dream of national rejuvenation. To achieve this goal, we need to seize opportunities, tackle challenges, balance the domestic and international situations, and promote the development of a more just and reasonable global governance system. This will create more favorable conditions for China's development and world peace.

The development of a more fair and equitable global governance system is in the interest of all countries around the world. The rapid growth of emerging markets and a large number of developing countries, which have gained increasing international influence, represents a significant shift in the global power dynamics in modern times. With the deepening of economic globalization, the interests and destinies of countries are becoming more intertwined, and many challenges can no longer be addressed by individual nations alone. As the world becomes more interconnected, issues require joint consultation and cooperation among countries. The establishment of international mechanisms, adherence to international rules, and the pursuit of international justice have garnered widespread consensus among the majority of nations.

China is a participant in, builder of, and contributor to the current international system, as well as an advocate for international cooperation and an active participant in international multilateralism. China is committed to promoting innovative development in global governance and actively seeks resonance between the positive approaches to life and governance in Chinese culture and the needs of the present era, making efforts to contribute Chinese wisdom and strength to the improvement of global governance. China takes into account both the demands of our own development and the expectations of the international community, while maintaining a balance between rights and obligations based on our national conditions. We strive to combine the protection of China's interests with the protection of the common interests of developing countries.

The "Recommendations" passed at the Fifth Plenary Session of the 18th Central Committee of the Communist Party of China put forward a series of targeted planning measures and specific action goals, which have pointed the direction for China to form a new pattern of opening up to the outside world and deepen its mutual-benefit cooperation with the world. Firstly, it proposes actively participating in the formulation of international rules in new areas such as cyberspace, the deep sea, the polar regions, and outer space. This is based on hard power to enhance China's institutional discourse power in global economic governance. Cyberspace, the deep sea, the polar regions, and outer space represent emerging fields of modern high technology, the importance of which was not previously evident. However, the development of the world economy and technology in contemporary times has increasingly highlighted the significance and role of these areas. Whoever controls the initiative in these areas largely dominates the development of international economy, politics, technology, military, and other fields. With the improvement of China's scientific and economic strength, it has already become a world leader in some of these new fields and has the necessary conditions to participate in the formulation of international rules. Active participation in the formulation of international rules reflects the enhancement of China's institutional discourse power in the new emerging fields of high technology.

Secondly, it proposes to promote the multilateral trade negotiation process, facilitate the balanced, win–win, and inclusive development of the multilateral trading system, and establish a fair, reasonable, and transparent international economic and trade rules system. It also supports the equal participation of developing countries in global economic governance and promotes the reform of the international monetary system and international financial regulation. Today's world economic development cannot do without cooperation and inclusiveness among countries, which inevitably involves various interests. And these interests are largely arranged through the international trade system. The existing international trade system has been formed and continued through long-term historical development, and the old international economic and trade order still has traces. Although China cannot yet be called a world trading power, it is already a major trading nation. Multilateral trade has become the mainstream of international trade, and China plays an important role in promoting the balanced, win–win, and inclusive development of the multilateral trading system, and establishing a fair, reasonable, and transparent international economic and trade rules system. China should and must make efforts in this field to reflect its institutional discourse power in global economic governance.

Thirdly, it proposes to accelerate the implementation of the free trade zone strategy, promote RCEP negotiations, advance the construction of the Asia-Pacific free trade zone, and form a high-standard network of free trade zones facing the world. This is based on comprehensive national strength to enhance China's institutional discourse power in global economic governance. China's innovative practice of implementing the free trade zone strategy adapts to the overall trend of regional economic development and conforms to the trend of world economic regionalization. China leads and promotes RCEP negotiations and the construction of the Asia-Pacific free trade zone with an open concept and takes the lead in regional economic development as an initiator or founding member.

Fourthly, it advocates for actively shouldering international responsibilities and obligations. It stresses the principle of common but differentiated responsibilities, fairness, and respective capabilities. China should actively participate in global climate change negotiations and fulfill its emission reduction commitments. This is based on China's influence, self-confidence, and the responsibility of a major power to enhance its institutional discourse power in global economic governance. Although China is a world power, it has yet to become a world leader. While being a major power is a fact, becoming a world leader is an aspiration. As a world power, China has the responsibility and obligation to participate in international affairs, exert influence, and demonstrate the responsibility of a major power. However, it's unrealistic to expect China to solve all the problems in the international arena, as we don't have the ability to do so. Instead, we should undertake responsibilities and obligations to the best of our ability. This is a pragmatic, proactive, and responsible role for a major power to play.

Fifthly, it proposes expanding the scale of foreign aid, improving the way aid is delivered, and providing more free consulting and training in areas such as human resources, development planning, and economic policies to developing countries. It also aims to expand cooperation and assistance in fields such as science and technology education, healthcare, disaster prevention and reduction, environmental governance, wildlife conservation, poverty reduction, and increase humanitarian aid efforts. China actively participates in the United Nations' 2030 Agenda for Sustainable Development. In the context of globalization, no country's development can be isolated and independent of others, and it cannot do without the development and support of other countries. This is the global environment for development, which applies to both developed and developing countries alike.

During his address at the 70th United Nations General Assembly, Xi Jinping highlighted, "In today's world, countries are interdependent and share weal and woe. We should uphold the purposes and principles of the UN Charter, build a new type of international relations featuring win–win cooperation, and create a community of shared future for mankind."[7]

China will always be a builder of world peace, a contributor to global development, and a defender of international order. We need to work together to create a regional order that is more favorable to Asia and the world and promote the construction of a community with a shared future for mankind by building an Asian community with a shared future. We should adhere to the spirit of the Asia-Pacific family and the awareness of a community with a shared future, work together to promote the prosperity and progress of the Asia-Pacific region, and build a future-oriented Asia-Pacific partnership.

[7]Publicity Department of the CPC Central Committee (2016), *Op. cit.*, p. 264.

Postscript

Understanding the Development of China's Political Economics is a book written at the invitation of the China Renmin University Press. It elaborates on the new developments in the political economics of socialism with Chinese characteristics since the 18th National Congress of the Communist Party of China in 2012.

The term "political economics of China's development" in the context of political economics of socialism with Chinese characteristics emphasizes the "development" aspect. It is based on China's national characteristics and the practical experience of socialist economic construction and development. The theory explores the reform and development of the socialist economic system, as well as the improvement and progress of the socialist economic institutions. It signifies the new theoretical achievements of a "systematic economic doctrine" with Chinese characteristics that combines the basic principles of Marxist political economics with China's reality. Since the 18th National Congress of the Communist Party of China, the Party Central Committee, led by Xi Jinping, has adhered to and developed socialism with Chinese characteristics. They have been courageous in practice and adept at innovation, forming a series of new concepts, ideas, and strategies for governing the country. This provides scientific theoretical guidance and an action plan for furthering reform and opening up, as well as accelerating the construction of socialist modernization under new historical conditions. The political economics of socialism with Chinese characteristics has achieved new developments within these new governing concepts, ideas, and strategies, opening up new horizons for contemporary Marxist political economics. The primary purpose and theme of *Understanding the Development of China's Political Economics* is to elucidate the latest advancements in the political economics of socialism with Chinese characteristics since the 18th National Congress.

Understanding the Development of China's Political Economics is co-edited by myself and Professor Wang Tianyi. The assignment of tasks for the contributors of each chapter is as follows:

Chapter 1: Gu Hailiang (Professor at the Collaborative Innovation Center for the Chinese Path and Sinicized Marxism, Peking University)

Chapter 2: Zhang Leisheng (Professor at the School of Marxism, Renmin University of China)

Chapter 3: Zhang Kai (Associate Professor at the Department of Economics, Party School of the Central Committee of the Communist Party of China)

Chapters 4 and 8: Wang Tianyi (Professor at the Department of Economics, Party School of the Central Committee of the Communist Party of China)

Chapter 5: Zhang Yujie (Professor at the Department of Economics, Party School of the Central Committee of the Communist Party of China)

Chapter 6: Li Peng (Professor at the Department of Economics, Party School of the Central Committee of the Communist Party of China)

Chapter 7: Jia Huaqiang (Professor at the Department of Economics, Party School of the Central Committee of the Communist Party of China)

Chapters 9, 11, 12, and 14: Zhou Yuehui (Lecturer at the Department of Economics, Party School of the Central Committee of the Communist Party of China)

Chapter 10: Chen Yuxue (Professor at the Department of Economics, Party School of the Central Committee of the Communist Party of China)

Chapter 13: Shi Hong (Professor at the Department of Economics, Party School of the Central Committee of the Communist Party of China)

Chapters 15 and 16: Gu Yumin (Professor at the School of Marxism, Fudan University)

Understanding the Development of China's Political Economics is also an interim result of the major project "Research on the Political Economics of Socialism with Chinese Characteristics," which I led as the chief expert under the Central Marxist Theoretical Research and Construction Project.

The publication of *Understanding the Development of China's Political Economics* has received strong support from friends at the China Renmin University Press. I would like to extend my heartfelt appreciation to the entire team, particularly Editor Niu Jinfang, whose dedication and hard work have been instrumental in the success of this project.

Gu Hailiang
January 31, 2025

Index

D

E

Q

R

S